MATTERS OF INSCRIPTION

Matters of Inscription

Reading Figures of Latinidad

Christina A. León

NEW YORK UNIVERSITY PRESS
New York

NEW YORK UNIVERSITY PRESS
New York
www.nyupress.org

© 2024 by New York University
All rights reserved

Library of Congress Cataloging-in-Publication Data

Names: León, Christina A., author.
Title: Matters of inscription : reading figures of Latinidad / Christina A. León.
Description: New York : New York University Press, 2024. | Includes bibliographical references and index. | Summary: "Matters of Inscription: Reading Figures of Latinidad argues that Latinx inscriptions require us to read at the edge of materiality and semiosis, charting a nimble method for "reading" various forms of Latinx marks and even the word Latinx across art, performance, poetry, plays, and fiction"—Provided by publisher.
Identifiers: LCCN 2023040743 | ISBN 9781479816774 (hardback ; acid-free paper) | ISBN 9781479816781 (paperback ; acid-free paper) | ISBN 9781479816798 (ebook) | ISBN 9781479816804 (ebook)
Subjects: LCSH: Spanish American literature—History and criticism. | American literature—Hispanic American authors—History and criticism. | Identity (Philosophical concept) in literature. | Latin Americans in literature. | LCGFT: Literary criticism.
Classification: LCC PQ7081 .L452166 2024 | DDC 860.9/38—dc23/eng/20240511
LC record available at https://lccn.loc.gov/2023040743

New York University Press books are printed on acid-free paper, and their binding materials are chosen for strength and durability. We strive to use environmentally responsible suppliers and materials to the greatest extent possible in publishing our books.

Manufactured in the United States of America

10 9 8 7 6 5 4 3 2 1

Also available as an e-book

CONTENTS

Introduction: Latinx Remarks
Inscription, Reference, and Catachresis   1

1. Source Materials: Reading the Matter of Ana Mendieta's
Catachrestic Inscriptions   49

2. Exorbitant Dust: Manuel Ramos Otero's Queer
and Colonial Matters   91

3. Gut Checks: María Irene Fornés's Visceral Pedagogy
and Dangerous Nerves   139

4. Losing the Pack: Tracking Loss, Tracing Animals,
and Longing for Belonging   177

Coda: Knots in the Throat
Roque Salas Rivera's Ballasted Entanglements   223

Acknowledgments   247

Notes   253

Index   289

About the Author   297

Introduction

Latinx Remarks

Inscription, Reference, and Catachresis

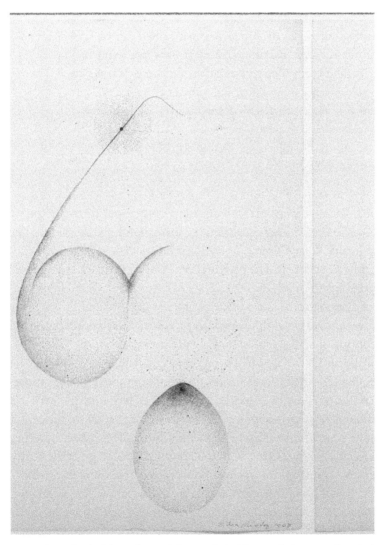

Figure I.1. *El significado del significante* (*The signified of the signifier*), 1968, Zilia Sánchez

Part I

A DOT, A NIB

What attracts our attention is the migration of one sign (or symbol) to another, however minute (a dot for example). And, little by little, the widening displacement of graphemes—this extraordinary repertory of objects extending, for example, from a cave painting to calligraphy, or to a rug, a tattoo, a basket or an embroidered scarf. Yet, this tremor of signs is nothing other than the productive motif (itself itinerant) of our interrogation: the displacement of signs in a wandering series whose graphic representation sometimes vibrates in an efflorescence of meaning, and sometimes freezes this migration in place, effectively erasing the gyratory space that is thereby reduced to a dot, a nib.
—Abdelkébir Khatibi, trans. Matt Reeck, "Tattoos: Writing in Dots"

In 1968, Zilia Sánchez pressed an ink pen to paper to create the most basic kind of mark: a dot. By arranging many dots into three larger, undulating forms, *El significado del significante* appears at once abstract and discernibly corporeal. The minimal dot is the only mark that composes the larger forms of this drawing. The dot here cannot be the period at the end of a sentence because this dot gathers density and grows in saturated thickness, then it thins, radiating, creating edged borders and radial projections. Inscribed into an off-white background, these dots gather and disperse. Or perhaps better put, they emanate; they disseminate and seemingly self-organize into clefts, folds, and mounds that are connected and contoured only by the dots. These shapes beget other forms, other movements. It is radically unclear which is the first mark, though concentration and density can be discerned. Some dots cluster together to form folds, evoking buttocks. In the bottom right corner of the drawing, we see another form. Is it an ovum pollinating or a breast fertilizing? We see, in almost pointillist form, the space of migration, the pollination of a buttock, the fertilization not *of* but *from* an egg. The more one looks at the piece, the more one is confused about where the punctum may lie and what forces make these undulating forms. One zooms in to see the mark, the textured minimalist pointillism, and then takes a step back to see the larger, loose, abstracted but perceptible composition in this drawing. What connects these dots? And where do the forces of concentration and brittle delineation lie? How is organic form rendered from the most basic mark of ink? And how does the title of the drawing, *El significado del significante* or "the signified of the signifier," inflect how we may begin to make sense of this abstractly evocative drawing?

Sánchez's erotic signification morphed from stippling to three-dimensional modes in her prolific, inspired, and undernoted career. She came to be known for her erotic topologies: undulating paintings created by stretching canvases over hand-molded wooden armatures and painting them with spare, acrylic colors: usually pastels, neutrals, and black. Her taut surfaces and visual abstractions withhold as much as they suggest, and none can be said to clearly represent her in relation to ethnicity, gender, or desire. This is not to say that her biography or her life is insignificant to her work; instead, what this suggests is that her work is not immediately legible as Latinx, queer, Caribbean, Cuban, or Puerto Rican. Questions of latinidad have evolved over her very long career and her late reception, a reception that would be understood, at times, in identarian terms—especially when her work is considered outside of midcentury Cuba and Puerto Rico.

This introduction turns to Sánchez's work, career, and artistic life to think anew these persistent questions of identity that we cannot resolve *nor absolve* ourselves from considering. So, a warning to the reader: while Sánchez's taut surfaces, migratory path, and evolving formal and interpretive observations will structure and unfold in this introduction, and while these pages will be primarily concerned with questions of representation at the level of figurativity, her figure is not meant to be representative as such—she is neither totem nor misfit. I take her work and her artistic life as an occasion to consider issues at the heart of this book—namely, how figurativity and materiality require us to read Latinx art and literature in ways that resist total appropriation into political programs and do not translate readily to road maps to liberation. It would only be with the 2018 exhibition *Radical Women: Latin American Art, 1960–1985* that Sánchez's work would start to gain traction in the US—years after inclusion efforts to diversify museums and canons have led to the institutionalization of what we now call "Latinx studies."

Hence, we may read Sánchez herself as Latinx only metaleptically. This after-the-fact designation renders the category of Latinx or latinidad precarious, requiring that we read its risky signifying operations. And yet, that reading cannot utilize the moniker "Latinx" or "latinidad" as helpful heuristics for thinking about the incommensurate heterogeneities that underlie these terms. Cristina Beltrán puts this succinctly: "Characterizing a subject as either 'Hispanic' or 'Latino' is an exercise in opacity."[1] This opacity may provide an opportunity to make the category more relational. But relationality may itself become so flexible and open that it engulfs and elides; moreover, its adherence to residual colonial taxonomy rehearses racializations that are anti-Black and anti-Indigenous.

"Latinx" is a panethnic category that is only known through its catachrestic figuration. It at once represents no one; at the same time, as an ill-fitted, imposed, or forced metaphor, latinidad has serious and variegated material fallout for those who dwell under its nominalist designation and for those who encompass its unacknowledged, constitutive outside. What this means is that we are summoned to read, or encounter, these cultural productions knowing that, while such categories bear on the material conditions of inscription, creation, and instantiation, they fail to match the material complexity and figurative quality of any of these works or lives. *Matters of Inscription*, then, aims to think at the interstice of the figurative and the material at the site of inscription. In this book, *inscription* is meant to be a capacious term that denotes mark-making, writing, etching, and identity markers. The term echoes deconstructive insights about the materiality of language from Paul de Man and Jacques Derrida,[2] but so too does the term carry this deconstructive tradition into the corporeal by way of Judith Butler and Hortense J. Spillers,[3] as well as illuminate contemporaneous concerns.[4] To read inscriptions, then, takes the task of reading capaciously—analyzing inscriptions across art, theory, literature, performance, and even taxonomic designators. Each of these varied discourses offers occasions to understand how inscriptions can only function if read. Inscriptions operate as entanglements of mark and reader, of substrate and figure, and offer a way to think both at the level of the figurative and the material without necessary rank or delineation between these two categories. Inscriptions partake of sedimented discourses and grammars, of frames of reference with unwieldy outcomes; nonetheless, power is palpable through and through. Recent questions of trope, figurativity, form, and aesthetics ask us to reconsider forms of difference at a level of nontransparency and with nuance, without the colonialist call to either reproduce stereotypes or represent mythologies of race for voyeuristic consumption.[5] This attention to trope, figure, rhetoric, and grammar troubles aesthetic ideology and grapples with material forms of difference that cannot collapse neatly into linguistic notions of difference. Such attention to inscription is neither a new turn in theory nor the creation of a new concept that promises to solve current political problems. Solution-based approaches to difference can be necessary and effective, but they do not find felicitous interlocutors in literary studies and the humanities. Moreover, the demand that scholarship that addresses racial/sexual/gender/ethnic difference also always must provide pathways to liberation asks too much of the marginalized. This demand seeks a solution where one also expects to find disenfranchisement.

Disenchanted with idealism, this book holds fast to the ongoing task and charge of reading. Reading, of course, has been a mainstay of the humanities and, more particularly, of literary studies, from which field a reading of difference would emerge in the late twentieth century. The linguistic turn afforded a thinking of semiotics that exploded the linguistic beyond the parameters of the parameters of language as previously understood—that is, as reflective of the material world. Ferdinand de Saussure revised linguistic thinking in response to colonial encounters with linguistic plurality, which inspired new interest in linguistic study and occasioned a revisiting of how we think language works. In this context, language became importantly understood as having only negative, relational value forged in a field where concepts, or signifieds, are arbitrarily assigned to sound-images, or signifiers. These questions were revived by late structuralists and poststructuralists. Concomitantly, student protests, popular protests, and anticolonial movements fostered the institutionalization of fields such as ethnic studies, gender studies, critical race studies, and postcolonial studies.[6] As such, theories of difference collided: difference thought of as abstract alterity and difference indexed forcefully in the lives of those who are racialized, gendered, and colonized. In the early aughts, many theoretical schools of difference turned to surface and affect. More recently, we may say there was a return to formalisms and aesthetics that was thought to be in tension and tandem with difference. Once discarded as elitist, these formal modes of inquiry find felicitous afterlives in scholarly conversations specifically around questions of racialization, gender, and abstraction.[7]

Indebted to these various turns and schools of thought, *Matters of Inscription* takes the question of inscription—rather than form or aesthetics as such—as its site of reading. Strict formalism can err by presupposing a disentanglement of form from content—by imagining a generic, universally appropriable abstraction. The questions of new formalisms and new aesthetic theories have been germane to thinking beyond a foreseeable sociopolitical imperative in the humanities, and my project aims to consider similar questions from the vantage point of figuration, inscription, grammar, and rhetoric. Thinking with inscription allows us to grapple with the entanglement of writing, foundational epistemes, the matter of medium (whether linguistic, performative, or the plastic arts), and most importantly, reading—that site where every mode of inscription is taken up by an other insofar as it can be taken up at all. Every inscription is an entanglement, then, of matter and meaning that finds its figurative power in how reading interprets these inscriptions. And every inscription is written and read in an interregnum, or a context, that may not be recoverable.

Matter impinges upon our ways of inscribing story, art, and theory, and the recent turn to the more-than-human world occasions a way of rereading works as they negotiate, themselves, the relation between matter and meaning. How we interpret and read has incredible material consequence; so too does the figurative quality of language create unwieldy material fallout. With this in mind, *Matters of Inscription* sets off on the task of reading these figurative entanglements of matter and meaning, attentive to the tropological choices of artists and authors who often defy notions of the human as either sovereign, self-same, transparent, fully volitional, individual, or nonporous. Thinking figuratively through various materials that entangle humans in configurations that defy rectitude or pleas for recognition, I track how material tropes and metaphors allow us to see how figuration is neither human nor posthuman. Rather, inscription's figurative work allows us to think the human as entangled and, as such, wholly unavailable as a referent that figures a singular representation of a homogeneous people. We see now what Cristina Beltrán calls the "trouble with unity" in latinidad and how this trouble necessarily unmoors *how* we read terms and works.⁸ Such considerations may seem démodé, but recent attention to the statuses of metaphor and trope has been percolating across various fields attuned to demographic difference and theory. This resurgence is coeval with recent thinking of representation from the perspective of modern raciality via Denise Ferreira da Silva and a critical uptake of Sylvia Wynter's work on Man1 and Man2. Wynter and da Silva call our attention not only to aesthetics but also to the grammars that determine how we articulate difference. Such considerations are charged with the fresh urgency of undeniable dispossession throughout the world. In a similar way, *Matters of Inscription* aims to consider the structuring grammars and rhetorics through which Latinx cultural producers create work—work that can only be read within the frame of received letters. These letters do not dictate the telos of all work because inscriptive figurativity very swiftly errs, veers, and shifts with each iteration.

To return to Sánchez, I am interested in attending not to the meaning of Sánchez's life or even her works but to the status of the signified, to the problem of reference, and to the ongoing quandary that is signification and reading—both understood capaciously (under the aegis of the trace structure). The drawing at the beginning of this introduction hails from a series of drawings: *El significado del significante*—the signified of the signifier. The title evokes another layer of signification that is, at once, a suggestion and an abstraction. How do these shapes represent, index, or refer to a conceptual framework that deals with marks, graphs, and graphemes? How does this drawing evoke a theory so thoroughly linguistic? Correspondence, tightly and organically orchestrated in the composition of the drawing,⁹ seems amiss when it comes to the correspondence of the title to its referent, since the signified itself appears eponymously, which is to say, referentially (as what does the referring and also what is referred to). But here, in graphic form in 1968, Zilia Sánchez takes a different approach, since the title itself is an inversion of what we would come to know as late post-structuralism's fetish of the signifier.¹⁰ The conversations around signifiers and signifieds—in the wake of the linguistic turn catalyzed in Europe by *Tel Quel*, the French literary magazine that ran from 1960 to 1982—would lead critical theorists to analyze arbitrary and performative signifiers. If signifieds were once taken for granted, then in the late 1990s and early aughts, signifiers (as arbitrary, as empty, as floating, as performative) were all the rage. To show what a text does, rather than what it means, became consonant with critique. But so too do we recall that each signified is tied to its signifier in a chain of synchronic relations—relations further complicated by time and dissemination. My point here is not to reclaim a natural form of reference. Far from it, the return to questions of rhetoric and grammar asks us to consider how we read the referential aspect of language, marks, and inscriptions. This question haunts and limns every debate over what terms mean and how they do or do not do justice to those whom they purport to represent.

Representation as signification has been one way to think through the operations of difference at the level of language and at the level of peoples. But the strangeness of signification, of language, often pushes beyond any easy representative force. Sánchez's drawing takes this a step further by translating the vocabulary of semiotics into graphic form. How can a painting—itself a graphic—refer to another system entirely? Or is it another system? How does a title, surely inspired by *Tel Quel*, migrate onto this suite of drawings? The signified of the signifier seems an unlikely appearance visually, since we tend to think that we read signifiers alone. That is, we often think of the signifier as the discernible mark and the signified as the meaning. Here, in this rendering, the signified is actually the most abstracted graphic mark one can make: a dot. The canvas beneath looks more like atmosphere than base, and the relative opacity that the dots produce gives form to shapes at once organic and abstracted. These shapes seem to be in process, in a kind of autopoiesis: the dot replicates itself through a fractal dissemination wherein it takes on organic shapes; dots concentrate to create force and the impression of cleft flesh; a spore-like dispersal radiates, creating a wave, a lined apex, a descent sloping toward unfinished buttocks. To make a mark of the signified of the signifier aligns the signified with the movement of the signifier—thus allowing us to see why Jacques Derrida states early in *Of Grammatology* that "there the signified always already functions as a signifier. The secondary that it seemed possible to reserve for writing affects all signifieds in general, affect always already, the moment they *enter the game*. There is no signified that escapes, eventually to fall back, the play of signifying references that constitute language."[11] In this formulation, the signified functions as a mark, as a signifier, which means that the supplementarity of writing subtends what we imagine to be concept, meaning, or referent. To inflect the signified as a mark—as in Sánchez's work—is to consider the purchase that signifieds as concepts that operate referentially have on our ways of perceiving the material world. Always mediated, inscriptions ask us to think a signified that carries the residue of the referential, or the promise of index, in its conceptual terrain. For this Sánchez drawing, the signified is both the most basic visual mark and a mark that gives rise, when gathered, to abstracted corporeal forms. We can both register these marked clefts and remain uncertain as to what, precisely, they transmit or index. And yet it seems no surprise that this linguistic exercise rendered graphic would turn to corporeality. Often, thinkers of race and gender use inscription as a way to think about how a body is marked upon by a grammar never consented to, a larger sedimentation of grammar and race that precedes subjection/subjectivation.[12]

Again, I return to this perplexing title, *El significado del significante*, which evokes a baffling scene of reading. The title demands and obstructs reading, insisting on multiple interpretations across discourses, times, and networks; it pushes at opaque representation rendered in sumptuously abstracted corporeal form. Why the signified of the signifier? Of the piece, Sánchez settles on not one but three things that "this" might be: "This is an egg. It's the world, and it's a breast. Three things."[13] So the signified of the signifier is not one but three things: two indefinite and one definite—the only definitive thing being the world itself. The statement starts with the specificity of "this," at once a pronoun and determiner. It is a pronoun without gender, without anthropocentric assumption, and one of the most abstracted, general forms of grammatical referentiality. As both determiner and pronoun, it travels vastly and has a metareferential quality while living in almost diametric opposition to the pronoun "I." Semantically, Sánchez's answer demands more reading: Is "this" referring to the painting as a whole? One of the shapes? Is it naming the three largest discernible shapes? Again, we return to the drawing: no parallelisms exist between each shape; their near symmetry is ruptured by dots that trail off from a nearly complete form into another formation such that the flow is neither up nor down nor side to side, creating, rather, dispersed connections and arrangements that suggest the body and fertility (though it's unclear if it's seed, sperm, milk, or ink). One dot is most concentrated in the upper right corner of the piece, and from there radiant dots repeat themselves in patterns that are at once spore-like and organized. Buttock clefts disintegrate, or radiate, into constellations that suggest the abstract tracing of movement and internal organization. Three forms have uncertain relations to one another, but together they loosely gesture toward the movement of matter, matrixial qualities of bodies, and dissemination of both ink and biologic substance.

Three shapes emerge, and their triangulation speaks to a process that looks a lot like diaspora. This drawing is so abstracted, yet so interconnected, that it may offer us a way of considering the relationships between the three islands that Sánchez lived on: she was born in Cuba, and after a stay in Spain, she moved to Manhattan before finally landing in San Juan, Puerto Rico, where she has been working and living for some time. If we recall that the root of the word *diaspora* means "seed," then this transposition of the seminal into the feminine bears out in the trajectory of Sánchez's work. It bears out, not through a sheer rejection of the masculine, but rather through a movement that explores the tensions within sex and gender, that takes seriously divides and meeting points in form and content. This entanglement of form and content may be a moment to consider how life, theory, text, and art may correspond, but they do not readily translate marks of difference into one another. Reading rarely happens once; figurativity begets considerations over time, beyond the moment of inscription, signaling with each dot and nib the radial distance a mark makes from its maker.

I wonder, then: what would the artist herself make of the title over time? It is no coincidence that Zilia Sánchez's work would don a title so evocative of conversations afoot in France, though she wasn't in France in 1968 but rather in New York. This professional moment was a particularly fertile one for Sánchez, involving much reading about philosophies of sexuality and eroticism and working in restoration while in conversation with poets, writers, intellectuals, and other artists. Her New York City was a diasporic hotbed of production and conversation that gravitated around recently exiled Cubans in New York meeting with Puerto Rican and other Latin American intellectuals and artists. Her encounter with linguistic theories would come from her dear friend Severo Sarduy who summoned her to New York—another queer, Cuban artist who could read the bellwether of constricting life in Cuba and urged Sánchez to join him abroad. Sarduy's notable place in letters marked him as a neobaroque writer who, like Sánchez, explored corporeal fecundity and sensuality—a writer who would remain most Cuban abroad. So too was Sarduy a vital interlocutor for the group behind the literary journal *Tel Quel* in their reconsiderations of semiotics and the linguistic turn. In light of such connections, one would, should, and could expect a direct relation between Sánchez's title and this literary movement, but Sánchez replied rather coyly to the suggestion in a 2018 interview with Vesela Sretenovic, the main curator of Sánchez's retrospective, *Soy Isla*. Sretenovic asked about the 1968 suite of drawings and their evocative titling that "directly echoed French structuralism and the semiotics of the late sixties: Were you aware of those theories, or perhaps familiar with *Tel Quel*, a journal of literary criticism established in Paris in 1960 by a group of philosophers, writers, and poets [including Barthes, Derrida, Lacan, Francois Wahl (Sarduy's partner), and Sarduy]?"[14] To this equally erudite and Eurocentric question, Sánchez responded with an answer quite apart from her previous interpretation of the piece (breast, egg, world): "I don't think so, but given that Severo was in those circles, he could have introduced me to their ideas, because we would talk a lot. He was a little younger than me, but we had known each other from childhood. He was extremely supportive of me and wrote beautifully about my work. He was an exceptional person—he was also the one who said to me early on: 'Stay abroad.'"[15] Notice how Sánchez doesn't refer to Sarduy by his last name and places him into the intimate story of her life by using his first name. She then expands out to the circles and conversations they shared over a lifetime and their chain of associations. What her circumlocution lands upon is Severo as support instead of Sarduy as phallic fount. So too does she guide us back to herself, as an artist and person, and to her work. Sánchez's answer reveals a material set of connections that make her friend Severo exceptional. This exceptionality is underscored by his advice to stay away from Cuba's increasingly homophobic regime. Implicit in this simple statement is a world of queerness, diaspora, relative privilege, and erratic movement and a life of thinking across graphemes, signs, continents, and oceans. The safekeeping of two lives that circle around one another in the face of a constrictively homophobic Cuban government subtends this statement. Sánchez expressed no further interest in *Tel Quel* but rather in friendship as a reading: a reading of one's work, a reading of another's discourse, a reading of political climates. While others have carefully compared Sánchez's artwork to Severo Sarduy's—and there are undeniable thematic resonances—Sánchez herself opens up the possibility of influence in the conditional tense ("could have") and then shifts to the material and intellectual life their friendship encapsulated. I am interested in how Sánchez narrates her friendship with Sarduy as a material foundation rather than a theoretical source. And while Sánchez demurs over Sarduy's influence over her semiotic titles, she does credit him with influencing her work by way of reading its erotic aspects. When asked what books she had been reading about eroticism in New York, she answers, "I read so many books on sexuality, eroticism, and communication. And then, one day, Severo came to visit and whispered: 'Those are *tetas* [boobs]—you did breasts, Zilia!' That's why I started to use 'Eros' in my titles."[16] One can almost read the wry smile as Sánchez relates this story to Sretenovic, only compounded by a follow-up question asking the artist if she had thought of these as *tetas*. Sánchez exclaims, in a quick retort, that she had thought of them as mountains.

With this set of interpretations, the readerly task we may be charged with is to read even referential works with less assurance about the status of referentiality: to chart trajectory but not telos, connection but not causality, matrixial entanglement but not linear relation. The relation of Sarduy and Sánchez is indeed queer, but it's not carved out of identity; the expression of queerness here takes on radically differing forms. Sánchez, like many of her era, did not "come out" explicitly. In the interview above, Sánchez's answers are often pithier and more topological than content driven. As a taut surface, she is at once exposed and withholding—much like her iconic canvases. Sánchez transposed the linguistic turn onto the canvas itself—a canvas she would, at the same time, learn to stretch and contour. As felicitous, visual interlocutors for the linguistic turn, Zilia Sánchez's works push the page and the canvas into abstraction and tension that finds its topography in the erotic feminine. When asked if *Tel Quel* had made its way into her work, Sánchez responded by circumlocution—by taking the surface level of Sarduy and tracing his topological relation to her, his rich texture—and then returning to what counts: Sarduy, a fellow queer Cuban, giving her the best advice, to stay abroad. And it was abroad that Sánchez made her erotic topologies. In this moment of reading, one arrives at this painting that is already layered with various tensions and movements between signifier and signified—an inscription that exemplifies the ongoing problem of separating signifier and signified, messenger and message. My point here is not to rehearse, renovate, or moralize any one particular stance around the linguistic turn. Rather, I am turning to this lifelong friendship and encounter, or *encuentro*, as occasions to consider now, again, the status of what is signified and what is regarded as referent and to ask after what this provocative entanglement of mark and referent means for marked subjects of queerness, femininity, and latinidad. We cannot take these terms for granted precisely because of how they function rhetorically. The weight of both empirical evidence and lively theoretical discussion over the last few decades shows that race and referentiality, that sex and referentiality, have an especially fraught and economic relation insofar as our reading of reference brings weight, value, and expectation to those understood as referent.

The relation between Sánchez's art and life is anything but transparent. The larger contention of *Matters of Inscription* is that thinking about the status of referentiality requires us to contend with the materiality of language in at least two ways: (1) language creates material effects by dint of inscription's differentiation, its cutting, stitching, carving, or enfoldment into a fundament, substrate, canvas, page, or body; (2) how one is inscribed and one inscribes oneself entails profound material consequence. Attending to the status of reference requires that we not shy away from thinking index, meaning, grammar, and rhetoric. It also requires that we attend to how reference works, what it imagines, and what maintenance work objects, bodies, and environs have to do to keep inscription legible or protect its illegibility. The nontransparency of language matters profoundly at moments when our communities and classrooms demand that we account for language's violence; this attention to language has an implicit acknowledgment of language's mercurial relationship to material reality. And yet, to take language as being both violent and the solution seems to charge it with two diametrically opposed forces. Language seldom ameliorates what material deprivation has plundered. But it does require that we read and read dangerously.[17]

The term *Latinx* lingers as a question for reading in this introduction—not as a description of what's to come.[18] Rather, I want to think with *Latinx* the problem of reference in the twenty-first century's deployments of difference, which often operationalizes, flattens, and aestheticizes difference in order to sell or satisfy. The problem of reference has been haunting debates over the (un)gendered ending of *Latinx*—not exactly the latest ending, with the uptick of both spoken and written *Latine*. Previously, Sandra Soto situated a queer, Chicana intervention into the Latin terrain with *Latin@*—a term that made labial the "o," centered the "a," and spiraled the two, demanding the dipthonged pronunciation "Latinao."[19] This derived from *Latina/o*, which replaced *Latino*. Revisions of the word at the level of the signifier matter, and evermore inclusive language is part of the political process of vetting languaging. In this way, *Matters of Inscription* is neither calling for an embrace nor a cancellation of *Latinx*. By bringing our attention to the rhetorical work of inscription, we see how terms operate as a guiding frame of reference for persons, studies, and cultural production. *Latinx* has shifted lettered articulation, but its force is felt at the crossroads of configurations of difference both indexed to material history and abstracted into cultural semiotics. We may say that there are significant border wars around *Latinx* that this book cannot address in full nor ameliorate, much less represent.[20] Rather, I take heed of thinkers who have commitments to thinking difference indexed materially in a way not reducible to the alterity of the linguistic subject. Questioning referential purchase is a necessary critique for thoroughgoing engagement with any term thought to be descriptive of groupings of peoples. But to end the question there is to act as if denaturalization itself upends the ideologies waged against those who fall under an identificatory aegis.

Part II

REFERENTIAL QUANDARIES, REPRESENTATIONAL BOGS
One might say the angle of vision changes with "LatinX" and so it makes possible quite literally, new ways of seeing but as a term it does not make a substance miraculously appear that would definitionally represent it.
—Antonio Viego, "LatinX and the Neurologization of Self"

It seems a perilous time to employ latinidad as a frame for either identity or political formation. Recent exit polling data tells a familiar story to those of us who have lived in the folds of this unfolding process framed or hemmed in as latinidad: that Latinx peoples in the US are not monolithic, that, in many ways, there is little shared between the exilic Cuban bloc in Miami and the migrant woman detainee undergoing forced sterilization in an ICE (Immigration and Customs Enforcement) detention center just one state north in Georgia. And yet, as I write this sentence, I must revise: after the rescinding of the "wet foot / dry foot" policy of the Cuban Adjustment Act, some Cubans do sit in cells. Their migration patterns have changed from using rafts to brave the ninety miles of water between Cuba and Florida to following the footpaths worn by many Central and Mexican Americans across the US-Mexico border, and recently falling back again into the *balsero*/raft crisis—all paths leading to this carcerally driven nation-state. Forced sterilization, too, links these migrant bodies to bodies experimented on in mid-twentieth-century Puerto Rico, as well as to the plantation matrix from which all modern gynecology derives. Following this linkage, I must break again to say that while you won't find Puerto Ricans in the carceral hold of an ICE detention center, it is their distinctly colonial status that exempts them from those cells. Yet the island of Puerto Rico suffers tremendously as a cell of coloniality—the longest one in human history. This dizzying descent into latinidad is one way in which we may begin to hear, again, what Latinx scholars over the decades have been telling us: that this pan-ethnic category cannot be seen as a discrete racial formation, nor is it one wherein oppressions, issues, interests, and cultural practices cohere. Anything but a monolith, *Latinx* is a distinctly contemporary problem that requires a plumbing of the past and a critical approach beyond liberal and neoliberal ruses of visibility that have, in many senses, reigned over the thinking of most kinds of marked difference in the humanities.

* * *

Cristina Beltrán's work in *The Trouble with Unity* questions the supposed demographic unity of a Latinx sector as a convenient and oversimplified homogenization of an otherwise diverse, fragmented, and disputable set of subjects. She shows how the amalgamation that is latinidad poses itself as a sleeping giant, a leviathan, that cuts both ways: on the one hand, Latinx elites have used the overarching term to guarantee some semblance of rights and political purchase, on the other hand, conservative fear-mongering has used the term to amalgamate a threat and wash over inherent differences. In short, both attempts at using the term invoke a giant that never seems to have gigantic agency. Instead, this sleeping leviathan functions as a perceived threat to conservatism that wants to withhold national recognition and the "proper" place of Latinx in US democracy and to the very stability of the US as a nation that serves, primarily, a "proper" hegemonic center of European-descended whites. The trouble that the use of such a term proffers is not only the homogenization that tries to take many disparate groups (Cubans, Puerto Ricans, Dominicans, Mexicans, Chicanos, Tejanos, Nicaraguans, Peruvians, Argentines, and the list goes on) under one identificatory aegis but also the supposed transparency of the term—the ability for it to refer to one specific demographic clearly, with force, and to communicate their desires, aspirations, political leanings, and material needs.

This problem of identity categories, of course, is not new, politically or theoretically speaking. But recognition of these limitations often spurs discourses to expand in order to meet the demands of thinking the "not yet," of what identitarian claims reach toward in a less than acceptable political present, and to more fully account for the a priori assumptions that undergird identity. *Latinidad* remains a problem for reading. It is, at times, a problematic term, and yet its force does not stop mattering as a political category, as a colonial amalgam, as a descriptor that always expects too much coherence, as a category that does and does not conscribe the life chances of those who may be read under its aegis. And yet, this reading of *latinidad* as figurative is in concert with other turns to questioning the relation between matter and meaning.[21] These questions will be asked, but this book does not offer a solution or promise repair. It believes in the ethical task of reading and hopes to inspire a reading practice more attendant to the inscriptions of *latinidad*. Rather than reflecting on these inscriptions through the lenses of harm and repair, my reading attends to their various terrains as the force of these articulate aesthetic forms takes us beyond the representation of a people or an ethnic ontology. The constitutive margins of the category of latinidad fracture under the pressure of the debates about the term, its grammatical (un)gendering, the coloniality of Spanish, and the imperialism of English. These differences demand a careful reading practice attendant to ethnic inscriptions as scenes rather than as taxonomic categorizations.

In a discussion of reading, questions of consumption, consumerism, and extraction are far from easily avoidable.[22] Indeed, very few readers mean to read literary works or experience art as sociological fodder or political evidence. Feeling underrepresented, feeling unseen in most narratives, readers of all kinds yearn to see themselves, to identify with aesthetic objects. There is nothing inherently wrong with this desire; it structures much more than the opening of books, than attendance at art shows. What is at issue for my work is when the arts and humanities wield difference, race, class, gender, coloniality, disability, and so on in order to course-correct disciplines that have historically flourished under colonialism and that were entrusted with the task of teaching the stories that reproduce the nation. The urge to read for inclusion arises from a collision of student resistance, neoliberal policies, and the philanthrocapitalist approach to problems that rewards "solution-based" models. Too often, a thinking of representational problems is immediately paired with interventions that promise liberation by plumbing disenfranchised paths. These apparent solutions respond to very real political desires, but such critical reflexes limit much of the serious work on questions of race, gender, ethnicity, diaspora, area, gender, coloniality, and sexuality to describing the problem and posing a solution, often with the same terms.

This double bind places quite a lot of implicit work onto studies that correspond to marginalized and disenfranchised peoples, creating clines of value in the academy. Rey Chow succinctly diagnoses this problem as one that creates hierarchies of knowledge and discipline in the humanities, pigeonholing, even if unwittingly, those of us working as the cleanup crew on marked difference in order to save our various disciplines from their grounding in racism, sexism, and colonialism:

> The predominant idea of moral repair—together with variables of remedy, redress, uplift, rebirth, and remodeling—means that transcendental signifieds are once again activated but this time affixed to area-based and identity-based signifiers (be they peoples, practices, languages, histories, or cultures).... Although in one respect they are performing the task of

what Jacques Derrida calls the "dangerous supplement" (an addition that, once introduced, tends to unsettle the entirety of the preceding chains of signification), these other forms of knowledge are in effect made to shoulder what might be called the white academy's burden (of filth and guilt). For precisely that reason, within the knowledge economy of the university they are often perceived as lacking the prestige and respectability of the classical disciplines. After all, they have been brought in as a kind of cleaning service, and engaging with them remains, in the eyes of many colleagues, tantamount to intellectual slumming.[23]

By cordoning off material differences into transcendental signifieds, our university economies treat studies of race, gender, ethnicity, and sexuality as inherently reparative and wholly supplemental. Interdisciplines are asked to shoulder the white academy's guilt, recount the horror of the past, and chart progressivist futures. Such labors are not asked of classical disciplines, save for paltry calls to diversify our faculty and decolonize our syllabi.

And yet, Latinx literary studies has often been read beyond neoliberal gestures. Ricardo Ortiz reads Latinx literature expansively under the aegis of both deconstruction and a widened, capacious understanding of *Latinx* and *latinidad* as being caught between "evanescence and event."[24] Creating dialogue between thinkers like Jacques Derrida and Edwidge Danticat, Ortiz insists that the work of Latinx literature is to think the literary in tandem and tension with latinidad. In this way, Ortiz represents a felicitous interlocutor to *Matters of Inscription*, reading the questions of latinidad as not only literary but grammatical and rhetorical, since their iterability concretizes in words—words that need to be read recursively. Such a reading risks encountering potential blind spots inherited from nationalist and colonial discourses that silo literature and arts. Ralph Rodriguez writes that "instead of being a Linnaeus who squashes bugs that he cannot readily classify, I think we want to . . . blur them, because to hold them too tightly is to blind ourselves to the realities that surround us."[25] Both Ortiz and Rodriguez bring us back to the fundamental concerns of literary theory to ask critical questions of what we call Latinx literature. In these discussions, identity matters but is taken as a representational quandary rather than a taxonomic assurance—that is, identitarian terms become an occasion for reading. As Mary Pat Brady has shown, each scalar recalibration that has moved from the nation of origin to a hyphenated American designation, to *Chicano*, to *Hispanic/Latino*, and now to *Latinx* partakes of broader swaths of captivity, detainment, and carcerality.[26] When the scale of a term encompasses as much as *Latinx*, our reading must attend to particular inscriptions that might otherwise be lost in the largest swath of capture. *Latinx* is a term that borrows from previous markers of identity to intervene in a hegemonic tradition that didn't have the right terms to take stock of its difference. And yet, *Latinx* and its predecessors are seemingly always overdue for revision, always about to be updated. Like most of our terms, *Latinx* is operating on borrowed time. This borrowed time alerts us to the way in which identitarian terms matter little in the face of forced migrations, extinctions, rising waters and warming, and acidifying oceans—particularly precarious for islands. These terms are also inscribed under the rise of fascist forces, which create nefarious amalgams of ideology that blur race, coloniality, and gender as impure otherness.

Our terms and our experiences keep shifting, if not exactly evolving in any developmental or progressive sense. This observation shows how the problem of reference brings us back to one of the most knotted aspects of language: its strangely recursive and unwieldy ability to refer both faithfully and unfaithfully. Either way, the referential function of language occurs. This fundamental and ongoing problem for reading is why we need a critical account of reading, not any which way (though these different modes can stand in for clarifying method and affordance), but as a commitment to contend with the medium and the message that emerge from the entanglements of inscription—that is, a commitment to attending to the materiality of inscription. To do so is really to do justice to the act of reading difference. To do justice to difference, then, we cannot read the sign as having a felicitous or transparent relation to a referent. The critique of the biographical hermeneutic follows this necessarily, not to discard biography as context, but to refute that that context is knowable (or even reconstructible) in a saturated way that would explain literary and artistic works.[27] Here we can begin to see that *Latinx* and its progenitors require a thoroughgoing understanding of referentiality.[28] Assigning bios, life or lived experience, as the ultimate referent of Latinx cultural production assumes a necessary biopolitical utilitarianism of Latinx works.

Part III

AGAINST THE BIOGRAPHICAL HERMENEUTIC

One referential stronghold that I have grown to see as symptomatic of the transparency conceit is the immediacy with which students, readers, and audiences try to retrace the life of the author or artist in the work—explaining the aesthetic in terms of biography. The biographical hermeneutic, when deployed as the only, or dominant, interpretive lens, relies on taxonomic and ontological frameworks and grammars of material circumstance—a rhetoric overdetermined at the level of life chances and optics, scaled upon a value system that is vastly disenfranchising and also impoverished at the level of thought.[29] In other words, racist, colonial, and heteronormative values undergird how we come to designate difference unless we allow difference to interrupt our frameworks, to shift the discourse of grammars that are grounded in the worst forms of ontological debasement in order to toil the land that's thieved. If we tend to the a prioris, the elemental material, the grammars of dispossession, and the structures of power that reproduce such dispossession, we must read exorbitantly for any self. And while this may be an obvious statement, our readerly desires often betray other values with an adherence to the individual as exemplar, token, evidence, or prophet.

Matters of Inscription attends to a thoroughgoing reading of the complexity of (auto)biography as a form of translation and mediation, filtered by or through the personal, the material, the structural, and the linguistic. The temptation to read underrepresented literatures in general—and queer, Latinx writers in particular—as biographical is understandable. A certain consideration of life writing follows from the lack of those experiences being represented in traditional literary canons.[30] However, this canonical absence opens up an ethical problem: the demand for a life to be read as *the* frame of reference often requires making both the life and the story relatable by oversimplification, relying on circumstance and linear order to tell stories about lives that are actually far more plural, structural, and chaotic.[31] This is even, or, especially, the case when it comes to one's own story.

* * *

Manuel Ramos Otero, whose poetry I review in the second chapter, theorizes autobiography as a process of translation inflected grammatically—focusing on how grammar and gender collide in his native tongue. His formulation considers the poetics of autobiography as a process within what Walter Benjamin calls "the laws of fidelity in the freedom of linguistic flux."[32] Considering the particular grammatical laws dictating pronouns, Ramos Otero elucidates the gendered accents of autobiographical modes of writing with a nuanced, queer feminist approach to difference. He writes,

> *Sí*, la autobiografía es un "recuento retrospectivo," pero *sí*, todo acto de la escritura lo es. *No*, no es necesariamente en prosa, todo depende de la capacidad poética del que (de la que) quiere autobiografiar. *Sí*, el acento se pone sobre la vida individual, pero el acento siempre ha estado puesto gramaticalmente sobre el *Yo*, que también es *Tú*, que además es *Él* y que siempre es *Ella* cuando nos genera con el acento fundamental de la diferencia. Y *Sí*, pero también *No*. El acento se pone particularmente sobre la historia, pero no sobre la historia de la personalidad sino sobre la historia del personaje.

> *Yes*, autobiography is a "retrospective retelling," but *yes*, every act of writing is such. *No*, it is not necessarily in prose, everything depends on the poetic capacity of he (and she) who wants to write autobiographically. *Yes*, the accent is placed on the individual life, but the accent has always been placed grammatically on the *I*, which is also the *You*, which moreover is the *He* and is always *She* when we are engendered with the fundamental accent of difference. And *Yes*, but also *No*. The accent is placed particularly on history, but not on the history of the personality—instead on the history of the character.[33]

Pronouns matter in relation to gender, but pronouns create tricky terrains of reference beyond gender. I return to this question of pronouns and antecedents in the fourth chapter, but for now I want to think about Ramos Otero's insistence on the "fundamental accent of difference." Gender, race, and language all demand to be read, but their readability may not be predictable. Questions of accent and translation remain integral to the task of reading and encountering latinidad, and yet, this may not always be the provenance of the Spanish language as guarantor of belonging.

The task of telling one's own life, which always tends to fall short, disfigure, or be incomplete, is the very basis of ethical accountability for Judith Butler. As they explain in *Giving an Account of Oneself*, every person's account of themselves is necessarily incomplete. Far from saying that the autobiography is impossible or illegitimate, Butler writes,

> We can surely tell our stories, and there will be many stories to do precisely that. But we will not be able to be very authoritative when we try to give a full account with a narrative structure. The "I" can neither tell the story of its own emergence nor the conditions of its own possibility without bearing witness to a state of affairs to which one could not have been present, which are prior to one's own emergence as a subject who can know, and so constitute a set of origins that one can narrate only at the expense of authoritative knowledge.[34]

These origins, which we cannot know and thus depend on others to tell us, enmesh us in ethics. So, giving an account of oneself, being accountable by address, and using the autobiographical mode may very well prove that even one's own life story cannot be transmitted totally, comprehensively, and faithfully from the purported source: the self. Rather than anchoring the self as the sovereign author of one's own life, autobiography itself radically questions this authority. This ethical question of narration, especially as it pertains to telling the story of one's own life, also bears upon the task of reading. In such an articulation, the autobiographical mode gives us compelling grounds from which to ask how one might proceed with adequate caution regarding autobiographical modes of writing and reading. To be clear, I do not mean to say that reading for referentiality is always wrong. Instead, I want to emphasize that reading with an expectation of transparency is quite often an asymmetric demand made on racialized and gendered writers and texts. Instead of proceeding with caution, readers want or claim to know, ahead of time, what will lie between the covers of a book. This is a persistent problem for underrepresented work that often exists in the double bind of claiming truths heretofore untold, while simultaneously being read as a synecdoche for a whole people.

Certain texts, however influenced by the author's life, may not be read immediately as biographical. Reading—which entails a dwelling in the unknowability of a text's archive and referentiality—is often afforded to writers and texts for whom there are many representations of their supposed demographic. As such, those who don't have many tales told in the world of letters are often read as representative, ethnographically and sociologically, thus reducing the figurative force of their work. When fiction is read as transparent autobiography, we truly kill the author. Biographical hermeneutics foreclose the movement of narrative by enclosing it in a past that is melancholically sealed off. This is another instantiation of the problem of the metaphysics of presence, another consideration of the deadening of minoritized works. What if, instead, we seek not to understand the text but to risk reading it poetically, figuratively, and synesthetically?[35] What if we were to finger the rough edges where life and representation meet, to dwell in the traces of a desire to tell what can't be simply put, to linger in the unfulfilled longings that rage at the page like waves crashing, to allow ourselves to get carried away in the smallest particulate that floats off the page?

Part IV

READING LATINX INSCRIPTIONS
There are, ultimately, no positive terms in language. When the human organism inscribes itself in language it becomes a subject of language, and as a result of this inscription every determination of the subject will be by necessity indeterminate.
—Antonio Viego, *Dead Subjects: Toward a Politics of Loss in Latino Studies*

Thinking in terms of inscription would be unthinkable without the linguistic turn, and yet, at the same time, it consists of a reaction against it, since, for proponents of inscription, the levels of material and structure can no longer be differentiated as neatly. Instead, through the lens of inscription, thinkers focus their attention on how materiality and signification interact; and inscription becomes one of the models for theorizing this interaction.
—Andrea Bachner, *The Mark of Theory*

Latinx functions as an inscription with a long, variegated etymology, resulting from activist movements, incentivized and forced migrations, bureaucratic taxonomy, and market-driven demographic interpellation. By marking *Latinx* as an inscription, this book takes it as a mark to be read in general and under the pressures of how one makes marks as a marked writer or artist. In so doing, I hope to attend to the referential qualities located at the site not of the referent but of the signified. By accenting the signified of *Latinx*, I mean to say that the term requires not just thinking of the signifier and its strange relation to sounding out Spanish endings but also that we think of the suture of this signifier to a concept. *Latinx* represents an ethnic-racial concept with force: the force to describe a college class, a piece of art, a city, a sound, a set of studies. And yet, the material fallout of the term does affect supposed referents materially. Inscription has been a key word in much work addressing the quandary of how to read a mark in relation to its ground, substrate, canvas, or page.[36] Often, these grounds are groundless in the metaphysical sense—replete with overly sedimented logics of intelligibility and grammars of race and gender. The (anti)foundation of inscription is not background as such but rather entangled into each inscription. Negativity makes a mark readable. And marking concerns not only inscription at the level of word or etching but also how the one who marks is always marked by a grammar or rhetoric of race and gender. Though context cannot be saturated or recovered, readings must always grapple with the constraints contexts place upon inscription.

If we follow Sánchez's inscriptive drawing, we see that the signified is quite difficult to discern from the signifier—they are both marks. The signified of the signifier reminds us that a sign—a sound-image and a concept—at least in the wake of Saussure, cannot exactly be separated tout court. At this point, it is worth recalling a few things about Saussure—an initiating force of what would come to be known as "the linguistic turn"—in order to remind ourselves that this turn, like many other theoretical turns that would follow, was not understood as such in its inception. Tasked with teaching a course on "general linguistics," Saussure's radical insights—the arbitrary nature of the sign and the negative, differential value of the sign—could only be thought in a context where many languages other than those familiar to Europe were considered. So too do I want to draw special attention to how inseparable the signifier and signified are within the

Saussurian sign: "A language might also be compared to a sheet of paper. Thought is on one side of the sheet and sound the reverse side. Just as it is impossible to take a pair of scissors and cut one side of paper without at the same time cutting the other, so it is impossible in language to isolate sound from thought, or thought from sound. To separate the two for theoretical purposes takes us into either pure psychology or pure phonetics, not linguistics."[37] I rehearse this moment to direct our attention not just to signifiers but to the status of the signified, which, at least in a post-Saussurian semiotics, is a concept that requires an arbitrary relation to a signifier if it is to be understood at all. Prior to the paper metaphor, Saussure invoked language as a field of articulation—a mark-making against a backdrop of what might otherwise be nonsense. Sánchez's drawing, through choreographed marks, occasions a thinking of the signified as a mark. Rather than pretending to make a cut to the concept, Sánchez's drawing becomes a felicitous rejoinder to reconsider how signs create their force and value in the world. To inflect the signified in this inseparable sign is to think the purchase that concepts (which sometimes operate referentially) have on our ways of perceiving the material world. And though Latinx may not have strict referents, it is an abiding concept in our current episteme. To be clear, I am not endorsing a revision of poststructural insights into difference and the valences of language or a notion of referential materiality accessible by way of the signified. Rather, I am arguing that the sign's arbitrariness and negativity remain even at the level of the signified. The critical tendency to emphasize the signifier can conveniently drop the conceptual work that signifiers always incur, that lead one into either abstract or seemingly material referential terrain. When the signified is introduced back into the realm of the sign and signification, we can see the utter strangeness of how signifiers suture to signifieds and of how they traffic conceptually. But again, I want to consider the signified as different from the referent in order to think as linguistically and rhetorically as possible about the problem of reading and referencing *Latinx* as a sign. Always mediated, inscriptions ask us to think the signified as carrying the possibility of the referential and of the indexical. For Sánchez's drawing, the signified is both the most basic visual mark and a mark that gives rise, when gathered, to abstracted corporeal forms. If the signified and the signifier unite in the sign, they cannot be read as neatly apart.

Both partake in a sign that is sutured and cut, in a general space of possibility that is groundless, negative, *and yet* overdetermined by preceding sedimentations of meaning and grammar.[38] At least two remarkable phenomena become inscribed on the body prior to linguistic subjectivation: race and sex. We can both register these marked clefts and remain uncertain as to what, precisely, they transmit or index. And yet it seems no surprise that this linguistic exercise rendered graphic would turn to corporeality. Andrea Bachner reminds us that much of how racial and sexual/gendered difference has been understood, at least theoretically, is through models and metaphors of inscription.[39]

For Jacques Lacan, as for Antonio Viego, the emphasis in thinking the materiality of language resides in the realm of the signifier—a chain of associations that do not exactly capture the force of the real but wrestle with its ineffable capture in language. The question of language's inscription leads Antonio Viego to thoroughly attend to the problem of loss in his theoretical intervention into Latinx studies, *Dead Subjects: Toward a Politics of Loss in Latino Studies* (2011). There, Viego makes crucial and astute observations about how ethnic-racialized subjects are thought to be transparent signifiers, thoroughly known and understandable. As such, racist interpolative forces ask ethnic-racialized subjects to perform a fullness and agentiality that does not—indeed cannot—follow from poststructural and psychoanalytic accounts of subjectivity that understand the loss that comes with language as a loss of a relation to the real and of a polymorphous perversity prior to entry into the symbolic. This burden of representation becomes a burden of liveness[40] and then an unfulfillable demand for those disenfranchised, or at least those marked by nonwhiteness, to be more whole, more good, more agential. Viego's insights continue to charge Latinx studies with the problem of thinking its subjectivation and subjection to language. *Matters of Inscription* attends to this indeterminacy of language that Viego urges us to consider, especially for the sake of those who experience material loss after this linguistic inscription.

Language here is anything but romanticized, with "no positive terms."[41] This emphasis on the negative differential of language reminds us of Saussure's insights that language is only understood by what it is not. Human organisms inscribe themselves into language, but this inscription is not a humanist move. Language is privative and inherently linked to loss. Viego takes care to underscore that such loss may be universal to linguistic subjects, though racialization, gender, and coloniality produce profound material loss and deprivation that cannot be equivocated with that universal loss constitutive of linguistic subjectivation.[42] Such an emphasis on loss's incommensurability allows insights from the linguistic turn to be thought anew. Put another way, debates about *Latinx* as marker, as speech, as a term, allow us to see, once again, that the violence of language must be thought in tandem with material realities—without recourse to positivism. This is the charge of racial, ethnic, and gendered referential dilemmas that cannot be easily dealt with at the level of signifier if we understand the sign to be doing the work of both signifier and signified, especially if both are marks and exhibit a destabilizing supplementarity. The materiality of inscription does not give one referential access to material realities precisely because of this supplementarity, but it does afford a way of thinking at the interstice of language's materiality and its ability to refer to material conditions. Still, if language is de-idealized in inscriptions, and if it requires us to think materiality, then this thinking of materiality will not be the final, transcendental signified that gets us out of having to reckon with the problem of trace structure, writing, and inscriptive logics.

Why think referentiality as a material problem?[43] Reference is tricky terrain, but it is not unthinkable in the terms of deconstruction—despite critical emphasis on the signifier that seems to follow its early thinking. In a 1985 interview, Jacques Derrida offered the following consideration of reference: "The impossibility of reducing reference, that is what I am trying to say—and of reducing the other. What I'm doing is thinking about difference along with thinking about the other. And the other is the hard core of reference. It's exactly what we can't reinsert into interiority, into the homogeneity of some protected place. So thinking about difference is thinking about 'ference.' And the irreducibility of 'ference' is the other. It's what is other, which is different."[44] It follows, then, that reference charges us to think difference, even as we must tread carefully so as not to risk falsely anchoring language in the Real of the referent. To do so would be to endow radical alterity within a domestication of language. And this problem of reference is one that is particularly troubling in critical race, ethnic, and gender studies. Referentiality and race have a specific relation—a tight tether, often presupposed to be transparent and self-evident. We can see how *Latinx* already troubles this presumption—its racial reference being anything but clear. Accordingly, this book will not be about *Latinx* because, as Kandice Chuh reminds us, such a demand is most often a way to cordon off difference, to domesticate it as a known referent that can be managed.[45] Or, to think with Rey Chow, the positivism of difference in the aftermath of poststructural interventions in the North Atlantic academy was too often placed onto area and cultural studies and was not entirely dispelled by the critique of the metaphysics of presence.[46] So while this book will read and attend to *Latinx* as an identificatory sign with important referential concerns, I do not set out to define it as a category nor to carve out a specific set of aesthetic practices that dwell under its aegis. Rather, *Latinx* here functions as the most salient (but not the sole) identificatory inscription that conscribes the writers and artists in this book. But what kind of inscription or referential sign is *Latinx*? What I propose is that we read this sign, *Latinx*, as a trope—more specifically, as a catachresis.

Part V

TIGHT TETHER
Raciality, Reference, and Catachresis[47]

One of the contentions of this book, grounded as it is in an attention to aesthetic objects and literary theory, is that far from being past some of the most radical insights of the so-called linguistic turn, we still have trouble in the matter of reference and representation. These matters cannot be settled; instead, they demand anew that we return to the data—the given—of the literary and the aesthetic to question how we read.[48] This may feel like a return to the 1990s; however, the considerable work in postcolonial, decolonial, trans, queer, and critical race studies that has proliferated since that time gives us new resources that call for a revisitation of discourses on difference.

To that end, I ask, what does it feel like to be an overdetermined referent? Reference becomes a necessary literary element to consider, especially when underrepresented writers and artists are often charged with the task of telling us how horrible the past was and/or laying out a path for a liberated future.⁴⁹ Meanwhile, much of the systemic ontological imposition of raciality and the racialized gender of nonwhite, non-cis, non-male peoples renders their lives as figures necessary to maintaining the larger symbolic system itself.⁵⁰ It leaves the work of the past, the present, and the future on othered bodies, twisting and turning to fulfill various operations of meaning-making at once: to seamlessly transfer information, to excavate the past, and to drill tidy tunnels into the future. If we still have a problem of reference, it has less to do with the status of signifiers as either arbitrary or performative and more to do with how we collectively imagine the relationship between sign and referent, especially as it concerns the tight tether between raciality and a supposed transparent affixing the ethnic-racialized subject as object. This tight tether has been remarked upon by various scholars who show how the racial is taken as a transparent signifier, which is never transparent at all but instead mediated by a grid of intelligibility that is profoundly racist.

In *Poetics of Relation*, Édouard Glissant chastens transparent readings of difference. This problem of transparency finds its way into a number of texts, far too many to survey here, that grapple with questions of representation and racial difference. In Latinx studies, Antonio Viego argues that the field needs to account for loss at the level of psyche, language, and racial structure—a loss often denied to ethnic-racialized subjects who are lured by psychologies and activisms of ego-driven change and agential wholeness.⁵¹ Ethnic-racialized subjects are rendered "dead signifiers" when read in this transparent manner.⁵² Rey Chow, too, sees this danger as a "fascist longing in our midst"—reminding us that fascism's technologies rely on transparent, idealized images to love, not to hate.⁵³ She reframes fascism as a quintessential problem that requires us to question fetishes of alterity: "Emerging in postcoloniality, the new 'desire for our others' displays the same positive, projectional symptoms of fascism . . .—a rebelliousness and a monstrous aesthetics, but most of all a longing for a transparent, idealized image and an identifying submission to that image."⁵⁴ Both Chow and Viego charge transparency with conceit; it is an aspect and extension of the ruse of visibility that many have critiqued. Denise Ferreira da Silva takes transparency on as a thesis to be radically dispelled: "What is required, I think, is a radical gesture that clears up a critical position by displacing transparency, the attribute man has enjoyed since his institution as the sole self-determined being; consequently, it also requires creating a critical arsenal that identifies science and history as moments in the production of man without rehearsing either the logic of discovery or the thesis of transparency."[55] Da Silva notes that this "transparency thesis" has created the onto-epistemological status of the transparent "I" as the subject position of the racially white and global northern citizen. In order to displace transparency, one cannot merely include more racialized others because their ontic place is already built into the modern schema of representation. An acknowledgment of their difference does not throw these representations into ethical crisis,[56] even beyond the death of the subject. While transparency, even in its more colloquial sense, is often an important part of democratic processes, in and of itself it does not create an ethical relation, nor does it change material structure. In other words, when we're asked for transparency without accountability, we defer to grammar, legal codes, and symbolic orders that diminish many lives and relations. By what means might we consider the material need and the semantic gap that urges us to use identitarian terms in order to make claims on these hostile grounds?

Part VI

RISKING CATACHRESIS ON RHETORICAL GROUNDS
One of the offshoots of the deconstructive view of language is the acknowledgement that the political use of words, like the use of words, is irreducibly catachrestic. Again, the possibility of catachresis is not derived. The task of feminist political philosophy is neither to establish the proper meaning of "true," nor to get caught up in a regressive pattern to show how the proper meaning always eludes our grasp, nor yet to ignore it . . . but to accept the risk of catachresis.
—Gayatri C. Spivak, *Outside in the Teaching Machine*

Before we can answer the question of how to read identitarian terms as catachresis, we need to reconsider how language grounds itself in reference. If we follow the tracks of rhetoricians back to their origins and a certain foundation of language, we arrive at a rhetorical figure that has no grounding, no solid significatory purchase on reference, born out of necessity and lack: catachresis. Patricia Parker reminds us that "catachresis is a transfer of terms from one place to another employed when no proper word exists, while metaphor is a transfer or substitution employed when a proper term does already exist and is displaced by a term transferred from another place not its own."[57] Given metaphor's relationship to substitution and sameness, catachresis's abuse of metaphor exposes moments when metaphors cannot readily transport by means of one-to-one substitution. When I invoke catachresis, I am not heralding a new term—it is quite old—nor am I striving to assign progressive value to the term. Rather, catachresis is at work in many positional terms that seem to conjure difficult referential tethering, when the need to think something forges past the polished veneer of a poetic substitute or an unconstrained or natural referential claim. Posselt clarifies this idea: "Whereas metaphor is fundamentally related to substitution, in the case of catachresis no substitution takes place. Thus, catachresis is neither truly proper or literal, nor metaphorical or figurative; and yet it has something of both."[58] As a rhetorical trope, catachresis is used often and is more pernicious when underthought or naturalized. What I mean to say here is that I'm not developing a science of nor urging a turn to catachresis but reconsidering this rhetorical term—which has allowed scholars to think at the edge of reference, urgency, and meaning—in order to suggest how we might read overly sedimented terms.

Catachresis emerges as a way of talking about improper or ill-fitting metaphors that arise when one needs to name something but there is a dearth of proper terms for that something. As they sought to categorize a Latin translation of a Greek term, ancient orators from Quintilian to Cicero defined *catachresis* as an imaginative, desperate, and monstrous form of rhetoric. Catachresis, most often understood as an abuse or misuse of metaphor, is defined as a figuration that is improper; it signifies something for which there can be no literal referent. In this regard, catachresis emerges from the need to use a word where a proper one is lacking—proper in the sense of preexisting or proper to an order. If catachresis is the ground from which all metaphor takes flight, in one way or another, then its rather humble, desperate origin begs dissemination in full, because no one word will ever be enough.[59]

The relation between catachresis and metaphor is one that is slippery because the improper can be made proper and vice versa. Quintilian separates catachresis as *abusio* and metaphor as *translatio* but then concedes that poets often abuse language to add a flourish of meaning—that is, for poetic license.[60] If the two terms circle one another, this seems to have to do less with them being interchangeable and more to do with the force that catachresis imparts on how we receive metaphors; it can debase, misuse, abuse, and take up nearly dead metaphors. It can also reign in the realm of tropes as the originary figurativity of any language system—the tenuous gap and need from which language arises. But this origin would only ever be metaleptically known. Catachresis, it seems, betrays something of language: its misfits, its desperate needs, its lexical lacunae. Catachresis makes itself known through a forceful movement of language that both is and is not human: "The violent intrusions of catachresis and the possibility of transfers that, unwilled, subvert the very model of the controlling subject, are the gothic underside of the mastery of metaphor, the uncanny other of its will to control. And words taking on a life of their own not only conflates the abuses of metaphor with the *abusio* of *catachresis* but informs a potential linguistic return of the repressed, the insinuation of figures in the most 'familiar' and apparently 'proper' discourse, the *unheimlich* return of the dead or slumbering to life."[61] The economy of catachresis is linked to its strange and often contested status as metaphor. When identity functions as an analogical metaphor, sloppy comparisons glide over uneven terrain. Thinking in neatly metaphorical terms keeps political claims in the realm of the proper, the proprietary, and the polished. Put another way, while the personal is political, the personal is very seldom easily substitutable. If we think of catachresis as a misuse or abuse of metaphor, then we have less recourse to use analogs for explanation—which makes equivocation and one-to-one translation impossible. Because *analogy* and recovery of the true referent are impossible projects for catachresis, the figure qua figure draws attention to a vexxed referentiality with a particular injunction to think both need and loss. In this sense, to read identitarian terms as catachrestic would mean to read the contexts within which such terms make claims born out of the tense relationship between the lack of a proper word and the need to make a claim. Catachresis is born from the need to describe and the lack of a proper signifier, or lexical loss. Some losses are constitutive beyond any abstract sense of subject formation in language. Indeed, some losses are the grounding disenfranchisement that debases many while the weight of their dispossession supports a few, both symbolically and materially. For catachresis to be born of loss or lacunae does not mean we can equivocate those losses and lacks.

The following poem by Roque Salas Rivera shows how nothings can be multiple and incommensurate. The poem traffics in deficit by way of a consideration of Puerto Rico's massive debt—a debt that is both imposed, vastly disenfranchising Puerto Ricans on the island, and also actively invested in vis-à-vis a symbolically disavowed coloniality. The poem appears in *the tertiary / lo terciario*, which is written as poetic responses to Pedro Scaron's *El Capital*, the 1976 translation of Karl Marx's *Das Kapital: Kritik der politischen Ökonomie*. The poem underscores the ways in which nothingness, negativity, and loss cannot be equivocated:

> "*a material substratum will always remain*"
>   scene 4:
> cenex discovers there are multiple nothings.
>   like multiple infinities.
> no they aren't double nos.
> more like nothings each one excluding the other completely;
> the nothing of incommensurable fractions,
> the nothing of honey anthills,
> —quartz of snow and piss—,
> the nothing of pink plantains,
> the nothing of return,
> the nothing of my frozen hands they've cut
> and i carry like a rabbit's foot.
> cenex discovers there are worse worsts.[62]

"Pink plantains" do not exist as such—the naming here is a poetic catachresis that figures the incommensurability of these nothings. "Double nos" is a slippery move between English and Spanish. Is it double negation of two utterances of *no*? Or is it a double *nos*, which in Spanish would always be double in the sense that it functions as an enclitic, first-person plural pronoun embedded within some reflexive verbs and, therefore, as both the object and the tacit subject of the verb's work? To read this *nos* as a Spanish *nos* would mean to read this term as truncated, cut off from a phantasmatic transitive, reflexive verb. The poem already exists as double, since *the tertiary / lo terciario* is published in both Spanish and English, with the direction of the pages inverted—a queer relation between these two colonial languages, which seems most befitting for a work about Puerto Rico. The doubled enunciations of the poems create an echo and a chasm between the languages and disorder which is the original and which is the translation. Moreover, the incommensurate here emphasizes that negativities need not be assessed according to the same scale; there is a scalar and material difference between the privation of language, the lack of desire, and the vast disenfranchisement that racialized peoples have imposed upon them. The materialist insistence from Marx that a "material substratum will always remain" arises in the first volume of *Das Kapital* to remind us that matter comprises the stuff of the commodity and that material shifts in nature, as well as in labor, in order to create the strangeness of political economies that use commodities as social relations.[63] At times, catachresis can operate a bit like an amalgam—creating entities of seemingly disparate parts, the most notorious examples being the face of a mountain or the legs of a chair. We could mistake these catachreses as anthropomorphisms, but not all legs belong to humans. And anthropomorphism, rhetorically speaking, often has the effect of showing the limitations of the ontological parameters of the human rather than sheerly granting human form to another entity. As such, attention to the use of catachreses may bring about a different way of thinking key terms as arising in the dearth of grammars that can tend to these bodies.

In many ways, the lingering urgencies of the classical rhetorical considerations of catachresis hinge upon theoretical considerations that look to the limitations of extant words to describe disenfranchisement alongside the undeniable need to make such claims.[64] Catachresis enjoyed a revivification with deconstruction's consideration of the linguistic turn, and very quickly, thinkers reading at the edge of language and marked difference employed the term to consider what Gayatri Spivak calls "master words" (*women, proletariat*, etc.).[65] Catachresis emerges in Spivak's work as a conceptual companion to strategic essentialism and as a corrective to nostalgic yearnings for lost origins. If in "Can the Subaltern Speak" Spivak alerts us to two kinds of representation—speaking for another as political representative and re-presentation—then perhaps this tropological figure reverberates between the two kinds of representation that often plague the work of underrepresented literatures and art.⁶⁶ So too does the term limn conversations around gender performativity in Butler's early work. In both, catachresis is a risk of language precisely because language works through differentiation and deferral—neither of which creates predictable grounds for how language will be heard or read, and neither of which provides easy redress to injustice. Our identitarian terms fail to encapsulate the vast materiality and heterogeneity underneath their denotative provenance, but catachresis rhetorically recognizes the need to use a word where no proper one exists as such.⁶⁷ And when it does emerge in the tense relationship between this need to articulate an identificatory claim (of oneself or another) and the lack of a proper word to do that naming, catachresis draws attention to the quotidian problem of reference that haunts our political terms. The strangeness of its fit thus harbors the possibility of resignification: "Thus, catachresis might be conceived both as a figurative and a performative act of resignification which—in applying (abusively) a familiar term with a somewhat different signification—does not signify a pre-discursive object, but rather constitutes the identity of what is named."⁶⁸ What is named is granted its identity or its signified content by way of the name itself—alerting us to how this supplement, catachresis, can create the illusion of positivism. This abuse of metaphor, then, requires alert reading.

A quick glance at the status of metaphor tells us that the problem of figuration in relation to raciality and racialized gender remains.⁶⁹ Alterity and difference were the terrain of culture wars in the 1990s, and we see such warring factions reconfigured now. The critical value of a notion of language that operates off a fundamental difference, or *différance*, cannot simply be that meaning is deferred, that the original is a matrix, that gender is a performance of a repetition for which there is no original. The absence of a stable origin entails catachresis: a ground and an absence of ground all at once, where need and lack converge. Catachresis is a quotidian practice that exposes the limits of our thinking when substitution can no longer suffice—when analogical thinking violently collapses difference into sameness.

I understand catachresis to be risky in a few ways: there's risk of being misunderstood, risk of the signifier not doing justice to the signified, and risk of making a claim on shaky ground. But following Rey Chow's logic, we must risk bringing the question of referentiality to bear on the relation between loss and need.[70] Though signification works in modes of deferral, some forms of active disenfranchisement demand that we use terms more roughshod and more direct than eloquent metaphors and theoretical polemics. In the realm of social justice, the horizon of addressing disenfranchisement cannot afford to be perpetually *à venir*.[71] Words partake in the linguistic armature of ontological hierarchy. Modern grammars, especially of raciality, favor a form of idealism (metaphor) that is not ideal for those who have to do the work of representation. When thought in relation to race, critical Black studies has theorized these operations as that which harnesses the negative ontic in order to make modernity, civilization, and indeed humanity legible. The material and semantic supports that hold up hierarchies across the globe rely on a grammar that renders Black life as plastic and fungible.[72] Like iterability and performativity in deconstruction's thinking of *différance*, these two concepts have fundamentally transformed how we think about the ontological imposition of raciality.

Relatedly, the term *Latinx* has spurred detractors and supporters. In both camps, we find a need to specify what we mean when we employ the term *Latinx*. The "x" of *Latinx* may strive toward more inclusivity vis-à-vis gender, but the same may not be said for race, indigeneity, and coloniality. The need to supplement *Latinx* with a prefixal *Afro-*, for instance, shows something of the way in which *Latinx* requires specification, hinged upon a latinidad that is thoroughly colonial. Relatedly, we also see these critiques that show that perhaps the term erases Indigenous presence by being fully absorbed into Latinx iconography. In this manner, *Latinx* harnesses Indigenous figuration to conjure a prenational past through mythology. Following in this book, we may see why considerations of race and reference matter materially for how we read this term and its constituents. Put another way, the understanding of *Latinx* or *latinidad* as catachrestic keeps us from merging into *mestizaje* myths that engulf important and agonistic heterogeneities.[73]

New and challenging terms bring up stranger registers of feeling intra- and interpersonally. *Catachresis* draws attention to the discomfiture of the term.[74] The use of catachrestic terms can conjure a raw or crass affective register, off-putting feelings that align with catachresis's ability to cut, reconfigure, and metaleptically make meaning. This feeling has been referred to as ossification, reification, and congealment.

Judith Butler describes the operation in *Bodies That Matter*: "Catachresis is thus a perpetual risk that rigid designation seeks to overcome, but always inadvertently produces, despite its best intentions."[75] I follow Spivak's urge to accept "the risk of catachresis" by way of assembling a genealogy of thinkers who show how reference, transparency, and economy figure and structure the impact of referentiality upon the political use of identitarian terms.[76]

Part VII

GRAMMAR LESSONS

Black feminisms, in particular, have consistently paid heed of political rhetoric while still attending to material conditions. In this excerpt from Hortense Spillers's "Mama's Baby, Papa's Maybe," note the rupture that is both a beginning and a continuation as well as a grammar: "Let's face it. I am a marked woman, but not everybody knows my name. 'Peaches' and 'Brown Sugar,' 'Sapphire' and 'Earth Mother,' 'Aunty,' 'Granny,' God's 'Holy Fool,' a 'Miss Ebony First,' or 'Black Woman at the Podium': I describe a locus of confounded identities, a meeting ground of investments and privations in the national treasury of rhetorical wealth. My country needs me, and if I were not here, I would have to be invented."[77] Spiller's illustrative opening lines play with the ways in which being marked leads to a confusion of names and concludes that such marking structures an anti-Black national project. To be marked is to be a target, to have an ontological condition imposed. It also entails recalcitrance to any comfortable nominalization. Names inevitably disseminate to become different names, but the condition of the named stays in a loop of this originary violence that divests the marked, Black(ened) woman in service of a "national treasury of rhetorical wealth." In a dazzling set of sentences, we move from what we have to face, to being marked, to a list of names that range from violently intimate to disenfranchisingly euphemistic and constatively respectable. But in the meeting ground of confounded, recalcitrant identities, the Black(ened) woman is nonetheless necessitated as the substratum that grounds racist grammar.

If the grammars and modern representations we've received rest upon such radical debasement, then abuse of language may be one strategy for calling attention to that very structure of meaning-making. Perhaps this might be one reason we see attention to catachresis emerge anew in contemporaneous critical Black studies. Alessandra Raengo engages the trope of catachresis to explain the relation between seeing and saying, between the visual and the avisual, as catachresis.[78] Calvin Warren engages catachresis as a trope that can begin to figure the aporia of the "free" Black, a trope that may begin to allow how to think about important signs that do not have literal referents ontologically speaking.[79]

In catachresis, Paul de Man finds a monstrosity of figuration that can reorient our relationship to the supposedly given—to the referential status of reality itself:

> Abuse of language is, of course, itself the name of a trope: catachresis. This is indeed how Locke describes mixed modes. They are capable of inventing the most fantastic entities by dint of the positional power inherent in language. They can dismember the texture of reality and reassemble it in the most capricious of ways, pairing man with woman or human being with beast in the most unnatural shapes. Something monstrous lurks in the most innocent of catachreses: when one speaks of the legs of the table or the face of the mountain, catachresis is already turning into prosopopoeia, and one begins to perceive a world of potential ghosts and monsters.[80]

This positional power inherent in language reverberates forcefully when we consider the import of standpoint epistemology. Figuration is a matter of not just language but also bodies and other phenomena taken as referents that live with the marks of grammar enfleshed. Black feminisms and deconstruction, across different theoretical terrains, enable one to "dismember the texture of reality" with the hopes that it may reassemble into something unnatural, something not easily integrated into the lingua franca of hegemony.[81] A "world of potential ghosts and monsters" produces a hauntological resonance: figurations that dwell on the limits of signification. We should welcome such hauntings beyond proper meaning, with all the urgency of need.

Thinking with catachresis is less of a polemic for or against catachresis because it is in use all the time. Indeed, I admit that using a phrase like "the ground of language," as I have, is itself catachrestic. Attention to catachresis as a fundamental, rhetorical operation of figuration invites us to consider the politico-ethical ramifications of the pressures of signification for those who are overdetermined by their sign as a referent, as evidence. Identity markers like Black, brown, Latinx, Asian, native/Indigenous, woman, queer, person of color, when thought of as catachresis,[82] may give us a way to pause and linger over tensions between need and lack as "the process rushes on."[83] Perhaps the risk of catachresis comes when thinking referentiality at its limits cannot but attend to the status of the referent in addition to the sign. We may do well to think how the limits of referentiality haunt our political terrain. For Rey Chow, such work of limit-thinking would allow referentiality to interrupt the work of theory: "Let referentiality interrupt, to reopen the poststructuralist closure on this issue, to acknowledge the inevitability of reference even in the most avant-garde of theoretical undertakings, and to demand a thorough reassessment of an originary act of repudiation/exclusion in terms that can begin to address the 'scandal of domination and exploitation of one part of mankind by another.'"[84] To allow referentiality to interrupt is not to take as raw data those deemed to be demographic referents. Instead, Chow proposes an "ethics after idealism" that resonates with Denise Ferreira da Silva's imperative to de-idealize. De-idealized reading admits to our disturbing attachments—our potential complicity with modes of domination—and creates the possibility of an ethically responsible mode of reading.[85] Chow elaborates on this ethicality: "To propose a kind of ethics after idealism is thus not to confirm the attainment of an entirely independent critical direction, but rather to put into practice a supplementing imperative—to follow, to supplement idealism doggedly with non-benevolent readings, in all the dangers supplementarity entails."[86] Attention to catachresis allows the conditions of referentiality to be thought anew, to be thought with urgency instead of deferral or embarrassment. The crossing of matter and language in matter-metaphors produces monstrous amalgams, often making their referential status opaque or ambivalent.

Rhetorical terms draw attention to how language makes meaning, and this attention helps us to see how aesthetics can collude with idealized or fascistic aims. One cannot deny the aestheticization of politics nor the politicization of aesthetics, as Walter Benjamin shows in his germinal essay "The Work of Art in the Age of Its Technological Reproducibility." Benjamin's iconic essay considers how the masses interact with art. In our moment, rereading the essay brings up many anxieties around technology, as well as a renewed urgency to consider how fascism works and lures. Calling the masses a "matrix," Benjamin notes that "the increasing proletarianization of modern man and the increasing formation of masses are two sides of the same process. Fascism attempts to organize the newly proletarianized masses while leaving intact the property relations which they strive to abolish. It sees its salvation in granting expression to the masses—but on no account granting them rights."[87] He goes on to say that "the masses have a right to changed property; fascism seeks to give them expression in keeping these relations unchanged. The logical outcome of fascism is an aestheticizing of political life."[88] The enduring legacy of Benjamin's essay exceeds its moment of inscription—both in relation to its historical moment and its emplacement in Europe—to alert us anew to the danger of resting too easily in our thinking of the political and the aesthetic. The glossy aestheticization of politics is the flimsy veneer of diversity work in our universities—what Rey Chow calls "the fascist longings in our midst."[89]

In this manner, we may consider that the "matrix," as Benjamin called the masses, may be thought of in relation to current figures of racialized and gendered nondominance, often named through catachrestic invocations of demographics. These demographic inscriptions can be wielded falsely without changing the material substratum of property relations and life resources. Figurations and instrumentalizations of underrepresented peoples are key to the critical work of many who think at the intersections of race, gender, matter, and the humanities. Kandice Chuh translates this danger as a charge for those of us who work within the confines of the neoliberal university that would rather carry out the task of taxonomizing and technocratizing than shift the structure of racial capitalism. Still, she inhabits the humanities to consider what she calls "illiberal humanisms" that create an aesthetic sensibility "after Man," taking up Sylvia Wynter's charge.[90] In this respect, as we risk catachresis, we risk aesthetics, fully aware that the aesthetic has long been the arsenal of monolithic theories of art and humanity that exclude others. We must understand that transparent readings rarely attune themselves aesthetically to works created by the "others" of Wynterian notions of Man.

To create literature and art, especially as a minority or an immigrant in the United States, is to make cultural texts in a world that markets difference as adornment or appendage and siloes it in days of remembrance, awareness weeks, and tribute months. Difference is to be read under the sign of marked identity written in a grammar one did not consent to. At another moment of crisis, in the wake of the 2010 earthquake in Haiti, Edwidge Danticat stated that the immigrant artist should "create dangerously, for people who read dangerously."[91] And while the artists and writers in this book may not have been writing, at all times, in disaster zones, they did risk making aesthetic works, knowing the lay of the land, the weight of history, and the difficulty of finding expression beyond the silos of weak multiculturalism.

Chapter Overview

Such danger and risk are at play in each of the chapters that follow: the problem of sedimentation, the unruly movements of particulate, the mercurial affect that dwells in the gut, and the ambivalence of animality in relation to race and belonging. By drawing attention to the figurativity of both language and matter, this book centers aesthetics and ethics in order to nuance the political dictates around siloed difference. At the crossroads of matter and meaning, Latinx inscriptions hold the potential to consider how we relate to difference. This carries a different valence than considerations of art as a container of experience, rendered transparent and consumable by those with an appetite for alterity. Far from representing Latinx subjects as identifiable, whole, and self-sovereign, the repertoire of artists and writers in *Matters of Inscription* work through figurations of material metaphors that inflect scenes of referentiality with a haptic, fetid understanding of the relationship between matter and meaning. Put another way, they choose tropes that undo presumptions about origin (stone), diaspora (dust), pedagogy (viscera), and belonging (animal packs). In drawing our attention to the entanglement of matter and meaning, these aesthetic pieces rebuff any ethnographic or sociological claims born out of fiction. But in the modes of fiction, art, and the literary, these pieces do challenge us to think about Latinx literature as something more than a body of writing about Latinx peoples.

The first section of this book looks to dust and limestone—two material metaphors that function not only as guiding textures of the chapters but also as forms of sedimentation (limestone) and de-sedimentation (dust). My analysis of these matter-metaphors in the works of Cuban artist Ana Mendieta and Puerto Rican writer Manuel Ramos Otero shows how foundations and diasporas are never self-same, constantly shifting in the temporality of deep time and catastrophic futures—a time that exists in geological matter and enfolds human life into vaster and longer ecologies. But these larger ecologies also index eclipsed human cosmologies.

The first chapter, "Source Material: Reading the Matter of Ana Mendieta's Catachrestic Inscriptions," focuses on how Ana Mendieta positions matter at the foundation of the Cuban nation through her *Esculturas Rupestres*, a series of ten figures carved into limestone cave walls in Jaruco, Cuba, during the summer of 1981. These sculptures cite Taíno goddess effigies, functioning as an iterative genealogical mythology that uses matter and place to tell a deep history of colonial contact—a history that registers both ephemerally and materially the ongoing matter of indigeneity in Cuba. Carving these in proportions and movements that mimic the face of the soft, supple, and ever-changing canvas of limestone, Mendieta foregrounds the ground of her work, only to let the trace fade. Rather than taking earth, fecundity, and materiality as merely essentialist—as fixed and raw matter—this chapter considers how Mendieta complicates our notions of origin precisely by working with, rather than against, natural matter. As one of the few remaining relics of Ana Mendieta's earth works, many writers and artists have gone to Jaruco, Cuba, to try to find the lingering traces of her artistic signature. Once considered either fully lost or eroded by Cuba's humid ecology, her works have since been located. This chapter narrates my own journey to the caves in 2017, which fundamentally shifted my reading of the caves as the matter of place became more important than Mendieta's intentions with these sculptures. Her return to Cuba was set against a backdrop of Cold War politics and certainly registers a significant moment in her career. But rather than read these sculptures as Mendieta's claim on Cuba, this chapter reads the larger matter of limestone in Mendieta's *Esculturas*—her artwork that notoriously "returns" to the source of Cuba—as a material register of Taíno *and* Afro-Cuban resistance. Moving beyond the reigning political programs of 1981, Mendieta's use of highly fossilized stone matter entangles Cuban indigeneity and the afterlives of slavery that exceed Mendieta's own story. These caves echo the violent foundations of the Cuban nation that cannot be jettisoned into a tidy, linear story of progress.

The second chapter, "Exorbitant Dust: Manuel Ramos Otero's Queer and Colonial Matters" traces the figure of *polvo*, which translates to "dust," in the work of the New York-based, Puerto Rican writer Manuel Ramos Otero. Ramos Otero wrote through tropes of finitude long before his diagnosis with HIV, continuing until his eventual death in 1990 from AIDS complications. Writing defiantly and openly as a queer, feminist Puerto Rican, and as a *sidoso* (slang for someone with AIDS, known as SIDA in Spanish), his work invites death and desire to commingle through a figuration of dust, a substance that covers skin, coats translation, and dirties up conventional genres. Ramos Otero's work strikes a tenuous balance between the personal and the figurative through an insistence on aesthetic mediation—a mediation that he figures through *polvo*, a particular matter that exposes our porosity and yet still clings and hovers in the space between bodies, between the past and the future, between life and death. The forceful fragility of *polvo* is then not reducible to Ramos Otero's work on AIDS but is instead another instantiation of his oeuvre's commitment to thinking the persistence of that which is nonetheless finite: from dust to dust. And yet, through his essays, poetry, and short stories, dust also marks the vibrant dangers of desire—its undoing, disappointment, and salacious risk. His queer translations of autobiography turn the conventional wisdom of the genre on its head by refusing to consolidate a life into words—giving us instead an exquisite sprinkling of dust, a life both undone and made possible by desire. This figure of dust resonates as something both material and ephemeral, marking the bits of nearly imperceptible matter that move between bodies, borders, and genres. So too does dust become exorbitant to Ramos Otero's own life when we read its charge in the register of coloniality and climate change. Ramos Otero's affinity for finitude, figured through *polvo*, counterintuitively conjures a relational desire that moves beyond distinctions between life and death in order to privilege the porous, the marginal, and the always precarious possibility of survival. As the dust settles in the aftermath of Hurricane Maria, I read this trope that not only figures the world of Ramos Otero's Puerto Rico but also prefigures how coloniality persists and lingers in its present-day, dusty atmosphere.

The second part of this book, comprised of two chapters, moves to think of biological matter through the organizing matter-metaphors of viscera and animality—focusing on the fraught terrain of intra- and interrelation. Charting the works of playwright María Irene Fornés and author Justin Torres, this second section shows how our biological frames for understanding humanism are limited if we only pay attention to the life of the mind as opposed to the visceral feelings that dwell in the gut. By focusing on animality, too, we begin to see how entangled our metaphors of belonging are with a constricted notion of who counts as human.

The third chapter, "Gut Checks: María Irene Fornés's Visceral Pedagogy and Dangerous Nerves," considers the corporeal pedagogy at play in María Irene Fornés's 1977 play *Fefu and Her Friends*. Fornés's forged this commitment as a teacher of playwriting at the INTAR (International Arts Relations, Inc.) workshop, which she led for many years in New York. There, she came to be known as the pedagogue of a future generation of Latinx playwrights, including Cherríe Moraga, Eduardo Machado, and Caridad Svich. Much writing has been done on Fornés as a pedagogue, but what has not yet been considered in depth is how she also used her legendary workshop lessons to write many of her own plays. This chapter considers the lessons inherent in *Fefu and Her Friends* as a way of redirecting critical attention back to her own oeuvre. Her plays are often difficult to comprehend, conjuring the absurdist tradition of Antonin Artaud and Bertolt Brecht with the particular accent that Fornés brings as a Cuban immigrant, lesbian, and feminist. And while this accent matters, much of Fornés's lessons at INTAR pushed against realism and ethnic expectation. Instead, she taught the strange terrain of creativity to mostly Latinx writers by allotting them stipends and communal space to learn playwriting, a skill she mostly taught herself. These workshops provided material structure for Latinx writers to develop their own creative voices without asking them to deliver anticipatable Latinx themes. This commitment to her own communities and resistance to their typification is resonant with the way Fornés wrote and staged *Fefu and Her Friends*. I examine the erotic and charged relations between women in this iconic play, which features characters in constricted circumstances wherein they must navigate the negative affects, lost love, and unaccountable violence that dwell in the gut and that complicate any politics based on the possession of a stable or shared identity. The world of a Fornés play is often a lesson in object relations, wherein the terms of engagement remain as opaque on stage as they are in life. For *Fefu and Her Friends*, these are both internal and highly volatile games of danger and excitement that register at the level of viscera and teach us difficult lessons about being together.

The fourth and final chapter, "Losing the Pack: Tracking Loss, Tracing Animals, and Longing for Belonging," looks to the movements of animals, language, and affective bodies in Justin Torres's 2011 novel *We the Animals*. I contextualize the novel within the aftermath of California's 2008 Proposition 8, whose passage momentarily banned same-sex marriage. The media speciously and erroneously blamed Black and brown communities for this voting outcome, assuming that such communities are inherently homophobic. *We the Animals* undoes overly sedimented expectations that families of color are inherently homophobic, all the while showing familial relations as tender and violent in turns. In this chapter, I read Torres's novel alongside critical race and queer theories that engage animal studies to show how Torres figures ambivalent animality as a tropological resistance to upstanding family morals. The novel flirts with genres of progress and development born out of the Enlightenment and liberalism—the bildungsroman, evolution narratives, and the coming out story—only to render them as harmful, lingering myths of humanism. Formally, the novel consists of stringed-together vignettes that function as clipped close-ups of a family enduring structural violence in racial capitalism and heterosexism. In these scenes, we see the aftermath or shadow of violence. We read of a family loving and hurting one another, rendered through animalistic prose that depicts how loss can be both terrifying and necessary to witness. The chapter engages receptions of Torres's novel that tend to read it as liberatory; in contrast to these readings, I suggest that the novel depicts a movement of eventual subjectivity that reverberates with loss rather than achievement. The oddly linguistic animal ecology of the text reveals how language's operations relate to and exceed taxonomies that entangle race, queerness, and animality without assigning a humanistic moralism to the narrative. Pronouns are queerly rendered as the animal pack thins to a solitary "I." Through an undecidable final vignette entitled "Zookeeping," the novel ultimately obstructs any of the progress narratives that it conjures, upending them as drunken dreams of neoliberal "progress."

This book ends on a coda that examines some of the tropes of Roque Salas Rivera's return to Puerto Rico—a return that registers in bilingual lyric anticolonial and trans movements on the island. By taking Salas Rivera's self-translation notes as a hermeneutic provocation, the coda concentrates on figural knots that both refuse and suture readings across *Preguntas frecuentes / Frequently Asked Questions* (2018) and *X/Ex/Exis* (2020). Translation often benefits power, and its work as exposure (as extraction) entails diminishing returns for the original language. Yet Salas Rivera steals back from English with his poetic and translation decisions to withhold or hold onto loss as itself incommensurable or untranslatable. One knot that Salas Rivera refuses to translate is the term for the blue stones of Old San Juan's roads, *adoquines*, which could be translated as "cobblestones." The coda tracks the material provenance of these *adoquines* to consider the weight of referentiality as a colonial problem. A common, mythological account holds that the *adoquines* of Old San Juan were originally used as ballast in Spanish colonial ships, but the bricks actually came from England between 1890 and 1896—before the island's relationship to the English language shifted radically. The literal translation reveals as much as it obscures. What does it mean to resist narrative, colonial, poetic, and linguistic closure to render cobblestones as *cobblestones*? English is doubly denied, whether by intention or linguistic felicity; it's denied both original emplotment and the weight of originality. English loses its ballast. These knotted, or refused, translations issue from the body not to create a fetish of Spanish as original language but to withhold the imperial prejudices of translation labor—the interpellation that often creates access, if not exclusively then mostly, for the Global North's consumption. With no comfortable gendered grammar in Spanish nor grounding of home in English, Salas Rivera figures in knots what is and is not—the entanglement of what is but has no proper name or home as such with the translation of terms that have no destination. As such, the coda ends on a thinking of the stakes of infrastructures of translation, negotiations of identities through a refused exposure in language, and the abiding problem of colonial foundations that haunt both English and Spanish in the thinking of anything Latinx.

Matters of Inscription attends to issues of dispossession and marginalization in latinidad with an insistence that these losses and deprivations be rendered incommensurate so as not to collapse difference in experience or scales of ontological debasement. Though the concerns in the pages of the book conscribe figures of queer, feminist, and Caribbean latinidad, the concerns laid out in this theoretical frame are not exactly indexed to these gendered and ethnic-racialized demographics. That is, while not representative, I have taken the case of Latinx literature and art as an occasion to read scenes of representation that undo what Ralph Rodriguez calls "ethnic expectation."[92] As the reader can see from the chapter descriptions, my readings of latinidad will be necessarily hemmed by the positionality and migratory paths of the writers and artists I read, who all hail from Puerto Rico and Cuba in various diasporic trajectories. Most of their supposed identities could easily be read as Latinx, even though for many of them this term was not a part of their identificatory lexicon. The move to consider the kind of Cuban and Puerto Rican writers and artists I do means that this book's archive represents a very small strand of the larger story of latinidad in the Americas. This assemblage of aesthetic objects all come from migratory patterns and ethnonational discourses that resulted from the wars of 1898. Cuba was granted supposed independence while Puerto Rico became colonized yet again, and these moments inflected migratory patterns from both nations in the twentieth and twenty-first centuries. And yet, the pairing of Puerto Rico and Cuba is an overdetermined move that risks centering the *dos alas* myth.[93] These readings, then, must be supplemented with the many works that urge us to think the often missing place of the Dominican Republic,[94] the important intervention of Afro-Latinx studies,[95] and the waves of Central American migrations.[96] While my theoretical approach gathers insights from critical Black studies, Indigenous studies, and border studies, my objects are not indexical of these discourses in a strict manner. I have chosen to take this approach to allow various exigencies to shift my analysis, rather than my objects, to begin to respond to the urgency around racial reckonings as an opportunity to shift our ways of reading.

My hope is that these considerations may not exactly cement a discourse so much as ask us to reread anew the question of difference beyond programs and heuristics that adhere to taxonomic monikers—to think at the interstice of semiotic difference and the difference that befalls those racialized and gendered outside of the norm. These chapters, then, create occasions for reading inscriptions that operate as entanglements, that move through figuration, and that name through the counterintuitive act of catachresis. They track material tropes to better understand the materiality at stake in reading these works and the material structures wherein their inscription can take place and be legible. These authors and chapters do not represent political programs as such; they do not provide blueprints for liberation. Instead, their textured inscriptions leave us mired in entanglements, disturbing attachments, glimmering hope, and difficult object relations that compose the landscapes of most lives and, more emphatically, of those who have lost nation and home, who never have stable categorical ground, and who may or may not understand themselves and their work as Latinx.

1

Source Materials

Reading the Matter of Ana Mendieta's Catachrestic Inscriptions

Stone is primal matter, inhuman in its duration. Yet despite its incalculable temporality, the lithic is not some vast and alien outside. A limit-breaching intimacy persistently unfurls.
—Jeremy Cohen, *Stone: An Ecology of the Inhuman*

A fact seldom highlighted about Cuban American artist Ana Mendieta is that, at the time of her early death, she was working on a book. This book was meant to exhibit photo etchings of the *Esculturas Rupestres*, ten life-sized figures that Mendieta carved into limestone cave walls in Jaruco, Cuba, in the summer of 1981.[1] She intended to take these photographic glimpses of her textured sculptures and place them alongside mythologies of the Taínos—the Indigenous people of Cuba—and descriptions of their devastating encounter with Spanish settlers in the very early days of the Americas. Mendieta's early work was performative—creating bold, corporeal, and elemental performances and installations outside of studios and galleries, for the most part. Her work was often staged in remote areas: in a river in Iowa, in obscure areas in Oaxaca, and in limestone grottos in Cuba. She complemented her ephemeral, momentary works with intense documentation through photography and film, often recorded using a Super 8 camera.[2] Because the sculptures were located in a park outside of Havana and would fade in the humid, ever-changing tropical landscape, Mendieta first shared her sculptural works through exhibitions of large scale black and white photos, as well as films that document the sculptures. Later, Mendieta had an idea that the sculptures would be best experienced in the form of an artbook. In some of her grant writing materials for the book on the Jaruco sculptures, Mendieta emphasized, "It really makes sense to view these very intimate works in the intimacy provided by the book format."[3]

Though Mendieta had nearly completed the book, oversaw the creation of print plates for it, and even printed the first few sets for this book and signed the front page of each, the book was not published in her lifetime. I take its incompletion as a prompt to reread and revisit her most notable work made in her homeland of Cuba. José Quiroga poetically renders Mendieta's particular relation to Cuba in a similar manner: "Mendieta's was a *cubanía* of interruption that had its own coherence: a sentence left in mid-phrase, a chapter left uncompleted, a book half read, a tale broken up into fragments."[4] Incompletion, erasure, and loss also happen to be some of the most persistent and haunting aspects of Mendieta's oeuvre. And as we will see, Mendieta's cave carvings are bound up with various histories and material sources that register finitude, rendering foundations as particulate assemblages of biological matter and recursive endings that, taken together, mark what others read as beginnings. This chapter takes her return to Cuba as an event that tells us more about the entanglement of coloniality, land, and people than it does about Mendieta's individual biography or "homecoming." It's true that her return to Cuba yielded much for her personally: a pivot in her art practice, a reunion with her family and land, and an exchange with Cuban artists that fortified and intensified her own craft. But her return also spurred a set of relations—aesthetic, political, and ethical—that existed far before and continue to persist beyond her own life span. And the temporality of her return is also remarked on, as it were, by the fading contours of her sculptures.

Ana Mendieta not only showcased an important evolution in her art practice with the *Esculturas Rupestres*; by making them when she did, she also became the first Cuban American artist since the Cuban Revolution to be granted permission by the Ministry of Culture to officially create and exhibit art on the island. But rather than make a memorial to either the revolution or the interests of Cuban exiles, she took her art practice to a national park and pointed to an indigenous past carved into soft, highly fossilized limestone, which produces cave-like formations of embankments, cliffsides, and grottos. Cuba and the larger Caribbean have an estranged relationship with indigenous legacy and presence. Until fairly recently, colonial tales of Indigenous extinction were the reigning narrative of indigeneity in the archipelagic region. The mythos of aboriginal extinction has proven quite powerful in Cuba, even if it is increasingly challenged by the growing Cuban, Caribbean, and diasporic movement to reclaim Taíno inheritance. Such a movement was not yet in full swing during the time of Mendieta, a far-flung, white-turned-brown artist based in Iowa who reencountered Cuba through the thoroughly colonial archive of indigeneity that spurred the '70s *indigenismo* movement. Within the context of such a high-profile, state-sanctioned visit to Cuba, the decision to figure indigeneity through Taíno iconography amounted to staking both a claim and an unclaim—a counterintuitive and perhaps risky representational move. As we will see, there is a density to the materialities, inscriptions, and histories that cohere and crumble in these caves.[5] That density exceeds easy political representation and places one at a prenational, extranational site. In what follows, I show how her work in Jaruco presents a not-so-new materialist approach—one that figures origins in relation to finitude and exile in relation to return. These sculptural works and their rock writing perform an ongoing, mutable, and highly porous act of witnessing that emphasizes the intimate and violent registers of material inscription against notions of historical veracity.

If people continually seek to find Mendieta, asking who she is and where she is, they often return to the site of Jaruco in order to do so. But Mendieta had not frequented the park during her childhood in Cuba, and so marking them as a source amounts to a perplexing move that demands rereading. Most acutely, many do search for traces of Ana Mendieta's works because of her untimely, early, and violent death—a loss that still reverberates. But this search for Mendieta and her traces are also a part of her legacy of relation, longing, and exploration—most viscerally felt in the very material unfolding of her artwork. José Esteban Muñoz marks this intimacy as the sharing of a sense of brownness in Mendieta's *Silueta* series, as her intense vitalism, and as an afterburn that lingers so forcefully that many see a glimpse of something necessary in her works and life. Mendieta's work continues to have a legacy that extends beyond her biography and instead shows how her work insists on witnessing violent inscriptions. Mendieta's biography gained intense public scrutiny due to the suspect way she died at age thirty-six in 1985.

Over the years since Mendieta's suspect death, feminist activists have often staged protests at Carl Andre's exhibitions, pouring blood in front of the museum or wailing and crying within Andre's exhibitions, with signs that ask "Where is Ana Mendieta?" which became the inspiration for Jane Blocker's monograph *Where Is Ana Mendieta?* Here I add to a list of questions that haunt her life and death.

Focusing on the *Esculturas Rupestres*, I ask, What are the implications of the site and shape of these sculptures for a Cuban (American) artist who returns to her homeland? What does it mean for Mendieta to carve into cave-like walls a form of indigeneity that she can neither claim nor retrieve? How does the location of Jaruco and the palimpsest of history that the limestone holds matter? Following the grooves that Mendieta carved into the Jaruco limestone, this chapter will move from the indigenous history and presence that complicates questions of origin and return in Cuba to the feminist critical reception of Mendieta's work, which often charged her with essentialism. My reading of these sculptures counters the heuristics of essentialism, inviting us to instead reconsider how nature and figures so often aligned with nature (those marked by race, indigeneity, and femininity) work within a matrix wherein matter and history collide in mutually constitutive ways. I take yet another look at Mendieta's work, to the *Esculturas Rupestres* as invoking a complex notion of return to her homeland. I am motivated, principally, by an ethical call to read marked cultural production, whether performative or narrative, in a way that extends beyond reduction to either biography or circumstance. I prefer instead to let the material and the semiotic guide my reading of an aesthetic object away from the biopolitical interest in identification and individual stories, which are always encased in material structure. To think through the intertextual connections of her life and her complicated choice of source materials, this chapter traverses many discourses, which is only fitting when discussing a figure like Ana Mendieta, who trafficked in many circles that, in turn, claimed her as their own. Mendieta's cave carvings invite us to ponder questions of translation that sully, rather than clarify, past violences, complicating claims to origin, source, or fundament. These works demand a careful reading precisely because they were inscribed under a thesis of Indigenous extinction. Jodi Byrd reminds us that "there is a fine line, then, between deconstructing a process of signification and reinscribing the discourses that continue to justify the codification of knowledge production that orders the native as colonized."[6] In Jaruco, on these limestone walls, Mendieta figures the return to a source that ultimately remains a receding fundament but leaves us in a rich entanglement of history and nature, of exile and return, of the ephemeral and the persistent. I would like to place an accent on the question of origins, endurance, and finitude in Mendieta's sculptures—turning our attention to her source material and how this careful choice continues to work on us vis-à-vis carving, or inscribing, onto a densely fraught matrix of matter and history.

Biological Frames

While Mendieta's work is compelling in its own right, most scholars engaging with her art feel equally compelled to explore her life's story—one that defies overly sedimented stories about Cuban migration to the US. Born in 1948 in Cuba, Mendieta came from a family of privilege and political prominence. Her paternal great-uncle, Carlos Mendieta, was the president of Cuba in 1934 for about a year until he learned that his presidency was being manipulated and undermined by his army chief, none other than Fulgencio Batista. Though her father, Ignacio, and family largely supported the early efforts of the Cuban Revolution, as many Cubans did, they became quickly disillusioned. Amid growing concerns about the control the Cuban state would have over young minds and with the backdrop of the failed Bay of Pigs invasion, Mendieta became exiled in the United States at the age of twelve due to the fraught Operation Peter Pan. Running from December 1960 through October 1962, Operation Peter Pan was a joint effort between the US State Department and Catholic Charities USA that removed roughly fourteen thousand Cuban youths from the island and brought them to the United States as unaccompanied minors. Parents volunteered their children for this lonely exodus in fear that the Cuban government would eventually send children to communist indoctrination camps. This fear was partly the result of the Catholic Church's anticommunist rhetoric—heavily influenced by the Catholic diocese of Miami—which instilled among many Cubans the worry that the revolutionary government would take over all facets of children's lives. As a result of this operation, Mendieta and her sister, Raquelín, were taken to a refugee camp, then put in foster homes and in various institutions in Miami until they were eventually placed in Dubuque, Iowa, where they both endured a toxic mixture of prejudice and isolation. Suffering slurs that were pointedly racist and sexist, Mendieta experienced the racialized transformation that comes with migration. She left Cuba a white Cuban, comfortably upper middle class, but upon entering the United States, she became racialized as brown. Migration transforms one's body, its inscriptions. In addition to the gendered and racialized disenfranchisement Mendieta and her sister faced in orphanhood, the forced exile would become a salient motivation for her artistic practice, which she began in earnest in Iowa. During these years, she created work that responded to the violence, both metaphorical and physical, inflicted upon women's bodies. At the University of Iowa, Mendieta studied with Hans Breder in his cutting-edge and influential Intermedia program, and there she began to hone a wholly singular artistic practice. From Iowa, she would venture to Mexico and the New York art world, which led her Cuba and Italy. New York's art scene also led her to Carl Andre. That end to her life has recently spurred a set of frustrating, overdetermining frames through which to view her life story and her life's work through a renewed media attention to dubious circumstances of her death. It is not the intention of this chapter to replicate that false frame which diminishes her life's work to her end, but it is one issue that raises the stakes of how endings and finalities become problematic frames of reference.

Understandably, Mendieta has become a figure that is read in relation to her many biographical figurations, some self-identified and others imposed. Instead of thinking about her work only through the framework of her life's story, I want to dwell on how the biographical hermeneutic has rendered the aesthetic and material force of Mendieta's artwork in overly simplistic ways, relying upon her life to tell the story of her art even after her death. Depending on the lens, the year, and the vantage point from which one views her, Ana Mendieta can translate into many figures: the adolescent exile, the bold feminist artist, the provocative performer insisting upon corporeality, the Latina who called herself "Tropic-Ana," or the tragic figure of an all too early death. Some of these readings reduce Mendieta's work to the toiling of a traumatized exile who desperately wanted to find home, while others see her works tracing the rich and prolific trails that she left behind. To be sure, Mendieta's positionality does matter, and indeed beyond any reduction of her works to her biography. Her relative privilege is important to consider, both in relation to her own origins and her artistic career.[7]

Indigenous Traces, Indigenous Persistence

Before delving into Jaruco's limestone, let me sketch a brief picture of the question of indigeneity in Cuba. Like in other parts of the Caribbean, modern Indigenous peoples in Cuba claim Taíno/Indigenous community in places like Guantánamo and in the eastern mountainous regions of the island.[8] But such claims challenge a thinking of indigeneity that requires diachronic purity—a colonial invention based on a metaphysics of purity and an easy reliance on autochthony. Cuban national discourse had been, up until recently, that the overwhelming majority of Taínos were nearly wiped out on the island within less than a century of Spanish colonization and that those who survived were absorbed into an increasingly creolized people. And though this tale isn't true, it results from a problem of both Indigenous denial and colonial taxonomies that linger in Cuba's racial imaginary. The *encomienda* system was exceedingly brutal, and island ecologies create different pressures around phenomena like outbreaks of disease, which led to a larger decline in Taíno populations in a short amount of time than what we track in North American history. Yet much of *guajiro* culture overlaps with Indigenous culture. *Guajiro* is slang for "Cuban peasant," somewhat similar to the *jíbaro* figure in Puerto Rico. The term *guajiro* was once rumored to be a Hispanicization of the English *war hero*, supposedly originating in the war of 1898. But contemporary scholarship traces it to Arawak and Wayuu languages—indigenous languages that would have circulated in what we today call the Caribbean, Colombia, and Venezuela. The year 1898 serves as a turning point in national narratives and also helps us to see how indigeneity became rewritten and reinscribed in the independent formation of Cuba. Indigenous caciques, or chiefs, resurface throughout historical documents and records of battles in Cuba. Notably, some fought alongside Afro-Cuban leader Maceo in the war for independence against Spain—but those fighters had Spanish surnames.[9] Forced adoption of Spanish surnames and identification as *guajiro/indio* seem to be ways in which genealogies of indigeneity in Cuba were both denied and absorbed by processes of *mestizaje*, or creolization, as well as indexed to the history of countryside peasantry, creating a folk indigeneity inscribed into national romance.[10] Taíno peoples, legacies, and rituals do persist, though not in ways that can be commensurately figured with

North American categories like First Nations or tribal sovereignty. Many find understandable confirmation in tallies of mitochondrial DNA that suggest a lot of indigenous presence in Cuba, as well as the larger Caribbean.[11] As Kim TallBear, among others, has shown, the concept of genealogical purity is itself a colonialist construct meant to defend the ever-elusive category of whiteness. Genetic coding offers problematic notions of origin: "Native American DNA as an object could not exist without, and yet functions as a scientific data point to support the idea of, once pure, original populations. Notions of ancestral populations, the ordering and calculating of genetic markers and their associations, and the representation of living groups of individuals as reference populations all require the assumption that there was a moment, a human body, a marker, a population back there in space and time that was a biogeographical pinpoint of originality."[12] Such a figure participates in scientific taxonomy that is dubious at best. For Cuban and Puerto Rican activists, the DNA tests do not portray new knowledge. It does confirm what they have been saying for some time—what colonial and ethnonationalist governments have figured as a historical closure. How does the inscription of DNA shift how we might read Mendieta's cave carvings? When I ask the question of what changes when we think about Mendieta's DNA, it is not to naturalize DNA as a marker of race. Rather, I raise the question to raise the stakes of contemporary readings of source matter in the form of DNA. As Kim TallBear shows, the inscription of DNA may require a reading that de-idealizes ancestry while also revising problematic colonial inscriptions that erase all Indigenous presence in the Caribbean. The referential quality of Indigenous DNA does not end the need to rearticulate new forms of understanding indigeneity in the Caribbean. My contention here is that it surfaces as yet another kind of biopolitical inscription that requires that we consider *how* it references and, perhaps, suspend a faith in thinking that *what* it references is stable and knowable. As such, this chapter does not wager to adjudicate these inscriptions as properly descendant from DNA. What I do argue is that the recurrent return to Jaruco creates a palimpsest of resistance and coloniality that requires several levels of reading that contend with the dense materiality and congealment within the site of Jaruco.

We do know that Taíno culture endures in many forms: whole communities, legends of mythology, archaeological traces, food practices, and Taíno words. Words like *huracán*, or *hurricane*, and *barbacoa*, or *barbecue*, derive from Taíno language. The Taíno, then, is not an invisible figure in the Cuban or the American imaginary—though in Mendieta's lifetime, it would have been a strange figure, rendered fossil and enshrouded in the fraught opacity of colonial sources. And these questions bring to the fore, once again, the reigning issues of *mestizaje* and how we read race in the Caribbean. The unfolding story of the Taíno peoples requires attention to what we call source material and how we read it.

The first person to write an account of the Taínos from a European perspective was a friar who accompanied Christopher Columbus on his second journey to the Caribbean in 1494, Fray Ramón Pané. Much of the scholarship on Taínos, up until the 1970s, has been derived from his account of the two years he lived with and learned from the customs of Taínos on the island we now call Hispaniola. Written in Castilian Spanish by a missionary priest whose first language was Catalan and translated from the indigenous language he was simultaneously learning, Pané's manuscript was from the start fraught with the many challenges of translation—both linguistic and cultural. The plot of translation thickens once we learn that the original manuscript has never been recovered and only exists as a facsimile copied into *Historia del almirante don Cristobal Colón por su hijo don Fernando*, a biography and historical defense of Christopher Columbus written by his son. This biography was never published during don Fernando's lifetime and remained unpublished until his death in 1539, since Columbus had fallen out of favor with the Spanish crown. The only full copy of the text survives in an Italian translation by Alfonso de Ulloa penned in 1571, seventy-three years after the document's completion and translated many times over. The first record of this colonial contact, which also happens to be the first book written in a European language in the Americas, becomes lost serially and only survives in the opaque haze of translation. Ramón Pané's successor, Bartolomé de Las Casas, commented upon Pané's translation challenges and even corrected some in his own writings on the Indigenous peoples of the Caribbean. As Las Casas came to be known as an ardent defender of the "Indians," he also came to be known as the very person to advise the Spanish crown to participate in the African slave trade. The catastrophic consequences of colonial contact for Indigenous peoples of the Caribbean are necessarily entangled with the transatlantic slave trade and Afro-Caribbean presence.

An important part of resurgent knowledge of the Taínos came from Yale professor José Juan Arrom's scholarship and republication of Fray Ramón Pané's book, *Relación acerca de las antiguedades de los indios* (*An Account of the Antiquities of the Indians*), during a period of a revival of interest in indigeneity in the Caribbean in the 1970s.[13] Arrom retranslated the *Relación* from a 1571 "poor Italian translation" of Don Fernando's text by Alfonso de Ulloa. While Pané's account was read in Spain, likely taken back by Christopher Columbus on his return from his third voyage, fragments only appear in one letter by a cardinal and as excerpts in Bartolomé de Las Casas's *Apologética de las Indias* in chapter 120.

By 1850, the last indigenous jurisdiction in Cuba was obliterated by Spanish rule, effectively sedimenting the extinction narrative at the level of political representation. But the message of eradication came prior to this, when Spanish colonizers claimed that Taínos were wiped off the island within less than a century of colonial contact. While it's true that many of the Taínos were killed off whether by the cruel conditions of the *encomienda* or by disease and that their worlds and cosmologies withered, it's also true that many of the Taíno peoples survived by retreating into the remote hill country of what we now call Guantánamo in Cuba—thriving as *guajiros*, mountain *indios*, who use verifiable indigenous rituals mixed with larger cosmologies in Cuba. There, caciques (Taíno chiefs or leaders) still carry out spiritual, agrarian, and medicinal rituals. The first roads built to some of these communities in Cuba were only paved in 1964.

Archaeologist and professor José Barreiro, a self-identified Taíno descendant and scholar of the area, has been working in the eastern mountains of Cuba, in the region of Baracoa, to help with the revitalization of Taíno legacies and survival.[14] He's created a museum in Cueva del Paraíso. In his work as an Indigenous activist, he has been a force in uniting Taínos with other native peoples across the hemisphere. During the 1970s, the revolutionary government prohibited many of these rituals, especially ones displayed to tourists. This stifling of culture prohibited many Santería practices as well. Revolutionary discourse, up until fairly recently, attempted to cathect more strongly onto forms of identification and liberation that produce possible progress narratives, welcoming a mythos of racial equality under the homogenizing telos of the revolution that all were first, and foremost, Cuban. Such strictures on spiritual and ethnic practices have diminished after the fall of the Soviet Union, which inaugurated intense scarcity on the island, known as the Special Period, translated and truncated from the official title "Período especial en tiempos de paz," which lasted from 1991 to 2000. During these years, the scarcity of food and hydrocarbon fuels incentivized the government to free up religious practices and institutions on the island.

Colonial contact in the Americas, and especially in the Caribbean, necessitates a thinking of Americanity as that which is the product of two entangled processes: Indigenous death and displacement and land worked with the stolen labor of the enslaved. This ungrounded foundation of the Americas is worked into the bedrock of nation-states we now take for granted as countries. In places like Cuba, the island ecology made it difficult for more numbers of the Indigenous to survive, and the cruel conditions of the *encomienda* proved merciless and a prototype for what Glissant calls the "plantation matrix."[15] In this cave that signals source and origin, we are called through matter to pay attention to the lithic traces of extinction and cycles of worlds ending. Place of birth is not a benign feminine maternal but the crossroads of contact, exploitation, and extraction that become the ambivalent "start" for settler colonialism and the shutting down of indigenous cosmologies. This led Spanish colonialists (like their British, Dutch, Portuguese, and French counterparts in the Americas) to legitimate the radical dispossession of land and Indigenous folks and enslave so many from Africa to extract their labor, rendering flesh fungible for profit, like the mineral riches of the Americas.

While Mendieta abstractly and loosely gestures toward pre-Columbian Indigenous presence, this question cannot be severed from a thinking of how the dwindling numbers of Indigenous people paved the way for the enslavement and forced migration of people of African descent in Cuba, the Caribbean, and the Americas more broadly. Tying Indigenous decimation to anti-Blackness makes sense with limestone, in a manner akin and apposite to the conceptual use of sand by Vanessa Agard-Jones or, more interstitially and proximate in ethos, the figure of the shoal in the work of Tiffany Lethabo King.[16] These two foundational violences surface in the limestone if we pay attention to the matter of history and the history of matter. Attending to the contours of limestone is not simply about empirically looking to the past or to the stratification of rock. Rather, such attention fundamentally throws into question much of Western metaphysics—focusing on the entanglement of all matter of persons, bodies, and ecologies that have been considered subhuman, inhuman, and nonhuman. Thinkers like Katherine McKittrick and Kathryn Yusoff show how geography and geology, as Western sciences, are also caught up in larger questions of Western metaphysics.[17] So here, I want to read the matter of limestone as itself a more apt figuration of the problem of origin—to understand origin narratives as necessarily catachrestic. As Zakkiyah Iman Jackson writes, "Whether machine, plant, animal, or object, the nonhuman's figuration and mattering is shaped by the gendered racialization of the field of metaphysics even as teleological finality is indefinitely deferred by the processual nature of actualization or the agency of matter. Thus, terrestrial movement toward the nonhuman is simultaneously movement toward blackness, whether blackness is embraced or not, as blackness constitutes the very matter at hand."[18] The limestone in Jaruco may have indigenous carvings on them, but such carvings are coevally inscribed into a bedrock of dispossession that urges us to consider the traces of Blackness in Cuba in the work of extraction and on the ocean floor of the Atlantic.

Mendieta's work alludes to many cultural cosmologies that she then translated into her own abstracted iconography—developing her own symbols and shapes that recall many cultures across space and time. In particular, Mendieta had worked with and studied Afro-Cuban iconography, looking to Santería as one densely Cuban site from which to explore her own corporeal engagement with performance, difference, and carnality. Perhaps her most notable engagement with this process was during an early performance in Iowa where she held a white, decapitated hen to her naked body—a sacrifice common to Santería. In this performance, her body became a canvas for the dying chicken's final, spastic movements that marked her with the spattered blood of her own violence. Mendieta was very aware of the particularities of Afrocubanidad but did not choose to focus on this explicitly in Jaruco. So in light of this, it's interesting that she chooses to register a more forgotten, less visible form of presence and loss on the island that cannot be subsumed by Cuba's politics, which has often used Afro-Cubans as a sign of the revolution's antiracism and benevolence.

The Cuban Revolution has often heralded itself as having overcome racism, but there are many material discrepancies between life's chances for Afro-Cubans and lighter-skinned Cubans. The foundational racialized violence of Cuba, especially anti-Blackness, persists. As recently as 2013, Afro-Cuban literary scholar Roberto Zurbano questioned the commitment of the revolution to antiracism in a *New York Times* op-ed, which led to his demotion as the head of Casa de las Américas.[19] Such is the tight dance of speech and art-making in Cuba, caught in the tension being interpellated into the revolutionary government's progress narrative or censorship. It is within this tension that Mendieta made her most prominent artwork on the island, away from Havana and its centralized institutions, in hills suffused with the bedrock of oceans unearthed.

The Matter of Essentialism

Following Mendieta's body of work has been a fount and a symbol for a good amount of feminist theorization and feminist art movements. But for some US white feminist critics of the 1980s and '90s, her work brought unease to those who balked at the fetid bodies, fire, dirt, and excessive allusions to nature in Mendieta's artwork. In the 1980s, theorists like Griselda Pollock and Mary Kelly warned that such explicit and graphic use of the female body in feminist art (i.e., works by Carolee Schneemann, Lucy Lippard, and Judy Chicago) was narcissistic and ran the risk of essentializing femininity through fetishism. Such antiessentialist critiques of Mendieta's work persisted through the 1990s. In that decade, Mira Schor wrote, "Mendieta's Woman, particularly in the later works, is only female, she represents a limited view of the form and experience of femininity out of the limitless possibilities of femaleness. Because dialogue and conflict do not flourish within a significant portion of her work, it does not have the depth of an oeuvre. In Mendieta's work there are many deeply moving and rivetingly memorable images, but, ultimately, the constant repetition of an unquestioned, generic (gyneric) Great Mother is deeply, and now, poignantly problematic."[20] I will return to Mendieta's work to consider how it is born out of and begets dialogue, as well as indexes conflict. For now, I move forward to see how critiques of Mendieta's essentialism pushed many other feminist critics to defend Mendieta. Jane Blocker's 1999 book on Mendieta, *Where Is Ana Mendieta? Identity, Performativity, and Exile*, works to undo some of the accusations that Mendieta's work was too "essentialist" due to its reputed representation of woman as primitive, earthly, and womb-like.[21] Eschewing presumptions about the work as naively essentialist in regard to gender or as the mere result of exilic trauma, Blocker argues the precise opposite, in a theoretical language very much endemic to the late '90s—namely, that Mendieta's work is performative and uncanny. Blocker's work provided much-needed nuance to the reception of Mendieta in art history discourse, specifically regarding her figure within debates contemporaneous to the 1990s. Yet feminist theorist Diana Fuss, in her 1989 scholarly focus *Essentially Speaking*, asks us to think longer and harder about how essence and essentialism are deployed rather than merely assigning all essentialisms to bad politics and bad feminism.[22] Shuttle forward to Eve Kosofsky Sedgwick in *Touching Feeling*, who asked us to move away from the dualistic, conceptual gridlock of debates of essentialism versus antiessentialism as the necessary starting point in feminist and queer analysis.[23] Such a guiding dualism often produces an allergy to considerations of the body, of femininity, and of origins. In this context, it seems worth noting two things: first, Mendieta's work is not, above all, a theory of gender; and second, an ability to eschew considerations of the body, origins, and femininity in relation to race and place is a privilege for few. Such allegations of essentialism tend to reduce Mendieta's work to a transparent mode of gendered representation—ignoring the nuances of place, matter, and race. Moreover, such allegations against Mendieta fail to see the figurative quality of matter in her work. Mendieta does not work on static matter but instead shows how matter also works on us. As such, her aesthetic alignments with nature may not necessarily be so deterministic or reductive. In the case of Mendieta, the very material of her canvas, though supposedly natural, may be no more stable, no more fixed, than gender itself. The question is of scale, of time, but also of who deserves to have a timescale of consideration. My salient point here is that what was perceived as essentialism, a form of positivism, is only essentialist if the art is understood as transparently referential and if the natural elements and processes that co-author Mendieta's work are considered mute, raw, and permanent.

Remembering Ana Mendieta, feminist artist Carolee Schneemann has spoken in interviews of the difficulty of making corporeally based feminist art during a time when there was such a dogma of antiessentialism: "The struggle has to do with the confines of essentialist theory, which was a way of constraining and marginalizing our fuller historic implications. Both of us were committed to the saturation of material, in that the body moves and is sustained by saturation within the extensivity of our sensory energy."[24] In this quote, you can hear a materialist critique of the terms of essentialism. Schneemann gestures toward the body as material, saturated, energetic, and sensorial, a complex system of force, affect, and flesh. She continues,

> In the use of our bodies we shared the confluence of being despised in the art world throughout our early experiments, as mine from the 60s were hugely resisted and then Ana enters the forcefield of feminist issues in the 70s where feminist theory and research begins to tear down the determinations of narcissism, exhibitionism, but what enters in the field at that moment is the abject and the essentialist! In order to recognize that we were facing a new construct of deflections, that if the identification of the vital energies with nature and the body can only be "essentialist or abject," we are still going to be denied full aesthetic authority.[25]

One cannot help but hear the double bind for feminist artists: You cannot own even your own body, and you cannot theorize from your body. Instead, even in feminist circles, your body will be suspect.

As Mendieta's work moved from her bloody, embodied performances, her body as such began to recede. With her *Silueta* series, she began to present only the trace of it. Rather than centering her body, she created these silhouettes in proportion to her bodily frame—a frame many critics cannot help but comment was rather small, not reaching five feet in height. This propensity to gesture toward an absent body marked a shift in her work, focused less on a metaphysics of presence and more on how bodies momentarily imprint and commingle with the elements. Many of these pieces were loosely held together and utilized natural elements like fire, dirt, blood, and sticks—showcasing her propensity toward a collaboration with natural forces, erosion, and ephemerality. Regarding the question of essentialism in this series, Ellen Tepfer comments, "In them, Mendieta does not take an anti-essentialist stance, which posits that there is no femininity as such. But neither does she take the opposite position—one that conceives of femininity as a fixed category, an entity that can be simply 'returned to' or embodied."[26] So while it may be true that Mendieta's art was not particularly interested in antiessentialism, as many critical trends desired, neither did she conceive of femininity as a static, essential, or particularly delineated category.[27] Rather, she worked with the abstract lines of goddess iconography, the aesthetic affordances of blood, the ways in which femininity is often met with violence, and the many worlds lost to strict dogmas and violent coloniality.

Into the Caves

The *Esculturas Rupestres* stand as the culmination of the earth-body work that encompassed the intensely corporeal performative and ephemeral art of Mendieta's *Silueta* series. Mendieta's art dealt with various incarnations and transmutations of the body. Situating the *Esculturas Rupestres* among the different phases of Mendieta's artwork, Olga Viso writes, "Mendieta's series of rock carvings in Jaruco would prove to be among her most significant works of the period. She had brought the Siluetas, a series of ongoing earth-body works devoted to the recuperation of origins and a lost homeland, to its very source."[28] Though Mendieta often spoke of origin and her own exilic status as one torn from her homeland, she did not use the language of recuperation. Instead of looking for a single point of origin located in a spatiotemporal index, Mendieta questioned the past as something that could be recuperated: "There is no past to redeem: there is the void, the orphanhood, the unbaptized earth of the beginning, the time that from within the earth looks upon us."[29] Rather than redeeming history, Mendieta looked to confront the abyssal voids—the gaps and fissures and silences—that often make up the foundations of what we consider to be history. Mendieta's words here allude to her readings of Mexican poet and thinker Octavio Paz, who writes of the historical inheritance of colonialism and coming after colonialism and the search for origins that are neither singular nor clear. He calls solitude a form of "orphanhood, an obscure awareness that we have been torn from the All, and an ardent search: a flight and a return, an effort to re-establish the bonds that unite us with the universe."[30] For Mendieta, art itself allows a return to a more cosmological form of abyssal origin, one that cannot be located in a nation-state. Recalling Mendieta and her own relationship to exile and return, María de Los Angeles Torres writes, "She often said that our returns were journeys to *our origins*, but her definition of this was not narrow. She expanded the *our* beyond our immediate historical selves; and the *origins*, beyond the borders of geography. As such, she gave us a way to lay claim to our past while becoming human in the present."[31] Moreover, returning to a source or homeland, *patria*, is a spatiotemporal theme well explored in Latinx studies. Many Latinx scholars have eloquently articulated the temporal structures that condition received notions of latinidad: how Latinx peoples seem to be at once the past and simultaneously the future—never allowed the plenitude and danger of the present.[32] But the future anterior for Mendieta would not find its return in a solid place or a firm reference. Her oeuvre instead moved through material processes and migratory paths that took her from Iowa to Mexico to Cuba to Italy.

After making the abstract carvings on the limestone walls and formations of the caves, Mendieta named them after Taíno goddess effigies, most likely taken from her own research on Taíno myths and legends, which would have included José Juan Arrom's research on Pané's manuscript.[33] Working across these translated sources, her sculptures function as an iterative, material genealogy of myth itself—invoking the aura of cave paintings, colonial contact, and the material sediment of millennia. Mendieta created the effigies in the limestone of the cave walls—a supple, soft, and ever-changing canvas—carving the *esculturas* in proportions and movements that mimic the face of the rock. In so doing, the *Esculturas Rupestres* foreground the medium—the very ground of Mendieta's work in Jaruco: the limestone itself.

The limestone grottos that create cave-like settings in Jaruco function as historical reservoirs of the locale and the seafloor. Oolitic limestone takes its name from oolite, derived from the ancient Greek ᾠόν for "egg," connoting the small grains that compose limestone. The soft, impressionable rock serves as a canvas that registers, layers, and blurs the traces of time passing. Olga Viso writes that "pre-Hispanic civilizations had inhabited the zone and the park's rocky outcroppings had served as refuge for pirates during the colonial era. At the end of the nineteenth century the location was a hideout for Mambíses."[34] In addition to providing an enclave to Indigenous civilizations and independence soldiers, the caves also held a place for more modern dissidents. In "Still Searching for Ana Mendieta," José Quiroga writes, "I am sure too that Mendieta learned that some of the Jaruco caves held many recent memories of clandestine homosexual weddings, and that they had been used as places where rockers and pot-smoking disaffected youth would meet."[35] These caves, then, are suffused with the traces of those who have never been fully accounted for within the Cuban state. This history of alterity troubles any simplistic rendering of Mendieta's notion of origin, exile, or return—or indeed any simplistic reading of Cuba and its proper subjects. Quiroga's elegant search for Mendieta's traces illuminates that the questions and journeys that surround Mendieta's work may be the very way in which one can encounter the ethos of her work.

Once declared vanished and gone by both the Guggenheim Museum in New York and the Ludwig Foundation in Havana, many have found the lingering traces of Mendieta's return to her supposed source. The filmmakers of the first major documentary on Ana Mendieta, *Ana Mendieta: Fuego de tierra* (1987) visited one of the sites at Jaruco, as well as Galeria DUPP in 1997 and Olga Viso in 2002. Canadian artist Elise Rasmussen exhibited her own photos of the weathered cave carvings in a project called *Finding Ana*. In an article in the *New Inquiry* on her project, the artist states, "Ana meant for the work to exist through her documentation. Her work was ephemeral, and I believe she enjoyed the idea of it returning to the earth. So finding the sculptures didn't mean I necessarily found the work, as the work lives on through the images. For me it was much more personal, of being able to actually touch and feel the same limestone that she carved. In a way it brought me as close to her physically as possible."[36] The material encounter here gets at the very matter of the ongoing search for Mendieta. More recently, Raquel Cecilia Mendieta, Ana Mendieta's niece and goddaughter, has located both sites of Mendieta's work and created a film documenting these findings entitled *Whispering Cave*.

Mendieta's return to the island was not singular, but multiple. Her plans to travel back home, to Cuba, developed within the larger context of Cuban exiles who sympathized with some, if not all, of the motivations for and aspirations of the Cuban Revolution. The larger sociopolitical moment of her returns signaled a brief aperture in US-Cuban relations known as *el diálogo,* fostered by President Carter with the partnership of Cuban American citizens during the mid-to-late 1970s, which hoped for a détente in the Cold War logic that kept the US and Cuba at odds. This hopeful moment opened up a slew of exchanges between the US and Cuba, largely galvanized by groups of young Cubans who moved beyond the strict pro- or antirevolutionary mythos. Though the dialogues did not fulfill their ideals of opening relations between the nations, several meetings did take place and some political prisoners were released, including Mendieta's own father in 1979. These openings set the stage for Mendieta, and other Cubans like her who did not share the Miami exile community's hardline approach, to make their own returns to the island of their birth. In these circles, Mendieta made seven trips to Cuba between 1980 and 1983 and, on occasion, brought artists and intellectuals from her New York City art world to her homeland. During this time, she met with a generation of Cuban artists focused heavily on Afro-Cuban mythologies as well as Indigenous ones. It is with these artists that she first made her trek to Jaruco.

Mendieta focused on artistic exchange, familial reunions, and lingering in the caves of Jaruco—working long days in near solitude away from the busy modernity of Havana and away from much of the cultural life of the island. Her visits coincided, rather felicitously, with an already moving shift to forms of art and aesthetic intervention that exceeded the strictures assigned by the Cuban government's increasing rigidity on all things cultural, following what many have called the *quinquineo gris*: the five years between 1971 and 1976 that marked the end of revolutionary experimentation and inculcated a more Soviet, insular type of ideological and cultural control. The group of artists, dubbed *Volumen Uno*, brought a change to the island's aesthetic production, one that refused overt political messages and instead erred on the side of abstraction, Indigenous, and Afro-Cuban iconography. The artists exhibiting in *Volumen Uno* included Flavio Garciandía, Tomas Sánchez, José Manuel Fors, José Bedia, Gustavo Pérez Monzón, Ricardo Rodriguez Brey, Leandro Soto, Israel León, Juan Francisco Elso, Rubén Torres Llorca, and Rogelio López Marín (Gory).

During Mendieta's trips to Cuba, she sometimes acted as an arts and culture ambassador or, more precisely, a bridge between US artists and Cuban artists through the Cuban Cultural Circle. This organization was very akin to the Maceo Brigade, named after the Afro-Cuban independence military official Antonio Maceo. She recruited folks to come with her, including poet Jayne Cortez and art critic Lucy Lippard. She traveled seven times to the island, sometimes acting as a tour guide for the Cuban Cultural Circle, sometimes to exhibit and create her own work. In writing of Mendieta's legacy on the island, the Cuban curator Elvis Fuentes, now at El Museo del Barrio in New York, declares: "Her ability to appropriate and synthesize aspects of Land Art, Body Art, and Feminism turned her into a kind of 'compendium' of the various experimental trends of the period. Hence, when she visited Cuba, Mendieta became a catalyst for young creators who were eager to try out new means of expression."[37] Luis Camnitzer rerouted this impact, calling her a mediator rather than an influencer: "Ana became the ideal mediator between the 1980s generation and the 'outside.' She did not influence artists aesthetically but provided a sounding board for ideas and gave moral support. She also became a two-way carrier of information about art between Cuba and the United States."[38] While the estimations of impact vary, what we do know is that this exchange was intense and fruitful for both Mendieta and the artists who lived on the island.

At this time, Mendieta was romantically involved with Carl Andre, and when he first visited the island in 1981, she arranged for Bedia and friends to dine with him. They were impressed with Andre's elegant manners but somewhat skeptical of his purported Marxist beliefs, grumbling that they had to live inside "la teoría" (the theory). Andre fancied himself an ardent Marxist and this confrontation signaled how his ideological beliefs were cushioned by the affordances of a successful New York art career. Materiality often undoes idealism. Bedia later summarized Mendieta's significance for them: "We were already formed as artists, but she gave us a look at the broad art world through the eyes of a Cuban like us."[39] While they argued over artistic movements, like minimalism, the exchange was immensely fruitful. Mendieta demystified the North American art world for the Cuban artists who had endured the intense isolationist years of the 1970s. In return, they shared with her their greater knowledge of Indigenous and Afro-Cuban traditions on the island. They also helped her scout out a location for her *Esculturas Rupestres*.[40] Vicki Ruiz summarizes this time on the island, drawing attention to the fact that this aesthetic encounter between Mendieta and Cuban artists had humming in the background a disruptive event in Cuba's revolutionary progress narrative: the Mariel boat lifts. Ruiz explains, "Her visit was deliberately used to increase the government's popularity, then in measurable decline due to the Mariel Boatlifts—a massive exodus, which forced as many as 125,000 Cubans to leave the island.... All of the attention given to Mendieta's visit was calculated to divert attention away from the forced exodus at Mariel. Although Mendieta realized that the Cuban government had used her, she found little sympathy at home in the United States for her situation."[41] The time was ripe for Mendieta's encounter with Cuba but also fraught with the ongoing turbulence that is politics. Nationalisms like to smooth over these rough, rocky moments—using anything they can to claim innocence and purity. It is within this context that I think it is worth noting how much Mendieta strayed from art institutions, choosing the location of Jaruco over the many ideological state apparatuses in Havana.

A Palimpsest of Returns

For many years, through teaching and research, Mendieta illustrated for me a way of feeling and being Cuban without the restricting, dogmatic politics that crowded around Cuba and its formidable diaspora. Yet also, my own visit to the island was only afforded by means of institutional affiliation. During June 2016, I accompanied twelve students from Oregon State University to Cuba. We departed from Miami to Havana just days after President Trump had tightened travel restrictions and remittances to Cuba, thus reversing the paltry progress in relations that had been made during the Obama years.[42] Conjuring Cold War ghosts to foment his populist base, Trump made his own Republican pilgrimage to the site that honors the Brigade 2506—the CIA-trained Cubans who fought against Castro's regime. When conferring about the trip's itinerary with our hosts, I asked that Jaruco be added to it. I gave as much information as I could about Ana Mendieta and these cave carvings. I was not sure if we would be simply visiting a state park or finding the caves and their inscriptive relics.

And so we ventured off from Havana in our small school bus, hopping along potholed roads and preparing for the midday heat to bear upon us. Jaruco is a place where *guajiros* still flourish, where modernity seems to have halted its project. Just about an hour outside of the densely populated, vibrant city of Havana, with its throngs of gatherings on corners or along the *malecón*, Jaruco looks more like an agrarian oasis—a different moment in the ever-changing Cuban palimpsest.[43] The striking countryside scenes en route to Jaruco are emphasized by how thinned out the population becomes. As we bumped along the road in our school bus, we were felicitously escorted for a short moment by a man on a horse galloping alongside the bus, whipping his stallion until they both reminded us that *horsepower* is not simply a metaphor and dashed away into the thicket of palm trees.

He seemed an apparition out of Virgilio Piñera's *La isla en peso*,[44] the *guajiro* who mounts his stallion, a sign that even the countryside bears the marks of coloniality—that shadowy precursor to modernity—and sustains ecologies of colonial intervention. But it also bears noting that during the Special Period years, Cubans would return to both colonial horseback and Chinese-imported bicycles when fuel was scarce, as was food. The bus ride itself was illustrative of the fortitude of Cubans who have remained on the island, a fortitude not yet reliant upon the twenty-first-century infrastructures and technologies we take for granted in the United States. On the way to Jaruco we got lost, not once,

Figure 1.1. On the way to Jaruco, author's photo

but many times. Or, better put, we got lost according to US standards. What we really did was find our way, which often meant coming to a fork in the increasingly unpaved road with no signage, asking a person on the side of the street which way to go. Each time our bus driver, Chino, would crank open the doors to our bus and gregariously ask some perfect stranger where to go, always addressing them with the diminutive, dulcet tonalities that are the lilts of stranger intimacies on the island. In Cuba, you address someone as your love, through a baroque lyric that surfaces in quotidian chatter, thanking them enormously, *mil gracias*, and wishing them well. We finally arrived at Jaruco, entered the park, and stopped at a *paladar*, a private restaurant, which specializes in all things pork. The bus stopped, our guide meandered into the restaurant, and we all took a look around.

Here, at the entrance, we were greeted by a statue of a "Taína"—painted in red, rendered feminine—a gendered and racialized trope of generic indigeneity.

The map's routes are, at best, abstracted and indiscernible, giving paths to restaurants and the hotel rather than nature trails. Situated diagonally from the Taíno statue that greets the park visitors, a statue of an escaped enslaved person, a *cimarrón*, ominously looms. The position of the *cimarrón* is telling. If you only stare at the entrance, you get the welcome

Figure 1.2. Taína at Jaruco park entrance, author's photo

of a peaceful, feminized Taína—a telling posture that says more about colonial myths surrounding the purportedly peaceful people who had actually eradicated other, earlier Indigenous Arawaks before Columbus's arrival on the island. You might not notice the *cimarrón* who is nearly escaped, up a hill and easily missed if entrance is your only goal. He is a reminder of marooning and survival, if hyperbolically rendered.

Physically much larger than the Taíno, the *cimarrón* poses with a machete in midswing, about to hack away at a dog who threatened to reveal the secret path of his escape. At the opening of the park, two human figures come to surface from the history of the locale, placing us, if unwittingly, in the very materials and bodies that made the modern nation of Cuba, and indeed the larger Americas, possible: the pre-Columbian Indigenous and the enslaved. These powerful figurations are and were entangled, and the limestone of this park tells one of their porously sedimented stories. The statues, in their diametrical position and scale, remind us that Cuba has a particularly caricatured relationship to its racial foundations. The indigenous past is often locked solely in the past, figuratively sealed and, therefore, enabling a link to or creating a need to think what Brathwaite might call the African presence in the Caribbean—both historical and present.[45] The *cimarrón*'s size registers more colonial fear than his open eyes seem to be meant to convey. And the Taína's passivity colludes with what missionaries tried to argue in contradistinction to the enslaved peoples, though most historical and archaeological evidence tells a more complicated story of indigeneity in the Caribbean. So too does some etymology deriving from the Arawak language allow us to see the overlap of these figures, even in the etymology of *cimarrón*. José Juan Arrom writes,

> The word cimarrón may very well originate from the Taíno root symara: When the símara root is modified with the ending—n, a durative sign ... símaran could be translated as arrow shot from the bow, escape from the dominion of man or, as Oviedo says, "fugitive." There, símaran equates to "sylvan," "of the jungle" or "savage"; applied to non-cultivated plants, to "runaway," "rebellious" or "ferocious" when applied to domesticated animals that become wild, and also to men, Indians first and blacks after, that run away and in their desperate escape searched for freedom far from the dominion of their master.[46]

Figure 1.3. *Cimarrón* at park entrance, photo by Roy Pérez

The entangled relationship between the Indigenous and the enslaved in relation to taxonomies of difference resultant from empire, law, religion, and sociogeny is explained in rigorous theory and deft historical attention in the work of Sylvia Wynter. These colonial caricatures attest to the descriptive logic of coloniality that Sylvia Wynter describes: "If the range of the Native Others were now to be classified . . . in terms of the multiple mythologies of the savage Other, the fossil other, the abnormal Other, the timeless ethnographic Other, the most salient of all these was to be that the mythology of the Black Other of sub-Saharan Africans (and their Diasporic descendants) . . . all of this was done in a lawlike manner through the systemic stigmatization of the Earth in terms of its being made of a 'vile and base matter.'"[47] As such, the matter of Jaruco's park engulfs the narrative of Mendieta's return—telling a story exorbitant to any source she could claim and marking a matrix of matter that proves recalcitrant to proprietary relation.[48]

Moving from these hyperbolically racialized statues, my gaze flitted away from the human to the lithic, engaged by the textured outcroppings and the plants that made their home in this park. A native and rare agave grows here, *Agave Jarucoensis*, which was identified as endemic to Cuba and more specifically to the Escalera de Jaruco.[49]

After roaming at the entrance of the park, we all climbed back into the bus, now accompanied by a park ranger who would take us to Mendieta's caves. We drove another ten minutes through dirt roads scantly signposted and stopped in a seemingly random patch of nowhere. Guided

Figure 1.4. Native agave, author's photo

by the ranger, we walked over to the barbed wire fence with stern, old posts, and our guide moved one off the side and pointed toward our path. We walked through thickets of thorny bushes and dense vegetation in a path that seemed more obscured than delineated, learning that the path had been closed five years prior because people would come to the site and paint graffiti over the walls. Our guide gestured that this betrayed Mendieta's wish that nature be the only co-artist involved in the *esculturas'* denouement. It is striking that her outdoor works may be institutionalized in Jaruco before, say, any of her remaining works in Miami, such as *Ceiba Fetish*, which she made upon one of her returns to Miami from Cuba in 1981.[50] Claims and origins reinscribe.

Finally, after walking through scraggly bushes on a veritably nonexistent path, we arrived at a small opening and the cavernous stairs that climbed Jaruco. Immediately, a few *esculturas* stood out while the others had faded to a point nearly indiscernible from the extant lithic formations. Rather than finding Mendieta in these cave-like settings, we came to her source materials, which stand in relation and contrast to colonial sources—dense vegetation and gorgeous formations of rocks that erred on the extraterrestrial at times.

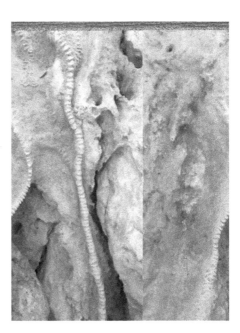

Figure 1.5. Limestone formations in Jaruco, photo courtesy of Matthew Rubio

In Taíno mythology, caves are the birthplace of humans. Importantly, people emerge from not one but two caves in this lore. When making their own marks on rock, Taínos worked with the suggestions of already extant natural formations. Caves also mark the birthplace of the sun and the moon, as well as a burial site for the human dead—a celestial cycle takes place in these caves. And like many other cultures, Taínos make art in their caves—art that deals with the sacred and moves with the natural formations in the caves. What was most revealing about this trip to Mendieta's sculptures was how she, too, worked with an already and beautifully textured canvas. Sculpting by way of fusing with natural materials, for Mendieta, meant honoring the extant formations and processes.

When I first arrived at the caves, I was elated to see two clearly delineated sculptures: *Bacayu* (*Light of Day*) and *Maroya* (I). Taíno mythology pointed to caves as the source of the sun and moon, and these two sculptures emanate from the caves with insistent force. The most striking and delineated of Mendieta's sculptures is *Bacayu*. I would speculate, too, that it was the most delineated when Mendieta initially inscribed it, during the summer of 1981. Note the way in which what has best survived is an island sculpture, created using a rock formation that already stood out from the walls of the limestone grotto in 1981. *Bacayu*, which Mendieta translated as "light of day," is indeed the first luminous figure that greets one after walking through thorny, tropical thickets and up into the cavernous hillsides where Mendieta worked. Note the details on the photograph taken in 1981. Here, what appears to be a delineation of possible black mold is actually black paint.

Rather than a masterfully polished sculpture, *Bacayu* illuminates the outlines of a body according to how it had already been made over the time of its stoney growth. This form persists in the present, now accompanied by a stalagmite tucked just behind the sculpture. Many, many years from now, it is possible that this stalagmite will grow into a column, thus shifting the aesthetic arrangement of these caves.

Just to the right of *Bacayu*'s well-illuminated figure, we see the outlines of *Maroya*. Both are represented as loosely feminine silhouettes, one emphasizing breasts and the other a vulva. Both signal a source, but in this matrix of maternity, we find many mothers, many sources of light, many points of departure and return. Hence, if these cave sculptures do signal a confrontation between Mendieta's work and its source, we must

Figure 1.6. *Bacayu*, 1981, Galerie LeLong

push the meanings of such loaded terms as *source* and *origin*. Take, for instance, the carving entitled *Guanaroca*, which can be found in another locale in the park.

Here Mendieta carves a goddess effigy to the purported first woman of humanity, according to Taíno legend. Mendieta carves the effigy with the contours of the cave, giving asymmetry to this goddess that conjures the figures of many other goddesses of fertility recognizable across cultures. The effigy is both specific and translatable, legible even beyond the specific locale of Cuba. The texture and shape of the wall dictate the movement of this static sculpture—it seems to both emerge and be a site of emergence. The focal point of the sculpture is a vaginal opening, which is also surrounded by a labial carving that may connote the legs. The southern hemisphere of this carving, then, creates a space from which movement springs. It is a first woman who herself seems to be a matrix, inextricably bound within this cave wall. And while she may be the first woman, her originary outlines have faded and been absorbed into the limestone walls.

In thirty years, the walls have mutated, and now only the barest traces of *Guanaroca* exist—absorbed, smoothed, and enfolded into a landscape

Figure 1.7. *Guanaroca (First Woman)*, 1981, Galerie LeLong

that has resculpted its own face. As I climbed through the caves, I was struck not by some ominous presence of Mendieta but instead by the ways in which her choice of matter and location tugged on ongoing questions in relation to Cuba, her legacy, and the temporal markers registered and blurred by such a vibrant, already marked canvas.

As we moved through the grottos, our guide showed us the various lingering traces of Mendieta's sculptural work. He explained that the path had been obscured to only allow nature to erode her works, also noting that there had been an upsurge in North American interest in the sculptures. There are plans to build an homage to Mendieta in the hotel room she stayed in while she worked in Jaruco. Feeling trepidatious, but ultimately too curious not to venture a question, I asked very cautiously about what Quiroga had written—if modern dissidents have frequented these caves in more contemporaneous times. I asked if Mendieta could have known of these occurrences. The state worker vehemently opposed my question and its assumptions, quickly responding, "Aquí? No" ("Here? No."). He explained that the place was very secluded, that there were no paved roads until the seventies, and that the agrarian location was mostly inhabited by *campesinos* who raised pork.[51] He then went on to remind me that the Mambí army used the caves of Jaruco as enclaves. After this, though, he did emit a signal that subtly underscores Quiroga's findings and my suspicions. He said that a few years prior, a police chief died about two hundred meters from the caves, and a band of counterrevolutionaries had killed him. I pushed this inquiry no further, turning my attention back to the grottos and Mendieta's astounding choice of location.

How was I to leave these caves that had been a source of searching, cover, and longing for so many? My students, ever perceptive to what really matters, left me and a few others to linger in the caves, as they sought out more water back on our bus. Three students, the most touched by Mendieta's work and legacy, stayed behind. We moved silently along the rocks and looked out at the impressive vistas that hillside caves and grottos afford: views of the luscious, green countryside. We moved through the formations like children, in awe of not only Mendieta's sculptures but also the strange, gorgeous textures that oolitic limestone produces. One student peered into a hole in the floor of an upper shelf of a grotto, slowly and gingerly excavating empty shells from the *hueco*. She started arranging them in her own *silueta*. I joined this silent ritual, helping to arrange the shells, and another student pulled a few strands of hair from her head, giving the tiny homage further texture. It was a small gesture, a tiny prayer, a simple tribute that is surely now disassembled, weathered, and rearranged.

What the Limestone Holds

Looking to the overlapping histories of Jaruco, we see how the locale is suffused with many stories that detail beginnings and endings. In particular, next to the most discernible *escultura*, a stalagmite is forming—growing upward from a stalactite's stream of sculpting water. Such formations in caves are markers of secondary mineral deposits, most often found in limestone caves. Most stalagmites are speleothems. Speleothems are studied as climate proxies because their location within cave environments and patterns of growth allow them to be used as archives for several climate variables. If rocks can tell us about climate and environmental changes, if they endure as a strange witness to deep time, they do not record mere presence but, instead, endings

Figure 1.8. Stalagmite, author's photo

and beginnings in layers and loops of finitude. Rocks register inscriptions with stratifications that index a time far longer than humans can remember or retrace. Dana Luciano reminds us that this is "the paradox of new materialist media theory as far as the rock record goes. Thinking about rocks as media makes them less alien to us; it allows us to see them as lively—and yet the information encoded in the 'rock record' is organized to a large degree by death and disappearance."[52] The source materials here gesture toward origins and endings—an unstable foundation or canvas, a stratification of that which traces former living organisms, whole underwater ecosystems. And while we may not think of stones or rocks as being able to die, they often become reservoirs of understanding origin. Yet such an origin is not singular and not really temporally identifiable as only an origin, given that most rocks derive from forms of sedimentation, erosion, metabolism, and eruptions from the molten interior of the earth.[53]

Limestone has a way of writing the shadowy outlines of finitude through registering the outlines of biological matter. This recognition can be an ethical one that asks us to look to the past to see the future, thinking through some of the harshest truths. Lynne Huffer, writing "Foucault's Fossils," considers how fossils register something of Foucault's genealogical and archaeological practice, one that would be enhanced profoundly by an attention to coloniality and race: "The mad logic of resemblance of a fossil record that proleptically tracks life's extinction ruptures the grids that make us—and life itself—intelligible. The fossil is an inhuman art, a lithic conviviality, an intensification of the monstrosity of the world's truths."[54] Limestone is the most fossil-dense form of sediment. It holds the traces of many oceanic creatures and worlds gone, thus linking the floor of the Caribbean and the Atlantic, resurfacing histories of dispossession, extraction, and forced labor. This stone is intensely conglomerate with stratifications of finitude. It is a rather strange canvas whose texture derives from the inhumanity, indeed the unliveliness, of fossils.

Caves, of course, gesture to many notions of source and origin, not least of which is the mythic beginning of art in Western culture. Such sites are imbued not only with the inhuman and loss but also with the possibility of gleaning truth from representation and art. In her essay "On Photography," Susan Sontag inaugurates her own take on visual culture with the following line: "Humankind lingers unregenerately in Plato's cave, still reveling, its age-old habit, in mere images of the truth."[55] What fundaments do images of truth rest upon? Luce Irigaray shows that Plato's allegory of the cave rests upon a degradation of the maternal and the feminine, a slaughtering of materiality and matter to make it a fertile ground upon which upstanding individuals, or more precisely men, may unyoke themselves from the shadowy underworld and emerge to the platonic ideals.[56] But this material fundament, in Irigaray, is only thought at the level of sexual difference. I will return to Irigaray shortly but want to note here that the cave-like limestone walls of Jaruco index more than just the feminine attributes of Mendieta's abstracted goddesses.

Like many other cultures, Taínos made art in their caves—art that deals with the sacred and moved, like Mendieta's carvings, with the caves' natural formations. The largest concentration of extant Taíno art is on the small island of Mona, located between Puerto Rico and the Dominican Republic. Such archaeological work has revived interest in Taíno culture across islands, reminding us of how the Indigenous folks who first dealt with the blow of coloniality still have lasting imprints and descendants, whether through DNA, agriculture, lithic trace, or linguistic loan, in a broader story of coloniality.

Caves cannot help but gesture toward several concepts at once, not least of which are origins and geology. But I want to take care and not claim these caves as originary in any simplistic manner, as a zero ground or single point of departure. Rather, these caves, like the limestone, gesture toward a different temporality that is neither linear nor singular. So too am I hesitant to assign these caves as yet another signpost of what geologists call the Anthropocene for the very same reasons that many scholars of color and postcolonial, queer, Black, and feminist critics have noted: that the world the Anthropocene worries over is a world that has already been radically inhospitable for many for a long time.

* * *

As Katherine McKittrick and Kathryn Yusoff have shown, the very ground or bedrock of the Americas rests on demonic grounds, a relation to the earth that renders the inhuman, or those outside of the domain of Western man—such as plants, minerals, and many other lives (and certainly Indigenous and Black life)—extractable and fungible for the purposes of colonialism, imperialism, and modernity.[57] Yusoff, indebted to McKittrick's work on Sylvia Wynter and geography, takes us to the mineral foundations that prop up maps and topographies, a geologic trace structure that has been made to mold to colonial expectations but also upends them. She writes, "If the imagination of planetary peril coerces an ideal of 'we,' it only does so when the entrappings of late liberalism become threatened. This 'we' negates all responsibility for how the wealth of geology was built off the subtending strata of indigenous genocide and erasure, slavery and carceral labor, and evades what that accumulation of wealth still makes possible in the present—lest 'we' forget that the economies of geology still largely regulate geopolitics and modes of naturalizing, formalizing, and operationalizing dispossession and going settler colonialism."[58] The ideality of a relationality that emerges from planetary threat erases the many who are not considered within a normative frame of ethics. More precisely, the relational structure that is exposed as relational, or interdependent, in ecological considerations often marshals a "we" that precludes many lives and life-worlds that have already been vanquished, upon whose bodies many forms of accumulation rise. Axelle Karera makes this point forcefully: "Under the ongoing conditions of surplus violence, in which mundane activities (like playing in a park) or one's attempt to secure a safer life (asylum seekers) can easily result in one's death, we must opt to be suspicious of a discursive ethical establishment that appears unable to register these deaths."[59] So while "we" or one cannot and should not identify with the lithic, we can witness something absolutely necessary about layers upon layers of finitude, which should caution us against rendering this compilation of death as a source that will compost and, ultimately, fertilize emancipatory futures out of death, or the threat of death, itself.[60]

Caves and Catachresis

Mendieta's caves beg for a careful reading, not only because of the multilayered temporality of these particular caves or because of the complex task of archiving returns and ends as recursive, but also because her work has a tendency to push figuration to its limits—or as she might say, to its source. If she is going to the source, then she is also digging around in the source, getting dirty with the very stuff of what grounds her work—its ability to figure. These caves and their inscriptions remain resistant to the uses of political advocacy, remain opaque to propaganda that shouts across the ninety miles between the Florida Straits and Cuba, and remain a problem for reading.

Mendieta sculpts life-sized deities onto the Jaruco caves that have housed the very outlaws, the loose ends, of Cuban history. She creates a constellation of pre-Columbian myths, social dissidents, and her own "return" in the limestone that cocreated her works. Her setting choice of the sculptures in Jaruco alludes to many rock inscriptions and caves: the caves with paintings that mark the first evidence of art, Plato's allegory of the cave, and the caves of Taíno mythology that tell the origins of humanity. Mendieta's caves are both figurative caves and actual caves—colliding figuration with referentiality to the point that the caves can be neither solely figurative nor referential but overwhelmingly both. The figurations of these caves *cave in*. They can be neither simply referential nor solely metaphorical in meaning. As such, they function as a catachresis, conventionally defined as a figure of strain, misuse, or abuse of words and metaphors. Jacques Derrida categorizes *catachresis* as that which names all original incompleteness, and Gayatri Spivak extends the category to words that figure monikers like women, wherein no exemplary example exists.[61] These caves, as installation art pieces that conjure up myriad artistic, metaphorical, historical, and political scenarios, function as a catachresis that shows how matter at once makes meaning and lets it fade away.

Attention to catachresis breaks the metaphorical economy of equivalence, all too easily subsumed into logics of politics that operate on false, violent analogies—analogies that often operate in an effort to usher, or urge, movement toward a known horizon, a homogenizing telos. Such would be the case with the reigning binaries that have historically governed how one would have related to Cuba—either moving toward Castro or away—both using freedom as the marker of value, both white mythologies. And yet this catachresis commingles the literal and the figurative in an evocative way to suggest a kind of breakdown in erosion, in exposure, and in reading.

Catachreses are not always necessarily good figurations—the abuse of metaphor may not be politically viable and may become weathered, worn out, overwrought. These catachrestic caves perhaps hold engravings that were assumed to be lost objects, lost worlds. Barbara Johnson writes that "every lost object is always, in a sense, a catachresis, a figurative substitute for nothing that could ever be literal."[62] Calling attention to the work of catachresis in Irigaray's writing, Lynne Huffer defines catachresis as "the extension of metaphorical meaning beyond the figural . . . a figure that lacks original or proper meaning."[63] Such a move to push figuration to its limits through catachresis is precisely what Irigaray calls for in the *Speculum of the Other Woman*, to "unmask the figures, forms and signs, that ensure present coherence."[64] This work of catachresis, from Irigaray to Spivak, both invokes origin and undoes its ideal status—rendering metaphor, language, and analogy an incomplete project, a hystericization of ideals. The work Mendieta and Irigaray call for is a work of genealogical translation that refuses to read origin myths as one-to-one correlations (or correspondence)—both unearth caves of origin in philosophy and national discourse. Moreover, both feminist thinkers have been the subject of many translations, have been called essentialist, and have found odd fits in the various discourses of Anglo-American feminism. Against this charge of essentialism, Naomi Schor writes that "it is on the rock of materialism and not of essentialism that Irigaray seeks to establish the truth of her claim."[65] I gesture toward Irigaray as a felicitous interlocutor to Mendieta in order to reroute the feminist reception of Mendieta's work away from debates about essentialism that reigned over the nineties and early aughts to a more materialist critique of origin and historical truth. Like Irigaray, Mendieta focuses more on the overdetermination of origin stories rather than the deterministic characteristics of origins. But Mendieta's own return is overdetermined by coloniality, one that may be interested in materiality's force and the material/maternal collapse, but one that also indexes racial and colonial exploitation.

Even lost objects can become melancholic attachments, infused with nostalgia all too often inked into inscriptions of indigeneity, especially in pursuits of origins for those who think themselves *mestizo* or *criollo*. María Josefina Saldaña-Portillo asks us to consider, "In what ways might the psyche of a subject be shaped by the foreclosure and repression of indigenous 'lost objects'? How might the Indian-as-lost object—banned or repressed not only from space but from psychic life—nevertheless remain in the psyche? How might the foreclosed, lost, or repressed racialized Indian not only remain but also animate the subject formed by fictive notions of whiteness or mestizaje?"[66] In reading these caves, we find ourselves in a vertiginous problem of origin, which enfolds endings into source materials, finitude into fundament. If we understand each origin as a catachresis, we may develop a way to both read the retrieval of source materials for homecomings after exile and also keep the question of source open for reading, such that we may not easily reduce the matter of land in Mendieta's work to either background or to being properly autochthonous to her life. The source materials that inspire these cave carvings, these rupestrian inscriptions, are complicated and complicate any claim to an origin or loss.

The agency ascribed to meaning-making in these caves does not, and cannot, be solely given over to Mendieta. The work here is collaborative—given over to the mutable limestone and the histories that have been sedimented in this inaccessible locale. Feminist theorist Vicki Kirby gives us a provocative set of questions to reconsider this question of the sedimented natural alignments of nature with the atemporal, the feminine, and the indigenous. In *Quantum Anthropologies*, she reworks Derrida's oft-cited deconstructionist provocation that "there is no outside of the text" with a revision that "there is no outside of nature."[67] This inescapable entanglement asks us to consider nature as porous and encompassing and to contend with the fact that what we often presume to be raw background contains a trace structure. This has profound implications, specifically for those already aligned, in a Western view, with nature.[68] But this alignment cannot mean a collapse of figure into fundament, or of the lithic traces of finitude with a renewed program of ethics or politics. The shadowy outlines of death seldom afford liberated, emancipated futures.

Rather than seeking recourse to a prelapsarian notion of nature or indigeneity, Mendieta's caves carefully carve out a past that is not necessarily her own—not her source, not her origin. Her catachrestic inscriptions revisit a location and historical matter that, whether wittingly or not, place us at a very dense site of human and inhuman material histories that recount the violent foundations of the Cuban nation. As was her signature, Mendieta's marks in these caves became lost, and this loss spurred incredible returns to questions that haunt the Americas.

These losses—the losses of exiles, the losses of Taínos, the losses of the enslaved—are not commensurate. Her inscriptions move with the limestone, not against it, to engage in a dialogue with matter that *matters*. The limestone of the caves is significant in that the material canvas acts on Mendieta's carvings, morphing them and complicating them rather than preserving them. Most of the grains that compose limestone are skeletal fragments of marine organisms like coral. Limestone holds the traces of the sea as a historical place and as a relational space for the Caribbean, chiming in with Derek Walcott's provocation that the "sea is history" and Edward Braithwaite's notion that "unity is sub-marine."[69] Such use of the limestone conjures a particularly Caribbeanist version of what Wai Chee Dimock calls "deep time"—one that enfolds material with traces of histories of violence.[70] This alignment with that which has been denigrated as mere matter opens us up to a matrix of ethical entanglements that still work on us. The geological force of Mendieta's cave works brings us into the spatiotemporal mattering of limestone, a sediment of the sea that appears, millennia later, as caves. These caves remind us that the time of coloniality endures, that the matter of Indigenous denial and the transatlantic slave trade are imprinted in stone as the bedrock of Americanity, modernity, and Cuba in particular. Read through coloniality and limestone, Mendieta's inscriptive return to Cuba offers a way to de-idealize political terms while engaging with them as a material and fraught source. They also offer an occasion, when read beyond the context of their inscription, for de-idealizing nationalism and the nations of origin of all diasporic Latinx peoples in favor of material engagement, to be instead more concerned with material life than political ideals, which do indeed fail and kill. These caves echo.

Mendieta's caves and their effigies figure the fundament of her work as a source *only catachrestically*. For her, the source reveals the universe as springing forth from a matrix, a *mater*, from which we can never fully recover. Rather than a simplistic return, her work suspends a place of searching that is markedly feminine and unrelentingly corporeal: "I have been carrying on a dialogue between the landscape and the female body. Having been torn from my homeland (Cuba) during my adolescence, I am overwhelmed by the feeling of having been cast out from the womb (Nature). My art is the way I re-establish the bonds that unite me to the Universe."[71] Mendieta's work relays between the material and figurative to offer a conversation between the landscape and the female body based on the most abstracted and vacated outline of her person—a silhouette. Emptied of content and insistent on impermanence, her abstracted lines and loose silhouettes create a way for her to reintegrate herself not into the source, origin, or nation but into a fading erosion. Whether at the level of the sculptures, their colonial sources, the limestone, or the locale, Mendieta's inscriptions illustrate how fundaments absorb and morph marks. Her works require a thinking of myth, history, and matter as entangled in their participation in exposure and erosion. They may be weathered; they tend to fade into the dynamism of the material substrate. Our reading of them requires us to consider how her inscriptions are read over time *in situ*—over time and yet indexed to a time-space of 1981 Cuba that summons questions that precede coloniality and that register the eclipsed futures of whole cosmologies. The fundamental grids of intelligibility have shifted radically since 1981, requiring a reading that exceeds Mendieta's biography as sufficient context for reading these catachrestic caves.

Recall that this chapter began thinking about the book that Mendieta never made of these sculptures. She proposed that the dimensions of the book be quite small because "although the works overpower they are intimate in feeling."[72] Mendieta worked through arrangements of extant material texture—of dirt, bodies, blood, and limestone—to enfold the past within the present through a register of materiality and feeling rather than stable knowledge about the historical sources we read, about claims on land or body. Working with matter according to its own timeline, Mendieta's inscriptions demand that our readerly attention pay heed to that which has, in the Western imaginary, been rendered background, raw material and matter only made valuable through forced extraction. Lithic finitude and entanglement as fundament elicit movement, homage, return, and contemplation—in other words, the material recursivity required of reading myth and matter as entangled. What remains, as we read these caves, are important ethico-political questions for Latinx studies. How do we read Latinx cultural production? How do we assess our source materials? What origin stories do we return to by way of indigeneity? How are forced movements and exiles forms of loss that are radically incommensurate? And how are we challenged, in these caves, to account yet again for the incredible grounding violence of anti-indigeneity and anti-Blackness in the Americas? Rather than finding and grasping, Ana Mendieta's material inscriptions require us to read again—this work of reading inscriptions that beckons one to stay with what may never be fully recovered but what remains.

2

Exorbitant Dust

Manuel Ramos Otero's Queer and Colonial Matters

Dust is the effect of contact between skin and world, and also what buildings catch and the ground gives up. Pinged and hurt and inflamed by contact we've become disoriented together, and breathed it out jointly, even when overwhelmed by what's too hard, or too embodied. This dust, that sand, that perturbing grain and the smooth surfaces and soft air too, act as resources for others. They are in us but the space they make is in a new alien zone of inexperience that might become something if we follow its tracks.
—Lauren Berlant, "The Commons: Infrastructures for Troubling Times"

Filtered through retinas, eyeballs, and optic nerves, the world reaches us in a series of "dark riddles" or "obscure sayings" (the literal sense of enigma) that hide more than they disclose. Indeed, the enigma of physical sight is akin to that of dust. Both withhold much in the course of presenting themselves and the things that appear around or through them.
—Michael Marder, *Dust*

Pero yo soy un animal de tentación y en la ribera de la vida hay algo, alguna voz que me seduce y me traduce, que me oraculiza con enigmas que buscan ser descifrados.

But I am an animal of temptation and in the shore of life there's something, some voice that seduces me and translates me, that oraculizes me with enigmas that yearn to be deciphered.
—Manuel Ramos Otero, "Ficción e historia: Texto y pretexto de la autobiografía"

On the shore of life, Manuel Ramos Otero's writing career indulged in the trope of dust as both matter and metaphor for the marginal, porous edges that crumble between life and death, between lovers' bodies, between fiction and history. This commitment to perceiving endings as particulate and plural renders Ramos Otero's literary work less available to overt and stable identifications of neoliberal subjectivity. As an organizing trope, the chosen and privileged matter-metaphor of dust disaggregates—marking the force and charge of Ramos Otero's poetics. He wrote defiantly and openly about his queerness, his status as a Puerto Rican subject, and his fascination with the margins. Later, in *Invitación al polvo*, he writes as a *sidoso*: a term he coins to describe a person replete with SIDA (the Spanish acronym for AIDS). What strikes me as particularly uncanny or haunting about tracing dust across his writerly career is that he presages death far before he could even know that his own would be the result of a ruinous encounter with the genocidal "management" of HIV/AIDS. What remains eerily familiar, though, is that a Puerto Rican writer like Ramos Otero shows us that Puerto Rico has always been on the brink of exhaustion and has always been precarious given its colonial status. This condition of slow, exhaustive precarity is featured in the work of thinkers like Sandra Ruiz, who theorizes what she calls "Ricanness" as a form of exhaustion, an exercise in endurance, and a perpetual waiting.[1] In the aftermath of Hurricane Maria, I revisit the dusty atmosphere of Puerto Rico with Ramos Otero's thinking of *polvo*, or dust, taking up his invitation. Dust's force and fragility poetically register the dispossession that forces many Puerto Ricans to invest in the cruel optimism of waiting for relief—knowing that the colonizer is no savior, knowing that the Jones Act makes oceanic borders rigidly withholding, knowing that survival lingers in the quotidian acts that become dusty in the wake of a storm that is less of a hurricane and more of an apotheosis of five hundred years of colonization. The attention to dust in Ramos Otero's work entangles larger questions of material need and recursive crisis.

The swerving bits of dust between two genocidal events, HIV/AIDS and Hurricane Maria, enmesh bodies, matter, and policy and invite us to think through the prescient figuration of *polvo* in Manuel Ramos Otero's oeuvre: a figure that places us in the entanglements of coloniality, racialization, and queerness—one that sullies, rather than clarifies, our understanding of these categories as either separate or predictable. To think of these crises as resonant and recursive, though, is not to analogize HIV/AIDS and Hurricane Maria but rather to see how attention to the matter of dust as both literal and figurative allows one to consider questions of porosity, homeostasis, and precarity. The small matter of dust is the conglomerate, nonidentifiable remains of intimacy, violence, and exposure. To read dust as both material and tropological brings one to the work of matter-metaphors—showing how matter figures our poetic vision and how poetic vision may impact our material pursuits. In the ethico-political landscape of Ramos Otero's literary works, the invitation and attention to dust as a guiding matter-metaphor draws our attention to how finitude is materially felt *particularly* at the crossroads of queerness and coloniality. The cross-contamination of matter and metaphor allows us to consider this enduring precarity at the level of aesthetics—namely, the senses and the body.

In what follows, I analyze the use of *polvo* in three different genres and moments in Manuel Ramos Otero's work: his 1971 short story "Hollywood Memorabilia"; his essay posthumously published in 1990, "Ficción e historia: Texto y pretexto de la autobiografía"; and also posthumously published in 1991, his poetry collection *Invitación al polvo*. Tracing the figure of dust over these textual moments, I hope to elucidate how concentrating on this figure and matter challenges conventional notions and genres of life as sovereign, transparent, and homogenous. Moreover, I attend to how the figuration of matter or dust entangles both queerness and coloniality, which urges us to shift our focus from the individual to the structural and from effects on subjectivity to material constrictions. It is, ironically, through a person who writes himself into his own fiction—centering his life as an experience from which to translate and ultimately making his life's work an aesthetic relation figured through dust—that we come to understand these matters as ontologically, temporally, and spatially plural and porous.

By articulating Ramos Otero's poetics of dust, I home in on how this matter poetically disaggregates narrative conventions that tend to consolidate life. In the first section, I concentrate on how a dusty poetics allows Ramos Otero to consider autobiography and translation as intertwined processes of mediation and transmogrification. In order to attend to this theorization, I then read Ramos Otero's final collection of poetry, elucidating the stakes of an invitation to dust as a forceful vigil and rageful detritus as he approaches his own life's end with ferocity. Moving from Ramos Otero's writing to larger ecologies that also demand attention to dust, I end with a tracing of dusty diasporas from across the Atlantic to Puerto Rico. Ecologies of dust in the Caribbean function as an aggregate, swerving matter that entangles the globe with Puerto Rico and vice versa. *Polvo* invites us to shift our focus from the individual to the structural and from effects on subjectivity to material constrictions that affect many. Dust is a minor matter of grave importance.

Part I

DUSTY TRANSLATIONS
Or a Poetics of Transmogrification

Dust finds its way into the material messiness of the relationship between fiction and history in Ramos Otero's theorization of autobiography. "Ficción e historia: Texto y pretexto de autobiografía" (Fiction and history: Autobiographical text and pretext) appeared posthumously in an homage to Manuel Ramos Otero in the San Juan newspaper *El Mundo* on October 14, 1990, precisely one week after his death on October 7. Ramos Otero articulates his ludic and insistent assertion that he has always been the protagonist of his writing. He then adds, "Yo creo que al fin y al cabo, lo único que siempre he hecho, desde que asumí la escritura, ha sido la traducción de la autobiografía (After all, I believe that the only thing I have done, since I started writing, has been the translation of autobiography)."[2] If Ramos Otero is translating his life through aesthetic means, what does this translation process do to our notion of the referential status of his life? His queer translations of autobiography turn the conventional wisdom of the genre on its head by refusing to consolidate a life into words—giving us, instead, an exquisite sprinkling of dust, a life both undone and made possible by desire.

The politico-ethical stance of Ramos Otero's work is neither nihilistic nor utopic—it is a mode of writing that conjures porosity and, hence, the pleasure and risk of exposure. Dust is not nothing; it is many somethings, but it is minor and not self-identical. This plurality figures in Ramos Otero's thinking as the crumbling matter at the edge or shore: a limit-matter. Ruminating on poetics, he writes,

Los hombres y las palabras son lo mismo. Solamente la poesía libera a las palabras y los hombres. . . . Por eso he sido Ulises, pero también Penélope, en cada *polvo* he comprendido el *polvo* y que la ribera de la muerte es la ribera de la vida. El poema es el médium, la puerta secreta, el espejo sacrílego y sagrado, el único ahora entre el antes el después, la sesión espiritista de la historia.

Men and words are the same. Only poetry liberates words and men. . . . Because of this I've been Ulysses, but also Penelope, in each fuck I have understood dust and that the shore of death is the shore of life. The poem is the medium, the secret door, the sacrilegious and sacred mirror, the only now between before and after, the spiritualist session of history.[3]

Poetry and dust figure similarly here as that which undoes sedimented dualisms, gender binaries, and conceits of self-sovereignty. Poetics transforms, translates, and mediates, while dust functions as the detritus of such material transformations. While Ramos Otero himself conceives of his writing in relation to autobiography, he does so by deliberately refusing a hard distinction between his writing and his life. He achieves this aesthetic translation by crafting texts that reverberate so frenetically between life and writing that the distinctions between the two begin to disintegrate, leaving us with the notion that neither can be approached via simplistic referentiality. The dusty, frayed outlines and borders between these modes begin to blur.

Often, Manuel Ramos Otero's prose and poetry did echo the facts of his life—one he rendered exorbitant through a prolific, storied, and theatrical writing career. Critical attention has made evident the autobiographical tendencies, moments, and elements of his writing that perform seductive ruses—flirting with the exquisite edges where Ramos Otero's life and fiction interact aesthetically.[4] In his engagement with Ramos Otero, Lawrence La Fountain-Stokes has shown that "by highlighting a self-referential, autobiographical 'mask' or 'persona' in his fiction, nonfiction, and poetry, Ramos Otero constructs a highly stylized, particular, yet striking image of a displaced, exiled gay Puerto Rican man in New York."[5] This aesthetic intervention, of a highly stylized image, disrupts pure notions of referentiality and links La Fountain-Stokes's readings to the work of Arnaldo Cruz-Malavé and Jossianna

Arroyo, who have both characterized Ramos Otero's work as masks and personae rather than Ramos Otero as such.[6] These critics show how autobiography functions as a complex poetics for Ramos Otero that exceeds individualistic writing. In concert with such critics, I consider the imbricated theorization of autobiography and translation in Ramos Otero's oeuvre. I trace the dust where Ramos Otero translates his own life through aesthetic form—rendering his autobiography opaquely resistant to a straightforward reading of his life. What we read instead is a dust writing that reaches lusciously toward its own frayed edges.

Born in Manatí, Puerto Rico, in 1948, Manuel Ramos Otero moved to the capital of San Juan at the age of seven as the island was undergoing massive modernization that promised many new life pathways. The governor, Luis Muñoz Marín, launched a modernization campaign on the island that brought sweeping changes; industrialization kicked up a lot of dust. During these years, the United States "invested" in its colony through "Manos a la Obra," or "Operation Bootstrap," as an effort to secure more control in the Caribbean (partially due to the Cuban Revolution in the background) and radically shifted the island's economy, sociality, and quotidian life. Once the holdover of monocultural plantocracy, sugar mills turned into factories. This wave of industrialization meant that former agricultural laborers, many of whom were Afrodescendants and *jíbaros* (rural peasants), moved from the countryside to urban centers. The United States' intervention campaign brought highways and suburban neighborhood developments that started to connect the island, but it also had a pernicious agenda, instituting "educational" campaigns that sought to discipline the new urban inhabitants into "proper" sexuality. These efforts resulted in the massive, nonconsensual sterilization of many Puerto Rican women. These years also inaugurated an era of Puerto Rico being a testing ground for US markets, which resulted not in the reproduction of the benefits of modern infrastructure but rather in profound neoliberal dispossession: poverty and debt. In Ramos Otero's lifetime, Puerto Ricans were incentivized to look for work beyond the island, moving to far colder cities in the United States, on the mainland. This history of modernity in Puerto Rico encases Ramos Otero's biography and provides some material understandings of his migratory path back and forth from the island. With infrastructure comes cement, with industrialization comes construction—all of which create an environment for dust precisely through trying to flatten and stabilize dirt. Michael Marder explains, "By disturbing and depleting topsoil through construction and intensive agriculture, we interfere with the stability of the earth, which is the substratum of our lives, forcing its upper layers, together with the molds and fungi they contain, into the air."[7] When we cannot abide a dirty foundation, we manufacture a precarious atmosphere. And atmosphere is precisely what drove Ramos Otero to leave Puerto Rico.

After completing a bachelor's degree in social sciences at the University of Puerto Rico, Río Piedras, Ramos Otero moved to New York in 1968 to continue studying cinema and escape the feeling of persecution for his open sexuality in Puerto Rico. His migratory move was overdetermined and conditioned by many material desires, political constrictions, and aesthetic drives:

> Primero, era la alternativa para salir de mi casa. Segundo, no aguantaba la atmósfera de Puerto Rico. Me había dado cuenta que Nueva York era una ciudad donde podía vivir sin sentirme perseguido todo el tiempo. En Puerto Rico sentía muchísima persecución debido a la apertura de mi sexualidad. *Pero no fue sólo eso*. Quedé fascinado con la ciudad y con la posibilidad de independencia total que me ofrecía. . . . Además, quería seguir estudiando y hacer cine.[8]

> First, it was the alternative in order to leave my home. Second, I couldn't stand the atmosphere in Puerto Rico. I had learned that New York was a city where I could live without feeling persecuted all of the time. In Puerto Rico, I felt a lot of persecution due to my open sexuality. *But it wasn't just that*. I was fascinated with the city and the total independence it offered me. . . . In addition, I wanted to continue studying and to make movies.

Ramos Otero left Puerto Rico because he couldn't stand the atmosphere of homophobia—but atmospheres are never singularly composed.[9] Ramos Otero's desire to flee homophobic persecution was compounded by his desire to pursue film. This desire for material resources writes a familiar script for a particularly American nightmare. His move to New York City would place him at the crossroads of queer desire, immigrant aspiration, and a homophobic, genocidal state that sanctioned so much death from HIV/AIDS.

In New York City, Ramos Otero began to study cinema but quickly learned that the equipment would be too costly and thus left the School of Visual Arts to study theater with Lee Strasberg. This other island of Manhattan granted Ramos Otero aesthetic resources and a diasporic distance from Puerto Rico—a distance that he described contrapuntally as archipelagic and one wherein he further strengthened his anticolonial identification as Puerto Rican.[10] With the exception of a brief move back to Puerto Rico and the short amount of time leading up to his early death from AIDS-related complications, Ramos Otero spent the majority of his writing life in New York City, while most of his writing remained linguistically in Spanish. His stories, poems, and novel moved between the island and the city, between themes of death and sexuality, between his life and his fantasy. Given the shifting quality of his work and its steadfast linguistic commitment to Spanish, it comes as no surprise that placing Ramos Otero within literary histories dominated by concerns with national canons and identity politics has proven tricky.[11] That said, with the increasing attention recently paid to the aesthetic contributions of underrepresented writers and specifically queer writers of color, Manuel Ramos Otero's legacy is starting to become one in the ongoing story of Latinx literary studies.[12] Yet he remains a misfit for heralding an exemplary subject of identity, since his works tend toward a dangerous disintegration through dust. Particulate assemblages show less the ontological contours of a person and more the atmospheric swerve of encounters where supposedly discrete forms become brittle, porous, and decayed. Through a fragmented assemblage, *polvo* pulverizes our preconceived notions of that which would feign to disentangle history from fiction and death from life.

Ramos Otero's writing asks us to linger at the margins of life and genre, putting particular pressure on how we read authors biographically. What we mean by autobiography has important political and ethical dimensions, especially when assigning it to a marked, underrepresented writer who insists upon aesthetic innovation and dazzlingly theatrical writing. An unquestioned autobiographical reading practice focuses on individuals and has the danger of turning the assumed referential experience of the person in question into either a token success story or an exemplar of oppression. And moreover, the biographical hermeneutic so often ascribed to Latinx writers in particular becomes the reigning mode of engaging writers' works—often neglecting form, material history, and theoretical nuance that finds its force *not* in the writing itself but in the supposed empiricism of the life of the author. Ramos Otero's work strikes a tenuous balance between the personal and the figurative through an insistence on aesthetic mediation—a process that he figures through *polvo*, a particular matter that exposes our porosity and yet still clings and hovers in the space between bodies, between the past and the future, between life and death. The forceful fragility of *polvo* is not reducible to his work on AIDS but is instead another instantiation of his oeuvre's tropological commitment to observing the persistence of that which is nonetheless finite.

For his published works, Manuel Ramos Otero often put theatrically staged photographs and visual renderings of himself on the covers. And on his collection *El cuento de la mujer del mar* (The story of the woman of the sea), he featured a photograph of his mother. While it remains a bibliographic sin to judge a book by its cover, Ramos Otero—sacrilegious as he is—invites us to do just that with his ornate covers. This move acquires even more intentional flair when we consider that it is not completely audacious for author images to be featured on fictional books; they just usually appear *as* authors on the back or inside the dust jacket. Moving his image from the location conventionally legible as "author" to the cover, Manuel Ramos Otero playfully invites us to read his image as the aesthetic and fictional subject of his works. And yet, these images are highly stylized, theatrical performances of visuality—rendering the possible biographical implications of his image in the terrain of aesthetic uncertainty.

Take, for instance, Ramos Otero's penchant for staging himself through the mode of visuality on the book cover for *Invitación al polvo* (1991), his last, posthumously published collection of poetry. Manuel Ramos Otero stands behind a statue of a woman in a cemetery wrapping his arms around her with one hand suggestively close to her groin while another gently rests upon her chest. His head is slightly cocked back, his eyes peering down to meet the gaze of whoever might happen upon this cemetery scene as he entices us to open the book. One could perhaps read the embrace of Ramos Otero as a sexual one with the feminine statue. Or, as we will see when we turn to his writing, this

Figure 2.1. Cover of *Invitación al polvo*

embrace may be more in line with the campy, cross-gendered identifications of his fiction. One could also read this as a moment of possession, wherein he assumes the role of a woman at the tragic moment of her death, beckoning desire through this cross identification. Heavenly light emanates from Ramos Otero's head, cascading from his hairline and onto a tree line interrupted only by a strange interloper's head. Just behind Ramos Otero's embrace, an adolescent straddles a cross that serves as a headstone. Our attention is drawn to this cross that we awkwardly face from the side, only fully registering its crucifixion iconography from the way in which it makes this adolescent's shorts rise up on the inner thighs—awkwardly approximating the invaginated folds of the foregrounded statue. This androgynous child at once bears the innocent face of a cherub and strikes a pose of sacrilegious masturbation—acting as a strange interloper or an irritant. Finally, the visual uncertainty of this scene echoes the double entendre of the book's title. *Invitación al polvo* translates literally to "invitation to dust," a phrase that resonates with religious undertones and that perhaps most obviously means death. At the same time, the Spanish term *polvo* carries a sexual connotation and can mean "semen," while *echar un polvo* is a common phrase that means "to fuck."[13] This theatrical cover image, beautifully and ambivalently orchestrated, conjures up the salient motifs of Ramos Otero's work and should caution us against any simplistic reading of autobiography in his prose and poetry.

As we can see from this photographic scene, Ramos Otero's penchant for camp and theatricality nuances what we mean when we assign the tag *autobiography* to his work. Though Ramos Otero never made films or acted in Hollywood, he did employ a cinematic and performative quality in his literary works and also started a short-lived theatrical group. His move from prose—both short stories and a novel—to poetry coincided with his ability to write and perform, which, at the time of the writing of this poetry collection, was waning due to his advanced stages of AIDS. This energetic shift surfaces in his work through forceful, insistent, and increasingly aggravated dust writing. Instead of assuming that visual representation has a more literal referent than linguistic representation, dwelling on Ramos Otero's visual register may in fact get us to a place of understanding how his use of the autobiographical is elaborately aesthetic. Furthermore, the visual offers a different register of representation through which to consider how his work functions as a reverberating set of translations between different linguistic *and* semiotic registers.

I begin with this visual reading because Ramos Otero's visual self-representation has led many critics to consider his work autobiographically. I investigate how autobiography works for Ramos Otero because his notion of autobiography is anything but simplistic or commonsensical. In her essay "A Community in Transit," Mónica Lladó-Ortega explains the impulse to read Manuel Ramos Otero's work as autobiographical: "The tendency to read his writing as too autobiographical is partially due to the fact that Ramos Otero inserts himself in his texts, literally, through pictures of himself and of his mother on the covers of the books."[14] Using Ramos Otero's own writing about autobiography in order to highlight the use of the first person as a gesture of performativity and multiplicity, Lladó-Ortega complicates the notion of autobiography in his work to show how it is transitory and relational. While Lladó-Ortega's overall essay nuances much criticism of Ramos Otero's use of the autobiographical by showing it as performative and complicated, this mistaken conflation of the visual as literal seems to diametrically oppose visual and literary representation. By reading the visual as having a simplistic referentiality, such readings of Manuel Ramos Otero run the risk of reducing the complex and highly mediated relationship between his life and his work.[15] Though the designation of the autobiographical must be complicated in his work, one cannot avoid the question, or the referential interruption, of his life's story. Rather than reading his fiction as transparently telling, I show how Ramos Otero translates his own life through a poetics of dust—rendering his autobiography opaquely resistant to a straightforward reading of his life. What we read, instead, is his afterlife, a dust writing that reaches lusciously and dangerously toward its own end. This figuration and literary translation is rendered metanarratologically by taking what should appear on the dust jacket, a simple author photograph—that which keeps the author's life somehow separate from aesthetic mediation and yet more in the sovereign position of writer—and placing it on the surface of his work in order to invite the dirty work of mediation. Visuality becomes a semiotic register for bold translation in Ramos Otero's literary works.

Dusty Projections

POLVO IN THE LIGHT

Permit me to relate an anecdote about a misreading of my own, which in its mishap may hopefully elucidate the stakes and promise of rereading the oeuvre of Manuel Ramos Otero now, in a more entangled, materialist manner in the dusty wake of Hurricane Maria in Puerto Rico. My first encounter with Ramos Otero's work was in an avant-gardism class in graduate school through his story "Hollywood Memorabilia"—a deliciously campy, yet also macabre, story of a solitary gay man living in New York, where he works as both a social scientist and a projectionist in a second-run cinema. This story is part of Ramos Otero's first collection of short stories, *Concierto de metal para un recuerdo y otras orgías de soledad* (Brass concert for a memory and other orgies of solitude). In "Hollywood Memorabilia," the protagonist incessantly, almost obsessively, becomes seduced by imagining himself as golden-age Hollywood starlets in the crescendo of their denouement, as they die and perish on-screen. His own projected fantasies commingle with these fantasies as he anticipates his early death, one he's sure will arrive soon and one he tries desperately to glamorize. His campy defiance, his certainty of an early death, and his walks through New York City all prompted me to interpolate this text into an already woven canon of queer writers who wrote during the HIV/AIDS crisis in New York, San Francisco, and Los Angeles. The felt precarity with which the protagonist anticipated his death seemed part of this tapestry—that is until I realized that the story was written in 1971, a good decade before HIV/AIDS or GRID/SIDA would come to be known acronyms uttered as both diagnosis and death sentence for so many people living in these metropolitan areas. In 1971, Ramos Otero had already been living and writing in New York for four years—working as a social researcher, taking classes with Lee Strasberg, and shifting from cinematic studies to writing. So here, my mishap is one of interpretive and tropological overdetermination—one encouraged by pinkwashing and homonationalism—a thinking that death, camp, and New York City were allegorically collapsed. And yet, a return to this story brings me back to a trope that foretells the felt risk, the lonely walks, and the precarious desires that surface—*polvo* or dust in the light.

"Hollywood Memorabilia"—written in Spanish except for the title—certainly bears a striking resemblance to Ramos Otero's life. He was, like the story's narrator, a social researcher who lived in New York. Yet the story's very structure resists any notion of the narrator as self-same, self-contained, or transparent—showing instead that the line between fantasy and reality can become dusty and result in the dispersal between what *is* and what is *desired*. Rather than a direct mapping of his life as a point of referentiality to his fiction, Ramos Otero's writing shows how the autobiographical tells the tale of its own undoing and dissolution through dust. The dissolution in this short story becomes one of translation through fleeting, metonymic and thickly pleasurable identifications with campy Hollywood stars. The 1971 short story relates the tale of a young man who lives a solitary life in New York—working various jobs and fantasizing about lost lovers and Hollywood starlets. The whole of the story takes place in the narrator's interior monologue, fluctuating between his own life and the lives he watches on cinematic screens. In his solitude, the two registers begin to blend and culminate into an indistinguishable, atomized suspension between his body and the screen.

The process of both figuring and disfiguring the first-person narration in this story begins to unravel, pleasurably and queerly, from the narrative voice's very first enunciation as both authoritative and authorial. Given the inaugural lines "Yo soy Dios" (I am God), the story opens with a promise of narrative sovereignty that will toy with the very limits of narration. One could read this story and its disintegrating deity of a narrator as a poststructuralist critique of authorial intent—but this story is much more convoluted and more polemical, both in its relation to politics and its dance with death. Fairly quickly into the narrative, one is struck by the excessive references to English language signifiers of camp (as the title itself remains in English, in homage to one of the most important components of camp—Hollywood's past).[16] The *yo* of "Yo soy Dios" sets up the campy theatricality of writing and language; indeed he plays up the performative aspects of language to bring things into existence.[17] Like the God of Genesis, the narrator creates with words—the ultimate performative summoning. But instead of creating light or establishing the natural order of things, this narrator creates a character who will be named Angel . . . and John and Paul. The act of narration, of naming, sets the stage for a flood of fantastical relationships to these three men whom the narrator calls "la Divina Trinidad Parasitaria" (the divine parasitic trinity).[18]

Aside from being an author, our deified narrator also works as a researcher in a governmental program that seeks to create "una sistema perfecto de movilidad" (a perfect system of mobility).[19] Defensively, as if in conversation with a more "politicized" interlocutor, Ramos Otero's narrator quickly responds,

> No. Las deficiencias de capitalismo no me interesan. ¿Por qué? Porque tengo veinte y tres años y pienso que a los treinta moriré con un ataque imprevisto de tuberculosis (como Greta Garbo en *Camille*).
>
> No. Capitalism's deficiencies do not interest me. Why not? Because I'm 23 years old and I think that at thirty I'll die of an unforeseen attack of tuberculosis (like Greta Garbo in *Camille*).[20]

After this rather flamboyant dismissal of normative politicization, which the actual Ramos Otero indeed takes up in his more overtly political essays,[21] the narrator announces that he also works as a projectionist in a second-run movie theater. Working two jobs for our narrator means that he never has the time for chance encounters with men, an economic scarcity that confines desire to the screen. This reminder that material constraints or capitalism make it difficult to date is then rather quickly called into question:

> Tan tarde salgo que camino hasta casa y no me queda tiempo para conocer a nadie en el camino, entablar una relación espontánea y rápida e invitarle a que pase a casa a tomar café (también tengo té de jazmín porque conocí un chico que adora el té de jazmín pero de todas formas no importa porque dijo que llegaría a las ocho y después de esperarlo hasta la madrugada supe que no vendría; aún no he abierto la caja con sobres individuales de té de jazmín).
>
> I leave so late that I head home and there's no time for me to meet anyone on the way, commence a spontaneous and quick relationship with him to come over to the house to have a cup of coffee (I also have jasmine tea because I met a guy who adores jasmine tea but anyhow it doesn't matter

because he said he would come over at eight and after waiting for him until dawn I figured he wouldn't come; I still haven't opened the box with its individual bags of tea).[22]

The story begins with the performative work of narration, details a social research job, and then signals a blatant disinterest in politics that is explained by an anticipated death that simulates Hollywood. Then we arrive at the narrator's failed romantic life. Gliding along and punctuated by references to an early death that resembles melodramatic Hollywood movies, the larger narrative that follows operates in a metonymic, conversational, and contradictory way. Though seemingly chaotic at first, this movement gains significance throughout the narrative and develops into a textual relation to death, politics, and camp that refuses to be subsumed under a liberationist project.

During the day, the narrator works as a social researcher—the data on social mobility, he tells us, is not very promising. So while his days are filled with facts, his nights are filled with fantasy and projection as he works in a second-run cinema. The secondhandedness of these films not only gives them the appeal of the vintage or the old but also creates a temporal distance that frees them up for a kind of infusion of fantasy and mythologization that departs from the banal and quotidian. Sontag explains that "time may enhance what seems simply dogged or lacking in fantasy now because we are too close to it, because it resembles too closely our own everyday fantasies.... We are better able to enjoy fantasy when it is not our own."[23] Fantasies of an older time and place are more accessible. "Hollywood Memorabilia" interpolates the reader into this game of illusions and desire—centering the play of fantasy. To project one's own fantasies onto another often renders them more legible as desirous—as with the temporal distance gained from camp. Likewise, to project one's own identity, death, or lovers onto démodé Hollywood stars may seem delusional, but it also renders that identity, death, or those lovers unavailable to be co-opted into a pathos of sympathy or oppression. The metonymic movement of desire advances alongside the many imagined deaths of this narrator and keeps desire always out of reach and, well, desirable. This cross identificatory mode is made material through the intricate descriptions of projection in the story, which shows how camp functions as a kind of translation that eschews any literal resemblance.

This lack of resemblance, through a campy translation, creates a mediated form that puts pressure on the pathos of the politics that Ramos Otero has so wittingly criticized. Old Hollywood becomes a set of citations within which to negotiate a relation between "realidad e ilusión," which the narrator names as the two most important words for him to understand because the "felicidad externa de saber que se nos aprueba el comportamiento, para mí no existe" (external happiness of knowing that our behavior is approved of doesn't exist for me).[24] Campy signs make available an affective register and a disguise from which to explain a life. Noting again the failure of his own biography, the narrator reveals that he writes it with disguises.[25] Such an admission gestures toward the love of adornment and costume in camp. Philip Core reiterates Sontag's aphorisms on camp and writes,

> CAMP is a form of historicism viewed histrionically.
> CAMP is a biography written by the subject as if it were about another person.
> CAMP is a disguise that fails.
> CAMP is a lie which tells the truth.[26]

In this biography of disguises, we do not have direct access to the person who takes on the proper name of Manuel Ramos Otero. And yet, through the failure, the disguises, and the histrionics, we do receive an archive of affect within which to relate to the life hinted at in the story: "Escribo mi vida que es un recuerdo de emociones reconstruidas a través de Rita Hayworth en *Gilda*, de Gloria Swanson en *Sunset Boulevard*, etc. etc." (I write my life, which is a retelling of emotions reconstructed by means of Rita Hayworth in *Gilda*, of Gloria Swanson in *Sunset Boulevard*, etc. etc.).[27]

What does it mean to write adoringly about and identify with Joan Crawford or Bette Davis in Spanish *as* biography, as the translation of autobiography? Perhaps the campiest and most artificial aspect of "Hollywood Memorabilia" is the demystification of one's own memory by using Hollywood's memory instead. The cinematic tradition that the narrator brings up is not contemporary to the early 1970s nor is it markedly Latin American. Instead, it is an older Hollywood—the 1930s and '40s Hollywood of great stars and high glam.[28] In noting this, I do not intend to erase the presence of Latinx peoples and Latin Americans in the history of Hollywood, but instead I aim to highlight that camp is used here as a mode of translation that is not predicated on resemblance.[29]

José Esteban Muñoz writes of "an opulent scene of cross-identification that is, in one manner of speaking, *queer* . . . the word *queer* itself, in its origins in the German *quer*, means 'across'; the concept itself can only be understood as connoting a mode of identifications that is as relational as it is oblique."[30] In "Hollywood Memorabilia," Manuel Ramos Otero translates autobiography through these oblique cross identifications with starlets. Like most campy gestures, he does so not to identify with an unfettered idea of feminized beauty but to create a constellation of complicated adoration mixed with identifications with Hollywood women in the moment of their denouement—feeling somehow like Gloria Swanson's role as the late-career actress grotesquely and maddeningly clinging to her legacy. Seeking pleasure in failure, this work of camp shows the affective attachments and crossings of desire that compose the autobiographical mode of Manuel Ramos Otero. His work created its own camp—one that resisted both total assimilation through its linguistic register that remained in Spanish and recognizable politicization through its aesthetic choices. The choice to write openly queer and campy stories defied the political center of the Nuyorican scene during Ramos Otero's time in New York. The complicated translation and aesthetic issues within Ramos Otero's work, perhaps best exemplified by "Hollywood Memorabilia," offer us dense layers of cultural and linguistic semiotics that do not precisely line up.

What seems particularly provocative about the terrain of the story is the privileging of a camp aesthetic over and against a more recognizable form of politics. With a defiant and polemical near-monologue, the narrator announces himself as not at all interested in race or class:

> La investigación social y la movilidad y el problema de los negros (escucho el ruido de varios suspiros de pechos insultados que consideran el racismo el issue universal) no me interesa tanto como el cine y Joan Crawford en *Grand Hotel* . . . (varios ¡ahhhhhhs! vomitados que al fin y al cabo me tienen sin cuidado porque ya no resisto a las señoras que se levantan temprano en la mañana y acuden a misa vestidas de negro sin

nada en el estómago y se golpean el pecho tres veces con interrupciones, ni a la gente que critica al presidente de la Universidad del Estado por sospechársele homosexual reprimido debido a sus manerismos desbocados durante los discursos de graduación, ni a la gente que opina que estudiante es sinónimo de sometimiento tradicional y que la revolución en los países coloniales y el comunismo son lo mismo). Todo me parece tremenda porquería burguesocialista, izquierdoderechista. Después de todo la mierda es mierda es mierda (revisando a Gertrude Stein).

Social research and mobility and the problem of blacks do not interest me (I hear the sound of many sighs from the insulted breasts that consider racism the universal issue) as much as cinema and Joan Crawford in *Grand Hotel* . . . (many vomited ahhhhhhs! that when all is said and done don't matter to me because I can't stand any longer the matrons who rise early and go off to mass dressed in black with nothing in their stomachs and beat their breasts three times with pauses, or the people who criticize the president of the State University suspecting him of being a repressed homosexual because of his coarse mannerisms during graduation speeches, or the people who hold the opinion that a student is synonymous with traditional subjugation and that revolution in the colonized countries and Communism are the same thing). It all seems a lot of bourgeoisocialist, leftrightish rubbish to me. After all shit is shit is shit (to revise Gertrude Stein).[31]

Much like the rapid disintegration of the authorial voice's omnipotence, this railing polemic against normative politics camps the whole bit by portraying it as both melodramatic and theatrical—the sighs from insulted breasts and the vomited "ahhhhhhs!" seem rather fitting descriptions of the kinds of reactions that camp provokes. The flippant dismissal of politics gives way to a more nuanced critique of politics that can no longer abide the liberal humanist projects that equate students with the traditionally subjugated and confuse revolution with Communism. This statement is somewhat heretical, and intentionally so for Ramos Otero. He had a personal and staunch commitment to Puerto Rican culture and the independence movement that had been galvanizing over the midcentury. Instead of denouncing politics in general, Ramos Otero critiques here, in quite a subtle manner, the slippage between student resistance movements in the United States and subaltern struggles as well as the slippage between Communism and revolution in colonized spaces. The narrator then gives us a campy revision of Stein's "Rose is a rose is a rose is a rose" to further develop his queer citational practices and further inflect his abject aestheticism that refuses to take the shit of politics, preferring instead to indulge in fantasies of the end.[32] And while the critique of politics as usual is welcome, I do not want to glide over the anti-Blackness of the above statement in order to indulge in a queer aesthetic that looks away from ontological dispossession. Rather, this is where the camp aesthetic meets its limits as a politico-ethical practice that resists. This kind of fixation on glamorized death and feminized abjection still smacks of relative privilege that provides the foundation for the allure of negativity. This marks camp as a queer form of translation but also a disturbing attachment. By inserting this racist polemic that ends in a disentanglement of college classrooms and third-world struggle, we find a de-idealization, not only of politics as usual, but also of the protagonist himself.[33] He is no hero, no leader, no saint, but he is complicatedly queer and begs for a nonbenevolent reading.

This diffuse and multivalent camp practice also translates the autobiographical impulses of the first-person narration. The narrator parodies the role of any "I" in a narration:

> Bueno, el personaje se llamará yo. Porque después de varias recapitulaciones de la memoria, aún no se me facilita el comienzo.... Ocurre que el comienzo y el final pertenecen al mismo espacio y ya no se distinguen sus formas.
>
> OK, let's call the character I. Because after several recapitulations of memory, the beginning is still not made easy for me.... It so happens that the beginning and the end share the same space and their forms can no longer be distinguished.[34]

Drawing our focus to the limits of any narration, the narrator reminds us that no "I" is witness to its own beginning or end, drawing our attention to the limits of any one person's ability to self-narrate a whole, complete story—such would be a writing beyond the grave that exists in the speculative. The beginning and the end are precisely the part of one's own story that one cannot be witness to—they are the radical absence of the self from its own narrative and the necessary limitations on any autobiography. Rather than covering up this limitation, "Hollywood Memorabilia" takes pleasure in fantasizing about many possible, glamorous deaths—letting Hollywood starlets take the lead roles in the protagonist's own cinematic vision of his memory and eventual death. If camp is, as Sontag's notes tell us, a failed seriousness, then Ramos Otero employs such a failed seriousness with regard to death and the autobiographical mode by camping both.[35]

Accepting death and fantasizing about it means confronting the grandest illusion—the thing we cannot know. Ramos Otero and Freud both know this: we may fixate on death, fantasize about it, visualize it, but we cannot know it. Death is radically opaque to our consciousness, yet it is also unavoidable, nonnegotiable. Which is perhaps why the final star that appears in this story is Greta Garbo of *Queen Christina*.[36] The narrator is starting to disintegrate; the end is drawing near, and he feels himself changing roles with images on the screen:

> Hace algún tiempo que al quedar hermético en la cabina siento cómo cambio lugares con alguien en el film. Lo vengo haciendo con frecuencia (he tenido resultados estupendos con *Queen Christina* en la escena final).
>
> For some time, now, remaining sealed in the booth I feel how I change positions with someone in the film. It's been happening to me frequently (I've had incredible results with *Queen Christina* in the final scene).[37]

This final scene—Greta Garbo's stalwart face at the bow of a ship—is not a scene of death but instead a scene of survival. The titular queen's Spanish lover, whom she met and fell in love with while passing as a man, has been murdered. It was for him that she had given up her throne, though this supposed heterosexuality becomes crossed and dissolved by the fact that it's a rare moment in Hollywood's memory wherein two women kiss on-screen. And this is the fleeting cinematic image that Ramos Otero leaves us with, a bittersweet ending, an exiled figure that has loved and lost, that has reigned and relinquished power, that stands alone but determined, staring at the sea.[38]

Roland Barthes famously analyzed this final image of Garbo's face as a moment when we understood cinematography as primarily being about the face rather than the body. An actress who gained celebrity from silent movies, Garbo speaks in this movie, survives, cross-dresses, and kisses men and women, and the movie ends on this stoic, solitary, unflinching scene of her face at the helm. Solitude figures often in Ramos Otero's work, a trope that seems to be in constant tension with dust, *polvo*. Perhaps solitude is never truly solitary but rather a condition that phenomenalizes an exposed body in an open, arid field or a harsh atmosphere that makes one brittle, vulnerable to erosion and turning to dust. Perhaps this projection of a solitary face, withholding her desires and difficulties, becomes too risky of a projection, too solitary of a fantasy of self.

Though "Hollywood Memorabilia" does have a relation to politics that extends beyond its reactionary proclamations and campy identifications, the text does not have a politically normative telos of liberation or revolution. The campy aesthetic here pertains to a desire that exceeds sexual identity and simplistic notions of liberation—risking not only ridicule but also that the campy subject may stay dispersed and suspended. As the narrator draws near to the end of his own story, he narrates his dissolution toward his desirous image:

> Pero ya comienzo por desvanecerme. El autor, el proyeccionista, Dios, parecen quedar desintegrados en átomos constantes de luz y siento un impulso flojo que me proyecta con suavidad en el lienzo. El tiempo del proyector al lienzo nunca fue más largo y siento partículas perdidas que aún no terminan su viaje. No quiero pensar en la posibilidad siempre presente de que la proyección se interrumpa sin que los átomos logren integrarse en la ilusión esperada.

> But I'm already beginning to dissolve. The author, the projectionist, God, seem to be disintegrating into lasting atoms of light and I feel a weak impulse that gently projects me onto the screen. The time from the projector to the screen was never longer and I sense particles that still do not finish their journey. I don't want to think about the always present possibility that the projection may be interrupted without the atoms managing to integrate themselves into the desired illusion.[39]

This dispersal becomes a figure for reading both the failure and the survivability of the text—the possibility, always already there, that the projection of one's desires and the achievement of them may not in fact become "integrated" into each other.[40] And yet, the consistent failure of integration—into a cogent autobiography, into a sustained romance, into a political vision—is the very textual machination that propels the text. The perpetual crossings of ideas, genres, and identities offer Ramos Otero, and us, a way of configuring a nonintegrationist, perhaps disidentificatory, practice of persistence drenched in aesthetics and pleasure. This early short story of Ramos Otero's has asked me to read and reread an anticipation of death that is not reducible to HIV/AIDS but may also mark the precarity of the Puerto Rican and queer condition figured both lusciously and riskily as dispersal. This dispersal is a figure of dust caught in light, illuminating the space of relation that is the space of risk. In a treatise on dust, philosopher Michael Marder puts it another way: "Dust flakes hovering in a ray of light (say, under a lit lamp) reveal that ray, its extent and direction, along with our lived space, never as transparent as we believe."[41] *Polvo*, dust, *átomos*, and particles fill the air at the close of "Hollywood Memorabilia," reminding us of the space between the self and the self's fantasies, the porosity of the self, and the gaps and lacks populated with floating bits that both illuminate and obscure relations. Desire, writing, life, and death commingle in dust. Dust hovers over the outlines of what we see, placing us in a phenomenological register that conjures fantasy, opacity, and erotic relations with an attention to plural, quotidian mixed ecologies of particles barely seen.

Dusty Traces

TRANSLATION AND AUTOBIOGRAPHY

A simile may help here. Just as a tangent touches a circle lightly and at but one point, with this touch rather than with the point setting the law according to which it is to continue on its straight path to infinity, a translation touches the original lightly and only at the infinitely small point of the sense, thereupon pursuing its own course according to the laws of fidelity in the freedom of linguistic flux.
—Walter Benjamin, "The Task of the Translator"

I now turn from a short story's oblique depiction of *polvo* to a discussion of autobiography. "Ficción e historia: Texto y pretexto de la autobiografía" (Fiction and history: Autobiographical text and pretext) appeared posthumously in an homage to Manuel Ramos Otero in the San Juan newspaper *El Mundo* on October 14, 1990, precisely one week after his death on October 7. In the article, Ramos Otero articulates his ludic and insistent assertion that he has always been the protagonist of his writing. Feeling the need to further refine this statement, he adds, "Yo creo que al fin y al cabo, lo único que siempre he hecho, desde que asumí la escritura, ha sido la traducción de la autobiografía" (After all, I believe that the only thing I have done, since I started writing, has been the translation of autobiography).[42] Given the complexity of this statement about his writing being a *translation* of autobiography, this section considers the role of both translation and autobiography theoretically in order to better understand how Ramos Otero plays on two modes often thought apart. The porosity between fiction and history is Ramos Otero's frame to consider autobiography, which will then lead us back to questions of gender, bodies, and dust.

One of the motivating contentions for this chapter is a thoroughgoing reading of the complexity of autobiography as a form of translation and mediation, filtered through dispersal like dust. Autobiography and translation bring up similar theoretical and literary questions. Both make us think and complicate any notion of origin while simultaneously invoking it. Both challenge us to reconsider the referent—how the referent does not emerge from the process of either translation or autobiography unmarked. For Ramos Otero to claim that he has only ever written a translation of autobiography highlights the intricate connections between a life and the writing of it. What does it mean to be the translator of one's own life? Moreover, what does it mean to translate not from one language to another but from a life to the written word? Ramos Otero's comment alerts us to the necessity of thinking translation beyond mere linguistic difference and makes us consider the different registers within which translation occurs.

Conventional wisdom assumes that the ultimate referent and origin of autobiography is the writer's life. Speaking of translations as autobiography puts a very different kind of pressure on the status of the origin. Walter Benjamin's landmark essay "The Task of the Translator" reminds us that the "essential quality" of a good translation, like a good story, "is not communication or the imparting of information";[43] information is that which is "incompatible with the spirit of storytelling."[44] And storytelling is how Ramos Otero figures himself as a writer, as a *cuentero*. Benjamin remarks on the relationship between the original piece of literature and its translation, noting that the former is transformed through the very process of having been translated: "For in its afterlife—which could not be called that if it were not a transformation and a renewal of something living—the original undergoes a change."[45] This notion of an echoed afterlife gives a spatialized materialism to works of art.[46] The articulation of the life and afterlife gives us a way to think more densely about the work of Manuel Ramos Otero. If it is that the translation gives afterlife to a life, then his articulation of the translation of autobiography means that his work, even in its writing, conceived of itself to be read posthumously. Indeed, Ramos Otero's autobiographical mode has, to a certain extent, given him more readers and appreciation in the afterlife of his texts than he had during his own lifetime. Moreover, the flirtations with death, epitaph writings, and figuration of *polvo* urge us to consider that the posthumous gesture is entangled with a critique of certain versions of humanistic life attainable unevenly across the globe. The posthumous gesture precedes death.

While Benjamin writes of the importance that the afterlife of a translation brings, he does not see it in a mimetic relationship with the source or the original. Instead, he uses the word *echo* to denote how the translation has something of a reverberating relationship to the original. He writes, "The task of the translator consists in finding that intended effect [*intentio*] upon the language into which he is translating which produces in it the echo of the original."[47] In order to elaborate, Benjamin invokes the image of a "language forest": "Unlike a work of literature, translation does not find itself in the center of the language forest but on the outside facing the wooded ridge; it calls into it without entering, aiming at the single spot where the echo is able to give, in its own language, the reverberation of the work in the alien one."[48] The question here, for the purposes of this chapter, is, What if the translation is at once a translation and, to a certain extent, an original piece of literature? What happens to the notion of the origin and the notion of translation?

Ramos Otero imagines the process of autobiographical writing as both impersonal and singular, contingent on the laws of grammar and the particular positionality and poetic capability of the writer. If "translation is a form," as Benjamin reminds us, then we may find that this form translates life into literary writing through registers that are not merely interlinguistic.[49] Rey Chow takes up Benjamin's essay on translation in order to move beyond a notion of translation that only considers the phenomenon between different linguistic registers and think about translation between cultures and media. In "Film as Ethnography: Or, Translation between Cultures in the Postcolonial World," Chow explores the resistant work of Chinese documentarians who undo the orientalist frame of looking; "'viewed object' is now looking at 'viewing subject' looking."[50] In order to consider further the complex moves of autoethnography, Chow turns to theories of translation: "Precisely because translation is an activity that immediately problematizes the ontological hierarchy of languages—'which is primary and which is secondary?'—it is also the place where the oldest prejudices about origins and derivations come into play most forcefully."[51] Indeed, Chow sees such a relation between the original and the derivation as not only traditionally hierarchical but also conventionally oversimplified. As such, she does not seek a reassertion of the primacy of an original that is precolonial, Eastern, and authentic but instead invokes the coevality of different linguistic and semiotic registers to get at the inescapably imbricated ways that meaning is made in our postcolonial world: "Instead, cultural translation needs to be rethought as the co-temporal exchange and contention between different social groups deploying different sign systems that may not be synthesizable to one particular model of language or representation. Considerations of the translation of or between cultures would have to move beyond verbal and literary languages to include events of the media such as radio, film, television, video, pop, music and so forth, without writing such events off as mere examples of mass indoctrination."[52] Given Manuel Ramos Otero's penchant for writing film, camp, and popular culture into his own writing, our task may be to trace the moments when his writing uses different semiotic registers that precisely do not line up to get at what he calls a translation of autobiography. Rey Chow's capacious understanding of translation, as well as her insistence upon the inherent hierarchical strictures of thinking translation as merely linguistic, provides a point of departure to consider the differing semiotic, linguistic, and cultural registers of Ramos Otero's mode of translation.

Noting the figurative qualities of autobiography, Paul de Man's 1979 essay, "Autobiography as De-facement," deconstructs conventional notions of autobiography and its relation to reference. Early in his essay he asks, "But are we so certain that autobiography depends on reference, as a photograph depends on its subject or a (realistic) picture on its model?"[53] De Man productively blurs the hard and fast border that seems to distinguish fiction and autobiography. First, he contests the categorization of autobiography as a genre, specifically because he claims that such a designation takes an aesthetic category (genre) and melds it with a historical category of life (biography or autobiography). Considering the complex relation between aesthetics and history, Ramos Otero sets up his essay on autobiography by figuring translation as the process that frames the difference between fiction and history:

> Yo sé que toda traducción es una reescritura. Yo sé que nuestra definición de lo que es ficción y de lo que es historia está matizada por ese fenómeno habitual que nadie parece tomar en cuenta, llamado traducción.
>
> I know that all of translation is a rewriting. I know that our definition of what is fiction and what is history is tinged by this quotidian phenomenon that no one seems to take into account, namely translation.[54]

For de Man, the figurative dimensions of writing put pressure on the category of autobiography, which is so often deemed self-evident. De Man further shows the performative aspects of autobiography that do not simply come down to a simplistic notion of referentiality: "We assume that life *produces* the autobiography as an act produces its consequences, but can we not suggest, with equal justice, that the autobiographical project may itself produce and determine the life and that whatever the writer *does* is in fact governed by the technical demands of self-portraiture and thus determined, in all its aspects, by the resources of his medium?"[55] The answer to de Man's rhetorical question is, of course, yes. Autobiographical writing figures the life that it claims to merely reference and in so doing comes to disfigure the life as much as it figures it. Much like

J. L. Austin shows that all language is to a certain extent performative, de Man goes to show that the autobiographical is an element of all reading and writing. This point touches upon the process of autobiography as one that is essential—it takes place as much on the level of reading as it does on the level of writing.[56]

Furthering his theory through a reading of Wordsworth, de Man links the writing of life to death and the giving of face to defacement: "Prosopopoeia is the trope of autobiography, by which one's name, as in the Milton poem, is made as intelligible and memorable as a face. Our topic deals with the giving and taking away of faces, with face and deface, *figure*, figuration and disfiguration."[57] In order to communicate this dual function of autobiography, de Man chooses the trope of prosopopoeia, the figure of speech within which an absent, dead, or fictional person is speaking. De Man proffers this trope as exemplary of autobiography to eschew transparent or literal notions of the mode of writing, to trouble the seemingly assured referential relation between the autobiography and the life of the author. Prosopopoeia, which de Man describes as both a headstone and writing from beyond the grave, resonates well with Manuel Ramos Otero's literary and visual penchant for the macabre. While we have already seen the visual representation of Ramos Otero fondling death in a cemetery, his complex relation to death is already on display in his first collection of poetry, *El libro de la muerte* (The book of death).[58] Though death remained a spectral center in his work, the gravitas of his poetic engagement with death shifted in confluence with his HIV diagnosis. Over the whole of his oeuvre, Ramos Otero told his life by narrating and poetically envisioning his relation to death, which straddled, like de Man's notion of autobiography, a consistent tension between figuring and disfiguring his biography.

Writing more specifically about autobiography in Latin America, Sylvia Molloy chimes in with de Man's notion that the autobiographical mode "is as much a way of reading as it is a way of writing."[59] Though Molloy writes more of a historical and political investigation of autobiography than a philosophical one, she contends that

> autobiography is always a re-presentation, that is, a retelling, since the life to which it refers is already a kind of narrative construct. Life is always, necessarily, a tale: we tell it to ourselves as subjects, through recollection;

we hear it told or we read it when the life is not ours. So, to say that autobiography is the most referential of genres—meaning, by reference, a somewhat simplistic referring back to "reality" and to concrete verifiable facts—is, in a sense, to pose the question falsely. Autobiography does not rely on events but on an articulation of those events stored in memory and reproduced by rememoration and verbalization. . . . In a sense I have already been "told," told by the very story I am telling.[60]

Such an articulation of autobiography figuring not events but memories that one has already been told further complicates the process of writing an autobiography by showing how it is mediated through the work of memory. Such a translation bears upon the work of Ramos Otero insofar as his articulation of autobiography relies as much upon the end product as it does upon the supposed source of his life.

Manuel Ramos Otero used a mixture of poetics and narrative to bear upon the question of biography, indulging in the errant and figurative qualities of writing. In an interview, Ramos Otero claims,

> En mi literatura coexisten poesía y narrativa porque siempre he concebido la escritura como mi biografía. No hay diferencia entre lo que soy y lo que escribo.
>
> In my literature, poetry and narrative coexist because I have always conceived of my writing as my biography. There is no difference between what I am and what I write.[61]

Refusing a difference between his self and his writing, Ramos Otero highlights the performative qualities of writing and reduces the difference between life and writing to a generic difference: being and writing—writing ontologizes him. When he claims there's no difference between his writing and his life, he precisely guarantees a singular notion of difference. By refusing recourse to a stable referent, his writing dodges reading practices that want to know his marked difference. Moreover, this writing of autobiography as translation provides a double mediation, a dusty filter through which one cannot find a pure (stable) referent of biography. My concern here is that the marketing, reception, and critical apparatuses of Latinx letters should try to distance themselves from what I will call the biographical hermeneutic: a method of reading stories as ethnographic information rather than aesthetic creation. However, to read literary works and artistic creations as if they are reducible to a fully graspable life renders both the life and the art rather constricted, transparent, and more dead than dusty. Scholars like Elena Machado Sáez have long noted that historical novels tend to do best in the market for Caribbean diasporic and Latinx literary production.[62] Underlying this combination of zeal for the historical via the novel is an abiding desire for wholeness, empiricism, and truth—a stock in realism that, at times, seems to veer away from the aesthetic encounter insofar as it replaces a desire for fact with fiction. This market drive, in turn, creates anticipatable aesthetics—and this might be one reason among many others that Ramos Otero's work did not make quite as much of a boom as other Latin American writers.

Rather than choose between history or fiction, Ramos Otero writes in the liminal shoreline between them—a dusty writing that obscures while telling, that translates while withholding, that immerses one in a poetics of finitude without liberation. In Ramos Otero's hands, translation becomes a kind of chemical transmogrification of life and word. Ramos Otero writes that the genre of autobiography lies between fiction and history—hovering there and distilled through a process of translation. Ramos Otero writes a translation of himself that's at the interstice of fiction and history to figure his stories, history, and self not as self-same but rather dispersed and desirous, as the dust that both settles onto and sloughs off skin:

> Yo estoy entre mi ficción y la historia, no estoy fuera de ninguna de las dos sino entre ambas, y todo lo que he escrito, todo lo que escribo es un intento de atrapar, irónicamente, la voz de mi liberación, esa voz que al aprehender las otras voces de los otros cuenteros de la historia definirá mejor los bordes temporales de la lengua, ese órgano tan humano que lo mismo hace el amor con la piel polvorosa de otro cuerpo que con la piel polvorienta de la fábula.
>
> I am between my fiction and history, I am not outside of either of the two but between both, and all that I have written, all that I write is an attempt to trap, ironically, the voice of my liberation, this voice that in

apprehending the other voices of other tellers of history will better define the temporal rims of the tongue, this organ, which is so human, that it makes love with the dusty skin of another body just as it does to the dusty skin of a story.[63]

Ramos Otero renders liberation as something to be trapped and caught—an ambivalent coimplication of liberation and entrapment such that they are flipsides of the same coin that holds them in productive tension.[64] To trap the voice of liberation renders poetically the ruse that exposure, writing, and demarcation give us visibility that sheerly presents a life and with that frankness comes freedom. Liberation must be trapped. Instead, dust writing evades such entrapment by indulging in the recursive cycles of finitude and meaning that commingle in the writing of a life that is always a translation, a mediation. Dust maintains a material and tropological commitment to "temporal rims" of the tongue, perhaps the limits of language—demanding an echo from other storytellers.

Ramos Otero locates himself lodged between fiction and history in order to reduce himself to neither pure abstraction nor pure referentiality; instead, his life becomes translated by means in a space between the two registers. This space is a space not only of the self but of others. This liminal space returns him to the ambivalent and desirous figure of *polvo*—something that conjures both death and desire. Full of dust, this tongue is that which makes love to another body. It is made up of particles that commingle with the other body and thus lessen the distinction between the two. This bordered tongue is then likened to the dusty skin of a story. This embodied page forms a dustiness that is actively dusting—decaying, perhaps, and crumbling at the edges. Here, Ramos Otero not only positions himself between fiction and history; he also figures desire between bodies and the page through an erotic invocation of *polvo*. Desire, for Ramos Otero, is figured as a dispersal, as the particles between bodies making love, between a self and its projected ideal, between life and death. Dust limns the tongue, which is finite and which will find its limit and end in death and dust.

To trap the voice of liberation renders poetically the ruse that exposure, writing, and demarcation give us visibility—and then life. Instead, dust writing is ludic and dangerously indulges in the recursive cycles of finitude and meaning that commingle in the writing of a life that is only ever a translation, a mediation. This, too, reminds us that though Ramos Otero was unabashedly queer in his writing, he did not understand this openness as a means and ends to liberation. Ramos Otero's politico-ethical stance is neither nihilistic nor utopic; it is, rather, a mode of writing that conjures porosity and, hence, the pleasures and dangers of exposure, desire, and diaspora. When faced with his own imminent death, Ramos Otero summoned his darkest angelic energies to witness what he knew he could not, leaving us with posthumous writing.

Part II

INVITING DEATH
A Dusty Vigil at the Shore of Life

Ramos Otero's literary signature becomes increasingly commingled with the dirt, the dust, and the ashes of love, sex, and death in *Invitación al polvo*. The collection, posthumously published in 1991, contains three sections: "Polvo enamorado" (Dust in love), "La víspera de polvo" (Dust's eve), and "La nada de nuestros nunca cuerpos" (The nothing of our never bodies). Through these sections, the collection of poetry takes us on a journey from the narrative arc of a love gained and lost to the diagnosis of HIV/AIDS to the eventual vigil that ominously, yet lusciously, anticipates death. *Invitación al polvo*, according to Rubén Ríos Ávila, "se trata de invitarnos a sentir, y sentimos, con él, la esperanza terrible de amor y el miedo, no ya *a la* muerte, sino a *mi* muerte" ([*Invitación al polvo*] deals with inviting us to feel, and we feel, with him, the terrible hope of love and fear, no more *to* death, but to *my* death). This feeling, the coimplication of love and death, of fear and hope, certainly corresponds overwhelmingly to AIDS in *Invitación al polvo*, but as our glimpses at his earlier work show, the feeling is not reducible to it.

If, throughout the second section of *Invitación*, Ramos Otero understands his anticipated death through the temporal figures of vigil and insomnia, in the last poem of this collection, the main figure is both temporal and spatial—namely, that of travel or of a trip. "La rosa" figures this trip as one that has no apparent arrival, no teleological conclusion to this life that is fading away, and no end point to desire except desire itself. The poem inhabits a circular structure, a revolving consideration of death and desire, wherein the ambivalence remains suspended without being resolved. The four lines that end and begin the poem are identical:

> El martes que viene voy de viaje.
> No es necesario hablar de mal agüero.
> Regreso al pan, al mar y al aguacero.
> A humedecer con *polvo*s mi homenaje.[65]

> This coming Tuesday I am going on a trip.
> It's not necessary to speak of bad luck.
> I return to bread, to the sea and to rainfall.
> To dampen my memorial with dust.

Here, *polvo* functions as the final sprinkling over a memorial, an homage, and also a mist that lubricates a passageway to the next realm—or stubbornly clings to this one.

Within the poem, the lyrical voice indulges in a fetid desire:

> ¡Oh delicioso lodazal terrestre, cama prohibida
> de los ángeles perversos, costra olorosa de quesos
> genitales, manos labriegas surcando en entretelas
> la libertad mortal que nadie entiende![66]

> Oh delicious muddy bog, prohibited bed
> of perverse angels, fragrant scab of genital
> cheeses, farmer hands ploughing in heartstrings
> the mortal freedom that no one understands!

The muddy bog of an ambivalent desire and death, of the danger of desire, becomes something to which the speaker must surrender if he is to understand the pleasures that persist even in this quagmire—which cannot be resolved or understood, even as it belies the freedom found in finitude. Rather than an understanding of the liberty that comes with finitude, one has the tactility of bodies: worn hands, the smell of scabs, the places on the body where life has been lived, where work has been done, where illness has left its mark, and where desire has rubbed up against all these experiences.

> Qué más quieren de mí sino este libro abierto
> que a todos asegura el clímax de sus penas,
> este fúnebre ramo deshojado, este mapa de piel
> que profetiza la órbita de otra cuarentena?[67]
>
> What do they want from me but this open book
> that assures all of the climax of their sorrows,
> this leafless, funeral bouquet, this map of skin
> that prophesies the orbit of another quarantine.

Here, the poetic voice exposes the hermeneutic desires for others to read his open book. The last line heralds a trenchant critique of false empathy that actually desires abject experience to be swept away, out of sight, and quarantined. This line asks us to remember how *sidosos*, or people with HIV/AIDS, assumed the genealogical role of lepers.

A few lines down, the lyrical voice wants to assure that things will be known, in the open:

> Quiero que sepan que estoy desorbitado,
> como siempre, que sigo enamorado de la orilla,
> que sigo sentado en el balcón del sueño
> tirándole saliva al dios de la pureza;
> y digo quel fuego no tiene funerales
> que no verán pasar jamás al enemigo
> si no es en rojo vivo, en crepúsculo, en sangre,
> si no fuera la vida de la misma manera.[68]
>
> I want them to know that I am exorbitant,
> as always, that I continue to be in love with the margin,
> that I stay seated at the balcony of the dream
> spitting saliva at the god of purity;
> and I say that fire does not have funerals
> that they will never see the enemy pass by
> if it is not red hot, in twilight, in blood,
> if it was not life in the same way.

In these lines that lead up to the repetition of the beginning lines, which end the poem in a looped fashion, the lyrical voice marks persistence in his queerness and a love of the limen. Desire, figured as fire, does not have a death and does not have a way of being commemorated but continues in a way that cannot even be detected by those who oppose it. On the edge of a dream and spitting saliva at the god of purity, of decency, the defiance that claims pleasure in the bed of perverse angels persists in order to arrive at its own memorial and homage. The ambivalence here functions as the tactile, the sensorial, that which escapes known distinctions between life and death—writing a radically posthumous and posthuman materiality that marks an angry vigil of death.

In this sense, the writing is an energetic death drive that refuses the current order of the living. In this work, situated as it is in HIV/AIDS, Ramos Otero uses his waning time and material resources to produce this angry, fetid vigil of his own death. HIV/AIDS is caught up in larger, longer questions of porosity, dust, and germs, especially within the colonial archipelago of Puerto Rico and New York City. In her genealogy of germ science and the mythos surrounding germs that has dominated domestic and scientific attitudes toward disease and contagion, Nancy Tomes shows that early science on tuberculosis inspired folks to consider dust deadly. The dust theory of infection came about from research in the mid-1880s by Georg Cornet, who "took finely powdered dust from consumptives' sickrooms, dissolved it in liquid, and injected the fluid into the abdominal cavity of guinea pigs; within a few weeks, almost all the guinea pigs had died from tubercular infection."[69] These findings led Cornet to believe that dried germs, as opposed to fresh sputum, posed the greatest risk for contagion. Although this work was refuted by another German scientist, Carle Flugge, who suggested that direct droplet infection—transmitted through coughing, singing, and/or talking—was more risky, the dust theory of infection remained common lore until the twentieth century, as Tomes suggests, "because it so neatly reconciled older beliefs about the air's infective properties with newer views of the germ."[70] One scientist who came out of Koch's laboratories wrote a book in 1890 called *Dust and Its Dangers*, which came to be the gospel for housecleaning at the turn of the century, premised on the notion that dust accumulated in more concentration in smaller spaces like a home than, say, a city. This theory of dust and contagion permutated over the years and resurfaced with the HIV/AIDS epidemic. Tomes ends her piece with an epilogue that considers how the gospel of germs, in fact, pervaded public sentiment in the early years of outbreak—so much so that public health officials had to dispel this antiquated thinking on germs, contagions, and other microbes by putting out pamphlets educating people about how the virus is *not* caught: casual contact, handshakes, toilet seats, dishes, and doorknobs. As she notes, though, "Ironically, because of their impaired immune systems, people with AIDS are at much greater risk from breaches in sanitary protection than are the people who shun them."[71] As Tomes illustrates in her epilogue, there are two key differences between the time of tuberculosis outbreaks and early germ theory and the onset of the HIV/AIDS crisis: (1) the reformers at the end of the nineteenth century understood that germ spread was indifferent to race and class, and they rallied, as an imagined community, against the spread of germs and (2) this public consciousness turned into public health campaigns and infrastructure. In the wake of the HIV/AIDS crisis, only the most rudimentary lessons of the gospel of germs prevailed, and instead of interpreting germs as a threat to all, those living with HIV/AIDS were left figured as lepers and pariahs. Consequently, public health services and institutions were depleted one by one. There were also new threats in the form of superbugs and environmental issues—issues that a lack of infrastructure and increasing privatization would not end. This story of the dust theory that made some lives less worthy of attention resulted in state-sanctioned mass death. HIV/AIDS, in many ways, has become an ecological problem as well as a medical one. One that undermined any narrative that the United States was less homophobic than other places.

While "La rosa" shows us the recursive tripwire of death, it also displays the amassing rage that Ramos Otero infused into his writing as he advanced toward his own turning to ash. The writing performs a grave melody that moves from the personal to the impersonal, according to Luis Othoniel Rosa.[72] Ramos Otero used his waning time and material resources to produce this angry, fetid vigil of his own death. As his time on this earth came to its final act, he still performed readings—sometimes in his hospital bed. One of those poems read from his bed was "Nobleza de sangre" or "Blood nobility." Perhaps the emphasis on HIV/AIDS writing in the United States made this poem more popular, one of the few of his translated works into English. It also appears in the first anthology of queer Puerto Rican writing called *Otros Cuerpos*. In this poem, as in the whole of his work, queerness and colonial status become fascinatingly entangled through genocide and through a further critique of sovereignty and purity. "Nobleza de sangre" considers all the particularities of blood and bloodline—figuring two forms of blood that put queers and Puerto Ricans at the crossroads of biopolitics, necropolitics, and uneven precarity.

Appearing late in *Invitación al polvo*, Ramos Otero moves from dust to blood. His apostrophe is to God, in the form of a prayer of thanks, and he infuses his words with palpable anger at forces who deem themselves sovereign enough to let some live and some die. The poem begins:

> Gracias, *Señor*, por habernos enviado el SIDA.
> Todos los tecatos y los maricones de New York,
> San Francisco, Puerto Rico y Haití te estaremos
> eternamente agradecidos por tu aplomo de Emperador del Todo y
> de la Nada (y si no me equivoco, de Católicos Apostólicos Romanos).

> Thank you, Lord, for having sent us AIDS.
> All the junkies and faggots in New York,
> San Francisco, Puerto Rico, and Haiti will be forever
> grateful for your aplomb as Emperor of All Things and
> The Void (and, if I'm not mistaken, of Apostolic Roman Catholics).[73]

Here, the poetic voice infuses bitter vitriol with mocking irony, creating a coalitional archipelagic relation between the places most notoriously affected by HIV/AIDS—linking two cities in the United States with Haiti and Ramos Otero's *otra isla* and home of Puerto Rico.

This poem, at this initial moment, glances across the Atlantic. The poetic voice continues—morphing his prayer into a scorn that puppets the hyperbolic imaginaries of the homophobic and racist attitudes attached to the virus:

> Los heterosexuales del centro de África, creo,
> que son ingratos al no reconocer quel SIDA

> les ha permitido entrar a la modernidad sin prejuicios,
> aunque ya sí saben que la falta de lluvia y de alimentos
> son tus justas artimañas de purificador y arquitecto de almas.
>
> The heterosexuals of central Africa are, I think,
> ungrateful not to recognize that AIDS
> has allowed them entrance into modernity without any prejudice
> though they already do know that the lack of rain and food
> are your just stratagems as purifier and architect of souls.

Assuming a mockingly moralistic tone, the poetic voice betrays that such attitudes kill. They kill precisely by summoning the subaltern and Global South into modernity. Here, lack of rain and food serve as the genocidal desires of a wanton deity, an architect of souls, a biopolitical enforcer who purifies through torturous means. And this purifier of souls is indeed sadistic. Moving from the two flagship cities of the outbreak to the Caribbean islands affected and then to central Africa, Ramos Otero also includes bisexuals in his community of *sidosos*:

> *Señor*, perdona a los bisexuales por su confusión innata
> de creer quen la variedad de cuerpos está el gusto,
> y sobre todo perdona a la mayoría moral, intachable y serena
> que aún ignora la dulce cortadura de tu espada de carne.
>
> Lord, forgive bisexuals for their innate confusion,
> for believing that pleasure is to be found in the variance of bodies,
> and above all forgive the reproachable and serene moral majority
> that still ignores the sweet incision of your sword of flesh.

Pleasure "in the variance of bodies" in this stanza translates bisexuality out of binaristic thinking and into a multivalent terrain of bodies and pleasures—a confusion that sounds more like a multitude of desirous relations. This barely concealed revision of Christian logic gains force when, in the next lines, the moral majority (those who would do most condemning through judgmental scripture and wanton lust for this plague) is the population most bereft of "the sweet incision of [the Lord's] sword of flesh." Positioned now as a sadist, a sadist who withholds his pleasurable cutting from his most devout followers, God and his discourse is what is innately confused.

Confusing who names and who is named, the poem continues to say that the poetic voice knows many who think that because humans are supposedly made in God's likeness, he must have endured the "caterva de enfermedades infecciosas" (swarm of infectious diseases) and that God has endured "ese asco collectivo de Kaposi Sarcoma" (the collective disgust of Kaposi's sarcoma and tuberculosis). The poetic voice here undoes these beliefs, saying, "As if there's night for you." But he does signal, in this litany of complaints, that his unending fatigue is making it difficult to walk or write his poetry. And yet, the writing proceeds and does so through the power of naming:

> Señor, me voy a tomar la poca libertad que me queda, colonizado al fin,
> y definir nuestra identidad: ¡Que nos llamen sidosos de una vez y todas!
>
> Lord, I'm going to take what little freedom I have left, colonized after all,
> and define our identity: Let them call us the sidious once and for all!

This seemingly sovereign act of naming, addressed at the Catholic God, flies in the face of creation stories wherein naming was handed to Adam—but this naming is in the subjunctive. Freedom becomes an imperative, rather than a given, in this poetic syntax. Ramos Otero didn't seek acceptance or normalization but rather figured himself as "the angel of a furious pen of another history," as he writes in "Vigilia."[74] In this marginal realm, he finds his poetic address and form. After naming himself with an identity few claimed with zeal at the time while also not conceding to the politically correct term of *person with AIDS* (PWA), the poetic voice seeks to ask a few questions of the sovereign God, infusing his line of questioning with finitude:

> *Señor*, sólo me queda bregar con el asunto de tu identidad.
> No voy a entrar en cuestiones personales ni a invadir tu intimidad (que es inviolable), pero ¿qué te llevó a otórgales la franquicia

de la segunda destrucción de Sodoma, a los americanos? Freud diría:
¿Será, tal vez, tu soledad total, tu colosal hastío, tu complejo de culpa
   con tantos genocidios, tu frustración sexual con los apóstoles,
o la ingenua ilusión de creer quel derecho al amor, a la carne secreta,
a la vida y la muerte aún te pertenecen con affidavit de cuna?

Lord, all that's left for me is to deal with the matter of your identity.
I'm not going to get into anything personal or invade your privacy
(which is inviolable), but what made you give the franchise
of the second destruction of Sodom to the Americans? Freud
   would say:
Was it, perhaps, your total solitude, your colossal boredom, your
   guilt complex
about so many genocides, your sexual frustration with the apostles,
or the naive illusion of believing that the right to love, to the secret
   flesh,
to life and death still belong to you by entitlement of birth?

A glitch occurs, poetically, when identity, the personal, and the sovereign God collide in figuration, producing a god who thinks of himself as a person. Here AIDS and US imperialism are entangled in the matter of HIV/AIDS figured as the second destruction of Sodom (an allegorical translation of coloniality). This biblical reference becomes another in a string of genocides assigned to God and to sovereignty. Summoning and camping psychoanalysis, the poetic voice asks if it is solitude that led God to destroy so many lives. Or was it boredom, a guilt complex, or sexual frustration with the apostles? But the ending of the poem opens by ending on a question that challenges the naive illusion that anyone would have the right to life and death, to secret flesh still, by birthright. Here Manuel Ramos Otero poetically renders an inversion of Nietzsche's dictum that "God is dead. God remains dead. And we killed him."[75] This dictum notes that the project of the Enlightenment killed God, and this project would also give us the fiction of sovereign subjectivity. A poetic variation on this theme of finitude, Ramos Otero figures and questions a god as a being that can be born. This still perhaps signals a death, a death foretold by the possibility of being born, a relation to finitude that is perverse when talking to the Roman

Catholic God. This God only exists in narration, only with the performative magic of language, which Ramos Otero had already exploited in "Hollywood Memorabilia." There is an overt sacrilegious tone that turns queenly and catty here, figuring God more as a mortal sovereign and less as an immortal one—bringing him to finitude as Ramos Otero approaches his own. And above all, he questions God's identity problem. Dust and death both make identity a difficult project.

Though *Invitación al polvo* signals a privileged relation to death generally and HIV/AIDS in particular, the collection does not see death as a final telos that determines a foreclosure of desire and relation. In Ramos Otero's writing, desire persists—whether it be through memory, fantasy, or materiality—in the trope of dust. The ambivalence of *polvo* is dispersed throughout the collection and becomes a figure that, through its registers of finitude and persistence, transforms into a motif of danger, of that which illuminates the risk of exposure. If dust had seemed particularly prescient about the HIV/AIDS pandemic, it now flashes as a figure that portends both the effects of coloniality and the raised stakes of thinking finitude, relationality, and precarity after Hurricane Maria. It is in this entangled figure that I dwell, showing the echoes of Ramos Otero's work and his luscious renderings of many kinds of undoings—those that are pleasurable and those that are damning.

Part III

MATTERS OF DUST AND DIASPORA
I've always thought about this yearly migration of dust as a diaspora of sorts: displaced grains of sand from the Arabian Peninsula lifted up by the dry winds and forced into exile from the desert. Almost imperceivable in their individuality, these little specks of dust register only in their collectivity, in their perseverance to stay together even as they are forced into far-flung lands.
—Yarimar Bonilla, "La Calima: Diasporic Dust"

Dust is dirty. Dust is always a minor matter that claims grand importance when matter is not assessed or valued on scales that always lie about how powerful or sovereign any self may be. Dust shows the scales of relation at the global level but also at the level of the almost imperceptible bit of dust that makes its way into our always porous bodies, our bodies that contribute to this business of dust without our consent and without option. It is everywhere, making strange and fleeting assemblages of the movements of matter, of story, of bodies, of skin, of breath. Dust may settle slowly or quickly lift up, as fires blaze, as libraries gather mold, as sands blow across the Atlantic Ocean. Dust populates relation not simply as space but also temporally, in a swerving entanglement—the tiny bits that bear witness and register how inter- and intrarelation impinge upon us and expose our porosity through the particulate. This deeply ambivalent matter of dust resonates as something frustratingly material and recalcitrant to sovereign efforts to purify and to seal off the self from a broader world of the senses, haptically seductive and debilitatingly invasive. Ramos Otero's dusty writing elucidates the vibrant dangers of desire—its salacious risk and aggregate particularity through a matter akin to what Deborah Vargas calls "lo sucio."[76] *Polvo* moves across the different genres and phases of Manuel Ramos Otero's work as a matter that refuses to disentangle the material realities of queerness and coloniality. Making love and reading dusty, dangerous, and desirous, the work of Ramos Otero invites us to think beyond a sealed self, a sovereign life, and the supposed distinctions between fiction and history. Porosity can be erotic and can also quickly turn to precarity, as we have seen, and it is in this charge of desirous risk that I think the perverse figure of *polvo* holds for Manuel Ramos Otero and for us. As Ramos Otero became more and more ill as a *sidoso*, one of his dear friends took him home to Puerto Rico to die. And there he did die, a telos that undoes the directional prejudice behind the term *sexile*. Instead, his ashes would be sprinkled at sea in his hometown of Manatí, a final return to his shore of life. His exorbitant dust still rages on the page, an urgent reminder that finitude comes for us all, but with a crucial and cruel distinction: it does not come for all of us with even speed and force.

To follow Ramos Otero's dusty afterlife, I now move to consider how dust works within the atmospherics of the Caribbean. Dust grants matter to a thinking of opacity and relation, inspired by the work of Édouard Glissant. Opacity functions as an ethical imperative to not reduce or flatten others in order to sustain relation itself. Dust is often thought of as insignificant remains, the dried remnants of what was once life.

Consider, then, that Glissant begins *Caribbean Discourse* with an epigraph that betrays the colonial attitude toward the archipelago through a quote attributed to Charles de Gaulle: "Between Europe and America I see only specks of dust."[77] For Glissant, such specks of dust become a way to imagine relation itself, to think the irreducible opacity of matter that keeps us in the pull, tension, and risk of relation.[78] Dust is that which, in its small, fragmented opacity, has the haptic ability to texture relation that is often underthought, underfelt, and under the radar of the blatantly visible. Glissant writes, "Relation contaminates, sweetens, as a principle, or as flower dust."[79] Employing the material metaphor of flower dust, or pollen, Glissant offers a felicitous reminder that relation means the possibility of cross-pollination and cross-contamination. This tiny particulate matters in his work, almost in an inverse calculus to how it had been deplored by Charles de Gaulle. Clouding vision, dust may show that what seems sheerly transparent is not a void but rather a populated and material relation with the play of physics, of light, of so much chance. Dust sullies vision. It is seemingly inert but moves frustratingly easily—a swarm or flurry of particulate matter that rearranges itself up in the air. Tracing *polvo* throughout the oeuvre of Manuel Ramos Otero enmeshes one in the material *and* tropological consideration of a multitude or swarm of dust that better matches both diaspora and its contrapuntal phenomenality, that better understands the excitations of de-sedimentation and dispersal. *Polvo* attends to the unevenness of modernization processes and cataclysmic events. *Polvo* provides a dusty lens to consider how Ramos Otero's invitation opens up a space-time configuration that shuttles, ecstatically, between the HIV/AIDS outbreak in Manhattan and Hurricane Maria in Puerto Rico. *Polvo* presages on the material grounds[80] of what is already felt—the difficulty and pleasure of being queer and (anti)colonial.

A curious aspect of Puerto Rico's climatology is *polvo del Sahara*, or Saharan dust, a phenomenon that occurs most often from May to September, thus significantly overlapping with hurricane season. The dust storms originate from the Saharan desert in northern Africa, where winds churn clouds of sandy dust up into the sky, then move over the Canary Islands, and then to the Caribbean, landing often in Puerto Rico and sometimes making it all the way to Mexico. These dust storms are ambivalent: they reduce visibility, leave a layer of dust over everything, and signal a threat to bodies that also suffer from autoimmune disorders and asthma. Yet Saharan dust works as a desiccant, a drying agent, that reduces the spread of fungal spores and dries the atmosphere in the Caribbean, thus halting the constant churn of cyclones and stunting the growth of tropical storms. The particulate matter is often iron-rich, and studies have found that these particles reflect solar radiation, thus cooling the otherwise warming oceans, deterring the humidity and heat that act as catalysts for hurricanes. Many have pondered over this migratory dust, which precedes the transatlantic slave trade, since the very same winds that bring tons of dust from the Saharan desert also blew wind behind sails of ships that brought massive social death and dispossession to the Antilles.[81] Edward Kamau Brathwaite writes, "Even before the first slaves came—bringing, perhaps, pre-Columbian explorers—there was a wind: an implacable climatic, indeed, geological connection."[82] This historical reminder urges us to consider who profits from suffering and what connections can be made across the globe.

Yarimar Bonilla writes movingly about this dust phenomenon as it pertains to Puerto Rico, calling the dust migration a performance. Her use of the term *performance* resonates with how dust moves in and out of Ramos Otero's work as process rather than being: "Perhaps through performance we can view otherwise unperceivable connections between Arabia and the Tropics: how each of these regions are the products of displacements, migrations, indentures, forced labor, extraction and the constant transformation and commodification of the natural landscape—the battle with dust storms, desert sands, hurricane winds, and the putrid humidity of the mangrove."[83] Dusty entanglements of matter, place, and power reveal the possibilities and difficulties of relation, leaving us with so many questions:

> What is and isn't possible in the connection between here and there? And how can these connections be performed, by which I mean brought into being? As both globalization and global warming forces us all to reckon with the threat of displacement and the impossibility of return to a previous state of affairs, I wonder: . . . Can our shared vulnerability to the winds of climate change help us reimagine the nature of our borders and our binds? Might we perhaps become able to recognize each other in the whirlwind and to explore where the wind and dust might take us?[84]

Bonilla and Brathwaite create an echo chamber around dust and its force, charging us with a thinking of diaspora that is more attentive to materiality and material conditions.

In concert with Jasbir Puar, both in her critique of homonationalism *and* in her call to consider the uneven spread of debility over the globe, I propose thinking with dust, or perverse *polvo*, as one way to consider queer diaspora against the idealization of individuals moving northward from the Global South to more white, queer metropoles.[85] Thinking with dust means attending to its swerving movements, its flurry after being struck, its dance during descent, its settling into cracks, its movement in and out of lungs, land, and water. Such movement better corresponds to both the material exigencies behind diaspora and its multidirectional, contrapuntal flows. The particulate matter here is one of a *sucia* sociality—a dirty, resourceful mode that looks to waste as archive. In theorizing the necessity of the aesthetic for queer diaspora curatorial and archival projects, Gayatri Gopinath claims, "These minor histories can be carefully extracted from informal archives made up of discarded or devalued objects, in haptic journeys through dust, dirt, and detritus."[86] Porosity can be erotic and can also quickly turn to precarity. It is in this ambivalent, relational charge that the perverse figure of *polvo* calls out to us.

Dust sullies vision; it has an abiding ambivalence and a strange temporality. It is seemingly inert but moves frustratingly easily, conjuring a register of movement, a swarm or flurry of particulate matter that rearranges in its dance, nearly suspended, in descent. Tracing *polvo* throughout the oeuvre of Manuel Ramos Otero enmeshes one in the material *and* tropological consideration of multitude or swarm of dust that better matches both diaspora and its contrapuntal phenomenality, that better understands the flurry of de-sedimentation and dispersal. Given the temporal play in Ramos Otero's writing on life and death, this closing section meditates upon the strange matter of dust. It is a matter that is never just one matter and that has entangled temporal pulses and draws. In this sense, *polvo*, too, becomes a thinking of matter, life, death, and vulnerability that signals the unevenness of modernization processes and cataclysmic events. Considering the ambivalent legacy of quantum field theory as both a deconstructive ontological or hauntological project and that which gave us the apocalyptic explosion of time and matter in the atomic bombs, Karen Barad considers the strange spatiotemporal matter: "The past is never finished and the future is not what will unfold, the world holds the memories of its iterative reconfigurings. All reconfigurings, including atomic blasts, violent ruptures, and tears in the fabric of being—of spacetimemattering—are sedimented into the world and its iterative becoming and must be taken into account in an objective (that is, responsible and accountable) analysis."[87] Barad insists that temporality is not merely multiple but instead radically entangled. As such, I take the occasion of *polvo* as a dusty lens through which to consider how Ramos Otero's insistence upon this material trope renders the space-time configurations that shuttle, ecstatically and damningly, between the HIV/AIDS outbreak in Manhattan and Hurricane Maria in Puerto Rico.

I imagine dust as a material metaphor that works in tandem and tension with Vanessa Agard-Jones's work on sand and queer desire in the Caribbean. Her theorization of sand works less with diaspora and more with those who do not, whether by choice or circumstance, flee the Caribbean to emphasize their queerness in exile.[88] This trenchant, materially attendant critique shows how the directional prejudice of the figure of the sexile tells a tale too limited, too individualistic to fully encapsulate queer relations in the Caribbean, especially as they are entangled with questions of coloniality. Moving away from watery metaphors that dominate literary tropes in the Caribbean, Agard-Jones finds in sand a different temporal register of disaster, one that links the eruption of Mount Pelée, which historically rendered Saint-Pierre Martinique as the Sodom of the Caribbean and the marked eruption as a divine punishment for sexual libertine ways, to the contemporary beach of Saint-Anne, where queer cruising occurs on the island. For her, sand works as a kind of archive that can attend to the material conditions of emplacement: "Rather than invoke ideas about absence and invisibility as the condition of same-sex desiring and gender-transgressing people, turning to sand as a metaphor for the repository of memory may help our analyses engage more fine-grained and ephemeral presences than our usual archives would allow."[89] One reason, among many, that I remain so rapt, so enthralled with Ramos Otero's tropological commitment to dust is not because it abides finitude and death, those undoing matters that make teleological projects all for naught, but because his dust writing is a dust thinking—that is, he abides dust, he indulges its deep ambivalence, its exposure and porosity, it's conglomerate parts, its bits that never amass to a whole, its matter that doesn't mind human issues of binaristic thinking. Dust is, instead, wholly nonplussed about binaries—or, perhaps less anthropomorphically, dust dissolves dualistic thinking. It is neither good nor bad but often both at the same time depending on the context, matter, time, and bodies involved. It is always particulate, particular, singular (yet radically plural)—never self-same, never single origin, never pure.

Polvo's Postscript

Through a poetics of dust, Manuel Ramos Otero summoned his darkest angelic energies to witness what he knew he could not. When I found myself in San Juan during the island-wide protests of July 2019, I could not help but feel that I was hearing Ramos Otero's invitation anew. Puerto Ricans on the island rallied across class, race, gender, and sexuality to demand respect for the dead through the ousting of Governor Ricardo Roselló. Many protesters graffitied the colonial walls of Old San Juan and held signs with the number 4,645—which accounts for the governmentally unacknowledged but confirmed number of Puerto Ricans who died in the aftermath of Hurricane Maria, tallied by the Harvard T. H. Chan School of Public Health with the help of the Centro de Periodismo Investigativo.[90] This death count uses a calculus between fast and slow death to show the astounding loss of life in the aftermath of Maria.[91] How does death recur in a colonial atmosphere, like so much dust caught in the throat? How can we think of the aching resonance between the supposedly indifferent effects of hurricanes and viruses and their overexposure in queer and racialized populations?

As crises accelerate globally, this postscript will surely be rendered dusty soon enough—indeed, I am unable to cap off this history of dust. Recent attention to both HIV/AIDS and Hurricane Maria reminds us urgently that these crises are not over but rather are redistributed and scattered,[92] discursively cleaned up in the media while their material effects remain the quotidian reality for those who fall outside of the purview of attention to what gets registered as crisis. Writing on the entanglement of bodies, catastrophic events, and history, William Haver identifies the HIV/AIDS crisis as a limit that demands an ethical attunement:

Only if we can imagine that what we do in making what we make is sustained by nothing but the sheer improbability of it all, the fact that it could be quite otherwise, that we can think of the thought of the ethical. Which is to say that the question of the ethical is in itself a cruel question, a painful question, which always throws us into the limit-situation where the very possibility of speaking, of thought, is the most improbable of probabilities. For the ethical is the insistence of a demand, a call, a scream of abject terror, that comes to us from the sociality, the indeterminacy, the nonreserve, that is beyond every epistemological horizon. The ethicality of the ethical resides only in broaching the question of the ethical, and in the unremitting cruelty of a question that must be borne in the askesis of an unbearable silence.[93]

Death is, in many ways, otherwise to being. But death need not be a final telos—indeed it only is if we ascribe so much meaning and importance to the neoliberal individual. It can be understood as a limit or a transmogrification of matter. Death, in its recursive drive, does call out to us through ash, through fossil, and through posthumous writing. If we consider these quotidian deaths with dust, as that which we breathe and that which recurs, we may be able to cull an ethical reading practice. Thinking with the minor matter of dust not only decenters individual human life; it also invites us to think beyond the reach of our lives to the moment when we will not be able to keep vigil over them or over the lives of others. Dust entreats us to ask cruel, painful but necessary questions. As a modest response in the face of so much death, Manuel Ramos Otero's prescient figuration of *polvo* offers us a figure of material vigil. In dust's quiet repose, we haptically encounter a poetics of life at the shore of death and of death at the shore of life.

3

Gut Checks

María Irene Fornés's Visceral Pedagogy and Dangerous Nerves

To be in the presence of Irene and to face the blank page in her presence is to sit with not knowing. It's a bliss state. It is the source of all creativity. When we peacefully sit with not knowing, it comes to us. We know. We spring into action. We write. We move through the writing like a fluid world, not knowing what's ahead, and not reflecting on what's behind. It is in not knowing that we, finally, truly know.
—Elaine Romero, "Expanding the Chair: A Conversation on Fornés's Pedagogy in Action"

How am I to represent this complex embodied fugue? My skin is an organ of sense that runs imperceptibly from inside my body to the outside, or from outside to inside, which defeats the idea that I'm living in my body. There are 108 single-word prepositions in the English language, and none is adequate to representing the relation of mind to body. Body and mind are simultaneously one and the same and clearly distinct. Thinking my body, I am thinking in my body, as my body, through my body, of my body, about my body, and I'm oriented around my body.
—Christina Crosby, *A Body, Undone: Living On after Great Pain*

In the trailer of Michelle Memran's documentary on María Irene Fornés, *The Rest I Make Up*, the camera pans over the playwright's West Village apartment, showing a life of reading and writing—books on curiosity, stacks of papers—as Fornés' lilting, accented voice asks a provocative question about the film and her role in it: "Am I so interesting that I would be the subject of your film?"[1] And indeed, Fornés's legacy is one of great interest, most ardently supported by her students—many of whom call themselves her children, recalling her oft-mentioned status as "the mother" of Latinx playwriting. In the vibrant theatrical world of Latinx New York, playwrights and artists such as Cherríe Moraga, Jorge Ignacio Cortiñas, Paula Vogel, Migdalia Cruz, and Caridad Svich, among many others, emerged from her workshops at the International Arts Relations (INTAR) Theatre—playwrights who have all praised Fornés for her instruction, which helped them to open up, to get unstuck, to embody their words, and to move steadfastly into the world of the unknown, the opaque, and the not-yet determined. To those who know her and her work, Fornés remains a central figure in the world of experimental theater and a beloved pedagogue who inspired at least two generations of Latinx playwrights. Yet these accolades are often followed by the refrain that she remains shockingly unknown even though she won nine Obies (off-Broadway theater awards) and wrote over forty plays. Her relative obscurity may be the result of her fiercely difficult plays, which pushed the bounds of American theater and refused the genres of realism, identitarian-based plots, and commercialized plays. Moreover, her career started not as a playwright but as a painter—a background that many credit for her singular craft and visionary pedagogy.

While the reception of Fornés often centers her pedagogical lessons—lovingly preserved and disseminated by her pupils both in writing and in theatrical practice—this chapter wonders over other lessons that may be gleaned from her work. My concern is that what might get elided with the critical reception of Fornés as a master pedagogue is a careful and close engagement with her oeuvre—that is, with how her plays, too, inscribe lingering lessons. Moreover, Fornés had an oblique relation to her own identity as Latina, lesbian, and feminist. Eric Mayes-Garcia reminds us that "Fornés's latinidad evades critics working under a paradigm of Western universality because it is not announced through a single fixed identity category that can be comprehended or 'possessed' as an object of sublimation, or as 'Other.'"[2] While Fornés claimed her cubanidad and had relatively open lesbian partnerships, her pedagogical and aesthetic commitments eschewed predictable identity plots and sometimes plot altogether. Put another way, she disavowed her own ego and personality with her writing and instead employed a lack of volition and a corporeally grounded creativity, rather than her own markers of identity, using that as the engine of her creativity. And yet, the body of her work now remains underread and underproduced as her legacy becomes more and more aligned under the moniker of teacher—all tied up in the figure of the mother of Latinx playwriting.[3] I wonder if this is one gendered script that she would have eschewed. While she dedicated her life to teaching herself and others, to render a Latina woman a mother, as a particularly fecund womb, produces a particular kind of stronghold, reducing her to her reproductive role or her maternal function.[4] This chapter takes the critical reception of Fornés as a prompt to reread her most iconic play, *Fefu and Her Friends*, as pedagogical. As I argue, *Fefu and Her Friends*, like many of her plays, imparts lessons that dwell in the sensorium of guts and nerves—not always the central nervous system, aligned with reason, but instead the aggression of the guts and the nervous body's reflexive affect. As a play about women, *Fefu and Her Friends* introduces all eight in one speedy first part, separates them and the audience, too, in the second part, and then brings them together after we've learned of their rifts in the third. This results in a situation in which it is difficult to interpret the actions and words of any of these women characters as having any clear message *for* or *about* women. Instead, we see glimpses into their tenderness but also the ways they have provoked one another, failed one another, and loved one another. Focusing on the lower sensorium of visceral feelings through guts and nerves, Fornés's plays showcase a prescient thinking that aligns with more contemporaneous feminist thinking that contends with biology, that can account for violence between women, and that takes pain and hysteria seriously.[5]

It's not easy to listen to the body, as anyone who's ever had chronic pain knows. Pain is relative and singular, but hospital signs put up a universal scale that disregards that some live with pain daily and others very seldom. The feelings of body parts are hard to discern, but they are certainly articulate or forceful enough to be felt if not known or discretely quantifiable. To follow the insights of Elizabeth Wilson in both *Psychosomatic* and *Gut Feminism*, the psyche and biology are more radically entangled than previously considered in second-wave feminist readings of hysteria.[6] In earlier interactions with the figure of the hysteric, feminist attention treated the pathologization of women as hysterics as the problem in and of itself. Meanwhile, feminist theory has asserted the importance of bodies but has often considered that body to be inert, unmediated, and acted upon rather unidirectionally by culture. Wilson's work on the peripheral nervous system and gut feelings asks us to consider how biological substrata, especially the enervated gut, function as part of a larger ecology that feminists should consider as data worth minding. Thinking with viscera mires one in the terrain of negative affect, trauma, and politics less driven by sovereign intention and more by levels of serotonin production, which requires an attention to processes of secretion and metabolization. I take this cue to read the body as an invitation to read corporeality and carnality as serious pedagogical tropes in the work of Fornés, since her writing always started with the body, but also because her corpus and her body of work would be best considered through these tropes that persist across her plays even when they are difficult to categorize either by familiar gender and ethnic thematics, in genre or kind, or as realist or absurdist. What appears to be most absurd in a Fornés play may be a theatrical translation of the body's articulation as an acted and therefore always embodied reflection of the corporeal articulations that seem to have particular purchase on feminized bodies: chronic pain, anxiety, hysteria, depression, and autoimmune disorders. In and of themselves, these ailments are not absurd, but that's only so if we devalue the possible trace structure of bodily expression. And these expressions would and should lead us to further delve into the crosshairs that emerge as entangled, intimate relations between porous bodies and the more-than-human environments that dwell within and beyond any body. They also direct our attention away from the provenance of an intentional mind and into a minded lower sensorium, away from the central nervous system and into the peripheral nervous system that dwells within the gut. In what follows, I track the figurations of enervation, viscera, and corporeality in Fornés's *Fefu and Her Friends* to show how this play espouses a visceral pedagogy that cedes mastery and mimicry in favor of the risk of learning.

Before moving into some thoughts on the Fornésian lessons that linger in the corpus of her plays, a brief biography is in order. María Irene Fornés, fondly called Irene by those closest to her, was born in Havana, Cuba, in 1930. Fornés came to the States at the age of fifteen in 1945, which she says you can hear in her accent—an accent she also claims permeates her plays at the level of language and discourse. While identity markers are often troubled in Fornés's inscriptions, she does insistently identify as Cuban by birth. Noting her relationship to language, Fornés often remarks upon her Hispanophone roots that give her plays an "off-center quality that is not exactly deliberate, but that [she has] not tried to change because [she knows] its origin lies in the temperament and language of [her] birth."[7] Her accent, though, does not transmit easy lessons on identity,[8] and indeed, her own relationship to Cuba is one that falls outside of the scripted binary that would have ruled most Cuban exiles in the latter half of the twentieth century. Consider the following anecdote from Fornés herself:

> I remember shortly after the Castro takeover [in 1959] there was a group of Cuban exile artists. They wanted me to go to meetings, to have readings, and they said, "It's not political." So I went. Then one day they passed an anti-Castro manifesto around that we were supposed to sign. It talked about the Red monster and the language was extreme. I said, "No, I don't want to sign." They were indignant and asked, "Are you in favor of Castro?" I said, "Not really. I'm not in favor of Castro but I'm not against him either. I don't know enough." And they said, "If you're not against him, you're for him."[9]

The harsh binary that Fornés receives—if you aren't against Castro, you're for him—is a familiar dictate following the Cuban Revolution. Such a binary has been hardened into policy through the US trade embargo on Cuba, adding to the difficulties of life on the island. Fornés, in an act of humility (and in a different temporal logic) refuses this binary, saying, "I don't know enough." I read this response as one that slows down the need to know that often aligns itself with the legibly political. Rather than claiming recourse to ignorance as an end to dialogue, Fornés's answer places an accent on *enough*—she does not yet know enough to come down on either side of a rather impossible binary, enough to add fuel to an already raging imperialist fire, enough to say with certainty and conviction what was happening in the late fifties and early sixties in Cuba. Instead, her response was one that kept open the space for learning in the face of not knowing enough, for looking at the nuances of a tense political situation, and for encountering Cuba beyond this violent binary. Such ethical attention to the unknown would mark the genius of Fornés's creative system, which she culled for herself as an autodidact and which she generously shared with others through her plays and her teaching.

While she's contemporarily described as a Latinx and queer playwright, Fornés's biography doesn't follow the overly scripted latinidad that cubanidad tried to dictate to its overdetermined diaspora. Fornés's story of migration happens prior to the revolution and becomes one more woven into immigrant and queer lives that circulated in New York City's Greenwich Village bohemian milieus. She and her mother both worked in factories, and yet, postwar New York City afforded Fornés a life of creativity and risk during a time when a bohemian lifestyle was a material possibility for some immigrants. Moving between New York, Paris, and Provincetown, Fornés overlapped with figures like Norman and Adela Mailer and, of course, her most famous lover: Susan Sontag. In Provincetown, the young Fornés studied abstractionist painting with Hans Hofmann in his studio. Notoriously a visual teacher, Hofmann shared many sensibilities with Fornés—they were both immigrants and exceptional teachers. She would not go on to be a painter, but she did transmute the visual education and painterly forces of push and pull that Hofmann espoused through brushstroke.[10]

Fornés left New York in 1957 with her lover Harriet Sohmers for a short stay in Paris. Though trained in painting, Fornés would return to the States before the decade was over and start writing her plays. This turn in her artistic practice was inspired by Beckett's *Waiting for Godot*, which she had seen in Paris, in French; this sparked a love for theater even though, or perhaps especially because, she did not understand the French language. During her time in Paris and New York, Fornés also had open relationships with women and men—earning her the nickname Don Juana. While these relationships were more or less open, Fornés did not often identify with predictably queer, lesbian, or homosexual scripts. After she established herself in the off-off Broadway scene, she began imparting lessons—ones she had created on her own as an autodidact—on the craft of playwriting to Latinx playwrights through the Hispanic Playwrights Workshop in Residence Laboratory at INTAR. This workshop asked students to tap into their creativity and, importantly, paid them for their time in the workshop—making the space materially possible for those often otherwise reliant on wage work.

In over four decades of prolific teaching in New York, punctuated by brief pedagogical stays at Yale and in California, Fornés produced a vibrant theatrical legacy that shifted what could be done in American theater. A typical Fornésian day at her infamous workshop would start with basic yoga exercises, what she called "old lady yoga," and then move into writing exercises that she engineered, ones that inspired writers to move beyond their routines and beyond what they already knew. About these exercises, Fornés claimed that "they take you to a place where creativity is, where personal experience and personal knowledge are used. But it's not *about* your personal experience."[11] For Fornés, these exercises used found materials (she infamously incited Sontag to write her first novel with a random line from a cookbook) and the body. Indeed, this corporeal foundation for creativity is echoed in a book she meant to write but never finished, which would have included her workshop lessons and would have been titled *The Anatomy of Inspiration*.

It is difficult to write *about* Fornés in a categorical manner. But that aboutness, that tight tether between signifier and signified for those who live under the aegis of named difference, is precisely the overdetermination that Fornés defies. So instead of relying on her maternal, reproductive function, her motherly role as a metaphor, I'm more interested in how the matter-metaphor of viscera and nerves help us understand her corporeal lessons. Performance studies remains acutely aware of how all too often we try to extract meaning from bodies, especially bodies marked by named difference. In this sense, when we teach underrepresented literature and art, there's an implicit injunction to show what the text or aesthetic piece is really "about." Inspired by the thinking and pedagogy of José Esteban Muñoz, Kandice Chuh remarked on Muñoz's queer optic that finds uncommon beauty that is "atmospheric as it is analytic; it is a sensibility and a ground for politics as much as it refers to an erotics and a critical method."[12] For Chuh, following Muñoz, the aesthetic marks a sensuous form of relation that attends to the material *and* the ephemeral without knowing what the art object is necessarily "about."[13] When we turn markers of difference into moral lessons, we reduce the field of what marks racialized difference and turn it into predictable content. In *Fefu and Her*

Friends, the character Emma claims that opening the senses is the task of the educator—not to enforce rote memory of banal facts but to open the senses to environment. Chuh calls this Muñoz's pedagogy of sensibility rather than identity.[14] The senses perceive affect without always turning them into discrete lessons that can be rendered as information clearly delineated.

While Fornés often plays with the themes of latinidad, feminism, and poverty in her playwriting, she tends to place an accent on the ambivalences, ambiguities, and difficulties inherent in these issues—often figuring them through fleshy, fetid attention to the body's viscera, worms churning beneath stone, and through strange animal references. Like Chuh, Fornés also eschewed the "about" imperative, and *Fefu* was never meant to be a play to make points "about" women: "I don't sit down to make a point *about women* if the central character of my play is a woman, any more than I intend to make a point *about men* when I write a play like *The Danube*, where the central character is a young man."[15] Here, her ludic and defiant remark shows how much the interpretive or hermeneutical frame renders plays by women with women as necessarily about women. It is a referential dilemma Fornés discards as "party line" thinking. For her, this facile instrumentalism of character would be tantamount to conceding to a "tyranny of well meaning."[16] Instead, as Sontag reminds us, Fornés's characters "are revealed through catechism," through acts of learning.[17] Such lessons in learning permeate many scenes in Fornés's oeuvre, and Sontag links this to her status as an autodidact: "Fornés elaborate sympathy for the labor of thought is the endearing observation of someone who is almost entirely self-taught."[18] One can detect a tone of condescension in Sontag's usage of endearing here, and many have commented on the difference between the two: Sontag was infamously scholarly and bookish and Fornés seldom read, preferring conversation to solitary reading, because she was dyslexic. The language of her plays is one many comment upon—assigning it to her propensity for chatter, her status as a nonnative speaker of English.[19] But what may be notable here, too, is that the success of her pedagogy gathers its energies because of, and not despite, her neurodivergence and her immigrant status. Fornés not only had sympathy for "the labor of thought," she also had an immense capacity to harness, on stage, how thought, in its formation, looks and feels.

Such thought rarely conformed to what people expected of her and her students' demographic. While the workshops served Latinx playwrights, Fornés did not ask her students to create based on their identities: "And never did Fornés ask dramatists to write 'as' a Hispanic, female, homosexual or whomever because in her opinion to do so would forever cripple the playwright and make him dependent on the expectations or acceptances of others. Likewise, Fornés resists the use of identity categories because in her words, 'just as you go to McDonald's and expect a certain kind of meal, you come to expect a certain kind of writing from a chosen category of writers.'"[20] Fornés crafted a space for a suspended tension between aesthetics and politics—a space of writing and craft where certain members of a demographic, one often stereotyped and confined to anticipated modes of cultural production, could convene and create works that need not be about their lives in a straightforward, predictable manner. This was a pedagogical venture fueled not by the known but the unknown—what latinidad had not yet transparently yielded. It is the crucial intersection of ethics and pedagogy—an ethical pedagogy that refuses to be pedantic and that traffics in a certain kind of opacity that creates a space of unknowing that fuels creativity and the imagination. Fornés's pedagogy extends beyond her workshops to her plays and back to the reader to create engagements with difference that not only inflect the scene of writing with aesthetic autonomy but also demand that we encounter and feel difference differently. What I want to emphasize is that Fornés's workshops created spaces for playwrights marked by ethnic-racial difference but did not turn that difference into a tokenized hailing with predictable content.

Live Wires

OF GUNS AND LOATHSOME WOMEN

How does this particular pedagogy surface in Fornés's own plays? Consider that her most popular play, by far, is the 1977 *Fefu and Her Friends*, a play that some have signaled as feminist while others have questioned its feminist commitments. So too is it a play that finds cache on university campuses in the United States. The play is set in the spring of 1935 and introduces the audience to eight women gathering at their friend Fefu's New England home in order to rehearse for an educational fundraising campaign. Formally, the play is divided into three sections: "Noon," "Afternoon," and "Evening." Each section of the play is called a *part* and not an *act*. This simple word change redirects how we read the play according to theatrical convention and also encourages a bodily reading along with the script. While the play itself does not overtly address questions of latinidad, an accented note inaugurates the play itself. In the opening pages of the play, there is a directive that precedes the play itself and reads, "Author's Note: Fefu is pronounced Feh-fooh."[21] This would be how a Spanish speaker would pronounce the name *Fefu*. The accented name has no explanation, no context in the play itself. Instead, it remains a curious detail that hovers over the play—beckoning one to consider what difference this accent makes. Listening in detail, according to Alexandra Vazquez, allows us to be affected as critics rather than mastering interpretation or extracting knowledge from art: "Instead of ossifying them into evidence for a totalizing argument, details can affect listing, writing, and reading practices in ways not immediately apparent or thought possible."[22] Vazquez reminds us that during the writing of *Fefu and Her Friends*, Fornés was listening to Olga Guillot's *Añorando el Caribe* on repeat, so much so that her neighbors must have thought she was "out of her mind."[23] Thinking outside of the central nervous system that so often privileges reason, sound spills like an accented voice into the play and provides the sensorial landscape for this bizarre story to come forth. As Fornés explains, "The play had nothing to do with Olga Guillot . . . but her voice kept me oiled." Of Guillot's voice, Vazquez writes, "It is a voice that's always too much, excessive, queer, deep, one that is unashamed to devote work and time to heartbreak, unrequited love, and revenge fantasies on behalf of those done wrong."[24] Rather than read this record as a direct source or a hidden message, Vazquez reads Guillot's voice and inspirational influence on Fornés as a kind of force, as a "sound that generated material effects on the writing. The proof of this sound effect is not made clear on the surface of the work, but we can nevertheless be certain that Guillot is an active part of the writer's soil, the generative material that gave it life."[25] The accent of *Fefu* is not accentuated in the play itself; the stage direction or cue already absorbed into the body of the play itself arises anew with this quintessentially Cuban music (of another time). In the most recent, professional production of the play, directed by Lileana Blain-Cruz, Guillot's boleros were used in the interludes between acts and scenes, an accentuation that acted as both sonic suture and sound spill.

The play itself mostly takes place within Fefu's home, but like Guillot's song, what hovers around the house and on the fringes of the play is palpably present. Violence is a specter that haunts *Fefu and Her Friends*—the violence of patriarchy, the violence of intersubjectivity, the violence of heartbreak, and the violence of group logics. Fefu inaugurates the play with a flamboyant polemic: "My husband married me to have a constant reminder of how loathsome women are."[26] After announcing this statement, Fefu says she concurs. Her interlocutors at this moment, Cindy and Christina, are aghast, and Fefu tries to assuage them, saying it's just a thought, something to grapple with. And indeed, the play more largely grapples with a group of women whose stories appear to us through glimpses into their conversations—conversations that all precede the rehearsal of a feminist campaign for education, though the content of that campaign remains obscured. Fefu explains that she likes to tarry with unpleasant and even revolting thoughts because "you see, that which is exposed to the exterior . . . is smooth and dry and clean. That which is not . . . underneath, is slimy and filled with fungus and crawling with worms. It is another life that is parallel to the one we manifest. It's there. The way worms are underneath the stone. If you don't recognize it . . . (whispering) it eats you. That's my opinion. Who's ready for lunch?"[27] This turn from a philosophical treatise on underlying abjection—of slime, fungus, and worms—to lunch is indicative of the delightful movements of Fornés's characters and their banter. Shortly after this announcement, Fefu asks Christina, the newcomer to the group, if she's met her husband. Christina says no and looks outside, offstage, where the play ironically confined the only two men in the play—men we never meet, who get along well and converse about low-stakes matters like lawnmowers. Christina looks offstage, outside, asking Fefu which one is her husband. Fefu says that one and picks up a shotgun and fires at him. After the shock dissipates and Phillip, the offstage phantasmatic husband, gets up, Fefu explains that it's all a game, that Phillip loads the shotgun with blanks and that this game suits them. In this overt gesture to Chekov's gun, we are assured that it will reappear, but we may not be so sure how the gun works, if it's loaded with a bullet, and if it's the charge that will strike the final blow of the play. We will return to this matter, but for now let's note how a phallic gun gets put down and analyze the question of how plumbing surfaces.

Christina, new to Fefu and her antics, finds this game of marital Russian roulette revolting—an adjective quite similar to *loathsome* or *abject*, the fascinating, wormy underside of a polished sociality and marriage. In this first act, as more and more women arrive and the men stay outside, Fefu explains her relationship to gender:

> Women have to find their strength, and when they do find it, it comes forth with bitterness and it's erratic . . . Women are restless with each other. They are like live wires . . . either chattering to keep themselves from making contact, or else, if they don't chatter, they avert their eyes . . . like Orpheus . . . as if a god once said "and if they shall recognize each other, the world will be blown apart." They are always eager for the men to arrive. When they do, they can put themselves at rest, tranquilized and in a mild stupor. With the men they feel safe. The danger is gone. That's the closest they can be to feeling wholesome. Men are the muscle that cover the raw nerve. They are the insulators. The danger is gone, but the price is the mind and the spirit. . . . High price.—I've never understood it. Why?—What is feared?—Hmm. Well . . .—Do you know? Perhaps the heavens would fall.—Have I offended you?[28]

Fefu moves from an essentialist polemic of gender, that women are fundamentally loathsome, to a more nuanced notion of gender and of women finding one another in danger fired in synapses. One could read this passage alongside Adrienne Rich's "Compulsory Heterosexuality and the Lesbian Continuum"—the continuum meant to understand women in relation to one another instead of in relation to men through values of heteropatriarchy. The danger that women recognizing one another poses is a kind of kinetic, charged, erotic explosion. Such danger, for Fefu and for the play itself, is scary—perhaps even revolting— but nonetheless fascinating. It is the unknown potentiality of a life outside of the men that covers the raw nerve—a thinking, feeling nervous system not reduced to the life of phallogocentric reason. Christina explains that she too has "wished for the trust that men have for each other. The faith the world puts in them and they in turn put in the world. I know I don't have it."[29] In the push and pull of conversation,

Christina moves closer to the core abjection of womanhood in a heteropatriarchal world and comes to understand that what Fefu desires may not be manhood as such but the affordance of privilege and ease that men have with the world. Upon hearing this, Fefu does not stay to bond, she does not further charge the room with danger, but leaves to attend to the lower sensorium of the house, its infrastructural support that allows the abject to vacate the home. As she exits, she rings out an axiom of her own and, perhaps, of the play: "Plumbing is more important than you think."[30] Upon her departure, Cindy turns to Christina to inquire what she thinks of Fefu's inflammatory speech. Christina falls off her chair "in a mock faint."[31] Christina responds with her corporeal comportment and not her central nervous system: "Think? I hurt. I'm all shreds inside."[32] Pain that is at once physical and emotional surfaces quite a lot in this play. Pain, too, is what spurs acting and writing in the world of Fornés, if it can be channeled: "Pain can be channeled—it's like what actors do. Actors go into the most agonizing thing and they're shaking and you think, 'My God, how can they do this every night.' You want to say, 'My poor darling. Let me hold you for a while to comfort you.' And you go back to the dressing room, and they look like they've just been swimming in the Caribbean. They look radiant, and you're a wreck. So that's how I write."[33] Fornés often reaches across genres to explain creativity—here citing acting to show how writing, too, is an embodied act, one that may leave you looking like you've been swimming in the Caribbean. This leaves one in an ambivalent state: both radiant and a wreck. Fornés understands the creative process as a kind of channeling that takes risk, delicate risk, to articulate.

As the first part of the play moves along, punctuated by introductions to each new guest as they arrive at Fefu's home, we become acquainted with one character, Julia, in her absence. Through the hushed murmurs between Christina and Cindy, triangulated by Fefu's presence looming behind them as they speak softly to each other, we vaguely come to understand that Julia is figured as a hysteric—a word never used in the play but that nonetheless describes the collection of symptoms that Julia endures. By not calling Julia a hysteric, the play allows us to see how the biology of a hysteric may have something to teach us when it is taken seriously and is not reduced to a state of abjectness for women under the heteropatriarchy.

When Julia enters the stage, using a wheelchair, Fefu escorts Julia to her room and Cindy confides in Christina: "I can't get used to it."[34] We come to find out that Cindy was with Julia when the incident that impaired her walking occurred. Christina asks, "Was she actually hit by the bullet?" and, tentatively, Cindy responds no, adding, "I thought the bullet hit her, but it didn't.—How do you know if a person is hit by a bullet?"[35] This question is typical of a Fornésian play—an elemental and fundamental question that surfaces through an almost naive curiosity. In a play that flirts so steadily with violence, the arbiters of violence become so abstracted that we can't know how a bullet wounds a person. Christina replies that you know a person has been hit by a bullet because "there's a wound and . . . there's a bullet."[36] These seemingly ludic remarks punctuate the play, bringing comic relief to otherwise dire and tense moments. But their simple logic doesn't tend to add up. Further along, Cindy explains that a hunter aimed at a deer and shot. Cindy continues,

> He shot. Julia and the deer fell. The deer was dead . . . dying. Julia was unconscious. She had convulsions . . . like the deer. He died and she didn't. I screamed for help and the hunter came and examined Julia. He said "She is not hurt." Julia's forehead was bleeding. He said, "It is a surface wound. I didn't hurt her." I know it wasn't he who hurt her. It was someone else. He went for help and Julia started talking. She was delirious.—Apparently there was a spinal nerve injury. She hit her head and she suffered a concussion. She blanks out and that is caused by the blow on the head. It's a scar in the brain. It's called petit mal.[37]

So there remains a bullet and a wound, though the causal, physical relationship between these elements remains completely unknown. There was a shot and a bullet and a wound, though it seems that there's ambivalence around how Julia collapsed in tandem with the deer. The hunter is yet another abstracted male figure who enters the play only through the language of the women in the play. What we are left with is the impact of the exterior world of men upon women. This hunter plays dangerously, much like Fefu's husband, Phillip. He is the incarnate example of phallogocentrism—the underlying faith in reason and "the world." Though this hunter says Julia's not hurt, Julia is; there is a wound and a bullet and seizures. Her nervous system tells a different story than the hunter's. Petit mal seizures are also often called absent seizures—the short, interruptive absence seizures of less than thirty seconds where twitching occurs and the person seems to be vacant from the body, but consciousness is not entirely lost.

After these whispered conversations provide an enigmatic origin story of Julia's disability, Emma, Sue, and Paula arrive, and with them comes a fresh set of hellos and greetings. Emma, ever-flamboyant and flirtatious, starts drumming up her plans for the rehearsal campaign and sneaks outside to say hello to the men. Only Emma and Fefu ever walk outside of this highly domesticated set. Much has been made critically of this partitioning of space. As Emma exits, Julia spots the recently fired shotgun and smells the barrel. Cindy assures her that the bullet is a blank. The scene continues:

(Julia takes the remaining slug out of the gun. She lets it fall on the floor.)

JULIA: She's hurting herself. *(Julia looks blank and is motionless. Cindy picks up the slug. She notices Julia's condition.)*
CINDY: Julia. *(To Christina.)* She's absent.[38]

Upon waking from her short seizure, Julia repeats her ominous proclamation that Fefu is hurting herself. She lets out a "strange whimper" and heads toward her room, saying she needs to lie down. As Cindy and Christina struggle to get the slug back into the rifle, the final guest arrives, Cecilia. They do indeed get the blank back into the shotgun just as the first part of the play ends. Fornés was an ardent fan of Chekov, and so we know this gun will fire again, but so too do we now know that in a Fornés play, all is up for question. Blows are received without aim being taken at the wounded, and so the danger released in the first part of the play too exceeds the trigger-happy Fefu—it is instead systemic, enervated, and charged between these women.

One difficult aspect of reading *Fefu and Her Friends* follows from a strange pronouncement that Fornés made about the play. In an oft-cited remark during an interview, she explains why the play is set in 1935:

The women were created in a certain way because of an affection I have for a kind of world which I feel is closer to the thirties than any other period. Simply because it is pre-Freud, in the way that people manifested themselves with each other there was something more wholesome and trusting, in a sense. People accepted each other at face value. They were not constantly interpreting each other or themselves. Before Freud became popular and infiltrated our social and emotional lives, if a person said, "I love so-and-so," the person listening would believe the statement. Today, there is an automatic disbelieving of everything that is said, and an interpreting of it. It's implied that there's always some kind of self-deception about an emotion.[39]

Of course, we know good and well that Freud's work is dated prior to 1930, but in my reading, what Fornés signals is less a concern with psychoanalysis as such and more a concern with interpretation, a larger process of extracting meaning that her plays generally resist. And given that the play is concerned with women talking to one another, we have a feminist imperative to believe their reports on their emotional states. Perhaps, counterintuitively, this is why the play features a lot of relations, dreams, and jokes that feel very psychoanalytic. But this "pre-Freudian" pronouncement becomes even stranger when we consider that one character clearly presents as a hysteric: Julia.

The statement just quoted above becomes even more fascinating when Fornés claims Julia as the mind of the play: "Julia is a very important voice and there are times when I feel the whole play is about her. Although Fefu has more of a mind than Julia, Julia is the mind of the play—the seer, the visionary."[40] The mind of the play, then, is a hysteric mind, a mind that articulates itself well beyond the site of reason or the brain. In a play where the boundaries of the home and its innards are so discussed, we have the play's mind as prostrate, precariously conscious (Julia has seizures), and confined, after entry, to the first floor of the home. What does it mean, then, to cast a hysteric as the mind of the play? This body-mind, then, transmits even in the absence of consciousness and intention.[41] Fornés's statement about a pre-Freud world requires that we read the play in tension and tandem with Julia's somatic presentation. Which is to say that what Fornés asks us to do, in this statement and in the play, is to believe that emotions are real—a fundamentally feminist insight, and a psychoanalytic one too.

Heavy Entrails and Systemic Breakdown

Taking the etiology and materiality of hysterics seriously has been a relatively late conversation in two modes of discourse for which hysteria would seem to be a central problem: feminist studies and disability studies. Elizabeth Wilson has shown how the antibiologism of feminist theory has, inadvertently, dismissed some of the central lessons regarding the soma that hysterics might provide for a more robust feminist theory of the body and aggression. In particular, she articulates that "hysteria comprehends more about the body than just what is given by perceptual and tactile data; hysteria also enacts some knowledge of biological unconscious—the ontogenetic and phylogenetic impulses that motivate the body's substrata. Conversion is an immediate and intimate psychosomatic event. It is not an ideational conflict transported into the bodily realm; it is not the body expressing, representing, or symbolizing a psychic conflict that originates elsewhere."[42] This articulation of a biological unconscious goes a step beyond the more traditional approach of seeing hysteria as a direct result of a body enduring sexism, both because hysteria extends beyond the supposed female body and because the hysteric body is not symbolizing but somatizing. This thinking of hysteria, then, views the body's substrata not as immutable bedrock but as dynamic, contingent, and impure.

Anna Molloy similarly puzzles over the dearth of disability studies' approaches to hysteria. She revisits Freud's most famous failure and hysteric, Dora, in order to consider how the pain and suffering of undocumented disability may be a modern-day hysteria, one that requires us to acknowledge the unsavory aspects of bodies in pain and suffering. She asserts that Dora stands as the figure for a disability studies that reckons with the way in which disability is, itself, very hard to master; not only hard to master, but also resistant to interpretation—a way of rendering disability as unavailable to both tokenism and thematic instrumentalization. As a figure, Dora reintroduces suffering and pain into the theoretical terrain of disability studies. This focus on pain and suffering does not necessarily make it more abject but rather avoids sugarcoating what is, indeed, undesirable about living with a disability as a material and phenomenal reality. Disavowing suffering has conceptual fallouts, and as she explains, "such disavowals, rather than repairing disability's originary violence, instead repeat it, in a secondary form that we must recognize as coextensive with disability oppression: the covering up of suffering and loss and the removing from view of pain and incapacity exclude ways of knowing that I have been calling criphystemological and that might also be described as disabled. Disavowals of suffering thus block access to what is most disabling about disability: its unmasterability, its noncompliance, and its radical resistance to meaning."[43] Pain is not always curable, nor is it easily indexed to origin or cause. It transmits across bodies and scrambles cognition. What I want to suggest is that, despite Fornés's desire for a pre-Freud world, *Fefu and Her Friends* operates as a hysterical play, especially in its attention to pain, viscera, and even in its incorporation of jokes.

And even critics writing about the play use telling metaphors. "*Fefu and Her Friends* had an unusually long gestation period" Scott Cummings explains.[44] Fornés had started the play in 1964, based on a Mexican joke that repurposes a misogynist joke and lets it become metabolized by the play. Fornés explains,

> The source of this play is a Mexican joke: There are two Mexicans in sombreros sitting at a bullfight and one says to the other, "Isn't she beautiful, the one in yellow?" and he points to a woman on the other side of the arena crowded with people. The other one says, "Which one?" and he takes his gun and shoots her and says, "The one that falls." In the first draft of the play Fefu explains that she started playing this game with her husband because of that joke. But in rewriting the play I took out this explanation.[45]

This joke becomes the source of Fefu's shooting game with Phillip. Fornés keeps the gun and switches the genders and the status of bullets. She often worked with found sources, whether jokes, books, or thrifted dresses. Recall that the world of off-off Broadway required that everyone pitch in well beyond their role as actor, lighting tech, or dramaturg. So Fornés would often go thrifting for inspiration, props, and other items that could one day reveal their use. But origins and inspiration are often not singular, and Fornés fashions an altogether different origin story for the play in 2001: "I started it because I had six dresses that I bought in a thrift shop, 1930s dresses, chiffon, lovely. I wanted to write a play about women so I could use these dresses."[46] The dresses, like the joke, never made it into the play. What remains from the dresses is the era:

the 1930s. What remains from the joke is the ominous specter of violence, both heteropatriarchal and also something more complicated in the world of the play, where one bullet fired can kill more than one body.

Fefu and Her Friends is often marked as a shift in Fornés's playwriting where she moves from absurdism into something a bit more realist—though her take on realism differs tremendously from US theatrical standards. One may wager that this shift occurred because *Fefu and Her Friends* was the first play that she wrote *and* directed. After this play, Fornés stewarded the rest of her plays as both playwright and director. This directorial role also forced her, upon seeing the performance space, to rewrite the second part of the play. Part two of *Fefu and Her Friends* operates as a breakdown of the fourth wall, of pretense, and of systems. While Julia goes in and out of her hallucinations, which she affirms are real, the audience is broken up and asked to move into the interior of the house during this part of the play. Fornés adapted the structure of the play's first set in 1977 at the Relativity Media Lab.

After writing the opening scene in 1964, Fornés returned to finish writing the play again in 1972. But during that time, she had thrown herself into her work at New York Theater Strategy. In order to finish the play, Fornés realized she would need to take a break from her administrative work and did so in 1977. After completing the first part of the play and a selection of scenes for the second part, she went scouting for a venue. Here she explains how space shifted the writing of the play:

> When I had a date for the play to be performed, I had to start looking for a place to perform it. I saw this place, the Relativity Media Lab on lower Broadway, and looked at the main performing area and thought it wasn't right. But I liked the place and the general atmosphere very much. The people who owned the place took me to different parts of the loft and said, "This room could be used for a dressing room," and I thought this room is so nice it could be used for a room in Fefu's house. They took me to another room and said, "This you can use as a green room," and I thought this is nice, this could be a room in Fefu's house. They took me to the office where we were to discuss terms, dates, etc. I thought this could be a room in Fefu's house. Then right there I thought I would like to do the play using these different rooms. . . . So then I went home and continued writing the play with this new concept in mind.

In a play that's almost entirely set within a home, Fornés writes that the second part takes place in four rooms—splitting up the audience into four groups so they can cross the proscenium and go backstage, into scenes where the audience and actors share a space with four walls. This has proven a difficulty for many restagings of the play, but one that often incurs the same creativity that Fornés espouses. By splitting the audience into four groups in the second part, the actors have to perform one scene four times in a row with precise timing. This precision requires a map to choreograph how each actor may circulate through these scenes without throwing the timing off. But time does get thrown off as the audience, subdivided into four groups, sees four differing sequences of scenes in the second part of the play. In this way, the audience enters into the play and becomes disaggregated both in physicality and in the experience of how the play unfolds.

For *Fefu and Her Friends*' second part, this means that the audience must be broken up; enter the domestic space, encased by four walls;

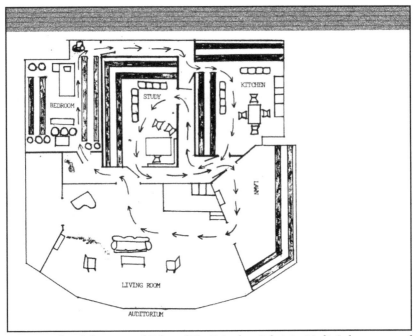

Figure 3.1. Sketch for part 2 of *Fefu and Her Friends* at Relativity Media Lab, courtesy of *The Rest I Make Up*

and be keenly aware of the lack of proscenium between audience and actor. So too does it immerse one into a house party. Audience members hear sound spills from other scenes that demand that we listen to kinetic dialogue conjuring a porously corporeal mise-en-scène. One overhears.

The affect of the play moves between characters quickly and earnestly after the immersive, intimate vignettes of part 2. Keeping up with these women together becomes as exhausting as it is elating. The play unfolds nervously—a larger nervous system with gut feelings that permeate the play. In the last production I was able to see in fall of 2019, directed by Lileana Blain-Cruz, the aural element of the play was amplified by careful dramaturgy and staging. In the second part of the play, the audience was divided into four groups, so each group had a different arc to the second part of the play but was able to overhear the other scenes. Such a sound spill allowed the audience to hear fragments that they would later see acted out in full—making us aware of the disjointed, fragmented scenes of intimacy and the scrambling of the audience. As I listened to Cindy and Christina's dialogue about what it means to be swept off one's feet, I heard murmurs of Julia's tortured monologue, Cecilia speaking of genitals loudly, and then Fefu telling Emma about the diarrhea a cat had expelled in her kitchen—a sign that animals do not conform to the tidy division of shit and food that plumbing so effectively keeps in check in "nice" homes. During this part of the play, the audience experiences both intimacy and a strange self-awareness. One is all the more keenly aware of one's body when the regular architecture of stage and proscenium breaks down, when you go backstage as the play continues. In this way, the second part is both immersive and distracting, a bit like being at a party where you hear a cacophony of sonic intimacies: arguments between former lovers, burbling laughter at reunion, and processing sessions between old friends. By moving the audience into Fefu's home, Fornés's first directorial debut shifted her staging of the play itself and introduced people to what would come to be known as environmental theater.[47] In this way, the home becomes corporeal.

Lileana Blain-Cruz is the first director to put on the play in a professional setting since Fornés herself first did in 1978. The difference of time, over five decades, collapses into 1935. Keenly aware of the importance of the second part of the play, Blain-Cruz recreated a stage with partitions—doing her best to turn a conventional play into one with hidden parts, like a staged backstage. Of this crucial architecture, she states in an interview,

> One of the things that I loved about the play is feeling like there is no one unified perspective. So when you look at these women, you can't say that you have an authoritative perspective on them because you're operating within a completely different relationship to time and space....
>
> Everybody's experience is unique. I think in terms of creating the space, there's also something about how the body functions as an organism. All of the spaces are connected.[48]

And indeed, the interconnectedness of the piece was most keenly communicated through sound spills and roving characters. Blain-Cruz assembled the cast as mostly women of color and styled Sue as butch—donning the sartorial garb of the masculine in tweed pants and a vest, with short-cropped hair. And yet, Sue is not signaled as a lesbian in the play's script—those overt designations better suit Cecilia and Paula, who have had a love affair—but rather as the only member of the group who hasn't enjoyed the comforts of upper-middle-class status. My curiosity was piqued regarding Sue's gender display, a character who is, upon reflection, the most solitary character of the play. Such a directorial gender translation brings the play into the contemporary—but not transparently and not for any clear referential reason. We may consider Blain-Cruz's casting, too, as an accentuation rather than an identity dictate. Because while the cast's racial and ethnic diversity was notable, it wasn't thematized. It just was. This seems to be a lesson in diversity that offers very little by way of predictable thematization, symbolization, or program.

Rather than considering a rational politics in the play, we find ourselves immersed in the fetid terrain of organs—in, perhaps, a hysterical form of communication. The audience is metabolized by the second part of the play, moving through this domestic body and feeling both intimately aware of the scene unfolding and also sensorially attuned to everything else occurring. In this second part, characters move between rooms with careful timing, emphasizing a skilled choreography between the simultaneous scenes.[49] Piper Murray characterizes the fluctuation between seriousness and play in this portion of the play as a hysterical communication of pain: "In the merry-go-round of Part Two, for example, we encounter in each of the scenes a kind of hysterical production through which, into all the play and laughter, erupts a pain neither purely physical nor purely emotional: Cindy relates a dream in which she is nearly strangled by a man who rubs her nipples, while Sue sucks on Fefu's ice cubes before returning them to the freezer, declaring 'I'm clean.'"[50] Part 2 generally features breakdowns into laughter, pain, and emotional processing—all of which are accompanied by jouissance. The women not only separate; they circulate: Fefu offers Paula and Cecilia the opportunity to play croquet. Paula also offers Julia soup—the only interruption to her monologue, which is itself studded with different voices and responses to absent judges—another set of spectral men that infiltrate the play without their presence being materially incarnated. While Julia retires to her room, Emma and Fefu are on the lawn. Emma discusses her obsessive rumination that people have genitals, and yet they act like they don't. She then launches into a theory about divine sex acts and the registry in heaven that assigns high marks to faithful acts of pleasure. Fefu humors her, takes relief in the profane theory, and then confesses her own pain—one allegorically rendered through a sick black cat that comes into her kitchen with "foul diarrhea." Upon her exit, Emma recites Shakespeare's Sonnet 14, addressed to the fair youth, one that first says fate cannot be divined. It goes on to say that through the youth's eyes the lyrical voice can divine that without procreation, without a child, the truth and beauty of the youth will die. Such an homage to Shakespeare is strange and also highlights that in a play about eight women, there is no mention of children. In fact, we don't know if Fefu, or any of the women, are mothers. How's that for an added level of the Bechdel test? The women do talk to one another about their husbands in small moments, but much of their conversation and movement focuses on one another.

    A newcomer to the group, Christina stays focused on Fefu and her scandalous polemics. Her fascination with Fefu emerges in private, in a scene that shows Cindy and Christina reading together in the study, trying to interpret each other's jokes. This conversation turns into a veritable crash course of Freudian slips. In this parlay, intimately encased by walls, Christina admits that she finds people like Fefu dangerous,

dangerous to convention. She says, "I don't think they are dangerous to the world; they are more useful than I am, more important, but I feel some of my life is endangered in their way of thinking."[51] In bringing together these women and uncovering raw nerves, danger is afoot, skewing convention and threatening modes of being that feel safe—that, perhaps, feel covered by men's muscles.

And though some of the women, like Fefu, are quite heterosexual (or at least have husbands), we come to learn, in the kitchen scene, that Paula and Cecilia have been lovers. As Paula and Sue prepare soup for lunch, Paula speculates, much like Emma, on her own idiosyncratic theory of love and grief over breakups, a processing session that underscores her lesbian ways. Her theory of breakups moves through bodies and objects: "Well, the break-up takes place in parts. The brain, the heart, the body, mutual things, shared things. The mind leaves but the heart is still there. The heart has left but the body wants to stay. The body leaves but the things are still at the apartment. You must come back. You move everything out of the apartment but the mind stays behind. Memory lingers in the place. Seven years later, perhaps seven years later, it doesn't matter anymore. Perhaps it takes longer. Perhaps it never ends."[52] In this mode of grief, we have an uncannily material theory of cathexis—of how the psyche attaches to objects and how such bonds endure beyond the physical presence of the lover. This theory of the breakup is in parts, much like the play, but also like bodies and like libidinal attachments. And this theory of breakups is broken up by none other than Paula's ex, Cecilia. She enters the kitchen and begins to process how she and Paula have become strangers to each other. This intimate moment between exes becomes interrupted, broken up again, by Fefu, who enters the kitchen to invite everyone to play croquet.

Though Fefu seems to get a thrill from provoking her friends with her extreme behavior, she also tends to them, brings them together, and even fixes the plumbing, rather obsessively, as she hosts them in her home. Between the metaphoricity of sexual difference through plumbing and the obvious phallic play with the shotgun, some have read Fefu's character as male-identified.[53] In these readings, her foil character is the hysteric Julia, who persecutes psychiatrists whom she calls her ghostly judges. The external force of the outside, as patriarchy, leaks into Fefu's home, clogs up the plumbing, and seeps into the affective traffic of the stage through sadomasochistic games—games of power that thrill and debase in turn. But the play centers embodied women who philosophize in intimate, quotidian conversation. At times they verge on nervous chatter, but these nerves allow us to learn and think with these women—not to extract knowledge from their flesh but to become wiser as we witness their intimacies putting them into the danger of dialogue and the risky eros of friendship. In the readings that concur with this continuum that opposes hysteria to feminism, there's an implicit telos or valuation—a continuum, by dint of registering hysteria as in relation to but separated categorically from feminism—that refuses to think that there might be a feminist learning that dwells within the bodies of hysterics.[54] This strikes me as particularly ableist and more concerned with a vetting of one's station than one's corporeal knowingness within that station. This tendency to disregard Julia as merely a hysteric, as silent, clashes with the movements of the play itself, which asks us to take pain, whether systemic or inexplicable, seriously. What if we listen, truly listen, to the bodies of people of marginalized genders and races? The pain of these women only becomes revealed after the pleasantries of arrival, through the live wires of processing, intimate catch-ups, and consciousness raising.[55] And while our attention, in this play, is directed at the viscera rather than the surface, we must pivot quickly and concertedly away from a tendency to see viscera and fleshy bodies as so visceral that we don't have to talk about gender and race.[56] Rather, I'm interested in how the play more broadly shows the porosity of skin and the gut—both kinetically linked through the sensorial and the nervous system—as very much affected by and affecting questions of difference.

In this part of the play, Julia leaves the sociality of the play and retires to a room to process her monologue-like, hysterical visions. Julia's scene is the most intense of the durational performances, quadrupled by the iterativity that the second part of the play demands. For this scene, she lies in isolation, prostrate—as the audience enters into her room as her only physical witness. Julia's room is on the first floor, and the stage directions take care to make the play's architecture accessible to her. Her stage directions may be the most poetic stage directions of the play:

(A plain unpainted room. Perhaps a room that was used for storage and was set up as a sleeping place for Julia. There is a mattress on the floor. To the right

of the mattress there is a small table, to the left is Julia's wheelchair. There is a sink on the wall. There are dry leaves on the floor though the time is not fall. The sheets are linen. Julia lies in bed covered to her shoulders. She wears a white hospital gown. Julia hallucinates. However, her behavior should not be the usual behavior attributed to a mad person. It should be rather still and luminous. There will be aspects of her hallucination that frighten her, but the hallucinating itself does not.)[57]

If Julia is the mind of the play, as Fornés claims, her mind is not at all separated from her body, and it speaks through the minor gestures of those with chronic pain, seizures, and neurodiverse relations to sight and reality. Her perceptions and hallucinations foreshadow the anxieties and pains that well up in the third part of the play. She has a foundational, fetid mind here, and Fornés's stage directions take care to respect her neurodiversity, displaying it as sensible, sensual, and sensate. She's out of place, at once in another season of fall as leaves turn to compost, and also out of the house, through set design that takes her deeper within the house and also into the clinic. There, she lays still and narrates the unnarratable through the persecution of the judges whom she dialogues with and pantomimes, saying, "I told them the stinking parts of the body are the important ones: the genitals, the anus, the mouth, the armpit. . . . He said all those parts must be kept clean and put away. He said that women's entrails are heavier than anything on earth."[58] These entrails are the terrain of the hysteric's somatic sensitivity. If we think through the etiology of hysteria—that is, if we take seriously that hysteria tells us something about the soma of the body and don't discard it as a mere symptom of living in the patriarchy—then we may be afforded an occasion to learn how the hysterical body works through somatic conversion. And in a play more generally concerned with worms that rot and plumbing, abjection often marks a place for fascination, provocation, and thought. Julia's inexplicable disability separates her from the others, and the audience witnesses the only interiority of the play revealed not through dialogue but through a trance-like set of hallucinations in which Julia speaks with persecutory judges. That is, the only access we get to her mind may be admittance that is less than conscious.

The extraordinary scenes and relations between the women in the play are far too numerous and too intricate for me to do justice to each in this chapter. What I would like to offer, though, is an analysis of the pedagogy that marks *Fefu and Her Friends*—one rather disinterested in identity content or rational knowledge. Much like how she crafted her workshops, Fornés traffics in a pedagogy that cedes intentionality and confession in favor of what remains unknown to the rational mind— what dwells in willful bodies that are not always clear on what they communicate. In "Six Small Thoughts on Fornes," Sarah Ruhl writes that "Fornes is doing something we rarely see nowadays—interrogating the limits and possibilities of the will rather than naming the neuroses that feed on a theatre of confessional intents and intentional confessions."[59] Naming neurosis means that one believes in the purchase of a pathological diagnosis—faith residing in an exposure of madness and a categorization of unreason. Interrogating the limits and possibilities of the will does something other than initiate the confessional mode. Rather than learn to understand the motives behind characters, like detectives or armchair psychologists, the audience affectively and physically traffics with characters in *Fefu and Her Friends*, peeking into intimate and incomplete windows of dialogue and sparks of debate. Ruhl writes that Fornés's characters operate with a "willful opacity."[60] Perhaps this willful opacity grants her characters a kind of complexity that an easy identity plot would eschew, because identity plots often overemphasize agency, confession, and politically expedient plots. In a Fornésian world, characters are not meant to be liberated or even entirely understood. We may not know why Fefu or Christina or Julia do what they do, but we begin to see the ensemble of their differences even though they are all women coming together under a common cause. They disagree, they tease, they flirt, they process old lesbian loves, they play with guns, they hallucinate, and they chase one another in a water fight punctuated by the infectious, thrilling noise of women's laughter. And all these interactions and intra-actions are kinetically expressed through reach, touch, recoil, and other bodily gestures. Sarah Ahmed reminds us that will and willfulness are deeply embodied as forms of political resistance: "Willfulness becomes a vital and shared inheritance: bodies can remember what has not been fully erased from themselves and from other bodies that have become parts of the social body.... Thinking of willfulness as embodied and shared vitality might help us to think of how willfulness is not always expressed as a no."[61]

And indeed, Fornés did not consider this play as something against men, or against anything.[62] She thought of it as an intimate gathering with friends, friends she was very happy to have, friends that breathed so intimately in her writerly mind that they eschewed plot, refusing to serve a storyline. In this manner, the women of the play cannot be reduced to archetype, symbol, or allegory. And this lack of significatory closure resists a politicization that is instructive on how to get out of these intimacies and tensions. One of Fornés's notable protégées, Jorge Cortiñas, adroitly sums up the work of part 2 of *Fefu and Her Friends*: "[a] play that divides its audience into four groups and makes each of them simultaneously see a different middle act is a play that is trying to avoid the ossification that haunts everything that is finished."[63]

Concerns of the Educator

In a visually striking play with almost too many women, we feel their togetherness more than we see it. We experience it. After the disorienting and upheaving scattering of the audience—now all the more aware of themselves as the audience after seeing and feeling the performative labor of these actors' repetition—part three of the play opens with the difficulty of difference itself:

> CECILIA: Well, we each have our own system of receiving information, placing it, responding to it. *(She sits in the center of the couch; the rest sit around her.)* That system can function with such a bias that it could take any situation and translate it into one formula. That is, I think, the main reason for stupidity or even madness, not being able to tell the difference between things.[64]

Cecilia here reminds us that to reduce all of these women to one formula would be madness, even stupidity. Asked for clarification by Sue, she goes on: "Like . . . this person is screaming at me. He's a bully. I don't like being screamed at. Another person or the same person screams in a different situation. But you know you have done something that provokes him to scream. He has a good reason. They are two different things, the screaming of one and the screaming of the other. Often that distinction is not made."[65] Here, we see affect and emotional outbursts being put into distinction of context and kind. Not all screams are alike. Not all men scream at women for the same reason. Cecilia takes this problem of reactivity—a formulaic mode of responding to difference and to difficulty—and develops this problem of distinction and information into group logics. These differences, their need for support, these are the difficulties of being together:

> We cannot survive in a vacuum. We must be part of a community, perhaps 10, 100, 1000. It depends on how strong you are. But even the strongest will need a dozen, even one who sees, thinks, and feels as he does. The greater the need for that kind of reassurance, the greater the number that he needs to identify with. Some need to identify with the whole nation. Then, the greater the number the more limited the responses and thoughts. A common denominator must be reached. Thoughts, emotions that fit all, have to be limited to a small number. That is, I feel, the concern of the educator—to teach how to be sensitive to the difference in ourselves as well as outside ourselves, not to supervise the memorization of facts. Otherwise the unusual in us will perish.[66]

This need for identification and analogical affect accrues into the most repressive and stultifying of group logics: nationalism. And nationalism in this logic is not wrong simply because it is idealistic or fantasy-driven, but also because the common denominator that needs to be reached to hold together such an affective system vastly diminishes affective possibility. And these issues—of difference, sense, and identity—are the concern of the educator. So rather than teaching knowledge, or supervising the memorization of facts, a sensitivity to difference within and beyond the self becomes the concern of pedagogy. Otherwise, "the unusual in us will perish."

Cecilia's theory of difference and identification poses an implicit critique of homogenizing group logics that makes the task of teaching race, gender, and sexuality risky. I want to pause and consider how this functions pedagogically, in order to render what's often seen as identity politics as a weak theory, a local theory. Students come to classrooms marked by the study of what Robyn Wiegman aptly calls "identity knowledges."[67] We know that these studies—Latinx studies, gender studies, postcolonial studies, Black studies, and so on—come from student protest and resistance. But when we, those charged with teaching these studies, rely too heavily on the clear referentiality of these terms, we absolutely perish the unusual. How do we make difference more than a theme? How do we keep its helpful articulation of community without policing membership or squashing dissent? And how might all this require not just a rational thinking of difference but also an acknowledgment of the embodied risk and uncomfortable feelings that arise in these spaces? How might all this entail a radical curiosity and loss of ego, a precarious balance of risk and vulnerability?

Julia's hysteria, her somatic conversion, is taken seriously, porously, and dangerously—she portends danger to Fefu, and Fefu tries desperately to shake her from her reveries, but her body is somehow already under the grips of what it already knows opaquely through her nerves and entrails—the weighty parts of an overdetermined and intelligent body. The play concludes with Julia's mysterious death. Always trigger happy, Fefu shoots and kills a white rabbit in the garden, which also, somehow, kills Julia. Recall that Fefu claimed Julia knew of some secret to their mutual persecution and mental torture. If these characters are foils, their desires, bodies, and psyches are radically entangled and porously linked—rather than existing on opposite poles. By the end of *Fefu and Her Friends*, everyone has come together around the body of Julia, who dies by proxy—a blow received in tandem, inexplicably, with the white rabbit that Fefu shoots and kills. We have no answers to motive, no recourse to blame, but we are left with a glimpse into the lessons of coming together that remain difficult as we look upon this tableau. Julia's death may register as phantasy (in the Kleinian sense) or as an extension of Fefu's violence toward her just a few moments prior when Julia announced herself as contagious. This announcement confirmed Fefu's fears, which led Fefu to get closer to her. Fefu asked Julia to fight and, as she asked her to fight, she started to physically fight with Julia—who had been suffering in her bodymind and was using a wheelchair. This scene is shockingly violent and tender—we witness an altogether abject scene, a moment in which care and aggression bleed into each other as Fefu's desperate love turns quickly to violence, with Julia occupying a terribly ambivalent exchange, redoubled a moment later by her death. If Julia's is the mind of the play, hers communicates in ways that do not represent an elsewhere but something connected to, if not within, Fefu.

What is transmitted here is not knowledge from stage to audience or from body to mind but rather something that resists both ideation and cognition. Because she is the bodymind of the play, it must end with Julia's death—a death she may have understood at the level of soma, a death that remains inexplicable to us in the audience.

We don't know who or what kills Julia, but we know it's not a causal relation in a one-to-one manner—it is, rather, systemic like many deaths produced by a multisystemic failure of the body and of society. More generally, the audience knows very little after experiencing and feeling *Fefu and Her Friends*. Rather, we are thrown into the physics and kinesthesia of people in tense relation. These are the violent dynamics at play under the polished rock of the Enlightenment, the worms that churn against polite presentation, the difficulties of any political commitment based on an avowed shared identity. Learning and how we learn becomes more important than the content of learning, and that is formally mimicked in the fact that we don't know the precise educational campaign that has brought these friends together.

Fornés's plays are often regarded as Lehrstück plays—defined by a Brechtian technique that enables the process of learning often through the breakdown between the audience and the play. For instance, Penny Farfan links this aspect of Fornés's plays in order to consider the lessons for feminists: "In this Lehrstück, then, Fefu's male-identification is ultimately as self-destructive and ineffectual a strategy of resistance to women's subordination within patriarchal culture as Julia's hysteria."[68] Yet we may pause here to note that hysteria is not a resistance as such if we take seriously Wilson's interventions. Secondarily, Fornés does not understand this play itself to be resistant, and indeed, it's hard to see it as a play from which one may gain political takeaways. Roy Pérez articulates Fornés's particularly subtle and formal engagement with gender: "Many of these strategies often enact challenges to masculinist ways of thinking and being: respectively, structures that break up the proscenium for more intimacy, poetic language that is more interrogative than declarative, and plays with mostly or only women characters."[69] Randi Koppen writes convincingly of Fornés's theater as philosophical, and it is often an experiment in understanding elemental aspects of language, violence, and the fraught operations of being a person in relation to others on a playing field that's anything but level. Yet, this philosophical inquiry does not yield discrete knowledge. Or put another way, we do not learn content in this play—instead, what is learned is something that registers at the level of a gut check. Koppen describes Fornés's approach as something akin to Gertrude Stein's poetics:

> On Fornés's stage representation does not invite mastery. Holding back, retreating as it were behind its own surface (its aesthetic materialism), this theater always leaves part of the spectacle unmastered. Fornes's pedagogical project is to transmit knowledge, understood as "wisdom," "illumination," "a charge of some understanding," that is inseparable from (and arises in) the spectacle, contingent on a viewing that is not the "protection against contamination" but that attends to the visual in another way. What we have . . . are not spectacles given to the all-encompassing gaze, but rather sightings which invite an entirely different way of engaging with the visual: a look which forgoes mastery.[70]

Forgoing mastery, Fornés's lessons manifest viscerally as feelings of truth that register at a level below consciousness.

I use the term *gut check* here, and also in this chapter's title, in order to conjure some of Eve Kosofsky Sedgwick's insights in her later scholarship on Melanie Klein. I do so to lay out how both Klein and Fornés present us subjects, or characters, that are unideal, hurting and loving one another in recurrent patterns beyond intention. In thinking about Klein in the realm of pedagogy, Sedgwick states, "I feel enabled by the way that even abstruse Kleinian work remains so susceptible to a gut check. It may not be grounded in common sense, but it is phenomenologically grounded to a remarkable degree. A lot of this quality is owing to the fact that Klein's psychoanalysis, by contrast to Freud's, is based in affect and offers a compelling account of the developments and transformations of affective life."[71] Sedgwick notes that Klein's work satisfies her on a visceral level—as something that may appear strange but is true. And while Klein does not have a theory of race or gender, the clunkiness of her work and the unideal relations it accounts for offer those of us who work on marked difference a way to account for interpersonal and intramural violence. Klein's work often brings up uneasy feelings, since she traffics in a thoroughly embodied and physical terrain, so much so that introjection becomes a quite literal and figurative process—which itself is a rather catachrestic operation, if we consider figures like the good and bad breast, the eviscerating aggression of an infant, and the internalization of real people into our psyches, all of which makes phantasy hard to discern at the level of the literal. Sedgwick highlights how, for her, Klein is a thinker of chunky, thingly psyche: "But the invitingly chunky affordances of Klein's thought probably have most to do with a thematic aspect of her view of psychology: it's she who put the objects in object relations. In her concept of phantasy-with-a-p-h, human mental life becomes populated, not with ideas, representations, knowledges, urges, and repressions, but with things, things with physical properties, including people and hacked-off bits of people."[72] This marks a wisdom that both Fornés and Klein, in their elemental configurations of object relations, allow us to understand: that we live in violent systems that seldom communicate transparently and also that aggression is built into this system. So rather than disavow our unsavory, fetid feelings, we may do better by turning over the polished rocks and looking at those worms, considering the risk of being in community, and reckoning with violences that permeate under the conditions of oppression and not always indexed to it.

It's true that one of the leading sources on Fornés is Fornés herself, not because of the coincidence of her person and her work, but because her pedagogical work, it seems to me, drove her to articulate some of her craft and method, as she herself was not traditionally trained. Reading Fornés on Fornés feels as ludic, as flirtatious, and as willfully opaque as reading her plays. The conundrum before me is that I want to tell you what I've come to know of this charming playwright. And I'm sensuously and indefatigably charmed by her biography—at times shamelessly so. My critique of the biographical hermeneutic is less concerned with getting rid of biography as a frame of reference or context. Instead, I would wager that when the biographical story becomes a hermeneutic, when the coincidence and supposed order and arrangement of a life are explained in a text, we're deadening both the life and the text. What if, instead, we treat the life and the art as porously related? This suggests that they may be related and communicative but still sensuously excessive in communication and correspondence: much like the relation between one's gut and one's peripheral nervous system.

These systems create inscriptions and entangle us in the crosshairs of nerves, guts, and marked difference with the suspension of a final, discernible meaning. Fornés sees plays and art as teachers fundamentally—and warns that if we want art to teach us, we shouldn't rush too quickly to understand it. For her, engaging with theater is an act of thought that is elemental and sensuously material: "The action of words coming out or forming in the brain is a delicate one. It is as if words are dampness in a porous substance—a dampness that becomes liquid and condenses. As if there is a condensation that is really the forming of words. I want to catch the process of the forming of thought into words."[73] Catching this process is delicate and requires a theatrical language of learning rather than knowing, of thought forming and condensing rather than thought congealing. Such a process entails risk. These risks are delicate but dangerous, and the act of creation must be spared from an overdetermined ego:

> The creative system is something so delicate and easily damaged that I would never impose anything on it. I know it has its own mind and its own will and that system is my boss. If I think I know what I want to write about, I soon find out I can't write at all. But if I start writing and am patient enough, I sooner or later find something which is in the lower layers of my being and that is the thing I should be writing about. These things are passionate yearnings that activate my writing and activate me as a person. Sometimes these things are minute, sometimes they are puzzling, but if I am patient and a good observer they will always reveal themselves to me and uncover the nature of the work I am doing, like pieces of a larger mass that crumble and reveal its nature.[74]

This creative system is minded, willful, and heterogeneous, guiding Fornés's creativity and teaching us about how to channel pain and passionate yearnings. These minute, enigmatic bits require patience and attendance. Like the worms under the rock, if we observe long enough, we may come to know them as fragments of a crumbled mass. In this manner, Fornés's pedagogy and theater traffic in difference without imposition, without authorial mastery, and without a dictate that coerces its difference into mimeticism or forces it to impart easy, moral lessons. Instead, her writing becomes a careful observation of thought forming, of women enervating one another, and of deaths that can't be explained with just one bullet and one person.

Creating dangerously as an autodidact is a decided talent of the immigrant artist, as Edwidge Danticat reminds us with her imperative: "Create dangerously, for people who read dangerously."[75] For Fornés, writing necessarily employs risk: "We must take very delicate chances—delicate because they are dangerous, and delicate because they are subtle; so subtle that while we experience a personal terror it could be that no one will notice. It is this danger which in my mind is very connected to what is truly creative."[76] This terror sounds akin to the raw nerves of women and to the forming of thought into language when that language is not the one you were born into. In the danger, we find the potential of the creative—a legacy of learning that refuses to translate into didactic lessons on difference. Both Fornés and Danticat charge creativity with danger—a danger all too easily diffused in our fields of study as they domesticate difference.

María Irene Fornés's pedagogical lessons on negative affects and uneasy relations that dwell in the lower sensorium—both through her teaching in the workshop and her plays embodied on the stage—always gravitate toward the mercurial, the difficult, and the underbelly rather than the underdog. Permit me to close this chapter with an attention to viscera in Fornés's own words. Though Fornés appreciated the critical claim academia did afford her when it glanced in her direction, she deplored the way academic analysis tried to capture a work of art in a categorical frame. She said this kind of analysis was like trying to "push the baby back into the womb," adding that "you cannot get back to the source from the extract."[77] If one cannot get back to the source, or *mater*, from the extract, we then need to take seriously the lessons gleaned from the extract itself. In this same piece of writing, Fornés aligns creativity with risk and aging through loss of ego. And though she acknowledges how her age has afforded here a cessation in egotistical control over work, she nuances this aging formulation and amends that she doesn't feel at all that she's aging because she's not a mother, but a daughter: "On the other hand, I don't think I'm aging an hour. Part of it is because my mother is one-hundred-and-two years old, and when I'm with her I'm a baby. In comparison to my mother I'm a kid."[78] Fornés's mother lived to 103 years of age and often accompanied her to plays and productions, helping in the background and with costumes.[79]

The pedagogical legacy of Cuban American playwright María Irene Fornés and her figuration as the mother of the American avant-garde as well as Latinx playwrights necessitates a rethinking of this pedagogy against the matricidal tendency to render mothers as fertile, dead ground for progeny rather than as writers in and of themselves. The problem of calling Fornés a mother is not simply rhetorical but also is an ill fit even in the metaphorical sense—it may be a catachrestic figuration of Fornés that is rather worn out. Fornés as a teacher and a playwright employed a pedagogy more akin to the explosive opacity and creativity that drives her aesthetic—one that refuses to be the programmatic ground upon which could be assembled nearly or neatly mimetic futures. If the maternal function becomes a techne of reproducibility, no one can claim to have reproduced Fornésia. Instead, her theater and pedagogical legacy invite us back into the ludic play of plays through her daughterly position. In her oeuvre, we find a theater that inscribes willful opacity, difficult object relations, and ludic flirtations with absurd and violent affects, translated from the world of Latin American letters to the off-off Broadway stage. Her privileged tropes of viscera and a potential biological unconscious abide such a pedagogy—insisting upon a material opacity as an invitation to plumb lower sensualities and visceral feelings. Her tropes feature the entanglement of guts, ugly feelings, and dangerous nerves that defy any simple relegation of a maternal host to futurity or to serve as a bridge to representational politics or liberated futures. Instead, Fornés's performative pedagogy operates through a willful opacity, a creative danger at the core of her plays and creative process that dwells within the murky terrain of unknowing, a lack of intention, and constricted object relations.

Perhaps this is what's most striking about the documentary I referred to earlier in this chapter—Fornés started collaborating with the filmmaker, Michelle Memran, as she also began to understand that she was suffering from bouts of dementia. She consented to keep being the subject of the film even after a loss of memory and sense of self, a heartbreaking commitment to the lessons that losing ego might teach us about what it means to be in relation to one another when self-consciousness itself leaves, when memory is strained. Memran's documentary, however, does not document Fornés in mental decline so much as the documentary becomes one last place for Fornés to inscribe her witticisms and ludic flirtations through the camera's capture—a lens to which Fornés often turns as not recipient but lover. Memran offered up the camera as a writing pad—creating an occasion for Fornés to captivate an audience through her words and gestures.

Fornés created a pedagogy in which it becomes possible to consider creativity as inherently porous, delicate, and corporeal, as akin to the nervous or digestive system full of forces, flows, and pulls. Of writing, she says, "In a sense, each time you're a baby who feels nervous about stepping on strange ground. You think you've lost it. You wonder, what is the place I'm in. You feel you will never be able to find your way back. You have to have that fear because you are always on new ground. You're always renewed, and young, and ignorant and afraid. But also you have the energy of feeling something is happening, and that gives you enormous courage."[80] How does this ethos complicate any figuration of Fornés as a maternal host to Latinx playwriting futures? How does it complicate feminist desires for mothers we can place in the past? Renewed, young, ignorant, and afraid become states that enable the risk needed to invoke the energetic forces of creation. Fornés's theater and her approach to creativity more generally desired the risk of creativity—creating a kinetic theater that enervates and frustrates desires for political content as indexed to identity or as understood by route of identity. Her larger praxis over her career of blending pedagogy with craft by writing alongside her students created the conditions, both aesthetically and materially, for a whole legion of Latinx playwrights to write their works. How can we who teach at the intersections of art and difference learn this lesson? How can we, too, create conditions whereby we may undermine the masterful discourse of difference adjudicated by a now increasingly threatened institutional practice of diversity, equity, and inclusion (DEI) and reinstall risk into our relations to institutional power? Antonio Viego charges Latinx studies with this very task of disrupting institutional deadening—asking it to employ hysteric critique that undoes the pretense to mastery.[81] Here, mastery is understood as a faith in the transmission of pedagogy in one-to-one communication and also as the possibility of fully grasping or capturing knowledge. That is to say, Latinx studies need not be exhausted by explanations of latinidad in order for it to do any disruptive work. To exhaust Latinx difference would be to consign it and its constituents to the terms of the university, which domesticates and nullifies difference—usually and often by naming it. Perhaps what we learn from Fornés's legacy as a playwright and pedagogue is the task of creating spaces and discourses where we may contend with the less-than-savory aspects of being in relation to others, where we may plumb our studies beyond the rational humanistic bent, and where we may hold spaces where others may write demanding texts that make the reader, or the audience, alive to an experience that cannot be captured by the words that cling to Fornés herself: Latina, mother of playwrights, queer. We would, then, be in the space of the daughter taking risks by forging inscriptions that do not mimic their source.

4

Losing the Pack

Tracking Loss, Tracing Animals, and Longing for Belonging

You do not have to be good. You do not have to walk on your knees for a hundred miles through the desert repenting. You only have to let the soft animal of your body love what it loves.
—Mary Oliver, "Wild Geese"

Living on borders and in margins, keeping intact one's shifting and multiple identity and integrity, is like trying to swim in a new element, an "alien" element. There is an exhilaration in being a participant in the further evolution of humankind, being "worked" on. I have the sense that certain "faculties"—not just in me but in every border resident, colored or non-colored—and dormant areas of consciousness are being awakened. Strange, huh? And yes, the "alien" element has become familiar—never comfortable, not with society's clamor to uphold the old, to rejoin the flock, to go with the herd. No, not comfortable but home.
—Gloria Anzaldúa, *Borderlands / La Frontera*

A raucous and clamorous want, in the face of scarcity, marks the opening lines of Justin Torres's 2011 novel *We the Animals*. The novel begins with a vignette entitled "We Wanted More," which is also the first sentence. The following line echoes and launches around a sonorous table that enumerates and pulses with a resilient desire for this "more": "We knocked the butt ends of our forks against the table, tapped our spoons against empty bowls; we were hungry. We wanted more volume, more riots."[1] The "we" here are three boys, brothers, exemplified through the sum of their parts: "We were six snatching hands, six stomping feet;

we were brothers, boys, three little kings locked in a feud for more."[2] As this opening vignette progresses, we see boys fighting for heat, blood, and flesh—aching under the spankings that their father doles out, hunting for tiny animals like frogs, asking captured birds "Who's your daddy?" and "always scratching for more." Then the opening vignette turns, abruptly, to other moments. If the previous ones were marked by boyhood, rambunctiousness, and daddies, the moments that follow flow into a mercurial time of stillness, quiet, and gentleness marked by calm mornings: "When the air was still and light, those mornings when silence was our secret game and our gift and our sole accomplishment— we wanted less: less weight, less work, less noise, less father, less muscles and skin and hair. We wanted nothing, just this, just this."[3] These mornings of "just this" become places of rest as they let their mother sleep— their night-shift-working mother, described as a "confused goose of a woman" with "mixed-up love," as if there's any other kind.[4] This vignette shifts in both tone and syntax, moving from thuds and bangs and short, syncopated, stabbing sentences into a flowing sentence twenty-one lines long that spills into places of stillness and mornings sprawled in silence and spent drawing, allowing their work-worn mother to merely sleep. This languorous and elongated style recalls Molly Bloom's soliloquy that marks the unpunctuated end of James Joyce's *Ulysses*. And in this space, the "we" of this brother pack elongates into a stretched-out space of tranquility—wanting less. In this opening vignette, we begin to see the different animalities, or animacies, and deep ambivalences that mark the tempos and modes this pack of boys navigate as they grow together in a terrain marked by femininity and masculinity,[5] latinidad and whiteness, and most prominently, the animal and the human.

This chapter tracks these ambivalent animal metaphors as a form of tropological resistance to genres of liberal humanism in the 2011 novel *We the Animals* by queer, Puerto Rican American writer Justin Torres. Set in upstate New York, Torres's novel immerses one in an architectonic of distilled vignettes—rendered through almost filmic flashback scenes—that, stitched together, create a tapestry of a family: three boys born to a set of working-class parents who are a white mother and an Afro-Puerto Rican father. Figured as mutts, among other animals, these boys blur the boundaries between animality and humanity through their experimentations with belonging. One figure, though, emerges later in the text as the unnamed narrator and separates himself from his "pack" as he comes to embody his own queer desires. In this novel, which is so far flung from Puerto Rican communities on the island and in New York City, we see the story of a bicultural home wherein three brothers navigate how they are read according to a world that is predominantly white. While most readers of the novel emphasize its queer liberatory potential, my reading centers on meditations of loss and ambivalence that do not map onto a political program. In what follows, I read this novel alongside queer of color and critical race studies that consider how animality figures in relation to marked difference. I do so in order to engage with matters of race, gender, and language that refuse to reduce all humanisms to the conceptualization of either the Enlightenment or the posthumanist turn that sees matters of race and gender as merely human concerns. I argue that the novel lures readers into familiar tropes of humanism only to refuse or frustrate them. Bear in mind that the novel was published only three years after the landmark Prop 8 legislation in California—a not-so-distant historical event that served as an occasion to sediment false notions that Blackness and brownness were (1) disentangled from queerness and also (2) homophobic. This knee-jerk, white supremacist analysis scapegoated Black families and other families of color, claiming they were deterrents to gay liberal politics' nearly obsessive telos of marriage equality.

While luring readers into this potential fiction, one that gets played out to exhaustion, *We the Animals* ultimately uses animalities, animal metaphors, and animacy as irritants to a strident neoliberal fantasy of Latinx familial relations that opposes latinidad and queerness. Rather than figuring the queer, racialized child as a victim of his family's composite structures of belonging, Torres ends his novel on a note of undecidable, radically ambivalent animality that takes the narrative beyond liberatory humanist promise and into the opaque, uncertain terrain of desire and loss. But the losses figured in Justin Torres's novel are not losses that we would even be able to recover. If, as Antonio Viego has so astutely observed, loss is precisely not a politics given to ethnic-racialized subjects, then the losses figured here are ones that are more often granted to subjects who indulge in the melancholic, the grief of growing up, and the difficulty of being linguistically fraught animals. What we see, instead, is a refusal of the telos of the bildungsroman—deferring the logos of man and the uprightness of self-sameness. This refusal partakes in a narratological mode of what Iván A. Ramos writes as unbelonging: "an attempt to go beyond states of injury *produced* by forms of inequality and instead linger on what it means to embrace a sense of illegibility that in turn makes the promises of belonging undesirable."[6]

In *Scales of Captivity*, Mary Pat Brady shows how racial capitalism and coloniality employ scalar imaginations in order to increase captivity. Her focus on the figure of the child is helpful for my reading of *We the Animals*. In particular, the critique of the bildungsroman shows how dangerous narratives of development and rectitude can be: "Moreover, if scale holds a lien on our imagination, so, too, does its literary minion, the novel of development. The bildungsroman—the story of an orphan, of a cast-out child's progress through trials and suffering to achieve social integration and assimilation—is profoundly familiar, which is to say resonant with the coercive tactics that produce racializing capitalism, including the castagories that limn rectitude: heterosexuality, white propriety, and civility."[7] In refuting discourses of development and rectitude, we come to a critique of humanism that considers queer density and a critique of scale as instituting a hierarchy of peoples through techniques of capture. Torres writes *We the Animals* in modes that lure us into thinking that we might be reading something like a developmental discourse across several genres (most notably, the bildungsroman, Darwinian evolution, and the coming out narrative) that promises something like progress. It is a progress or developmental narrative that Torres teases out, plays with, and ultimately thwarts with his animal metaphors—metaphors that tempt us to believe we will arrive at an upstanding human story, a coming out story, a story that liberates a young, mixed-race queer from a stifling homophobic family. But to read *We the Animals* in this manner is precisely not to read the strange and gorgeous articulation of a subject who only comes to know himself as uneasy. As the narrative progresses the relational, "we" gives way to the telos of the "I" with knuckles uncurled, standing upright, and breathing easily that marks something like the narrative's horizon and ambivalent ending, one that I argue exposes our own readerly trainings that go against a more complicated notion of kinship and desire. If there is a zoo in *We the Animals*, it's one that keeps us in the mindset of the possibilities of the pack, in the registers of multiplicity, and in the rough circuits that come with most families and certainly mixed families. The most culminative violence in *We the Animals* is not against a queer victim as such but is instead the drive toward the first-person singular "I" in a thinned-out pack—a narrator alone, exposed and exposing the pest that is subjectivity and the drunken dreams of liberal humanism. *We the Animals* is a novel whose glinting edges smart your eyes and whose crystalline vignettes send a wash of childhood feels over our otherwise trained readerly desires, rending us from assured footing as we work our way through uncannily familiar tropes—exquisitely tender and uncertainly articulated. The book is a gorgeous, fragmented, and choral backward glance at childhood, at queer becomings, at far-flung families, at growing up biracial and uneasy in a predominantly white culture, and in the economic tight hold of racial capitalism that affords so few a chance at escape. But in place of escape, we have reflection and reverie. The fragmented reveries suture together an amalgamation of childhood, boyhood, and queerness as jubilant and resourceful and shame-ridden and graceful—both wild and terribly confined, both loving and hurting, often in the same moment. The animality in *We the Animals* leaps beyond the page and into the mythos of growing up, as if we ever do.

Let's return to the novel itself and trace these animal metaphors as they move from the plural to the singular. In the face of scarcity, it becomes difficult to track precisely what the composite "we" of the novel desires. The wanting of less shifts, once again, when the boys start up their rambunctious play with condiments in the next vignette, "Never-Never Time." The narrative voice stays in the relational perspective of "we," of the boy-animal pack, and shows the brothers experimenting with Gallagher's version of a spoof on infomercials with his notorious Sledge-O-Matic: "We had seen it on TV: a man with an untamed mustache and a mallet slaughtering vegetables, and people in clear plastic ponchos soaking up the mess, having the time of their lives. We aimed to smile like that."[8] The movement of this vignette mimics the strange undoing that a night shift's temporality can induce. While explaining that their mother works the graveyard shift, the vignette slips into mercurial time to explain the ways in which the boys learn to accommodate the mother's untimely mothering. Instead of correcting her, which they had in the past and which resulted in her exclaiming that she hates her life, they enter into her temporal (dis)orientation. "Just this," the temporal space that marks the desire for less that the boys exhibit in the opening vignette, may be a stolen moment in the middle of the night making a cake or preparing a meatloaf for dinner at 8 a.m. When attuning to their mother's night shift worker rhythms, the collective boys "lived in dreamtime."[9] When the mother wakes up to this prop comedy full of expenditures—tomatoes slaughtered, lotion and creams squirted about, and three young boys covered in gruesome viscosity—there is a tense anticipation of maternal anger. After all, Ma wakes up to a mess when she has very little time for "just this." In her maternal time, cleaning time eats into sleeping time and loving time and caring time, when there is no spare time, nor spare money. And quite frankly, there's never enough time for mothering. But in never-never time you're not exactly in time or in sync.

This vignette unfolds under the title of "Never-Never Time," which is a poetic revision of Peter Pan's Never-Never Land where children cease to grow into adults. *Never* itself is an adverb of time, a negation of a temporal rupture. It may be that something has never occurred, thus illuminating what time has not allowed, or it can be that something should never happen again. It is a negative absolute of time transferred, at times, onto land. How can land be not ever? How can the time-space of maternal succor seem elusively unassimilable into progress, into development, and into the capitalist clock? The term *never-never* not only doubles a negative of time, remarking that this time has never happened as such, but it also recalls that *never-never* has its origins in place and debt: the Australian outback has been referred to as "Never Never," and "Never Never" has also been a form of high interest, installed payment for goods in the United Kingdom. In the more explicit allusion to Never-Never Land, remade here as a time-space, the text recalls that latchkey kids have different childhood spaces, with a parent or parents who cannot abide normative time-scripts for either maternity or paternity. Never-never time would be the time that remains unaccounted for in the quotidian capitalist temporal arrangements: the time of social reproduction, the time of maternal labor, and the time of night workers who maintain the illusion that an eight-hour workday, not night, would suffice to keep the machinery of capitalism afloat.

Upon waking at 8:15 p.m. on a Sunday, confusing it for 8:15 a.m. on a Monday, Ma exclaims "fuck" twice and finally wakes up enough to see the mess her sons have made: "She gasped no, finally noticing the tomato and lotion streaking down our faces. She opened her eyes wide and then squinted. She called us to her side and gently ran a finger across each of our cheeks, cutting through the grease and sludge. She gasped again. 'That's just what you looked like when you slid out of me,' she whispered. 'Just like that.'"[10] These gasping realizations reset time and optics. The boys wretch at that thought of being born and squirm away from being infantilized. After the boys endure her birth stories and she endures their expressive disgust at having been born, she asks the boys to assume a maternal role with this strange request:

"Do it to me."
    "What?" we asked.
    "Make me born."

Upon realizing that they've smashed all of the tomatoes in the house, the mother suggests ketchup, and the boys prepare her birth scene. On the ground, on her knees, with a chin on the kitchen table, the mother awaits her birth in a raincoat and remains still, having been told to keep her eyes closed. In preparation, the boys become one body, breathing the boyish imaginary version of Lamaze:

"On the count of three," we said, and we each took a number—my number was last. We all took the deepest, longest breath we could, sucking the air through our teeth. Everyone had his face all clenched up, his hands squeezed into fists. We sucked in a little more air, and our chests swelled. The room felt like a balloon must, when you're blowing and blowing and blowing, right before it pops.
    "Three!"
    And the mallet swung through the air. Our mother yelped and slid to the floor and stayed there, her eyes wide open and ketchup everywhere, looking like she had been shot in the back of the head.
    "It's a mom!" we screamed. "Congratulations!" We ran to the cupboards and pulled out the biggest pots and heaviest ladles and clanged them as loud as we could, dancing around our mother's body, shouting, "Happy Birthday! . . . Happy New Year! . . . It's zero o'clock! . . . It's never-never time! . . . It's the time of your life!"[11]

In this impossible primal scene, the three boys assume gendered possessives only in their individuated embodiment as "everyone": "his face" and "his hands." But birth demands collectivity, and they breathe as one body that extends past their individual and collective bodies, encasing their mother in a spatial register that fills the room with tension. This tension before the pop, before the mallet strikes the ketchup bottle, builds into the crescendo scene of celebratory chaos that follows the mallet's impact upon the ketchup. As she's born, the mother yelps, slides to the floor, and looks in amazement as the three sons turn from the ones who birth to the ones who name birth and the time of birth; that is, they move from the maternal function to the role of the doctor who, like a deity, uses language to declare the time of birth and the taxonomic designation of the birthed. Yet the time remains in the "zero o'clock" of originary, catachrestic time, the time of the new, which is no time at all but can be likened to times that reset time—that bend or exist despite normative clocks. Curiously, the mother is not born into gender but rather into maternity. She is having the time of her life. And the time of her life is never-never, is dreamtime.

There's never enough time for motherhood. Or perhaps it's best to separate an actual, physical birth mother and what Elissa Marder calls the "maternal function." Marder marks motherhood as a fundamental techne that is literary and speculative. The rest of the novel will have various forms of birthing that are radically disimbricated from any form of biological maternity and yet radically entangled with it, as well as raciality and affect. Marder explains that the effects of birth, to which we cannot be witness but which is our genesis, infuse the question of birth with multiple meanings: "The meanings of birth produce indelible psychic traces that return throughout one's lifetime in the form of *mechanical reproduction* that to some degree remain radically indecipherable."[12] Reproducibility itself effects a trace logic of a missed event that is one's origin, but that origin is unwitnessed by the object of birth. In this sense, the place of one's birth is also radically unheimlich—pushing the bounds of linear humanist conception and trajectory within a life: "The uncanny properties of the 'maternal function' often become manifest through disturbances of space and time."[13] The event of birth is radically opaque to the one birthed, and this aporia subtends and creates correlations between the maternal function and is indelibly linked to not only time and gender but also race. Not all forms of maternity enjoy the same affordances, or even frustrations. From the couple function to a singular parent to the feminized space of the maternal and into inheritance, the structuration of filiation has remarkable effects upon and for racialized subjects.[14] And while maternity scrambles time, resets clocks, and ushers in scenes of birth that themselves multiply in ambivalence and indeterminacy, so too does maternity here fill a room with corporeal multiplicity and labored breath.

In calling motherhood a place, Amber Musser moves us away from an Oedipal, patriarchal imperative to think the work of parenting as the work of making individual subjects. This implies that the "move way from Oedipus is also a move away from an ethos of recognition and a temporality of development."[15] If this family's story does not fit into tidy scenes of progression and development, it's because to a certain extent, this family does not participate in the kind of Oedipality that produces heteronormative subjects. In "Oedipal Wrecks," Richard T. Rodríguez finds the promise of a Deleuzian "becoming animal" that rends the narrator from Oedipal, heteronormative family arrangements.[16] Deftly reading the movement away from liberal humanist standards of masculinity, Rodríguez argues that the protagonist finds other forms of queer survival that stand in opposition to the family's more normative gender roles. At the same time, we should pay heed to Cathy Cohen's urging that we should not rely too easily on a strict binary between queerness on the one hand and heteronormativity on the other.[17] Many forms of racialization and class disrupt the possibility of enjoying full access to heteronormative privilege and so too does this binary herald the protagonist into the role of sheer victim that disregards his own violence. This fundamentally disacknowledges that all subjectivity is violent. Grateful for Rodríguez's attunement to the queerness of animality, I pivot to a Kleinian psychoanalytic landscape to explore the novel's affective force.

Something very complicated occurs at the level of intimacy, relations, violence, and development in this novel. In its early stages, the boys inhabit something more akin to Melanie Klein's psychoanalytic model of object relations: one wherein objects are infused with phantasy, where succor and harm circulate around each other, and where relationality is both promise and peril.[18] The maternal time is nonlinear, recursive, attenuated to violence and aggression while also nonidealized as a space.

This psychic as well as phenomenal time-space and the mother here can become both victim and oppressor, both hurt and hurting—in other words, a whole object. And as we'll see, this mother is not rendered as merely a hurt animal, as merely a feminine victim of machismo. There is an excess to these scripted roles that lives in the withdrawn aesthetics of these intimate vignettes. Transferred onto children who birth mothers, this dream time aspires to wish fulfillment. And what these children wish for is jumbled, as the opening vignette signals: it is a want for both more and less.

Birthing Shame or Gestures of Heritage for Mutts

While the shifts in feminine and masculine tones are noticeable in the first vignette, after that, the gender roles ascribed do not follow a strict binary: Paps cooks, dances, and bathes his children. This puts pressure on the binary from within intimate scenes where gendered work does not follow a dualistic mode of distribution tout court. So too do scenes of birth iterate and multiply throughout the novel. While the boys learn of their own birth, they in turn stage the scene of a mother's birth—a doubled or invertedly squared motherhood as matrix. And the closest scene we get to a birthing between legs happens not with Ma, but with Paps, who slides the boys between his legs one by one. In the vignette entitled "Heritage," we move from the never-never time of maternity, with its impossible scenes of birth, its mercurial time, and its retracing of a beginning that demands a messy multiplicity to the patrilineal lineage myths that Paps would like to pass on. These myths are ones that have been withheld from Paps himself, but nevertheless, they are the aspirational myths of humanism: linear genealogy, purebred rhetoric, and faith in bloodlines. Switching, again, from maternal time to paternal time, the boys that compose the "we" get home from school to find Paps in the kitchen, cooking while dancing to the beat of a Tito Puente mambo. Waiting in the entranceway to the kitchen, the boys watch on as Paps dances a particularly Afro-Caribbean choreography of informed hips and confident twirling:

> Paps staked staccato steps across the linoleum to where we stood and whipped us onto the dance floor, grabbing our wimpy arms and jerking us

behind him. We rolled our tiny clenched fists in front of us and snapped our hips to the trumpet blasts.

One by one he took us by our hands and slid us between his legs, and we popped out the other side. Then we wiggled around the kitchen, following behind him in a line, like baby geese.[19]

The poetic alliteration of the line and its nimble figures segue from Paps dancing in assonant steps to whipping his three sons onto the dance floor, grabbing their arms, confusing gender roles with them and with his own body. Paps renders himself as both a confident macho dancer and a mother goose—a bird descriptor first assigned to Ma in the opening vignette when she was called a "confused goose of a woman."[20] Paps communicates here through language but more so through gestures rendered ekphrastically in language. To write gesturally, Juana María Rodríguez notes, "is to engage that which exceeds language through language."[21] Language's animacies gesture to the body's semiotics—a gestural form of meaning-making that is sensuous, skilled, and social—a repertoire of body that sometimes sustains culture in diaspora. In a performative autoethnography of dance in her own Cuban-diasporic Connecticut community, Rodríguez writes, "These immigrants' bodies exhausted from the drudgery of factory jobs, the indecipherability of their first-generation children, and the everyday shame of 'no speeke inglish' were transported to other worlds of belonging and worship through dance."[22] Paps's dance takes him further away from his boys as he cranks up the volume and mambo transports him to a time-space where he may have a community of dancers who know how to follow the mambo's opaque commands and meanings, which derive from the Afro-Caribbean's syncretic relation to signifiers. Paps "listens in detail" to a style of music that Alexandra T. Vazquez notes derives from "a detail from Congolese dialect that means a command and an object that carries the pulse of things" and that "*wiggled*, maneuvered, and finagled its way" in the United States.[23] And yet, the transport of such dancing dialect needs more than one to transmit its directives—it needs a felicitous social space to fully resonate.

* * *

This gaggling birth scene functions, narratologically and affectively, as an inauguration through shame into the failure to properly mimic the gestures of this father who births. Shame and heritage are deeply intertwined. Heritage here uses the discourse of purist ethnonationalism while, boldly and ironically, indulging in the gestural and embodied *tumbao* of Afro-latinidad. The appeals are confusing and confused. In this moment, through attention to gesture and sound and its assessments, we are well served to remember that often the family is the site where patriarchal mastery vents its own unsovereign lament.[24] As Paps tries to teach his boy-goslings to mambo to Tito Puente, he more assuredly displays himself in twirls that confound. After the boys, in their goose line, dance as poor, as rich, as white, and as Puerto Rican in front of Paps, who is both judge and jury—emboldened by beer's false hubris and false tenderness—he taxonomizes them as mutts: "'Mutts,' he said. 'You ain't white and you ain't Puerto Rican. Watch how a purebred dances, watch how we dance in the ghetto.'"[25] While this slur stings, its impact on the boys motivates them to strain to learn what their father means, though they can't tell, from language alone and over the cacophony of cooking and the radio, if he's angry or just making fun. Heritage as dance from a diasporic ghetto underscores the notion of a purebred or a mutt as fleeting and ephemeral as the rhythms of corporeal movements, showing how performatives evoke more than the linguistic. Telling them to "watch how a purebred dances," the text then narrates the father's performance in an ekphrastic, whirling language that approximates the complex movements of dance in the Puerto Rican diaspora: "He danced, and we tried to see what separated him from us. He pursed his lips and kept one hand on his stomach. His elbow was bent, his back was straight, but somehow there was looseness and freedom and confidence in every move. We tried to watch his feet, but something about the way they twisted and stepped over each other, something about the line of his torso, kept pulling our eyes up to his face, to his broad nose and dark, half-shut eyes and his pursed lips, which snarled and smiled both."[26] The dance becomes its own kind of semiotics in this short paragraph, and the absorbent attention of a plural set of children's eyes allows one to see the beauty and terror of being shown what you come from but are not. The boys try to witness and yearn to replicate a dance that their father can perform with his eyes half-closed, as he melts into the mambo. With rapt attention, they do their best to study his torso and how it moves at once still and free, the hips being loose, the back being upright, this twisted movement that is *not* the stiffness one would expect from an upright man. It is rather the Afro-Caribbean beat that makes its way into diaspora without translation at the ready. Their eyes move up toward the face, away from the body, tracking Paps's racial register, a register that shows his lips as pursed—a feminine adjective that does indeed show a sensuousness that exceeds white masculinity's relationship to hip movement, to luscious lip appeal, and to dancing and cooking. As the boys try to track and trace his steps, they don't learn a lesson of dance but rather one of inauthenticity. And while shame can educate, in sparse exposure it validates unbelonging: "Instruction occurred through continual exposure and the socially witnessed humiliation of endless trial and error that would validate one's cultural authenticity, or regretfully confirm that the process of North American assimilation had been complete."[27] During his dance, the boys are trying to understand their separation from their father, a separation more often figured in psychoanalytic discourse as the distancing from the maternal body. But what if your mother tongue and mother dance come from your father—a father who shows but doesn't teach, who wins in the game of authenticity as if that's the goal of heritage, to vet rather than nurture his own children? And yet this is often the heritage that remains just out of reach to many first- and second-generation kids. It's no wonder, then, that Spanish, in this country, is often called a heritage language for the younger generations of Latinx peoples for whom their relationship to language carries loss and shame, a shame instilled by parents who wanted to assimilate, wanted to protect their children by only teaching them English, or who simply didn't have the time to teach their children Spanish because they were working.

 The text distances itself from letting this metaphor of heritage become concretized through the phrase "as if." After the father says, "This is your heritage," the text follows, "As if from this dance we could know about his own childhood, about the flavor of tenement buildings in Spanish Harlem, and projects in Red Hook, and city parks, and about his own Paps, how he beat him, how he taught him to dance, as if we could hear Spanish in his movements, as if Puerto Rico was a man in a bath robe, grabbing another beer from the fridge raising it to drink, his head back, still dancing, still stepping and snapping perfectly in time."[28] The "as if" here exposes the intergenerational trauma, violence, and complexity that is "heritage": both a dance and a beating, both flavor and grit, both love and violence. This damage takes part in what Glissant calls root logic, the false mythology that we can all trace our genealogies in a linear root stock. What the boys learn from their father, then, is something about masculinity that's not aligned with white masculinity but is expressed through dance, animality, and cooking—a semiotics of gesture rather than language as such.

The term *mutt* itself is a monstrous figuration, a chimera of animacy and animality with an errant etymology that tells us a bit about the interplay between linguistics variation, animal figuration, and the entanglement of meaning for "humanimals." Originally shortened from *mutton-head*—which is a British English way of referring to a sheep's head—the sheep's head, severed, dead, and ready to be consumed becomes a way of referring to a "dull or stupid person." This *mutton-head* is further clipped, and the head is removed fully to form the word *mutt*, which is a particularly US American slang. And yet, the word *mutt* has a few meanings clustered under its sign that all refer back to real animals, but of lesser value than a sheep, thus functioning like a derogatory that is both raced and gendered:

a racehorse, especially a slow one; any horse in poor condition
a dog, especially a mongrel; also occasionally a mutt dog
a person who is awkward, ignorant, or blundering; an incompetent individual, a fool
without negative connotation, a person, a fellow
an unattractive woman

Mutt and *mulatto* share animalistic, racialized etymologies—a figuration that entangles raced and sexed humans with animals of servitude and supposedly lower sentience. Mel Chen reminds us that language's animacy is largely considered through its relationship to liveliness and to sentience. Such entangled meanings swirl in the figure of the mutt. We will return to the figure of the mutt, as do the boys, when they begin to understand the specific configurations of their lives in relation to the larger, whitened terrain of upstate New York. This aptitude for plumbing the nuances of animistic language helps make clear the vexed terrain of animal metaphors and of racialized slurs. Chen, too, reminds us that slurs are "insults, shaming language, slurs, and injurious speech can be thought of as tools of objectification, but these also, in crucial ways, paradoxically rely on animacy as they objectify, thereby providing possibilities for reanimation."[29]

In a sense of queer animacy, this provisional, very ephemeral collectivity of us plays with properties of grammar akin to the ways in which Mel Chen considers queer animation: "If *queer* was previously understood to be a 'dehumanizing' slur figuring its subjects as abject or 'lesser than,' this formerly 'objectifying' term has taken a life of its own, with the power to *animate* some other object. Here this is meant quite literally, since grammatically speaking an action verb sets the object of the sentence into motion, engages its capacity to be affected. Arguably, the word in some vital ways is thus deobjectified."[30] Chen shows us that this muddled referentiality is not as simple as a put-down but rather operates according to a "reference cline."[31] The performative here functions in the gestural animality that choreographs and confounds humanist ideals of race, gender, and sensuality. The gestural invokes and enfolds animacy into the fabric of the quotidian—in the kitchen—domesticated in while also being exorbitant to that space. Diasporic sounds seep in, demanding a listening in detail that envelopes the senses, exceeding the sonic and the linguistic while invoking both. And this performative choreography is and is not felicitous, depending on where you stand and how you dance and who is there to keep time, to match the beat. Moreover, performativity's felicitousness is contingent on contexts that afford the sociality that would make this sensuous dance more communal—that is, less isolated and less isolating.

While it becomes difficult to keep up with time, numbers gain profound significance in the texture of this work, not least of which is the mobile triangulation of the boys in their tripled, collective "we"—a "we" that turns into three kings,[32] into the three musketeers, into a trinity that is not so much holy as ephemeral, a pack of roving, exploratory, growing boys who collectively come to learn the boundaries that mark their life chances collectively, but not exactly in a manner that translates to the individual. The boys switch between paternal and maternal time, and in the vignette "Seven," we learn a bit more about Ma's relation to boyhood and manhood. The boys have been prohibited from visiting their parents' bedroom because their mother has been convalescing after her face was horribly beaten:

> In the morning, we stood side by side in the doorway and looked in on Ma, who slept open-mouthed, and we listened to the air struggle to get past the saliva in her throat. Three days ago, she had arrived home with both cheeks swollen purple. Paps had carried her into the house and brought her to bed, where he stroked her hair and whispered in her ear. He told us the dentist had been punching on her after she went under; he said that's how they loosen up the teeth before they rip them out. Ma had been in bed every day since—plastic vials of pain pills, glasses of water, half-drunk mugs of tea, and bloody tissues cluttered the floor around her bed. Paps had forbidden us to set foot in the bedroom, and for three mornings we had heeded, monitoring her breath from the doorway, but today we would not wait any longer.[33]

Note the switch from active verbs in the first sentence to passive in the second sentence, and then back to active again in the third onward. This passive voice is telling; it is the evacuation of the subject position of how Ma arrived home with such damage. Paps only appears in the third sentence, after her arrival at home with bruises. We are not witness to the swing and impact of punches but are instead, much like children, witness to the aftermath, the bruises, the healing process that never fully heals or sutures over what's been broken. The boys tiptoe with the quiet reverence used around the hurt and the sick, hiding in the curtains like three monks studying not god but mother—source, matrix, yet vulnerable. Upon waking, she calls them her "beautiful baby boys." Such utterances embarrass her sons, who have learned to question their beauty, question their ease and movements in the world. The narrator has to press his hand against the cold winter glass to shock himself back into his body because "that's how it is sometimes with Ma; I needed to press myself against something cold and hard, or I'd get dizzy." One of the brothers, Manny, points out that it's the protagonist's birthday—a detail that upon utterance ushers the mother back into the temporality of maternal work. She responds in kind with "'Happy Birthday,' . . . the words slightly tinged with pain." The narrator's brother, Manny, feeds a parental detail to Ma, reminding her that today the unnamed narrator is seven, and this further entrenches Ma's pain. She winces and says that when boys turn seven, they leave their mothers by hardening against love and, hence, with the two older, named boys, she had to "let them go—had to harden my heart—they wanted to smash things, wrestle." This makes the two other boys, Manny and Joel, feel "oddly proud." The youngest, our protagonist, rebuts: "I don't want to smash nothing, . . . I want to study God and never get married"—a reference to the earlier performance of monastic life, but in our protagonist's mind, God and mother are entangled.[34] She softens to this statement, cooing at her youngest and saying that it's decided, he will never be seven. When he acts confused at her logic, her stopping of time, her impulse to never-never time, she responds by laying out the math, saying he'll be six forever by just saying he'll be six plus one, six plus two, and so on.

As Ma gets out of bed, she reaches for a hand mirror to examine the damage done to her face. Upon seeing her reflection, her eyes well with tears that stay on the brink:

> Ma could hold tears on her eyelids longer than anyone; some days she walked around like that for hours, holding them there, not letting them drop . . .
>
> Now, Ma held the tears and studied her ugliness. The three of us boys started to back out of the room, but she called for me, said she wanted to talk to me about staying six, but she didn't say much beyond that, just looked and looked in the mirror, turning her jaw at different angles.
>
> "What did he do to me?" she asked.
>
> "He punched you in the face," I said, "to loosen up your teeth."
>
> I jumped at the sound of shattering glass. My brother's two heads instantly appeared back in the doorway, smiling wide, running their eyes from Ma to me, to the broken pieces of mirror, to the spot on the wall where it had been flung, to Ma, to me.[35]

The problem of pronouns here is that they are loosened from antecedents, much like the figures of Ma's teeth. The lack of consensus around who "he" refers to, the dentist or Paps, turns the young son's speech radically excitable, ending in a shattering moment that's narrated in the passive voice. Indeed, the shock of the shatter is experienced precisely because the reader is not afforded the witness of the action. It happens too quickly, and we are jolted by the shatter without having seen, or read, the action of flinging—which is only rendered metaleptically, after the shock of shattering glass. Glass that reflects and glass that is transparent, as a window, feature strongly in this specular moment.

Motifs of eyes and glass stand in for the psychic interiority of characters that stay, at the level of the text, withheld from the reader. So much of this book deals with queerness and latinidad, but in a register that is too zoomed in and too exquisitely sparse and sutured to thematize with ease. Thus, the structure of the book itself affords a nuanced approach to these categories as sensual and violent, poetically rendered and brutally honest—a glinting, multifaceted, crystalline set of vignettes. The protagonist uses his "I" first as an interior reflection, just before he turns seven: "The light reflected back and forth from the white sky to the snow; the light caught in the frost on the window. Outside, it was too bright to focus on any one spot. I opened my eyes as wide as I could, and they burned with light, and I thought about going blind, about how everyone said if you looked right up into the sun, full on, and held your gaze, you'd go blind—but when I tried, I could not blind myself."[36] Light, reflected back in such a way that it interrupts sight and witnessing, figures the pain that one incurs when one looks squarely into the eyes of hurt and hurtful matrices, especially if these light sources are your parents. And yet, the ability to self-obliterate, to cut off witness, is to succumb to the numbingly blind faith of the enlightened. But so too does the self's wish to self-harm easily morph into the harming of another. These intimate close-ups show that the psychic terrain of object relations—a Kleinian sensibility where love, guilt, and reparation work in cycles and not as constants—make even more sense under the strictures of white late capitalist supremacy. My aim here is not to exonerate violence but to shift our frame from a supposedly transparent one that relies on the rhetorical framings of white supremacy to one that truly accepts that, while violence may be inevitable, surely it must be attenuated, and this attenuation as a reckoning exceeds the parameters and agency described within this book. In this way, the book dwells within the now of the child's witness but with an attention to the structures of violence that encase childhoods differentially.

Violence that is structural seeps into the seams of these vignettes, and we sense that just beyond the page, just beyond the tense moments we witness, other storms lurk with terror. Ma confides in her youngest, asking him to stay six, an impossible timeline for this young boy:

> She whispered it all to me, her need so big, no softness anywhere, only Paps and boys turning into Paps. It wasn't just the cooing words, but the damp of her voice, the tinge of pain—it was the warm closeness of her bruises—that sparked me.
>
> I turned into her, saw the swollen mounds on either side of her face, the muddied purple skin ringed in yellow. Those bruises looked so sensitive, so soft, so capable of hurt, and this thrill, this spark, surged from my gut, spread through my chest, this wicked tingle, down the length of my arms and into my hands. I grabbed both of her cheeks and pulled her toward me for a kiss.
>
> The pain traveled sharp and fast to her eyes, pain opened up her pupils into big black disks. She ripped her face from mine and shoved me away from her, to the floor. She cussed me and Jesus, and the tears dropped, and I was seven.[37]

Softness turns to hurt, and hurt spreads across these vignettes and can, at times, create a contagion of violence, a movement wherein the child witnesses his mother's pain and is "sparked" to investigate, through gripping embrace, how tender bruises really are, how kisses can hurt, and how to be thrown into the timeline of boyhood by trying to assuage this soft but also overwhelming need. Rather than dwell in the time of the feminine, in the time of the dream world of soft need, the narrator reaches toward his mother with a ravenous love that hurts, and for this she expels him into manhood, a growth spurt articulated through violence. In this way, the novel refuses a benevolent, sentimental, or ideal rendition of either motherhood or childhood.

In the following vignette, we see the family together seeking a lake's cool refuge during a hot summer night. Here again, survival, violence, and love commingle in such a way that confuses the youngest. Upon nearly drowning, nearly being drowned by both parents whether by force or neglect, he emerges as if in a birth scene "rising up to the light and exploding into the air, and then that first breath, sucking air all the way down into [his] lungs."[38] When he surfaces, self-birthed and safe, at precisely this moment, Frankenstein is invoked:

> I remembered how Ma burst into tears and Paps celebrated, shouting as if he was a mad scientist and I a marvel of his creation:
> "He's alive!"
> "He's alive!"
> "He's alive!"

This triplicate declaration exclaims the narrator's gendered pronouns but not his name, which had been spoken with softness but is entirely withheld from the reader for the whole of the novel. He becomes alive, monstrous, and conglomerate—aching toward language and family but somehow barred. Moving from "he," we come to the vignette "Us Proper."

Impropriety and Pronouns

The narratological legacy of *Frankenstein* carries over into the next vignette, entitled "Us Proper," through the opening scene where bodies are scrapped together to make a whole.[39] In many ways, this vignette deals with the monstrous revelations of having been born. But rather than move in a linear mode of development, with the protagonist raising himself up as a singular monster, the boys combine themselves to become bigger, to become taller, and to experiment with gender. The boys gender this conglomerate creation in the feminine, which has everything to do with ability and positionality:

> When we were brothers, when we were all three together, we made a woman. We stacked up on one another's shoulders and wrapped ourselves in Ma's long winter coat.
> Manny was the bottom, the legs, and Joel was the stomach, and I was the lightest, so I was the woman's head. We used a ladder to keep from tipping over, but Manny's knees buckled under our weight, so we had to lie down on the ground and do it that way; we were a fallen woman who could not get back up, a helpless woman, flat on her back.[40]

Because of his lightness, his diminutive stature vis-à-vis his other brothers, the protagonist does get cast, for a moment, in the role of a woman's head, only to realize there's already too much weight. Headiness is what he will pursue through linguistic acumen and through the pursuit of education. The initial clause in the plural is past, but if it was singular, it would be subjunctive, and it would be speculation. But in this conjugated dive into the past, we see three brothers creating a woman "flat on her back"—an object of sexual aggression, the position of a fallen woman. Invoking the fall, though, is less originary and tidy than the story of Genesis would have it. Here, the positionality is not about being thrown from paradise or even upright subjectivity, within which the boys do not live. Leo Bersani extols this same positionality in "Is the Rectum a Grave?"—a positionality that it might be nice to speculate about as a radical shattering, but such a shattering only creates resistance wherein one has been a proper subject.[41] These boys, this woman, this family have not enjoyed such a seamless relationship to sovereign subjectivity with a plenitude of choice. Choice is often the terrain of a particular kind of subjectivity. Such an assumption of an individualistic subjectivity will be the ambivalent telos of the protagonist, a trajectory that will later cause resentment with his brothers as they sniff out the protagonist's queerness, which is also entangled with the promise of upward mobility. We'll return to this point, but for now let us linger over the curious entanglement of whiteness and femininity with the braininess that will separate him from his pack, that will queer his relation to gender, and that will create a rift in belonging. This woman's head and the difficulty of ascent render this pyramid scheme moot for the boys. Instead, lying down in passivity—not fighting the forces of gravity to assume a monstrous man—allows them to transform into something larger, something differently gendered.

Frankenstein's monster's rage is precisely linked to a lack of heritage, a monstrous origin and taxonomic designation, in which he emerges as a kind of resourceful, though neglected, child—and language is one tool he sharpens to both understand his place in the world and address his maker. Like Frankenstein's monster, too, Torres's narrator remains nameless for the entirety of the novel. Yet this protagonist keeps such linguistic, sharpened thoughts in the realm of both fantasy and phantasy in the Kleinian sense. Frankenstein's monster's articulate rage has been taken up through the pen of many. In particular, Susan Stryker has used that figure to consider familial bonds withheld in normative plenitude as a particular rage that the misfit endures, even in the most intimate spaces of kinship.[42] We have no access to the content of this rage in *We the Animals*, this hurt, and this aggression, but that radical withholding does not evacuate it.[43] Rather, it does not enjoy a causal access and thus keeps the narrator's interiority, as well as name, radically opaque, with only glinting reflections of the depths and machinations below. Perhaps it could be found in the language withheld in the journal, and this withholding gives the narrator a space where his psyche cannot be plumbed in service of an easy morality or a traceable condemnation or teleology.

During this vignette, the boys play with their collectivity—turning a plural personal pronoun into something akin to a proper pronoun. But rather than using "we" in this vignette, the "us" tries to become proper and to monstrously and clumsily assume the subject of the sentence with a pronoun that is always an object. The boys call this their "cave language," and they speak in unison, in tripartite chorus, in the rambunctious clamor of boyhood, declaring things like "Us hungry" or "Us burglars" followed by "Us scared" and "Us fucked."[44] The proper use of "us," then, reminds us that these boys are looking to be subjects of the sentence, but they inhabit the object position—creating a clunky grammar that shows how the proper can be proprietary, how inhabiting the subject of a sentence may not always be available.

A turning point, not uncommon for the bildungsroman or narratives that play with the trope of childhood as Edenic refuge, comes by way of learning about sex:

> We were the Three Billy Goats Gruff crossing the bridge, we were the trolls that lived under the bridge. But after we learned about sex—after Ma sat us down on the carpet and opened the encyclopedia to "Reproductive Systems," after she showed us cross-section diagrams of penises and vaginas and explained how they fit, after all that—we played a new game. No one had explained sex to Ma when she was a kid—not the nuns at school and not her own mother. So when she asked Paps, "Can't I get pregnant from this?" Paps had lied; he had laughed and asked, "This?"

And then there was Manny, all up in Ma's stomach, growing, heart ticking like a time bomb (Ma's words, heart ticking like a bomb), and her only fourteen years old, and Paps only sixteen, both in the ninth grade, and then both dropping out.[45]

The way in which birthing, sexual difference, animality, and knowledge (specifically knowledge tied to language) occurs in this novel is intricate, slippery, and often counterintuitive. This vignette follows scenes of various births, and now we have the science of birth told in tandem with a complicated scene of pregnancy. When the boys learn medicalized terms for their own birth stories, such official knowledge is complemented by Ma's own violent impregnation, a knowledge that exceeds scientificity and enters into the singular *and* structural story of how young Paps and Ma were when the boys were birthed, which in turn allows the boys to see their parents as young and coerced (both interpersonally and structurally). These glimpses in reverse are spare in the novel, but they reveal that this story is encased by and invites an analysis of racial capitalism, geography, and heterosexism. And so too does Ma demarcate the specific gendered and raced corporeal positionalities both parents had to tarry with upon pregnancy and marriage: "She told us how she was eight months fat by then, and Paps was dark and Afroed."[46] This is an origin story told in both intimate confession and scientific discourse, a doubled origin story, biological with all of the weight of the biopolitical and biocentric behind it that enshrouds the material realities of the historicity of this biracial/bicultural young couple.[47] That is, we get both science and flashback, and the two are entangled in a larger sociopolitical, racialized, gendered, and juridical context.

After these two birth stories, the boys are no longer animal in their collectivity:

All three born in Ma's teenage years ("my teenage years," Ma repeated, as if that meant something to us)—after we learned all about that, we were no longer Three Billy Goats Gruff crossing the bridge, we were no longer the three trolls that lived under the bridge.

After that, we played a new game where the trolls tricked sex on the goats, and we were the babies—half gruff, half troll.[48]

From here onward, the boys observe animals and animacy—they learn through observation, through slur, and only a few times inhabit or try to assume animality. We may say they play less with animality and instead yearn to understand it as they come to understand themselves as born, as sexed, as mixed-raced (a tricky category—we will talk about this later in the context of upstate New York and the contrast of belonging, lineage, and language), and as ascending away from the relational pack and into disciplined, or unruly, individual men who use the word *I*. They play now with what they know about sex, relay what they've just learned about babies from both science and anecdote.[49] While the boys are figured as animals, and parts of humans are still remarked upon with animal figuration, the boys themselves halt their collective becoming animal. Their gestures become more attached to identifiable humanistic notions of race and sex, even when always in tension with animality, all the more so now that their impropriety is both felt and remarked upon.

Again figured as monstrously mixed, as "halfies," the boys now roam about, loitering at gas stations and asking for "troll things" like cigarettes, whiskey, and other items they're too young to purchase. Passing adults refuse their requests, saying they're too young; they're babies. This doubled usage of the term *baby* tropes into another significance when they happen upon a pregnant woman. Upon viewing her, instead of asking for their contraband, they ask about her pregnancy in true gruff, troll form, asking, "Hey, lady, you got a bomb in there?"[50] Intuiting that they need another lesson on birth, she corrects them—taking them, seemingly, at their word—and tells them to come feel her belly, to feel the baby move. Now focused on the most literal referent of *baby*, they feel to understand more. After asking a few gruff questions—asking if the baby has a father and if that father "tricked" this woman—she chides them, increasingly offended by their literal questions and patchwork references. They ask about whether or not it hurts, and she replies, "Some. It'll hurt real bad when they take him out." They respond with their most scientific, objective knowledge: "It'll hurt your vagina." And she quips, "Don't you know how to be proper?" At this moment, the boys glance toward their sneakers, the corporeal gesture of shame—an affective embodiment. They give the woman money for her child, money they would have spent on their gruff troll pursuits, saying it's "from us." They offer this new baby their own money, their meager capital, their only property, after they are accused of being improper. And then they run home to their mother to "kiss and blow raspberries onto her belly—so thin and tight now, no room for us—asking, 'Us hurt you?' knowing that we had lived there once, in Ma's belly, before we were three together, before we were brothers. And Ma? She didn't question, she just let herself be pulled down, flat on her back, laughing; she just gave in, our Ma, raising her arms above her head, surrender style; she just gave herself up."[51] The language of the book registers an ambivalent and haptic sensuality, one that we know is not free of violence or transgression but is not wholly reducible to these kinds of pathologizations either. Tenderness and violence dwell in close proximity—or rather, like a trope, they turn suddenly.

The monstrosity of language may be one of its more material features, whether considered through figuration, dissemination, fungibility, and/or catachresis. It is the inhuman and uncontrollable aspect of this medium that relates and rends—and it is precisely this reason why language and animacy gain traction for queer of color critique in Mel Chen's work. So too is this why it remains important to understand ethnic-racialized subjects as linguistic while not reducing them to mere representation, producing a hermeneutic encounter infused with the politics of loss seldom afforded to nonwhite subjects, as Viego so articulately theorizes. And so too does this not, at least in this text, occasion an invitation to extract from the interiority of the characters. Their opacity is theirs. The words on the page only allow for so much plumbing of the psyche—the character's unconscious motivations remain barely perceptible and not even exactly symptomatic. Rather, the psychoanalytic engagement that this text culls pays heed to constant psychic and structural violence.

The low hum of quotidian violence haunts the narratological movements of *We the Animals* in a register at once intimate and ominous, marking a psychic terrain wherein the ludic flirts dangerously with the violent. In my reading, I find one aspect of this violence to be of a Kleinian texture, wherein affects and positions change in a way that is violent and loving, in turns deeply ambivalent and confusingly non-Oedipal.[52] The previous chapter's engagement with a Kleinian register helps us to read the unavoidable violence at work in Torres's novel. Pain, both psychic and physical, composes the terrain of childhood homes—and this one is no exception. In this sense, the novel operates under Kleinian principles of object relations wherein violence and love, the paranoid and the reparative, commingle in hopeful and frightening ways. Each character inhabits this complexity in a fullness, caring and hurting in turns. In many ways, this is the close-up of subjectivity as violence that must be accounted for—but remuneration and justice do not come in the form of easy moralizing and individual policing. The question of justice is not answered in this novel, but the question gains nuance through these intimate glimpses because we understand how much of what has seeped into this family's home and heart is structural violence in the form of poverty, racialization, and heteropatriarchy, and yet, there's no easy out. A lack of justice does not exonerate any of the interpersonal violence. But this phenomenal orientation of the text does portray the different and damaging ways that respectability is predicated upon the privileged affective parameters based on moral codes that are highly racialized, much in the way animality itself is racialized.

If in "Us Proper" Ma gives herself up to her boys, in the next vignette, "Lina," she simply gives up after Paps has left her. We, the readers, following the elliptical tracks of this narrative, don't know why Paps has left. We come to understand Ma as depressed through a trail of cigarette butts: "Ma stopped showing up for work, stopped eating, stopped cooking for us, stopped flushing cigarette butts down the toilet, and let them pile up instead, inside of empty bottles and in teacups; wet cigarette butts clogged the drain of the sink. She stopped sleeping in her bed and took to the couch instead, or the floor, or sometimes she slept at the kitchen table, with her head in one arm and the other arm dangling down toward the linoleum, where little heaps of cigarette butts and empty packs and ash piled up around her."[53] We track the ashes after burning in this vignette, and our only evidence is aftermath. The narrative does not supply the lead up to these ashes that leaves the mother in a different kind of temporal never-never land of supine stasis. Is this the afterburn of violence or love lost? We just know it as loss. And because of the socioeconomic encasement of this family, we can't know if the teacups have held tea or something else, yet the trail of detritus lets us know there are at least bottles. Objects and positions, rather than narrators, often tell the story in its reverberating potentiality.

During this time, the boys fend for themselves, rooting through the fridge and eating "long-forgotten things," as they are momentarily forgotten.[54] A call arrives from Ma's workplace, a brewery this time, and her supervisor Lina inquires about why she has missed six shifts. When she can't hear the boys over the clamorousness of the brewery, she comes over, and though the boys try to keep her out of the house—using scale and breaking point as their logic, saying Lina is "huge" and "there's no room" for her—she wedges her way into the home, and the boys rush to her bag of groceries, ravenously devouring the contents. Lina has a looming and large presence from the perspective of these brothers: she is described as having "wide horse teeth" and as claiming to come from a part of China where people are built "like Cadillacs."[55] She wedges her way into the home to take care, and care she gives by hailing Ma:

> "*Comrade!*" she hollered, stepping over us, and Ma came running, throwing herself into Lina's big arms, burying her face in Lina's silky black hair, and crying.
>
> Lina stood there for a while, then reached into her smock and pulled out a tissue, taking our mother's face in her hands and wiping it down, tucking wisps of hair behind Ma's ears. We were kneeling on the floor, not two feet away from them, and the longer Lina stood there, grooming Ma, the less we paid attention to the groceries. Then Lina started kissing Ma all over, little soft kisses, covering Ma's whole face with them, even her nose and eyebrows. Then she put her lips on Ma's lips and held them there, soft and still, and nobody—not me, not Ma, not Joel or Manny, nobody—said a word. There wasn't a word to say.[56]

Ma's face here is held in the feminine, both in tone, syntax, and figure, a quiet hush that halts languaging. In previous vignettes, like "Seven," Ma had to hold her own tears; her face could not be held without some temptation of a love that hurts, and now another form of protection comes in that's both large, strong, and nurturing. Such nurturance spills over and hushes even a hunger for food. When these lips meet, they don't speak together, they don't even move. They hold; they hush. This worker alliance that exists along a lesbian continuum is not explained further; it has no other plotline. Like the narrator's journal, this, too, belongs in a place outside of signification and representation in any content-driven way. There is, in a sense, a sovereignty of quiet in the novel—a withdrawal and a refusal of entry into interiority for a different kind of aesthetic comportment that does not allow for a direct transmission of a political moralism or takeaway.[57] Both extreme violence and moments of joyous flight or peaceful reprieve exist in the gaps and elisions of the novel. There are private moments stolen away even from the reader, even from language.

Pauses of reverence create moments of reprieve in the text. These changeups produce animated tonal shifts that mark the glinting edges of these vignettes, giving way to refractions rather than reflections of childhood. The different animacies, too, bring different temporalities into the book, stitched together using syncopated and dissonant beats and tempos. The work of the animal metaphors here becomes less about symbols or representations. More pointedly, the metaphorical invocation of animals exposes the entanglements of race and class that figure the rhetorical thrust of ethnic-racialized difference. These designations do not only or sheerly register as simply racist, though at times the boys learn about their nonplace in society through these assignments of animality. In the vignette entitled "Other Locusts," their neighbor, whom they call simply Old Man, hisses that they are animals and then locusts when they trash his garden.

Instead of scurrying away from the insults, these young, hungry boys crave linguistic and taxonomic detail. Sticking around to hear more, they are described by the old man as "invaders, marauders, scavengers, the devil's army on earth."[58] Descriptors that could be animal or human move in rapid metaphoric substitution, an insulting chain of signifiers that betrays how Judeo-Christian morality depends on cathecting onto bodies seen as less worthy regardless of the threat they may pose. The boys are rendered invasive, as pestilence and threat that betray this old man's nativist stance. But instead of submitting to shame or being deterred, the boys insist that Old Man explain his meaning and the boys narrate: "Locusts, the threat and possibility of locusts, seized our imaginations."[59] Old Man's slur clearly invokes tropes of the swarming, invasive insects, ones tied to the Old Testament as well as to racialized/anti-immigrant fears about the browning of the United States, which always figures Latinx and other brown and Black migrants as either individual or hoard-like monstrosities; this becomes traction for the boys to precisely learn about language, ecology, and significance. Their imaginations are specifically piqued by the ambivalence of a locust invasion, "the threat and possibility of locusts."[60] Old man explains that locusts come in waves and, eventually, die off because there's nothing left to eat for the last wave.[61] He goes on in lurid detail, even drawing up a sketch of a swarm to explain what locusts do. The boys sit with him on his porch, not granted entry into the house but remaining in that border-space of his domestic home until evening. Manny tells the old man that the boys have run away, but the narrative has made no mention of this prior, so the reader is equally unaware if this is a real possibility or a threat from Manny. Instead of trying to fix the situation, Old Man gives them figurations: "Old Man told us we were on the lam. He had all kinds of names for us, castaways, stowaways, hideaways, fugitives, punks, city slickers, bastards.... He also called us sweets, babies, innocents, poor pitiful creatures, God's own."[62] Old Man gathers up the remains of his vegetable garden that this swarm of boys has left in their rambunctious, pilfering wake. Gleaning from his own garden, Old Man makes them a salad. They decide he's alright and stick around. Then the two older boys start fighting, turning quickly from jest to jabs. The youngest pleads for them to stop as he recalls how his mother asks his father to stop. The boys don't stop their "kennel fighting" until the old man calls them "Animals!" twice and tells them to scram. The slur, in totality, amasses the final expulsion from this garden of innocence; no longer viewing them as "God's own," Old Man banishes the boys. As they leave, the vignette closes:

> Millions of questions. Like, how come animals aren't afraid of the dark? Especially the tiny ones, the bunnies and little birds that are skittish enough during the day—what do they make of the night? How do they understand it? How can they sleep out there, alone? Were the trees and bushes and rabbit hold all filled with ears listening, listening, and eyes never daring to shut?
>   And the other locusts, what's wrong with them, why do they come last, and what's left for them to eat?[63]

This expulsion from Old Man's garden leaves the narrator with more questions, precisely by way of learning about the hierarchies and ambivalences of animality as it corresponds to oblique, yet decipherable, figurations of migration, latinidad, and the ambivalences of white sympathy.

While the animal metaphors are meant to pack a punch and condemn, the slur has an unintended yet impactful effect on the pack of boys that leads them to proximate concerns over scarcity, fear, and relations in the more-than-human world. Mel Chen's work on animacies shows us that while animals have been used in hierarchies and the order of things, the thrust of their animacy makes them slippery. Chen writes, "The animal figures—whether fictional or actual—that appear are themselves animate, mobile. The hierarchy slips not only because it iteratively renews itself; I suggest its slippage subtends its very fixture, and it calls for us to detect the ways it does so."[64] In this theoretical move that positions the figure of the animal precisely at the crossroads of linguistics, nature, discourse, and identitarian markers, Chen urges us to not move too quickly to portend that we could get "beyond language" and, instead, enmeshes us in the animacy of language as it pertains to animality's hierarchies and slippages—ones that tend to tell stranger, queerer stories than the ontological parsings of animals in Western thought, from Aristotle to Heidegger to Derrida. Instead of the hubris that marks many posthumanist gestures, ones that concomitantly eschew political and ethical differences that seem all too human (race, sex, ability, gender, etc.), Chen's work redirects us to understand the rhetorics that subtend liberal humanism but also expose its fictions.[65] The slippages and fractures of animal metaphors and similes in Torres's novel do not seek to exonerate the racist form of the animalizations, but neither do they seek the animal or the terrain of animacy as a safe space of liberal or neoliberal morals.

Rather, the animacy of language here meets the entangled ways in which animal hierarchies tell something of raced, classed, and gendered belonging. If slurs insult and place the boys in taxonomies of difference, these designations are always situational and refer back to their family of origin in deeply racialized and classed ways: "We were half as ugly, half as dark, half as wild. Adults were always leaning in and explaining that we must have inherited this from Ma and that from Paps."[66] Inheritance, rather than heritage, makes social Darwinists of casual observers. In this manner, we see that the shame that has birthed these boys, delivered through slaps and slurs by Paps, is a shame whose source cannot solely be Paps. This shame marks his quotidian movements outside of the home wherein he is not a patriarch but a dispensable, racialized worker. On the way home, after Paps has been fired for taking his sons to work rather than leaving them at home alone, the boys beat the car with their father, making syncopated beats to let out the tension that comes from being squeezed beyond one's resources. Their clamorous banging and chanting muffles over Paps's defeat, his shame, and his crying. These stifling structures that encase the narrative are never rendered explicitly but are figured elliptically as "this." Upon coming home, head hung low without work, Paps looks to Ma and claims, "Nobody," Paps said. "Not us. Not them. Nobody's ever escaping this." He raised his head and swept his arm out in front of him. "*This*."[67] Nobody escapes this: not us, not them. The antecedents to these pronouns become unclear. At first glance, we might surmise that "us" refers to the parents and "them" refers to the boys. But the grief, anxiety, and overwhelm experienced by Paps is radiant. He extends his arms outward, and "this" takes on magnanimous scale. Ma reigns him in, pulling his hands. Anyone who has run up against "this" will know "this" feeling all too well.

At the level of metalanguage, for the narrative itself, this is all we have as evidence. "This" grows to envelop the feeling of stifling unpromise, the nightmare of the American dream, the endless labyrinthine puzzles between debt and job, between care and work (as if they could or should be separate), and the undeniable difficulty of having two working-class parents who are rent by miscegenation and dislocation from networks of care. This, all of this, becomes too much. And indeed, the book does little by way of granting escape valves. The only place to retreat would be within, not outside—there is no outside to the text of dispossession. It's no wonder, then, that we never gain entry into the protagonist's journals or even to his most interior landscape. But what we do receive is the choreography of gesture, of corporeal stance and movement, which suggests more than what can be said in language.

With no way out, Paps cannot and will not concede to the rules that dictate "this." Or rather, the game of "this" is built for his failures with luring pitfalls of false promise, and so he indulges in them. He produces expenditures that are aspirational but not pragmatic. We can see this when he buys what Ma refers to as his "Big Dick Truck," an object and event that enjoys its own vignette in the novel. And the violence he experiences is differently configured at home. Aside from Ma's physical assault, of which we witness the bruises, she also endures sexual violence.

Paps comes home with "sleepy eyes and bloodflushed ears," making passes at Ma and trying to cajole her into his mood. When she protests, he picks her up and drags her to the bedroom:

> She gripped the banister, and he tugged at her from behind until she let go. He couldn't see her expression, but we could. Her eyes searched, wild and desperate, for something to grab, and for just an instant she looked at us with that same pleading look—she looked to us for help, but we stood there, out of her reach, watching. Then her face flattened and calmed some; she even smiled a sad, halfway smile. What did we see there? Disappointment? Forgiveness? All of this passed in a moment, and only a moment, before Paps kicked the door shut.[68]

The many facets of this novel show how partial witness can be, how hard it is to always hold the face of another in danger and in distress. Faces, in this novel, get held, kissed, and bruised and turn away. Here the boys see too much and not everything at once. And as readers, we only see what they see; we are reminded that this all flashed by in a moment. The task of interpretation here becomes less important than the register of facial gesture, the dénouement of defeat, and the feeling of knowing too much and not enough. Not enough in the least. We grow up, many of us, knowing our mothers have been raped, knowing that that rape was sanctioned by many, and feel a helpless rage or shame at that fact.

After this episode, Ma works her graveyard shift, comes home, and asks the boys to pile into the truck, taking them away from their home. It is a flight with no destination. Though Paps promises to return the big dick truck, this promise remains speculative, and he never returns it. Is it because of shame? Is it because of pride? Is it because of obstinance? We can't know, but we know that the truck follows upon a wish for escape from all "this." And this truck becomes a vehicle for momentary flight, even if all "this" stymies the path out of all "this." Remember, too, that "this" is a pronoun, and pronouns without antecedents are often the terrain of racialized and gendered others in the fight of "us" versus "them." But what if "us" and "them" are confused at the level of the family itself? What if the most basic unit of belonging carries within it the fractures and, hence, the rough sutures of overdetermined structures of racism alongside heterosexism, which pits family members against one another while they each face economic and affective scarcity, turning "we" into lonely islands of "I"? And this inability to escape, to truly leave with the truck or not, is paralleled in an attempted flight that takes place in the vignette "Ducks." This scene becomes one of the only scenes where we see the boys encountering actual animals: ducks.[69]

Ma takes the derided phallic truck and drives the boys to a park where "there were no children. All the children were at school."[70] And indeed, if shame birthed these boys further into a kind of telos of masculinity, then Ma's need also accelerates their growth—rendering them not exactly children, not babies, not innocents. The boys explore the park as their mother takes a nap in the truck, her escape already halted by the finitude that comes from working in never-never time, her escape interrupted by the overlap between corporeal need and material lack. The boys ramble across the park, play games of hierarchy with one another—thus playing with power in their collectivity, parceling two against one: "Two of us ganged up on the other, then one suddenly switched allegiance and a new brother was bullied and ostracized, then another betrayal, another. We spent the long hours of morning and early afternoon this way, talking nothing but dares and putdowns, saying 'Oh *yeah*?' and cursing. We didn't talk about what might happen next; we were tough guys, and brave."[71] They also gendered these power moves through trickery: "'Girl, I ain't never gonna let you go,' said Joel—but then he did. He jumped off and sent me crashing. My tailbone bucked and vibrated and tried to explode. Still, I got on again, saying, 'Promise you won't do it this time?'"[72] After making their way to an overpass and being chided by a well-meaning, concerned woman that this is no place for little boys, they learn how language itself can render them less innocent, less young in the face of adults, and assault her first with the words "Listen bitch" and then with the infrastructure, "picking up a chunk of pavement."[73] They plod their way back to a kayak and take a nap only to wake up to pretzels hitting their faces, their mother treating them like ducks—ducks that are paddling alongside their makeshift resting place. She exclaims that she thought they were kidnapped, and in gestural response, the boys "flapped [their] elbows and quacked, and she tried to land the pretzels in [their] mouths, but she was no good at feeding [them]."[74] They climb into the truck, with only beer pretzels from Ma's purse as their food for the day, and Ma begins to feed them with fantasy and story to fill up the moments of fear, quiet, and hunger.

She talks of moving to Spain and paints a picture of their lives there. The narrator tries to follow Ma's logic, her plan for escape: "I was pretty sure you couldn't drive to Spain, but I couldn't be positive, so when Ma talked about the bullfights and how all the kids would look like us, with brown curls, tan and skinny, and when she talked about cobblestone streets and the life we would build selling bread from wicker baskets in the market, I thought anything was possible. We listened, adding what we could, and made a life."[75] In this life, the "I" moves into the "we" as a specular space, one overdetermined by a kind of ethnic racialization that the mother is projecting onto the boys, onto their bodies, vis-à-vis only one strand of their Puerto Rican "heritage": one that cannot truly account for Paps's afro and blackened features. As the colonial story comes to an end, dusk and then darkness descend over the park. The smallest figurations that gesture toward Puerto Rico come by way of infrastructure and light:

> On the street, the lampposts blinked on their orange bulbs. The green numbers of the digital clock came to life. A car passed now and then, but overall it was a very quiet road and then suddenly very dark. The lampposts were T-shaped, and they loomed like palm trees, and the circles of light they projected were like small lonesome islands.
>
> The sea of dark reminded me of something Paps was always saying, "Easier to sink than swim." He loved saying that.[76]

Life turns from a specular transatlantic voyage to a *patria* that these boys cannot claim. Spain, as mythos, holds the spectral notion that somewhere you can make a life selling bread. Environs encroach as time shifts the light of day into night's penumbras and shadows. As darkness enters like a sea of separation, so too does this figuration of life morph into figures more akin to Puerto Rico's place in the Caribbean archipelago—lampposts transform into palm trees and their circles of light turn into small lonesome islands. And in this engulfment of raciality, we see anew Paps's claim that it is, indeed, easier to sink than swim.[77]

After these moments where Ma and her boy-ducks (*patos*) fantasize about other geographies, she comes back into the time of need, of hunger, because as much as stories give hope, we cannot live on them alone: "Ma tried to keep talking, tried to keep all of it—the silence and hunger and the idea of Paps—at bay, but she was running out of words."[78] Silence, hunger, and Paps all congeal into a sea of darkness, but as it turns to night, all of these forces come into the scene before Ma even runs out of words. In this sense, the porous, relational aspects of our psyches, of our object relations, enter first through association or metonymy even when we mean to keep them at bay. As she runs out of words to create worlds that can't be entered or sustained without far more material resources, she turns to the boys and asks them what to do:

> "We can go home, but we don't have to. We don't ever have to go home again. We can leave him. We can do that. But I need you to tell me what to do."
>
> No one spoke. I tried to listen to faraway noises and guess what they were—animals, satellites. The up-close noises were easy, Ma choking on words, the croak in her throat, the controlled breathing of my brothers.
>
> "Jesus!" Ma whispered. "Say something! You think this is easy?"
>
> "Something," Joel said, and Manny reached across the seat and punched him.
>
> Ma flipped the ignition, and the engine jumped to life. We drove back the way we came, and eventually we pulled into the driveway, home again. We had been terrified she might actually take us away from him this time but also thrilled with the wild possibility of change. Now, at the sight of our house, when it was safe to feel let down, we did. I could feel the bitterness in my brothers' silence; I wondered if Ma felt it too.[79]

The relationship to space, noise, and silence creates echo chambers where we may have expected to find answers, indictments, or even a plan. In the face of too few options, Ma turns a decision over to those who can only play at decision-making: her sons. Ma's need, combined with decision fatigue, becomes toxic, spills over the boys, and initiates them into feeling what Ma can no longer contain. It is a concession that Paps, cruel as he may be, is right about all of "this." In this scene, the protagonist concentrates on feeling and sound, noting that it's easy to see the close-up, or rather to sense what's close: sadness though the silence of constrained breathing. But what extends beyond it engulfs this family, what might be just outside of the frame may only be heard, barely sensed as either animal or satellite: that which can orbit and roam beyond these needs for human infrastructure, which limits all decisions in forced entry into the cruelty of capitalism.

"This" surfaces again in ominous tone in the vignette "Wasn't No One to Stop This" as the boys start going out on their own at night, breaking windows, venting anger at their father's slaps, and exploring their environs as a pack of roving, mischievous boys. The narrator begins to separate from his brothers quietly, signaling a fear that he's not able to verbalize. Upon breaking the window of a neighbor's camper, they meet another boy, described as a headbanger; they become introduced to a world that's only existed outside of the pack. The boys understand their place in relation to a white neighbor boy described as having "blond-white hair [that] fell long and stringy down his back but was cut short at the sides and the front. He was always pulling at his crotch and telling as many lies as he could cram into a sentence. This type of boy was everywhere around us, but mostly we kept separate, us three half-breeds in our world, and the white-trash boys in theirs."[80] This marker of whiteness comes late in the novel. This language of typology surfaces and hyphenates identifiers of whiteness that are not usually hyphenated. Marking whiteness in this novel is not merely a political move, but rather it is the necessary naming of the "this" that encases and surrounds this pack of roving "half-breeds." The headbanger steps into the pack, and through exposure to pornography—specifically gay, role-playing daddy porn—the pack, once "thick," becomes "thin." And thinned out, the protagonist becomes separated, unheld by his brothers' eyes. In swift, spare excerpts from the porn videotape, we hear a role-playing that dangerously mirrors the opening of the novel where the father's slaps are meant to make the boys men. With videotaped representation, the quotidian discipline and punishment turn perverse, become alive: "We had seen flesh, women, sex parts, and sex acts, but only in still pictures. This man, this teenager, they were once alive, or had been once—in this sparse room, just a bed, sheets, a book, one continuous shot, no angles, no cutting away, like a home movie."[81] Being alive, having been alive, means that the boys are seeing not a still image but a moving one that may resonate. The home movie with its "one continuous shot" is almost the exact inverse of the narratological architecture of *We the Animals*, which sharply cuts away at the level of sense, syntax, and plot. The gaps are less vacuous lacunae than faceted angles of crystal—with glints that refract light away through incision and precision, creating a dazzling mélange of dancing light made by precise, violent cuts. This, as a demonstrative that gestures either to time or to proximity, gives us a weak theory of referentiality in place of an exhaustive or strong theory of structure. Structural inequities encase the novel and percolate through signifiers that ultimately separate the narrator-protagonist from the "we/us" configuration of his brothers and his family. And yet, the "grace" of the novel lies in a poetics that looks back onto a terrain vexed with violence and love—the commingling that can turn toxic but that also requires something other than a moral indignation that takes the form of individual blame as its mode of conviction. But in this basement, with a fourth boy with blond-white hair, the inability to look away transitions to Manny and Joel not being able to look at their brother. The vignette ends with a question: "Why won't you look at me, my brothers, why won't you take my eyes?"[82] And this question is answered by the vignette's title, which is also a line tucked between diegetic sound from the videotape:

> "Bend over my lap."
> Wasn't no one to stop this. My brothers. Wasn't no one.
> "Daddy, please."[83]

This section has a refrain of "we had seen" and "I had seen." What has been seen, and what filters as a pedagogy of affect and licentiousness, is the shaming of nudity, of speaking against God, of each other's flesh:

> We had seen flesh, but still pictures, women. And, too, we had seen each other's bodies—all of us, me and Manny and Joel, Ma and Paps—we had seen one another beaten, animal bleating in pain, hysterical, and now drugged, and now drunk and glazed, and naked, and joyous, heard high laughter, squeals and tears, and we had seen each other proud, empty proud, spite proud, and also trampled, also despised. We boys, had always seen so much of them, penniless or flush, in and out of love with us, trying, trying; we had seen them fail, but without understanding, we had taken the failing, taken it wide-eyed, shameless, without any sense of shame.[84]

This litany of witness, of the crescendos and movements of the family, becomes interrupted again by the porn tape's spanking matched by the narrator's refusal: "Wasn't us. Didn't have nothing to do with us." And then the pack is thinned when the narrator asks, "Why won't you look at me, my brothers, why won't you take my eyes?"[85] Ma had held tears on the rims of her eyes, and the narrator averted his eyes previously; now he wants his brothers to take his eyes. Taking his eyes may also be a plea to take him away from the solitude of his "I"—to keep him in the "we," to take away what the eyes have seen but also to be taken in, to be himself witnessed as part of, rather than apart from, the pack.

The narrative further details the fracture of the boy pack, and this separation is marked by a vignette about a trip to Niagara Falls that the protagonist makes with his father. Paps must make this trip for work, and the older brothers, Manny and Joel, cannot accompany them because they're behind in school. After arriving to Niagara Falls, Paps leaves the protagonist in a curiosity museum where he becomes entranced by documentary footage of men rushing over the iconic falls in barrels—some survived and some died. He dances, twirls, and creates his own "mer-boy" dance at first to save the souls that crash to their fates, but the dance takes over and he lets his little body wiggle and writhe in the projected, cinematic waters as he is "consumed in the death dance."[86] When he wakes up from his macabre reverie, he sees the silhouette of his father, which he recognizes as Paps by his "close-cut Afro."[87] Later, on the road home, his father relates that, upon looking at him, dancing not as poor, rich, white, or Puerto Rican but rather taken over by the killing waters, he was struck by the realization of the striking beauty of his youngest: "*Goddamn, I got me a pretty one.*"[88] Being singled out as just one, as an object of Pap's gaze and possession, the narrator moves into a kind of individuation through objectification.

In this state of one with eyes unheld, the next vignette narrates the brothers as "They." The narrative shifts to a future tense, projecting Manny and Joel as sharing a masculinity that is rough and tumble but shared. That sharing, though, ends at the level of racialization: "Later still, they'll realize that those boys are actually nothing like them at all. Who knows this mutt life, this race mixing? Who knows Paps? All these other boys, the white trash out there, they have legacies, decades upon decades of poverty and violence and bloodlines they can trace like a scar; and these are their creeks, their hills, their goodness. Their grandfathers poured the cement of this loading dock. And downstate, in Brooklyn, the Puerto Ricans have language, they have *language*."[89] This loss is a loss of heritage, a loss of a larger sense of belonging, one that makes these brothers huddle tight against a world that sees them as half-ugly, half-beautiful—as either pathetically innocent or wildly violent. This mutt life and race-mixing is bound up with Paps. And though Paps's heritage is, to a certain extent, phantasmatic in his contention to being purebred, he showcases a facility with sensual comportment that moves in a rhythm inaccessible to the boys. This signals that he has a language and belonging that the boys don't, telegraphing a larger grammar of loss gestured in the lineages described above. Whether stiff or sensuous, there is an assuredness of gait that aligns masculinity in a felicitous way. And these gestures translate into a language that is somehow not available to the heritage learner, no matter how many limpid attempts there are to consider the many Latinx children who do not have a felicitous tongue that produces Spanish without deep shame. And yet, later, language will be what separates and comports the protagonist in his final monologue. Somehow this is an anticipated grief, because the brothers can remain comfortably in the discomforting position of the mutt, the mixed-race, whereas the narrator's facility with language is caste-ing him out, or rather positioning him upright into the ascendant "I," which begets a proximity to whiteness or concedes to its grammatical assurance:

> And me now. Look at me. See me there with them, in the now—both inside and outside their understanding. See how I made them uneasy. They smelled my difference—my sharp, sad, pansy scent. They believed I would know a world larger than their own. They hated me for my good grades, my white ways. All at once they were disgusted, and jealous, and deeply protective, and deeply proud.
> Look at us, our last night together, when we were brothers still.[90]

Here we have a scenic snapshot told in the literary present that we know is in the past. The subtle verb tense shifts remind us that this now is past, but this now is also presented on the page as a kind of testimony, and we're asked to bear witness to how a moment contains so much love and hate, so much envy and pride, so much togetherness and rending. The now is a flash of a moment, the signal of danger, the potential that can only be deeply ambivalent because it is a moment where togetherness, we sense, is about to dissipate, to thin out. The term "look" directs the gaze, asking us not to look away, increasingly ekphrastic and cinematic in language. As the narrator addresses a reader (you) that is implicit in the demand to look, to watch—a demand that reads akin to "imagine, relate, read on without looking away"—he assumes the position of object (me) while waging his most direct acknowledgment of the reader to look. He is first object before fully individuated subject, an object separated from his pack. This gap reveals a suspended object in isolation that is both violent and hurt, aggressive and masochistic. And this moment of thinning becomes the moment of witness that exceeds the plural children or singular child, extending outward as an ethical directive to the reader. We don't know the specificity of the trauma or the loss, but we see its contours, shadows, and bruises. And this night suspends onward, slowly pacing and tracking.

The narrator separates himself from his family through his journals. There, he takes his pen as his sword, mastering language and logos, and begins to separate himself from his pack. It is in his journal as well that he writes salaciously about his queer desires. Toward the end of the novel, as the narrator who will remain unnamed looks at his brothers, he lets the reader in on a secret: "Secretly, outside of the family, I cultivated a facility with language and bitter spite. I kept a journal—in it, sharpened insults against all of them, my folks, my brothers."[91] This marks a shift in the narrative—wherein the brothers come to sense the narrator's difference in a way that cannot be reducible either to his gender or to his desires. They showcase envy as they sense his parents' perceptions of his potential, his promise of upward mobility, calling him "a fucking crystal vase" and a "fucking sacred lamb."[92] They pick up on his "pansy scent."[93] In these gestural forms, too, his effeminate ways are picked up on, enfolded somewhat ambivalently into whiteness, language, and animacy. The overall thisness that thickens and encircles the boy pack, and the family becomes imbricated with more singular variations and variables. Venn diagrams of systemic disenfranchisement pull them together and sometimes place them at odds with one another. But much of these separations remain opaque and unnamed, rendered in small anecdotes, understood as tacit yet not entirely taboo. In this way, the relational structure between the boys and the family more broadly is akin, up until a certain point in the novel, to what Carlos Decena calls a tacit subject.[94] Many queer, Latinx scholars have critiqued a certain era of queer studies for being too reliant upon the closet as a central epistemological figure for gay narratives, or even a central issue for queer politics itself. The level of visibility and, more importantly, material and affective ability to walk away from one's birth family is a form of overdetermined identity narrative that serves only a minority of queers for whom it defines their most "liberating" of moments.

While inseparable from gender, the thrust of the journal's insulting daggers shows a more complex story than a simple rendering of homophobia. Indeed, the narrator notes, "Look at us three, look at how they held me there—they didn't want to let me go."[95] And yet, off he goes to cruise, "sleazing around the bus station's men's room. This was the scent they'd picked up."[96] There, the narrator finds a gruff bus driver who seduces him with the words "You want me to make you. . . . I'll make you. I'll make you." Occluding the scene of his making is not so much a cutaway but instead only the blank space between the truck driver's promise and the next sentence: "And I was made." The text points less to sex as truth or the revealing of some core truth and more to the play of pronouns. Here a "you" is made into an "I." At the end of this vignette—aptly titled "The Night I Am Made"—the "I" emerges first as an object while screaming, "He made me," then adopting the more assured position of the subject by uttering, "I'm made." Both animals and pronouns have a particularly piqued place of importance in queer world-making. There is a coy collusion between the slippery status of animality in the novel, especially one that invokes many figurations of specific animalities (both mythological and verifiable in the zoology we know) and pronouns. The title itself conjures a first-person plural of "we" (positioned as social, speaking in chorus, but unspecified and assuming a subject position) with a category of life that is similarly vague, that ranges from insects to humans and contains one and a half million species (a million of which are insects—showcasing how much anthropocentrism is also scaled to overacknowledge certain animals).

For Derrida, in *The Animal That Therefore I Am*, human animals are marked by an ability to feel shame, to feel unease with oneself. What marks the human in this terrain is a self-consciousness that understands oneself as at odds with, well, oneself, which Derrida describes as "that animal at unease with itself."[97] And the self is precisely the unease that crops up in this short novel, as the narrator becomes made and assumes the first-person singular pronoun and his family "discovers" his journal. After exclaiming "I am made!" to an onslaught of passing cars that would not hear his claim, that would rush past in a hoard or a pack or a stampede, the narrator returns home—to find the matrix of his family set up like a tableau. The narration of his family is detailed as a mode of ekphrasis—rendering them as an aesthetic portraiture. He writes, "They were gathered in the front room, and the air reeked of grief. The force of their eight eyes pushed me backward toward the door; never had I been looked at with such ferocity. Everything easy between me and my brothers and my mother and my father was lost."[98] Loss of ease, self-consciousness, being made, the bildungsroman, all of these symptoms and genres propel the first person. The family has read the journal wherein he not only detailed "in bold and explicit language . . . fantasies about the men I met at the bus station, about what I wanted done to me. I had written a catalog of imagined perversions, a violent pornography with myself at the center, with myself obliterated. And now it was on my mother's lap." Note the slippages here between fantasy and reality, between real sexual acts and "imagined perversions," between the self at the center and the self obliterated. This radical ambivalence, which threads through the animality, queerness, and racializations of Torres's writing, renders *We the Animals* a novel impervious to normative moral judgment.

Before we move to the final passage, we have yet another ambivalent moment to discuss, one that renders the culpability of the family radically indiscernible. Set up like a tableau, the narrator says, "Each was radiant, gorgeous. How they posed for me. This was our last time all five in a room together. I could have risen; I believe they would have embraced me. Instead, I behaved like an animal."[99] The narrator tries to rip the skin off their faces and then his own. In a shuffle of both verbal and physical assault, the narrator rages against his family and then notes, "I said and did animal, unforgivable things. What else but to take me to the zoo?"[100] The bildungsroman is meant to take a boy to manhood, and yet, this ending or telos is rendered in serious trouble, if not obliterated, by the end of the novel.

Choosing neither to end in the key of victim nor the trope of triumph, Torres instead ends with the final vignette entitled "Zookeeping":

> These days, I sleep with peacocks, lions, on a bed of leaves. I've lost my pack. I dream of standing upright, of uncurled knuckles, of a simpler life—no hot muzzles, no fangs, no claws, no obscene plumage—strolling gaily, with an upright air.
>
> I sleep with other animals in cages and in dens, down rabbit holes, on tufts of hay. They adorn me, these animals—lay me down, paw me, own me—crown me prince of their rank jungles.
>
> "Upright, upright," I say, I slur, I vow.[101]

Perhaps what the narrator has lost is less family or belonging and more a sense of the pack—a place where violence and love commingle in the first-person plural, a place where identity—that is to say, ipseity[102]—need not stand erect as the "I," the first-person pronoun singular. In a critical movement toward a politics of loss in Latinx studies, Antonio Viego asks us to follow the teachings of Hortense Spillers. Tracing the importance of her racialized and gendered revision of psychoanalysis, Viego argues that we would do well to adopt a "notion of 'interior intersubjectivity,' a species of practice that articulates psychoanalysis with politics that refuses to cede the entire range of understandings that ethnic-racialized subjects might adopt with respect to what it means to be a subject marked out in culture as 'ethnic-racialized' to the edifice of ego and social psychology and that might, in some way, interrupt the moribund lock-step movement between ethnic-racialized resemblance and ethnic-racialized social and cultural intelligibility."[103] One way Viego seeks to do this is to invest in Adam Phillips's provocation that psychoanalysis be thought of as a rhetoric rather than a metaphysics—articulating how psychoanalysis may unfold less as an ontological description and more as a series of tropes. Such rhetorical attention to loss considers the nuance and complexity of relations and material structure that refuses to idealize or sanitize difference into something known or even purposeful. Being Latinx becomes a rhetorical problem, one figured in *We the Animals* through animal metaphors that maintain an ambivalent relation to a humanist ideal of the sovereign self that, through confession, becomes an upright man. But these animal metaphors maintain an ambivalent relation to referentiality, since they do not, for the most part, refer to "real" animals. In this manner, I do not read the animality of this novel as especially ecological in scope nor as a movement toward what some scholars call "wildness."[104] Rather, the strange animal figurations function in a manner that refuses to be domesticated into an easily extractable and replicable politics. In a sense, the animal metaphors keep us from translating the novel into a purposeful politics. The withdrawn aestheticism of the novel operates as a strategic employment of opacity, especially around the confessional mode, which would chasten us from generalizing from this singular story of loss. Indeed, one of the most refreshing aspects of the novel for this critic is that the withheld journal signals to the reader that we do not have the whole story, we do not know the desires or interior psyche of the narrator, and we do not even know what the family knows.

This final lure of the journal remains withheld, and thus, the novel operates in a register that defies the confessional mode, which, in a Foucauldian register, means that the questions of repression and liberation may not be suitable or desirable for this novel's narratological terrain.[105] Rey Chow helps me to make this point as she reads the problem of confession for ethnic and sexual minorities as one that should not be too assured in self-referential gestures:

> "Such acts of confession may now be further described as socially endorsed, coercive mimeticism, which stipulates that the thing to imitate, resemble, and become is none other than the ethnic or sexual minority herself. When minority individuals think that, by referring to themselves, they are liberating themselves from the powers that subordinate them, they may actually be allowing such power to work in the most intimate fashion—from within their hearts and souls."[106]

Following Chow's insights here on the relation between coercive mimeticism and confession, I want to draw out how Torres's decision to gesture toward a journal that we never read amounts to a distancing technique that draws attention to the fact that we do not quite know the narrator's desires. We may be readers who desire to know, but this knowledge is withheld. Such a choice constitutes a refusal to inscribe interiority and to entertain developmental allegories. And because we do not know what the narrator wants, nor who he truly is, we cannot say with any assurance that he has found a queer utopia or liberation. While some have read the novel as a "blueprint for queer liberation," there's simply not enough data, in the legitimately necessary sense, to provide a model of queer liberation in the closing vignette.[107] Here, instead, we see a mourning and melancholia of family that registers violence—undeniably exponentialized by the systemic—at the level of the interpersonal.

Moving across personal loss and structural dispossession, the novel ends with a pronouncement of the loss of a pack—foregrounding a notion of belonging that is distinctly mammalian, that longing for belonging that may be unique to the human animal who looks to place themself in relation to categories of identity. In "Animal Body, Inhuman Face," Alphonso Lingis writes, "A pack of wolves, a cacophonous assemblage of starlings in a maple tree when evening falls, a whole marsh throbbing with frogs, a whole night scintillating with fireflies exert a primal fascination on us. What is fascinating in the pack, the gangs of the savannah and the night, the swarming, the multiplicity in us. . . ."[108] In this closing vignette, the final line proceeds an utterance, followed by a drunken slur and then a solemn vow, and renders the uprightness of the "I" as a horizon (that is by definition out of reach) into the dangerous fiction of the sovereign self that finally stands apart from the beast. If the narrator has lost his pack, it is radically unclear where he's registering this loss: the descriptors could be the cacophonous sounds of a psych ward or the raucous, sensuous clamor of calls and paws in a queer bar. This passage flirts with tropes of Darwinian evolution, with tragedy, with the bildungsroman, and with the coming out story—only to render each radically undiscernible, exposing our own readerly habits rather than giving us a telos that satisfactorily finishes off this story. While this novel is both queer and Latinx, it is difficult to thematize its relation to either identitarian term: queer or Latinx. The queerness of pronouns float without antecedents and more often denote race or class rather than gender or desire. Likewise, it is neither an exemplar nor the exhaustive epic of latinidad. It is instead deeply Kleinian in ways that Eve Kosofsky Sedgwick articulated: it both raises the barometer of paranoia and offers moments of reparation. It is a weak theory of Latinx narratology in that it is disinterested in allowing the one to stand for the whole, in allowing ipseity to be a teleological achievement. It is *this* story of *this* family in *this* world. The gestures, the raw sutures, the proximal intimacies and violences, the infrastructural, the interpersonal, and small hints of the intrapersonal amass into a refracted story that ends on an ambivalent vignette showcasing animals bedding down into perhaps madness and perhaps queerness.[109] The vignette aesthetics outline a story of a family that is at once an intimate, but also an uncertain, crime scene where each body experiences the vacillations of violence and love. This ambivalence becomes nuanced, rather than nullified, by the fact that racialized gender and class engulf one's person with storms of dispossession and conflict, rendering moot the conceit of the singular body assuming an "I" as comfort, as safety, as an achievement. The solitude of the "I" at the end of the novel says, slurs, and vows. Being upright, upstanding, and a man are the horizons both gestured toward and refused in the opaque, desirous, luscious landscape that composes this novel's ending—where we find our narrator feeling loss, prowling the jungles, sleeping in dank dens, and seemingly still while caught in the tension of wanting both more and less.

Coda

Knots in the Throat

Roque Salas Rivera's Ballasted Entanglements

Ordered movement, configured as liberal freedom corporealized, requires ballast.
—Mary Pat Brady, *Scales of Captivity: Racial Capitalism and the Latinx Child*

This condition of overlapping recurrences is indicated by the term "entanglement," which is invoked, first and foremost, to suggest a topological looping together that is at the same time an enmeshment of topics. Beyond this intimation of a tangle, of things held together or laid over one another in nearness or likeness, my aim is to ask if entanglement could not also be a figure for meetings that are not necessarily defined by proximity or affinity. What kinds of entanglements might be conceivable through a partition and partiality rather than conjunction and intersection, and through disparity rather than equivalence?
—Rey Chow, *Entanglements, or Transmedial Thinking about Capture*

Retracing and reading inscriptions over the course of this book has led me to the colonial foundations and gendered crossroads traversed in and through latinidad. Rather than conclude this inquiry, I turn to thinking about questions of translating gender—concerns that I glossed in the introduction. In order to do so, I return again to Roque Salas Rivera's inscriptions to think about the grammars and substrata that lurk beneath and permeate gender. I do so because Roque Salas Rivera's poetry offers a distinctly gendered translation of anticolonial ethos rendered in verse. This coda concerns itself with tropes and textures of Roque Salas Rivera's poetry that coincides with his return to Puerto Rico, a return that registers in a bilingual lyric of ongoing anticolonial and trans movements on the island and the diaspora. Most recently, he moved from Philadelphia around 2016/2017 (after having been the poet laureate of the city). Salas Rivera inscribes figural knots that both refuse and suture readings across *Preguntas frecuentes* and *X/Ex/Exis*. Salas Rivera's poetic self-translations withhold translation in a way that requires that we read across Spanish and English, which makes it a particularly important site to think about the "x" of *Latinx*. Here, I take Salas Rivera's self-translation notes to serve as a hermeneutic provocation.[1] Salas Rivera calls his use of untranslated words *knots*, which create a poetics of critical, anticolonial translation of the self *not* in service of the language of access—English. And while the self becomes translated as the textures of language become more felt, the relations between English and Spanish enmesh, such that no preexisting self comes to the fore. What does surface, in the place of self as poetic arrival, is a translational praxis and trans poetics wherein exposure and understanding are denied as telos. In place of the self-revealed, we find a material and poetic return to an island that yet again registers the tensions between two deeply colonial languages. We read negotiations of the "x" in Latinx in the particular place of present-day Puerto Rico—where the "x" is only ever at the hinge of two colonial grammars. The "x," then, delinks itself from "Latin" and becomes as unincorporated into the US or Latin America as Puerto Rico's current status as an unincorporated territory in Salas Rivera's poetry and asks us to consider it as yet another knot, an untranslated gender that truly has no original. These untranslated words, or knots, are weighted by the materials of coloniality: ballast carried from Europe to the island on ships, the foundational problem of their grounding allure in the form of Old San Juan's roads, and the colonial grammars that subtend most gendered terms. Recursive and ongoing coloniality endures in Puerto Rico, and Salas Rivera figures this material substratum that underlies so much of quotidian life.

In order to tease out the problem of translation for gender in coloniality, as exposure and as the problem of one-to-one correlations, Salas Rivera writes translation notes that concentrate on the figure of a knot. Offering a foundational, material example of what he refuses to translate, Salas Rivera comments on the stones of Old San Juan as one such knot:

"Even though *adoquines* are *cobblestones*, *my adoquines*, the ones I stumbled over on my way to and from the water, could never bear the word *cobblestone*. Sometimes the word in Spanish is so enmeshed with the poem's life that changing it would be painful. I call these untranslated words *knots*."[2] The fabled *adoquines*, or cobblestones, of Old San Juan share the color of the ocean—an iridescent, opulent blue that shimmers across the old colonial streets of San Juan. Most assume that the *adoquines* of Old San Juan came to the island as ballast from Spanish colonial ships, but the bricks came from England during a set of years before the island's relationship to the English language itself would shift radically, between 1890 and 1896. The literal translation, "cobblestone," reveals as much as it obscures. What does it mean to resist the narrative, colonial, poetic, and linguistic closure here to render *adoquines* as cobblestones? English is doubly denied, whether by intention or linguistic felicity—denied both original emplotment and the weight of originality. English loses its stability and foundational posture.

How do we then read the bluish or *azulado adoquines* as knots? What I am after here is neither finding the right referent nor even tracking down provenance to an origin for these *adoquines*. Rather, I wonder how the material provenance may inflect our reading of these beautiful, blue *adoquines*. This material history of the *adoquines* becomes all the more traceable when not translated. I want to consider the material and historical weight that pulls the reference of *adoquines*, or cobblestones, into the economic and violent exchanges of two colonialities. In this hostile meeting ground between two languages, we read various forms of transport, transition, and transmogrification—translating oneself across differently gendered language and torquing translational choices to reveal a gendered negotiation between two deeply colonial languages. *Adoquines* are a figure of untranslatability,[3] an exemplar of what would be painful to translate into English, and also an index to the material history of Old San Juan's trade and infrastructure. The colonial ballast acquired between 1890 and 1896 becomes the figurative resistance to English's considerable pull for translation, for exposure, for making oneself and one's foundations legible to the English language. This material history of the *adoquines* becomes all the more traceable when not translated. That is, the knot of translation in the decision to keep *adoquines* as *adoquines* in the English translation of the poem is, perhaps, the only reason I was able to chase after the matter of provenance of these *adoquines*. This resistance to translation, this knot-cobblestone, led me to see not only how British colonialism haunts imperial prejudice when it comes to trans terms but also how more than one colonialism haunts any conversation about Puerto Rico. The mythical colonial ballast is actually a waste product, and yet that blue mythos becomes undeniably part of the colonial allure necessary for a tertiary economy.

Material Tracks

The *adoquines* of Old San Juan were an early infrastructure project, with roads first being paved with wood, then granite blocks called chinos, and finally the *adoquines* that concern this coda. While many assume that these stones were once ballast from Spanish ships, in actuality, they were ordered from Huntly Brothers in Sunderland, England. A report entitled "Los adoquines de escoria en San Juan," or "San Juan's cobblestones of waste," shows an even stranger provenance:

> With the evidence found in the files that we examined in the General Archive of Puerto Rico we have determined that the cobblestones "bluish" that we admire so much—visitors, locals and foreigners alike—they were made of iron slag in some foundry in Sunderland, England or its vicinity. Later and in communication with the Sunderland Borough Library, we learned that Huntly Brothers was an export house, mainly of coal and not a factory. As Mr. Simon Weathers let us know of that library, "there were several iron companies within a couple of miles from Sunderland where the slag blocks could have been produced as a by-product; and it is likely given your business, that Huntley Bros. saw an opportunity to export them."[4]

The slag blocks are by-products of industry—they are the stone-like waste materials produced by iron smelting or the refinement of ore. Since Huntly Brothers was an export house of, mostly, coal, the archivists of Sunderland suggested to Puerto Rican researchers that it's likely that the *adoquines* came from iron companies that were within a couple of miles proximity.[5] Different companies' exportation of other companies' waste materials shows how what was exported to the colonies had an inverse relation to what was extracted. These *adoquines* were neither exactly cobblestones nor ballast; they are stones from England—stones of waste. Yet anything on a boat in the nineteenth century would have required the balancing of ballast to make the trip, and its weight must still have been accounted for. In the eighteenth and nineteenth centuries, ballast served as a material archive of commerce and cruelty—specifically in the form of coloniality and enslavement. Lolita Buckner Inniss reminds us that the legal register of ballast is a materiality that registers what the language of international trade law often obfuscated: trade in the enslaved, which necessitated more ballast on ships than ships carrying solid goods.[6] Buckner Inniss shows that ballast has served as a material that, when read in light of the transatlantic slave trade and international law, often registers this history—perhaps even more than the iconicity of iron shackles. Ballast often served a dual purpose on ships—for instance, water that both hydrated and operated as weight. More devastatingly and importantly, the enslaved were accounted for as ballast or *lastre* when thrown overboard *or* when ships wanted their trade in the enslaved to go undetected after legal abolition. Buckner Inniss explains how ballast entangles language, materiality, and peoples:

> Slave ships' ballast unites words, things, and people in the contemplation of transatlantic slave trade history and of international law more broadly. It is a tangible, visible reminder of the fundamental materiality of a historical world of African capture and enslavement that is often subsumed by discursive, rhetorical, and metaphoric renderings. The materiality of slave ships' ballast offers an active resistance to language and signification of transatlantic slavery and international law that threatens to dismiss the horrors of the trade as indignities that must be expunged from memory. Slave ships' ballast helps to recall the bodies, lives, families, and dreams broken in the transatlantic slave trade, all while the use of ballast helped to increase the viability and profitability of transporting captives.[7]

I am struck in this passage by the coimplication of words and things, of the ways in which the history of ballast has a much larger referential purchase than we have previously understood. In this way, the *adoquines* lose their ballast in either language, really, and become a larger index of trade in waste and trade in body that required cruel and exact measurements: physical balance by way of meting out body- and counterweight.[8] Whether literal or mythical ballast, the history of coloniality that trafficked in enslaved bodies haunts the *adoquines* that line the streets of Old San Juan as a material category that kept a ship afloat and upright. My invocation of *ballast*, here, operates as a referential pull—by saying *pull*, I suggest a way of perhaps figuring, through language, the force of material index. Reference is an unwieldy aspect of language because it needn't be lodged in felicitous conditions of truth. We may consider this especially since many have assumed, understandably, that the *adoquines* of Old San Juan are ballast—that they index ballast or *lastre*. We also have the material provenance that, at least in this reading, functions as another reference. And yet the ontological parameters of the *adoquines* as waste product would have still functioned as weight to be balanced by ballast. That is to say, both the material provenance and the assumed reference of the *adoquines* require us to think in terms of ballast. All weight on a ship during the late nineteenth century required ballast. Ballast then pulls us into the transportation infrastructure of Puerto Rico's last years as a Spanish colony, just before it shifted to US imperialism. It also registers the weight or pull of referentiality when we read not only etymological mutation but also material history into the words we hold dear. That reference needn't determine the final meaning or poetic iteration of *adoquines*. Rather, it is Salas Rivera's resistance to transportation of the word into English that allows me to track both semiotic entanglement and material provenance.

These *adoquines* may be figured by Salas Rivera as something too painful to translate, and retaining them in the Spanish marks a forceful resistance to translation. Material provenance shows that pain and violence are foundational to the colonial infrastructure that underlies this material figure. The untranslated *adoquines* allow one to track the British coloniality and mercantilism underfoot, which elucidates how the island of Puerto Rico always entered into a global market where even waste became imported. Salas Rivera's poetics often make deft translation decisions to resist the interpellation to translate for the pleasure and consumption of monolingual English speakers. Salas Rivera's poetry features negotiations with translation processes where anything other than exposure (as potential extraction) often features diminishing returns. In this indebted landscape, Salas Rivera steals back from English in the poetic decision to withhold, or hold onto, loss as itself incommensurable or untranslatable. I am struck by his attention to figuration, to the tension between Spanish and English, and through catachrestic evocations, to showing how loss itself is incommensurate.[9] These catachrestic figures, like pink plantains, are stitched into poetry that traffics in nothings that do not equivocate—that show there are "worst worsts."[10] By creating a nothing that doesn't exist, alongside nothings or debts that deprive, Salas Rivera's poem "a material substratum will always remain" (which I read in the introduction) discloses the difference between poetic figurations of nothing and material investments that create nothing, or less than nothing. Assumed to be ballast and revealed to be waste, what we once read as stabilizing or particular to Puerto Rico may in fact be the remains of a pernicious coloniality.

Salas Rivera's poetic thinking of incommensurability leads me to consider the weight of coloniality that paves the streets of Old San Juan, to consider material and historical weight that pulls the reference of *adoquines*, or cobblestones, to the violence of two colonialities that may entangle them with the bombs. In this hostile meeting ground between two languages, we read various forms of transport, transition, and transmogrification—translating oneself across differently gendered language and torquing translational choices to reveal a gendered negotiation between two deeply colonial languages. To read Salas Rivera's poetry, then, requires both a consideration of the "x" in "Latinx studies" and an intensification of its position between two languages that, while both colonial, create clines of power on the island of Puerto Rico.

In the above translation notes, which have been a fount for critically reading his poetics,[11] Salas Rivera writes,

> Translating my own poetry has been a way of healing my relationship with a bilingual self who struggled intensely to learn standardized dialects of both languages. After living out my elementary school years in the US, I was unprepared for high school in Spanish-speaking Puerto Rico. Having acquired an undergraduate degree in Puerto Rico, I was unprepared for graduate school in Philadelphia. . . . My bilingualism was treated by my teachers, professors and peers as something that had to be contained, a *dangerous and infectious substance*. Each language

could *spill* into the other, leaving unwanted traces and incomprehensible words.[12]

"Unwanted traces" of "incomprehensible words" are the mark of Salas Rivera's poetics, which may signal some kind of relational reparation in the form of language. And yet, this uncontainable and dangerous, infecting substance spills into another—sullying two colonial languages, English and Spanish, which have contention in the history of Puerto Rico's unincorporated commonwealth.

Salas Rivera's work is written under the shadow of debt, a debt that Rocío Zambrana reads as anchored or extracted from race and gender in the colonial maelstrom that promises oversight and instead divests difference for further speculative finance.[13] Colonial knots resurface in these poetics that posit a *cuir*, or queer, and trans difference—one that tarries with difference as a matter of translation. At the level of language, embodiment, and structure as so radically entangled, Salas Rivera figures these knots as visceral. By calling these knots visceral, I center the body in Salas Rivera's poetry in an engagement with Neetu Khanna's notion of visceral decolonial affect.[14] The knots register plural presents, and in them we may begin to see the embodied and enunciated entanglements of Salas Rivera's poems. He writes, "This translation's unruly *knots* resist assimilation and loss and, in some ways, visibilize it as illegibility. They are ghostly traces of the original poem and the traumatic linguistic labor of making oneself legible at the expense of losing connection to the world in which the poems once reverberated. Specifically, that world is Puerto Rico. While translation has helped me heal my relationship with a bilingual self, this has been possible because it has simultaneously given me the room to acknowledge that home is still measured in *yearned adoquines*." English loses its ballast and home is measured in "*yearned adoquines*"—this untranslated notion of desire for home steals from English and creates sutures where one often finds cuts. The *adoquines* here function within two radically entangled colonialities that necessitate a thinking of ballast and the weight of ship freight in the lead-up to the *adoquinando*, or paving, of Old San Juan. The poetic decision to keep *adoquines* in Spanish does not stay still in the realm of Spanish semiotics. By staying in Spanish, rather, it exceeds its own inscription when we read it materially, which leads us to fundamental questions that put pause on whether a figure registers as anticolonial or fundamentally colonial. These untranslated words, or knots, are weighted by the materials of coloniality: ballast carried from Europe to the island on ships, the foundational problem of their grounding allure in the form of Old San Juan's roads, and the colonial grammars that subtend most gendered terms.

Colonial Grammars

I now pivot to ask, How might gender's movements be indebted to colonial taxonomy? Thinkers like C. Riley Snorton and Meredith Lee showcase how sexology, eugenics, and coloniality were at play in the matrix and genealogy of *trans*.[15] In this vein of trans critique, Che Gossett and Eva Hayward think the task of a trans heuristic that accounts for the colonial and anti-Black underpinnings of all gendered articulation. They chart a trans heuristic as one that may help consider the operations of coloniality in the movement of a thinking of the impossibility of another order, of one that exceeds our order of things. The thinking from this order to another one that exceeds our own suggests movement and change: "This to that suggests transit, transformation, trans-differentiation as a trans-heuristic that does not transcend the colonial project but reveals the force, the process, and the material constraints of trans."[16] While *trans* does signal a movement in and of gender, this movement is not free of constraint, not untethered from colonial conscription. In this manner, we may think about how ballast operates to keep certain figures upright, in rectitude.

With this colonial grammar in mind, let us return to the question of *transgender* and *translation* in Salas Rivera's knotted pen—the two terms are most obviously connected through the prefix "trans-." If we understand the linguistic violence of English's dominance and its need for immediate and near-total access, then we also have a parallel (if not commensurate) problem of access to intelligibility for all trans folks who, by dint of being non-cis, are called to account for their gendered selves, experiences, interiorities, and proper nominalizations/pronouns far more than any cisgender person would ever be queried. We may read Salas Rivera's title *Preguntas frecuentes*, or *Frequently Asked Questions*, with some level of trepidation, knowing how often a trans person is questioned and asked to account for their noticeable difference. *Preguntas frecuentes* was published in 2019 by La Impresora, a small print press located at that time in San Juan,[17] as a stand-alone poem on broadside. The inverted folds of the broadside turn it into something that may resemble a pamphlet. The poem's form recalls the broadside distributed in streets between the sixteenth and nineteenth centuries— a technology of the print press and not of the digital world. My copy of the poem folds in such a way that there are two covers: one in black ink (English) and one in a green ink (Spanish). The poem's self-translated difference will be discernible not only in language and ink color but also in the physical act of reading across languages. This feat will require different embodied maneuvers to read the two poems in relation to each other, creating a disorientation that refuses the side-by-side of many bilingual editions, including some of Salas Rivera's own published collections. The background color is a light green such that the Spanish feels more merged with the page and the English takes on a bold look with its traditional black ink. Side-by-side comparisons require flipping the large page over and over again, a further embodied hindrance to seamless reading, seamless translation, seamless comparison. The Spanish and English have an inverted, asymmetrical scale, with the laughs paying off in Spanish. Equivalence becomes ruptured through choices that surface in self-translation. Often in these self-translations, jokes can be a bit bereft in English or, as Salas Rivera more aptly names it, "Inglich"—favoring the laughter that comes with recreating English's proper name with a phonetic spelling more akin to how it sounds with a Spanish accent. In this bilingually rendered and enfolded poem, to turn the page does not equate to making progress poetically or historically. The next page must be turned to and turned over again. To read both languages in any manner other than a linear one, then, gestures toward the physical demands for both printing and reading that the letterpress produced.

In opposition to this broadside, letterpress format, the poem's title conjures an almost corporate interface that, in its facade, creates a strange distance, since what follows is not the easily legible interface of frequently asked questions (with short and punchy answers). And yet the title phantasmatically conjures the frequently asked questions waged against trans folks. Here, what gets tracked are the possibilities of pronoun and gender in each language, but also more generally the problem of translation that gender maintains.

The poem begins with a line that invokes a line:

> PREGUNTAS FRECUENTES
> un nudo es una línea cuir
>
> en inglés
> línea no tiene género
> en español linea
> es feminina dentro del idioma
>
> un nudo
>
> FREQUENTLY ASKED QUESTIONS
> a knot is a queer line
>
> in english
> line has no gender
> in spanish line
> is feminine within language
>
> a knot

If a knot is a queer (that is, not straight and not untangled) line, then we understand that there might be something queer about the knots of untranslated words. This knot unfurls into different languages, the lyrical line split in a gendered way. Yet a line is only gendered in "spanish," marking it as a line that is only *grammatically* gendered. Note, too, that *queer* in English does translate to Spanish, where *cuir* replaces the constant English exportation of the Global Northern gendered vernacular term *queer*. Rather, this gender is within a language, doubly—and this doubling is doubled again in translation:

> dentro de un idioma
> dentro de un idioma
> (una x dentro

de un puerto rico
dentro de un español)

en el trap
un género

within a language
within a language
(an x within
a puerto rico
within a spanish)

in trap
a gen(d)re

Parenthetically, an "x" appears "within a puerto rico, within a spanish." Both the island nation and the language are given indefinite articles, rendered quotidian nouns rather than proper nouns. Puerto Rico becomes an island encased by a language, doubly. Within these two encasings, one may find an "x." But all of this we may find in "el trap"/"trap." Note the substitution and addition between the Spanish and the English. "Trap" in Spanish requires a definite article. This definite article could appear in English but does not. If it did, it would make *the* trap, a singular trap for capture, and could not connote trap music. The subtlety of an incommensurate translation in "trap" or "en el trap" creates a dissonance between the two languages. It also registers the sonic in Spanish and imports the English as its own beat. In the following line (and here we see lines unfurl and knot across languages), the balance is renegotiated with Spanish, making polysemous sense of genre and gender in one word: *género*. And yet every importation of gender as a concept is a recent intrusion or translation into language.[18] In this translation, Salas Rivera adds a "(d)" to the English version, making gender heard in *genre*, to bring out the Latin root that makes a confluence of generic form and grammatical gender. Gendered possibilities are radically different in each language, and we see, at least here, that English lacks some gender play in its supposedly neutered terrain. It is, of course, no trick or minor detail that *trap* looms as both music and as a mode of enclosure and attack. Trans studies, in particular, has thought through the trap of visibility—noting how the trans tipping point coincides with remarkable anti-trans legislation and transphobic violence carried out extra-legally.[19] Francisco Galarte marks the trap as a particular problem for the narrativization of racialized, trans lives, noting that such tropological encasements can often turn to traps.[20] And yet *trap* here is both music and captivity, both aesthetic form and gender's tropological encasements.

Here Salas Rivera reduces the properness of Spanish. Spanish becomes a more dialect-Spanish, within a language *within* a language. The figuration of "x" is not Spanish generally, but a "spanish" in "puerto rico," which renders these nouns improper. In other words, the "x" of Latinx travels in Salas Rivera's pen not as an answer but as a knot or provocation. Language doubly captivated, doubly and differently gendered and genred. It is in this knot that we may read the "x" as invention, as a song, but when it's sung in Puerto Rico, it's most often sung, or even spoken, as an "e." Language and gender keep in transit, in translation. This knot is not English and not Spanish, precisely, but at the hinge of the two, creating knots in the throat. These self-translations theorize a formal bilingualism that inverts colonial order and gendered expectation by creating figural knots that refuse to be disentangled from their embodied enunciation. These knotted, or refused, translations issue from the body not in order to create a fetish of the original language of Spanish but to withhold the imperial prejudices of translational labor—the interpellation that often creates access, if not exclusively then mostly, for Global North consumption. With no comfortable gendered grammar in Spanish nor grounding of home in English, Salas Rivera figures in knots what is and is not: the entanglement of what is but has no proper name or home as such and the translation of terms that have no proper destination. This knotted translation textures the binguality of these poetry editions, rendering them intimately sutured and messily woven—transgender, translated, and transferential.

What I find in Salas Rivera's knots is a way of thinking through the catachrestic invocation of the "x" of *Latinx*—what it may or may not do in the constrictions, or at the meeting point, of two languages that carry a bulwark of violence. Precisely by (k)notting an entanglement of matter and figure, we see the tension inherent in *Latinx*—both the "Latin" and the "x." The "x" only remains and "Latin" is absorbed into "a Spanish" and in "a Puerto Rico." In this space-time configuration, Spanish is far less powerful than the imperial English that sought to erase Puerto Rican accents and grammars in the mid-twentieth century. Salas Rivera's poetics operate at the limit and hinge of English and Spanish through the envelopment of a prior coloniality (Spanish) under the aegis of US imperialism. The "x" then is unincorporated here; it remains in the margins as a gendered aspect de-linked from "Latin" that precisely makes it an especially felicitous place to read the "x" without an overdetermined attachment to the lives that "make it" to the US. This knot, the queer line of the "x," issues at the hinge of two languages ensconced in colonial taxonomies at the dense site of Puerto Rico.

These knots become refigured through a movement of knots in the translation notes above to *adoquines*. The line between untranslatability and translatability is ever in flux—creating less an opposition than an apposition between the two. The withheld translation of *adoquines* does acknowledge the hierarchy of the English language's imperial reach, its lust for access and extraction, its constant engulfment in bereft economic promise or, better put, PROMESA (The Puerto Rico Oversight, Management, and Economic Stability Act): "By translating these poems, I am acknowledging that US imperialism's economic impact has led many Puerto Ricans to migrate to the US, where speaking English and surviving are synonymous. I am recognizing that their children have inherited that violent linguistic erasure, and within English, as well as Spanish, they still find ways to make the colonizer's language their own. . . . It is just as necessary that linguistic purism be read for what it is: violence against those who perform their difference."[21] Two colonial languages interface here in the shadow of US imperialism's economic extraction that created two twinned formations: Puerto Rican debt and the Puerto Rican diaspora. To put language and economic structure in overlay, or entanglement, does not equivocate the two, nor does it create an easy counterstance. Rather, Puerto Ricans still find ways to make "the colonizer's language their own. . . ." But here, we would perhaps amend to say the colonizers' languages. Regardless of the language, we see that purism is always a violence against those who perform difference and then we may ask after the status of the entanglement of anticolonial and trans movements.

Translating Limits, or Bombs Don't Write Poems

It is within this doubly enveloped coloniality that I attend to Salas Rivera's yearned *adoquines* to show how his knots of translation lead me to take him at his word. I argue that the material provenance of *adoquines* in Old San Juan demands that we take these poetics very seriously, to attend to matters that swiftly turn to figure, exemplar, and lore. Following this, I ask, How do material processes take on seemingly magical traits? What engines shift body and language? And what is the limit to thinking analogously between transition, translation, and transmogrification?

These questions become poetically explored in Salas Rivera's 2020 collection *X/Ex/Exis* (2020). In "Each Translation Is a Transformation," the title bleeds and spills into the text.

    CADA TRADUCCIÓN ES UNA TRANSFORMACIÓN
    la gente trans sabe que cada transformación
    es como si explotaran triquitraques
    en nuestras venas acordeónicas
    del ir y venir
    de vecindarios y familias
    más o menos escogidas
    pero cuando sueltas una bomba
    no quedan traducciones
    antes o después

    EACH TRANSLATION IS A TRANSFORMATION
    trans people know that each transformation
    is as if they threw firecrackers
    in our accordion veins
    made of coming and going
    from neighborhoods and families
    that are more or less chosen
    but when you drop a bomb
    there are no translations
    befores or afters

The translation is not figured as such but as impact, routed through what trans people know about the risk of transformation that evokes the perception of firecrackers in veins. If each translation transforms, then trans people know that their pops create small blasts—momentary blips in a larger colonial, racist grammar of gender. Translation as transformation becomes a way to think about a body in transition, becomes a way to think about how many read *trans* as a violent shift, *as if* hormones register firecrackers in veins. This series of metonymic associations creates a semiological chain that centers the perspective of a trans person who conduits both linguistic and biological change. But the risky promise of change is quickly halted by the figure of the bomb. The bomb does not represent anything. There is no "before and after" bomb, and therefore, the source of bombs becomes the limit of translation, of transmogrification:

>pero las bombas no representan
>son como el viento si el viento fuese bomba
>no llaman ni te avisan
>que quieren café o que venden bizcochos
>a cambio de donativos
>en puerto rico la huelga estalla
>las bombas no lloran
>las bombas no escriben poemas
>matan a generaciones de escritores
>pero no es una bomba
>en filadelfia los fascistas marchan en los museos
>no sé si me sigues
>las bombas son la medida de todo el dolor
>habido y por haber
>el gobierno las construye
>este gobierno
>las tira

>but the bombs don't represent
>they are like the wind if the wind were a bomb
>they don't call or let you know
>they want coffee or are selling chocolate bars

in exchange for donations
in puerto rico the strike strikes
bombs don't cry
bombs don't write poems
they kill generations of writers
but it isn't a bomb
in philly the fascists march in the museums
i'm not sure if you follow
bombs are the measure of
all past and future pain
the government builds them
this government
drops them

This limit of bombs also asks after provenance: *which* government makes these bombs? This government—which again entangles Puerto Rico and the US. In this transformation, the movement of *trans* becomes an entry into language's ability to transport and shift, to perhaps invent, but this ability to change does not have the weight of a bomb. This limit reminds us that Puerto Rico is a colony, yes, but also a military base (not unlike Guam) where bombs have been dropped time and again in Culebra and Vieques. Bombs obliterate and radiate—extending into nuclear coloniality. Meanwhile, Puerto Ricans strike and poems disseminate. These shifts are not nothing, but they stand against an annihilating fascism that requires us to see a bomb as a bomb. What I suggest here is that to see the bomb as a bomb and not a symbol returns us to the weight of the *adoquines*, the weight of waste, the weight of ballast. If we see in *Preguntas frecuentes* a thinking of the entanglement of a colonized Spanish language or Spanish within a colony and queerness, in *X/Ex/Exis* we see the entanglement of transformation and its limit, the bomb. These poetics and these readings return us to questions about the problem of collapsing semiotics with materiality—about attending to a material substratum that remains and radiates.

The thinking of incommensurability resurfaces here as an important limit to how we might think overlapping, but nonequivalent, forms of deprivation. Through a material provenance of Old San Juan's *adoquines*, we see the fraught site where myth and material meet. These matters accrue urgency when we hope to confront contemporaneous forms of fascism that entangle racist and colonial militarism with gender—whether by policing, legislation, pinkwashing by way of homonationalism, rampant transphobic violence, the increasing inscriptions of anti-trans policy, and the corresponding extralegal trans deaths. What I hope to show is that Salas Rivera's material tropes require that I read both knots—of untranslated terms, of queerness—*and* limits of reference, of bombs. These figures require us to ask, How much of coloniality still lingers in the shimmering blues of the *adoquines*? Are these seductions not the same as the smokescreen of beauty that cloaks over the suffering of the Caribbean—echoing Suzanne Césaire and, later, Jamaica Kincaid?[22] In other words, what does the blue of the *adoquines* obscure through camouflage in this small place? "A puerto rico" demands to be read not merely as beautiful abjection but also materially in the aftermath of slavery, as well as through the correlate colonial demands that force islanders to play native for tourists' pleasure, whether by official or unofficial means. What I mean to suggest in this reading of Salas Rivera's translation notes is a poetic thinking, a translation that unballasts English only to let its impact come through by way of nontranslation. This not/knot translation exceeds the language on the page if we attend to the material provenance of that which the poet refuses to translate. This effectively knots together two languages with immense and differential coloniality. Knots gets caught in the throat—as a problem of gender, as a problem of translation. Knots suture and cut across languages.

And the untranslated word demands a reading that takes seriously whether it is or is not, literally, translatable. As Murray-Román reminds us reading Salas Rivera's use of *adoquines*: "Because *adoquines* does have serviceable translation, it is not literally untranslatable. In this sense, the *knots* are untranslatables in Barbara Cassin's terms: an untranslatable does not designate a word that has no linguistic counterpart in other languages, but because those linguistic counterparts fall short, the untranslatable compels one to 'keep on (not) translating.' Recognizing what it would cost the poet to unlink the word from its context and put it through the operation of *trasladar*, the untranslatable instead offers more experiments, new contexts, and different solutions."[23] We read the knot of *adoquines* to see what is registered in the weight of ballast that comes to pave roads that may not be translated but must be read and read dangerously, since what seems most at threat, yet again, is the colonial pavement that allows bombs and fascism to obliterate difference and all possibility of entangled meaning.

What about all of this is anticolonial? The tension explored between English and Spanish as it concerns gender is not one that becomes dialectically resolved. Rather, Salas Rivera's material and poetic return home are coincident, but not collapsible, with trans movements and with anticolonial movements. Yet the figuration of these two ongoing and unresolved movements (in the sense of the political and in the sense of the poetics of these untranslated self-translations) inflect upon each other in ways that surface through figures of violence and nonequivalence that display two languages fraught with coloniality. I know each time I see one of the *adoquines* in Old San Juan, I, too, fall into the seduction of coloniality and time passing. And I know also that many resistance movements have marched over these *adoquines*. Even more closely related to the gender politics at play in Salas Rivera's work, we have seen queer and trans Puerto Ricans vogue and *perreo* (or twerk) on and near these streets during the 2019 *soberano* protests. These island-wide protests took place in the summer of 2019, when the public demanded respect for the dead and for Puerto Rico as chants called for Governor Ricardo Rossello to leave office during a time of massive strikes and protests—and he did. This created tiny fireworks, a change in political power. But time passes over well-trodden forms of disenfranchisement, and so I take Salas Rivera's poetic invocation of the untranslatability of *adoquines* as a provocation to consider both the material history of these *adoquines* and the ballast, or weight, that coloniality holds even in anticolonial poetics. I make this readerly move not to deny the poetic force of Salas Rivera's work but to think about his and other evocations that turn from transness to transmogrification in the colonial predicament. What I want to emphasize is that the weight of referentiality functions here as material ballast that underlies even transfigurations of gender—reminding us that nothing in a colony is inherently anti- or decolonial. Transfiguration is a force, but it is one that explodes as a mere firecracker in the face of a bomb. Transgender figures and queer sexualities cannot, in and of themselves, decolonize colonial foundations because the very stuff of their thinking often relies on colonial grammars.

Tracing a material metaphor, *adoquines*—marked as a figural knot in Salas Rivera's short essay on translation choices in a decolonial key—tracks a tension with referentialities and creates a dual register of myth and material. If the bomb is the obliteration of all figurations, of all scenes of reading, then a ballasted entanglement, like that of *adoquines*, requires us to take the force of untranslation not as untranslatability but as a resistance to transport—a perhaps deferred or delayed arrival of meaning that requires a reading negotiated between two languages at the interstice of Puerto Rico. Here we see how the "x" becomes a figural knot, too, for Salas Rivera, one that stays hinged between the intense locality of enunciation, "a Puerto Rico on a Thursday night,"[24] and larger questions of loss, unincorporation, and gendered crossings. Reading Salas Rivera's work requires an attendance to following convoluted, lyrical lines—ones that may seem familiar but quickly flit from scenes of gender to references to dire colonial conditions. How should we read the title, *X/Ex/Exis*, of this collection that invokes, while also isolating, an "x" that may be from *Latinx*? The first "x" gets caught in the throat because of the different sounds one makes when announcing the letter in two languages conjured and complicated by this letter. English skips to Latin, by pronouncing "x" as *ex*, while Spanish enunciates a syllabic difference: *equis*. The "x" remains a backslash away from Latin. And yet *ex* becomes redoubled in English, as the slang of an ex becomes the vernacular haunting of one's former erotic affairs. And indeed, an ex of the poetic voice is conjured in this section of the poetry collection. Finally, *exis* is one diacritical mark away from *vos exís*, a conjugation hardly used in Puerto Rico, that conjures *exir*. It could be read as a poorly transcribed command: "you take leave," "all of you exit." The "x" itself transmutates across the collection, a movement that commands that one leave—an inhospitable enunciation bereft of the diacritical mark that would make it a command. We may not be welcome to mine gender in a small place.

Transport is metaphor's tropological provenance. This may be one way to revisit Eve Tuck and K. Wayne Yang, who show us that words can only do so much in the face of enduring coloniality.[25] What I hope to show is that one way of responding to Tuck and Yang's critique may be to maintain a vigilance around the status of metaphor so that we may track what is being transported beyond intention. For if Salas Rivera's poetic lines are queer, trans, and knotted, they are also ballasted or referentially pulled—at least in the case of *adoquines*—into the colonial. Not unlike the limestone that grounds Mendieta's cave carvings in Jaruco, *adoquines* function, in this coda, as an inscriptive foundational problem. Salas Rivera's poetics create knotted inscriptions that suture the poetic to materiality at the level of reference, debt, loss, and foundations. As we will recall from the introduction, Salas Rivera invokes material substratum in *lo terciario* as a poetic citation of Marx that titles a poem that figures catachrestically several nothings, which is to say it thinks desperately and incommensurably, about loss. This insistent poetic attention to what we may call historical materialism, coloniality, and gender in Salas Rivera's work motivates why I end the book thinking at the interstice of Puerto Rico by reading his words. This poetics operate at the limit of and hinge between English and Spanish through the envelopment of a prior coloniality (Spanish) under the aegis of US imperialism. This edge occasions one crucial place to think *Latinx* as a catachrestic invocation of how we may begin to think the term in a densely colonially conscribed invocation. Like many other places in the Caribbean and the Americas, Puerto Rico does not enjoy an accessible, precolonial lingua franca with which to articulate colonial counterstance.[26] This is not to say that the Spanish language is only colonial—it suffers constant imperial threat from English's global hegemony and local imperialism.[27] In Puerto Rico, Spanish's precarity on the island was most deeply felt when the US government threatened to change the national language to English, which failed. This shows the limitations of the reach of English, including a limitation on demands to transition to a lingua franca of global commerce for either speech or political movements. And yet, celebrating the resistance of Spanish creates a colonial conundrum that cannot be adjudicated by way of gender without an attention to race. The larger context of the Caribbean necessitates that we think long and hard about claims for anti- or decoloniality, not simply because the region has suffered so much due to waves of historical and ongoing colonization, but also because the ability to defy such sedimented historical processes does not easily come by way of symbolic change.

In *X/Ex/Exis*, we see the entanglement of transformation and its limit, the bomb. That is, at the level of the untranslated knot, we see a reference to colonial infrastructure that creates a knot with that bomb. What I find in Salas Rivera's knots is more akin to what the "x" may or may not do in the constrictions or at the meeting point of two languages that carry a bulwark of violence. This violence is well beyond, but is also constituted through, a gender binary code that is differential in the languages wherein gendered utterances are grammatically nonequivalent. Both languages and the cosmologies they issue from traffic in a colonial and racial project that functions often through sexuation. This may be one way to think with Francisco Galarte's invitation to read with the "x" rather than assign it the work of representation: "We must, then, think of the 'x' as not relieving the burden of the binary; it represents an opportunity to interrogate the effects of binaristic and dualistic thinking. I ask that we challenge ourselves to read for and with the 'x.'"[28] Precisely by (k)notting an entanglement of matter and figure that exemplifies the tension inherent in *Latinx*—both the "Latin" and the "x"—"x" only remains in this poetry volume, and "Latin" is absorbed into Spanish and Puerto Rico. That is, the "x" is absorbed into undeniable coloniality and a language that, in this space-time configuration, is at least less powerful than the imperial English that sought to erase Puerto Rican accents and grammars in the mid-twentieth century. The "x" then is unincorporated here; it remains in the margins as a gendered aspect de-linked from "Latin" that precisely makes it an especially felicitous place to read the "x" without an overdetermined attachment to the lives that "make it" to English and to the States. In this way, the "x" is one knot between the two languages, one figured not as a gesture but as knotted speech—*un nudo en la garganta*, a knot in the throat. And when something is caught in the throat, speech becomes difficult. "X," too, is a letter best pronounced in the back of the mouth, near the throat. This knot connotes entanglement in its figural askesis, but so too does it conjure a homonym of *not*. This knot operates at the hinge of two languages and acknowledges that all gender is translation—issued in grammars that are all too often ensconced in colonial taxonomies.

Between knots in the throat, colonially paved streets, and governments manufacturing bombs, the lines of Salas Rivera's poetics unfurl scenes of violence that threaten to make all difference illegible. The embodied moments of resistance, then, lay bare that the foundations of these streets and lines are indeed colonial and that their legibility, even the refusal of them, finds a limit in the figure of the bomb. The line, either knotted or circled and always lyrical, creates possible entanglements of queerness and (anti)coloniality. Yet if decolonization is not a metaphor, as Tuck and Wang propose, then our task is not to readily align trans with necessarily anticolonial. If the line is queer and knotted, it is also ballasted or referentially pulled—at least in the case of *adoquines*—into the colonial. Then we have a very trans, very queer problem of colonial foundations that asks us to attend to two things that Salas Rivera's work reveals: no language has gender transmitted faithfully and neither Spanish nor English can detach itself from the weight of coloniality. This does not mean one won't find gender play, as well as peril, in these linguistic knots. Rather, our task is not to find the right language or even word or even letter but to read, to translate, to think through the status of the untranslatable (of gender, of a critique of coloniality). Or put another way, if we see in *Preguntas frecuentes* a thinking of the entanglement of a colonized Spanish or a Spanish within a colony and queerness, in *X/Ex/Exis*, we see the entanglement of transformation and its limit, the bomb. That is, at the level of the untranslated knot, we see a colonial infrastructure that creates a knot with that bomb. These are larger questions that return us to the problem of collapsing semiotics with materiality. The bomb as a figure, in Salas Rivera's words, does not represent—it does not transport meaning, and it perhaps resists, or should resist, metaphorization. The bomb, then, becomes both a fascist figure, an imperial instrument, and a radioactive remainder that will not dissipate fast enough. The bomb creates a dangerous threat that is not speculative, that has been dropped, and this fact lingers in both colonial dust and in the waters of Vieques. The bomb becomes a referential limit. Reference meets a kind of edge with certain material figures—one where we cannot but read the reference to a bomb as something that requires a consideration of material reference as necessary ethical and political work that extends us beyond the text through a word that has no natural relation to its referent. The *adoquines* remind us of the problem of material reference, of its pull into a past not always legible at the surface, of the grounding grammars that are undeniably colonial. Tying coloniality to fascism, Salas Rivera's transfigurative movements find a limit in the bomb that scrambles time and shuttles us into the past, present, and future of nuclear coloniality under imperialism.

We are asked to think this limit anew in the figure of the bomb—a figure of fascist force. Following the bomb's limit, the reading of Salas

Rivera's knotted inscriptions entails taking both figuration and materiality seriously. These tense poetics constantly shift, sometimes withhold, and frequently negotiate referential limits. This tension issues a foundational problem for *Latinx* and an urgent need to think referentiality and materiality anew—not as literal, not as the real, not as raw evidence. Fascism works perniciously as a faith in transparent ideals and can aestheticize politics in a way that does not think about the mediation of the aesthetic, whether it be poetry, a performance, or an identitarian term. Just as levels of loss cannot be neatly collapsed into one another, so too do fascisms vary in scale and structure. We may think of *Latinx* within the limits and pulls of language, which requires us to read beyond idealism and to question our source—to attend to material provenance that de-idealizes metaphorical flourishes as anticolonial. Attending to the limits of language may be reading's most urgent task.

Salas Rivera's untranslated knot of the *adoquines* requires consideration of the problem of material reference, of its pull into a past not always legible at the surface, of the grounding grammars that are undeniably colonial. Tying coloniality to fascism, Salas Rivera's transfigurative movements find a limit in the bomb that scrambles time and shuttles us into the past, present, and future of nuclear coloniality under imperialism. In reading these tense poetics, I articulate that the figuration of Latinx reveals itself within the limits and pulls of language, which requires us to read beyond idealism and to question our sources. This task of reading even language's limits may allow us to attend to the overlap and dissonance between linguistic and material forms of loss. Salas Rivera's poetics occasion a place to read a poem at its limit—asking us to feel the force, or weight, of the limit that is within the violence of bombs. Here, then, what becomes more important than stating difference is the material provenance and aftermath of large-scale violence. It is within inscriptions that we may imagine this violence, but the urgency of this reading would require an attendant material shift beyond poetry, beyond metaphor. Incommensurable loss knotted into the *adoquines* leads me to consider the weight of coloniality that paves the streets of Old San Juan, to consider material and historical registers that pull the reference of *adoquines* into the violence that, perhaps, entangles them with the bombs that in Salas Rivera's pen do not represent.

ACKNOWLEDGMENTS

The undertaking of writing a book takes more than a village. It takes endless conversations and questions, many other books, other writings, and other works. It takes care, generosity, patience, inspiration, and time. This book is the humble result of my being a node in a network of so many who inspire, support, and question. The moments where my own book meets limits are mine alone, but my limitations have been diminished by the many I would like to thank with utter sincerity.

I must begin by paying gratitude to Ronald Mendoza-de Jesús for over fifteen years of rigorously intense discussions. Our conversations have punctuated every pivotal moment in my thinking since we started talking in 2008 and certainly every stage of this book. *Mil gracias* for being all that you are, with equal parts danger and *cariño*, and also somehow also miraculously *mi hermanito*.

As I was completing this manuscript, we lost the great literary scholar and critical aesthete José A. Quiroga—and I lost someone much more than a dissertation advisor. My deepest thanks go to José for taking this cubanita under his wing. And, really, I don't know how to put into words my gratitude. I can name all that I benefited from: his brilliant aestheticism, his witty antagonism, or his relentless desire for more. But that hardly captures how and who he was to and for me. Let me offer a glimpse of his singular mode, since I have yet to find a way to honor the whole of this wonderful scholar and friend. We were in a cab in Buenos Aires in 2009, heading to some fabulously queer art show that, of course, José knew all about, and the cabbie asked us where we were from. Without missing a beat, he answered, "Somos cubanos." That moment, which registered in a language that was and was not mine, made it magically more mine—or, at least, inhabitable. And when I say language, I mean something like the trace structure of my belonging. So, to José, thank you for queering that most poignant and pivotal moment of my latinidad, such as it is. *Te extraño un montón*. This book could not be what it is without your many invitations to tables, to friends, to writers, to artists. You curated a wholly singular education for me, seemingly effortlessly, and have left a good many of us desolately desirous for more, much more. It is for this reason that this book is dedicated to José A. Quiroga, to his incredible queer, diasporic life and to his formidable and elegant scholarship.

This book project emerged from the dissertation I wrote under José A. Quiroga's guidance, along with Michael Moon and Lynne Huffer at Emory University. Thank you to Lynne Huffer who has read so many pages, vetted so many questions, and taught me more than I can express here. I find that I keep returning to Lynne's seminars and questions in my mind. And I am thrilled and humbled to now call her a friend. To Michael Moon, thank you for sharing a brilliant literary interdisciplinarity with me—one that knows just when to cheat on a discipline. Kim Emery and Leah Rosenberg inspired seeds that grew into a PhD and, ultimately, this book. Thanks to both for such remarkable teaching at the University of Florida—no small feat then and certainly not now. To Nishant Shahani and Mindy Cardozo, thank you for starting this critical theory 352 train by sharing your brilliance. Thanks also go to Suzanne Bost and Tace Hedrick for teaching crucial Latinx feminisms to a very young version of me.

My PhD years laid the foundation for many years of query that continue to reverberate. In addition to my superb committee, all of whom taught truly life-changing seminars, I had the pleasure to learn from Elissa Marder, Shoshana Felman, Mark Jordan, María Carrión, Cathy Caruth, Jonathan Goldberg, and Elizabeth Wilson. Thanks to each for creating events in the classroom and for modeling pedagogical and scholarly rigor. Ania Kowalik was key in turning me into a Caribbeanist, and I am grateful for her direction. I thank Rebecca Kumar for the privilege of being in proximity to her brave and resilient heart and mind. Many others from my Emory grad school days have my gratitude as well: Aaron Goldsman, Alyssa Stalsberg, Joey Orr, Nikki Karekalas, Melinda Robb, Mairead Sullivan, and Dana Irwin.

At Oregon State University, Mila Zuo, Lily Sheehan, Anita Helle, and Megan Ward were fantastic, even necessary, scholars to know early in my career. Mila keeps me on fire as a fellow Leo, and I'm so grateful for our friendship. During my time at Princeton, Catherine Clune Taylor, Autumn Womack, Monica Huerta, Russ Leo, Zahid Chaudhary, Gayle

Salamon, Eduardo Cadava, Rachel Price, and Irene Small created a community filled with sharp thinking. At Duke, I am both humbled and grateful to be with such wonderful colleagues in the literature program. Before I even started here, Antonio Viego, Rey Chow, Ranjana Khanna, and Robyn Wiegman shaped my thinking in formidable ways—putting to words and bringing to light phenomena felt but not articulated until I read their impressive words and bold thinking. I am grateful to them, as well as the rest of my colleagues in the Program in Literature and at Duke University, especially Maya Kronfeld, Jennifer Nash, Anna Storti, and Nikki Lane.

Many thanks to Alexandra Vazquez, Mary Pat Brady, and Licia Fiol-Matta for helping me discover that these pages may yet amount to a book and, also, for their nuanced and articulate feminisms. They each took time to face even more Zoom calls over the pandemic and cut through the noise to help me distill this book. Rocío Zambrana revealed herself to me as a reviewer of this manuscript at a crucial time. She is a scholar who never ceases to amaze with her passionate philosophical praxis. I thank her for taking the time to question my work while creating work that constantly helps me to question.

It is a privilege to work among scholars who expose me to frameworks of thinking that have kept me in the most vibrant of dialogues. I met Iván Ramos, Joshua J. Guzmán, Vivian Huang, Kareem Khubchandani, and Kemi Adeyemi in what can only be described as a performance studies summer camp at Northwestern University, and this became an aperture in my career and in knowing exciting academics. Each has stayed with me over the years, and though it isn't constant, I love how we manage to always find one another. To Iván and Josh, thank you for sharing the dance floor, the page, and the music. Through them, I met the incredible Summer Kim Lee, my GGG, who has read my work, shared hotel rooms, and given me the intelligent, feminist companionship of both laughter and vulnerability. At Irvine, I met the amazing Judith Rodríguez, *mi pana*, whose work continually pushes my thinking and whose friendship has become a vital part of my survival tool kit. Thank you, Judy, for the spirit of your fortitude and intelligence from which I have tried to learn a thing or two. I met Roy Pérez at a vegan dinner in Chicago that all of a sudden placed us in networks of Cuba, LA, Florida, and Oregon. His humor and intelligence have been a salve in this career. Greta La Fleur and Poulomi Saha have been guiding lights in this profession—and a really good time too!

Misty de Berry appeared over a Zoom screen and taught me the power of breath before writing; *gracias amorcita*. Dixa Ramírez and Ren Ellis Neyra have brought a critical Caribbean underscore to my scholarly life, and I am grateful for their friendship and support. RL Goldberg asked me about books enough, and we disagreed enough, that the foundations for a solid friendship were laid in the basement of McCosh. Many also read various aspects of this project, and I thank them for their kind and patient editorial eyes, especially RL Goldberg, Summer Kim Lee, Ronald Mendoza-de Jesús, Meredith Lee, Benjamin Brewer, and Melinda Robb.

So many have been instrumental interlocutors, and so I also thank Alberto Varón, Melissa Sanchez, Kyla Wazana Tompkins, Erin Graff Zivin, Deb Vargas, Kirstie Dorr, Sara Clarke Kaplan, Juana María Rodríguez, Rubén Ríos Ávila, Ramón Rivera Servera, Cristina Beltrán, Laura Gutierrez, Ricardo Ortiz, Rachel Galvin, Yogita Goyal, Carlos Decena, Amber Musser, Zakiyyah Iman Jackson, Nicole Morris Johnson, Olivia Gagnon, H. Rakes, Natalie Belisle, Kimberly Bain, Omari Weekes, Ren Heinz, Ralph Rodriguez, Joseph Miranda, Tommy Conners, Uri McMillan, Alberto Sergio Laguna, Leticia Alvarado, C. Riley Snorton, Perry Zurn, Shane Vogel, Axelle Karera, and Erica Edwards. Thank you to Brian Herrera and Anne Garcia Romero for their work on sustaining the legacy of María Irene Fornés. Thanks to Michelle Memran for supplying a crucial image, as well as for her work documenting *la Fornés*. Thanks to Norge Mendoza Espinosa and Roberto Zurbano for the work they do in Cuba, which I was able to witness in 2017. It is profound. Thanks also go to Chiara Merino for showing me her San Juan and for the poetry of her writing, her laughter, and her smile.

I have had the occasion to present this work at a number of universities, conferences, and symposia. Marcia Ochoa, Deb Vargas, and Kirstie Dorr generously conceived of and convened the Queer Hemisphere residential fellowship through the UCHRI, which afforded me intellectual community and time to think and write in the fall of 2016, which further allowed me to refine aspects of my chapter on Manuel Ramos Otero. This chapter also received helpful feedback from Cornell University scholars as well as graduate students and faculty at the University of Pennsylvania. Scholars at the University of Southern California allowed me to think through this book project on two occasions and helped me to refine the project's frame. My first chapter was a work in progress for some time and found extremely helpful audiences at the University of Maryland, College Park and with the Dartmouth Society of Fellows. At the Postcolonial Studies Symposium, at the University of California, Berkeley, at Yale University, and at the University of British Columbia, I was able to refine the coda. Scholars at the University of Indiana, Bloomington and at Williams College helped me to sense the direction of the chapter on María Irene Fornés. My fellow members of Women in Theory, in particular Zakiyyah Iman Jackson, Natalie Belisle, and Rocío Zambrana, helped me to fortify my interest in catachresis. I am grateful to Erin Graff Zivin for her labor in organizing us and organizing many other scholarly conversations.

Teaching affords such conceptual promise, and so I thank each of my students over the years and across institutions for reading with me. To read in community is one of the luckiest parts of my life. I am especially grateful to graduate students who have enlivened seminars and meetings: Lindsay Griffiths Brown, Annabelle Haynes, Alex Díaz Hui, Paulina Pineda, Angela Brown, Charmaine Branch, Jolaun Hunter, Shanna Killeen, and Anthie Georgiadi. I am grateful, as well, for the lessons learned while coteaching with Adam Schwartz, Zahid Chaudhary, RL Goldberg, and Annabelle Haynes.

During the conceptualization and writing of this book, many scholars left this world who bent the thinking in these pages in remarkable ways: Eve Kosofsky Sedgwick, Barbara Johnson, Édouard Glissant, Mara Negrón, José Esteban Muñoz, María Irene Fornés, Lauren Berlant, Jonathan Goldberg, and José Antonio Quiroga. I am grateful for what their work has made possible and for the many who continue their lessons—sharing their legacy with those of us who didn't spend as much time with as much brilliance. I can only hope that this work begins to answer a few of the many calls and provocations of their thinking.

Friends outside of academia kept me grounded, and such grounding made academia possible: Rose Khor, Jonathan Kern, Charlie Godwin, Lindsay Lége, Coco Conroy, Angel Phillips, Chloe Kupfer, Kate Tettemer, and Andre Keichian. I am so grateful to each of you for bearing with me over many, many years of time and space separation. I am grateful, as well, to artists whose work incites critical thought: Amina Cruz and Xandra Ibarra.

To thank the artists that dwell within these pages perhaps goes without saying, but I am enormously grateful for what their work has allowed me to think: Zilia Sánchez, Ana Mendieta, Manuel Ramos Otero, Justin Torres, and Roque Salas Rivera. I am grateful to the Sánchez and Mendieta estates and Galerie LeLong for gorgeous images, as well as to Matt Rubio and Roy Pérez for others. Thanks go to the NYU Press team, especially Eric Zinner, for seeing this project through.

Portions of the introduction, chapter 2, and the coda were developed in earlier essays and articles: León, Christina. "Risking Catachresis: Reading Race, Reference, and Grammar in 'Women,'" *Diacritics* 49, no. 1 (2021): 61–71; León, Christina. "Exorbitant Dust: Manuel Ramos Otero's Queer and Colonial Matters," *GLQ* 27, no. 3 (2021): 357–77; and León, Christina. "Knots in the Throat: Raquel Salas Rivera Ballasted Entanglements," *Representations* 161, no. 1 (2023): 109–24.

Finally, I want to thank the people without whom the questions that hover over this book would not have been asked: my family. My cousins might not expect to be here, but now, at midlife, I see how steadily they've accompanied me—even when I'm too busy to visit. Thank you to Raina, Matthew, Andy, Marcía, Iván, and Bill, *mis primos*. To my mother, thank you for teaching me my first lessons in aesthetics, for modeling an ethical life, and for showing me the power of intuitive intelligence—one that is equal parts kind and sharp. To my father, thank you for giving me a global imaginary, for teaching a very young me the concept of infinity while we lived in the Philippines. To my brother, thanks for teaching me an acute queer resilience—one that knows that words can endear as well as defend. To Spoo, Patrick, and Cosmo, thanks for all you've said without words and for all the moments of quiet and adventurous companionship. To Han, I thank you endlessly for walking into my life at just the right time, for giving me the feeling of coming home with such handsome charm and exquisite taste in music, for healing me time and again when my body and person falter, and for your ceaseless curiosity about and patience with my writing process. Your grace astounds, as does your Aquarian mind and your steady heart.

NOTES

INTRODUCTION. LATINX REMARKS

1 Cristina Beltrán, *The Trouble with Unity: Latino Politics and the Creation of Identity* (New York: Oxford University Press, 2010), 6.
2 Paul de Man, "Hypogram and Inscription: Michael Riffaterre's Poetics of Reading," *Diacritics* 11, no. 4 (1981): 17; Jacques Derrida, "Force and Signification," in *Writing and Difference*, trans. Alan Bass (Chicago: University of Chicago, 1978), 3–30.
3 See Judith Butler, *Gender Trouble: Feminism and the Subversion of Identity* (New York: Routledge, 2006), 163–80; and Hortense J. Spillers, "'All the Things You Could Be by Now, If Sigmund Freud's Wife Was Your Mother': Psychoanalysis and Race," *Boundary 2* 23, no. 3 (1996): 710–34.
4 See Paul Benzon and Rita Raley, eds., "Inscriptive Studies," special issue, *ASAP/Journal* 7, no. 2 (May 2022). They write, "Within the inscriptive, form and content collapse; across medium and genre, inscriptive works both hinge on and reflexively attend to inscription itself, broadly construed, as both means and end in varying proportions" (225). See also Avery Slater, "Materiality and the Digital Future of Inscription," *Symplokē* 26, nos. 1–2 (2018): 461.
5 In relation to thinking tropologically in Latinx studies, I am particularly indebted to Emma Pérez's insights on tropological overdeterminations of *Chicanidad* in *The Decolonial Imaginary: Writing Chicanas into History* (Bloomington: Indiana University Press, 1999) and an extension of this tropological thinking in Francisco Galarte's *Brown Trans Figurations: Rethinking Race, Gender, and Sexuality in Chicanx/Latinx Studies* (Austin: University of Texas Press, 2021).
6 For deft readings of these institutional histories, see Roderick A. Ferguson, *The Reorder of Things: The University and Its Pedagogies of Minority Difference* (Minneapolis: University of Minnesota Press, 2012); Robyn Wiegman, *Object Lessons* (Durham, NC: Duke University Press, 2012); and Sara Ahmed, *On Being Included: Racism and Diversity in Institutional Life* (Durham, NC: Duke University Press, 2012).
7 See Phillip Brian Harper, *Abstractionist Aesthetics: Artistic Form and Social Critique in African American Culture* (New York: New York University Press, 2015); and Kadji Amin, Amber Musser, and Roy Pérez, "Queer Form: Aesthetics, Race, and the Violences of the Social," *ASAP/Journal* 2, no. 2 (May 2017): 227–39.

8 See Beltrán, *Trouble with Unity*; and Ralph E. Rodriguez, *Latinx Literature Unbound: Undoing Ethnic Expectation* (New York: Fordham University Press, 2018).
9 Irene V. Small's reading of *El significado del significante* is instructive here: "Reference and association—but also tension and dispersal—thus build laterally, through an allusive spreading or unfurling in which marked and unmarked share equally in a given drawing's pictorial and affective force." I also want to thank Small for urging me to further plumb Sánchez's work. See Small's "On Zilia Sánchez's Surface," in *Zilia Sánchez: Heróicas Eróticas en Nueva York* (New York: Galerie LeLong, 2014), 7.
10 By diagnosing this sedimentation of critical thought after the linguistic turn, I am not critiquing important conversations around the work of signifiers. Rather, I wonder what happens to our critical attention if we circle back to the signified as an equally compelling problem for reading.
11 Jacques Derrida, *Of Grammatology*, trans. Gayatri Chakravorty Spivak (Baltimore, MD: Johns Hopkins University Press, 2016), 7.
12 I am thinking here of the work of Judith Butler, Hortense Spillers, Frantz Fanon, and Andrea Bachner, to name but a few.
13 Zilia Sánchez, interview by Stefan Kalmár and Richard Birkett in March 2013, Artists Space, November 7, 2013, YouTube video, 15:47, https://www.youtube.com/watch?v=9LRddY6f9Kc.
14 Zilia Sánchez, "In Retrospect," interview Vesela Sretenovic, in *Zilia Sánchez: Soy Isla*, ed. Vesela Sretenovic (New Haven, CT: Yale University Press, 2019), 22.
15 Sánchez, 22.
16 Sánchez, 22.
17 My thinking of danger is indebted to years of conversations with Ronald Mendoza-de Jesús about his book *Catastrophic Historicism: Reading Julia de Burgos Dangerously* (New York: Fordham University Press, 2023). There, he theorizes with a Benjaminian noting of danger: "Danger *endangers* the link between possibility and mastery that enabled the historicist and their cosmo-poetic narratives to declare themselves the ground of the historicity of the past . . . reading danger names a historical practice that interrupts historicism by reintroduction contingency and nonlinearity into the text of history" (13).
18 For a longer mediation on lingering in latinidad, see Joshua Javier Guzmán and Christina A. León, "Cuts and Impressions: The Aesthetic Work of Lingering in Latinidad," *Women & Performance: A Journal of Feminist Theory* 25, no. 3 (September 2015): 261–76.
19 See Sandra K. Soto, *Reading Chican@ like a Queer: The De-mastery of Desire* (Austin: University of Texas Press, 2010).
20 For excellent scholarly conversations on Latinx debates, see Claudia Milian, ed., "LatinX Studies: Variations and Velocities," special issue, *Cultural Dynamics* 31, nos. 1–2 (February–May 2019); and Claudia Milian, ed., "Theorizing LatinX," special issue, *Cultural Dynamics* 29, no. 3 (August 2017). See also Catalina (Kathleen) M.

de Onís, "What's in an 'X'? An Exchange about the Politics of 'Latinx,'" *Chiricú Journal: Latina/o Literatures, Arts, and Cultures* 1, no. 2 (2017): 78–91.

21 My thinking at the interstice of matter and meaning is indebted to many scholars who tarry with new materialisms while centering marked differences of either gender or race/ethnicity. Among many, I have learned much from Zakiyyah Iman Jackson's *Becoming Human: Matter and Meaning in an Antiblack World* (New York: New York University Press, 2020); Karen Michelle Barad's *Meeting the Universe Halfway: Quantum Physics and the Entanglement of Matter and Meaning* (Durham, NC: Duke University Press, 2007); and Mel Y. Chen's *Animacies: Biopolitics, Racial Mattering, and Queer Affect* (Durham, NC: Duke University Press, 2012).

22 Following the work of Macarena Gómez-Barros, I take her attentive critique of extraction and consider it in reading practices, cultural capital, and instrumentalist approaches to aesthetic encounters. See Macarena Gómez-Barris, *The Extractive Zone: Social Ecologies and Decolonial Perspectives* (Durham, NC: Duke University Press, 2017).

23 Rey Chow, *A Face Drawn in Sand: Humanistic Study and Foucault in the Present* (New York: Columbia University Press, 2021), 19–20.

24 See Ricardo L. Ortiz, *Latinx Literature Now: Between Evanescence and Event* (New York: Springer, 2019).

25 Rodriguez, *Latinx Literature Unbound*, 51.

26 In an elegant footnote, Mary Pat Brady writes, "Terminology here proves very difficult. Latina/o (and, eventually, Latinx) emerged as a scalar attempt to draw together different constituencies; it names a desire for a new collectivity, one that scales up people who may be hailed by their own or their great-great grandparents' nation of origin or their settler/colonial status or even their status as what Jodi Byrd in *The Transit of Empire* calls arrivants." Mary Pat Brady, *Scales of Captivity: Racial Capitalism and the Latinx Child* (Durham, NC: Duke University Press, 2022), 250–51. It is worth noting, too, that Mary Pat Brady considers scale, like border, to be a metaphor made material (19). That is, the idea of scale does not describe, nor does it replace, a material condition—it is rather a metaphor that materially clines and values its objects.

27 For a critique of J. L. Austin's logic around contextual saturation, see Jacques Derrida, "Signature, Event, Context," in *Limited Inc*, trans. Samuel Weber and Jeffrey Mehlman (Evanston, IL: Northwestern University Press, 1988), 1–24.

28 For an incredibly thorough history of how *Hispanic*—the progenitor to *Latino* and now *Latinx*—came to be, see G. Cristina Mora, *Making Hispanics: How Activists, Bureaucrats, and Media Constructed a New American* (Chicago: University of Chicago Press, 2014).

29 For a compelling critique of scalar logics, see Brady, *Scales of Captivity*.

30 For helpful work on Latinx autobiography and memoir, see Suzanne Bost, *Shared Selves: Latinx Memoir and Ethical Alternatives to Humanism* (Urbana: University

of Illinois Press, 2019); and David J. Vázquez, *Triangulations: Narrative Strategies for Navigating Latino Identity* (Minneapolis: University of Minnesota Press, 2011).

31 My thinking of relatability as a frustrating demand upon minoritarian subjects is inspired by the work of Summer Kim Lee, who shows how the sociality imposed upon Asian American subjects by whiteness is to be relatable and accommodating. She pivots to moments when said subjects "stay in" themselves in order to sustain the arduous work of relationality and political change. See Summer Kim Lee, "Staying In: Mitski, Ocean Vuong, and Asian American Asociality," *Social Text* 37, no. 1 (March 2019): 27–50.

32 Walter Benjamin, "The Task of the Translator," in *Illuminations*, ed. Hannah Arendt, trans. Harry Zohn (New York: Schocken, 2007), 80.

33 Manuel Ramos Otero, "Ficción e historia: Texto y pretexto de la autobiografía," *El Mundo*, October 14, 1990, 22. All translations are mine unless otherwise indicated.

34 Judith Butler, *Giving an Account of Oneself* (New York: Fordham University Press, 2005), 37.

35 In this manner, my approach considers matters beyond logocentrism or sociological thinking. This attunement to affect and sense resonates with the work of Ren Ellis Neyra, who writes, "Multisensorial poetic listening and sonically oriented close-readings yield synesthetic reattunement and generate swerving creative-critical movement. The copulations of possibility in the aforesaid adverbial and gerundive arrangements offer emotional refuges to imaginatively avow submerged sensorial solidarities inter alia that elude violent, monohuman, liberal, economic sovereignty." Ren Ellis Neyra, *The Cry of the Senses: Listening to Latinx and Caribbean Poetics* (Durham, NC: Duke University Press, 2020), 17.

36 "Within the inscriptive, form and content collapse; across medium and genre, inscriptive works both hinge on and reflexively attend to inscription itself, broadly construed, as both means and end in varying proportions." Benzon and Raley, "Inscriptive Studies," 225. See also Andrea Bachner, *The Mark of Theory: Inscriptive Figures, Poststructuralist Prehistories* (New York: Fordham University Press, 2018); Slater, "Materiality"; and Andrzej Warminski, *Material Inscriptions: Rhetorical Reading in Practice and Theory* (Edinburgh: Edinburgh University Press, 2013).

37 Ferdinand de Saussure, *Course in General Linguistics*, ed. Charles Bally and Albert Sechehaye, trans. Roy Harris (LaSalle, IL: Open Court, 1986), 111.

38 My use of the phrase "general space of possibility" comes from Jacques Derrida's insights into writing in "Signature, Event, Context," wherein the absence of intention, consciousness, and presence is presupposed in the graphematic structure of communication. This space is also the spacing, the "iter," of *différance*. That is, for Derrida, *différance* is not merely difference but introduces a radical alterity in the spacing, the iterability, that makes writing possible: the trace structure. Derrida clarifies "that general space is first of all spacing as a disruption of presence in a mark, what I here call writing." Derrida, "Signature, Event, Context," 19. That the space is generalizable takes it beyond what we may call empirical inscription or even language. For an excellent materialist reading of Derrida's trace structure, see

Deborah Goldgaber's "Programmed to Fail? On the Limits of Inscription and the Generality of Writing," *Journal of Speculative Philosophy* 31, no. 3 (2017): 444–57; and *Speculative Grammatology: Deconstruction and the New Materialism (Speculative Materialism)* (Edinburgh: Edinburgh University Press, 2020).

39 Bachner echoes my thinking with the linguistic turn while sharing concerns about the limitations of only thinking within the realm of signification: "Thinking in terms of inscription would be unthinkable without the linguistic turn, and yet, at the same time, it consists of a reaction against it, since, for proponents of inscription, the levels of material and structure can no longer be differentiated as neatly. Instead, through the lens of inscription, thinkers focus their attention on how materiality and signification interact; and inscription becomes one of the models for theorizing this interaction." Bachner, *Mark of Theory*, 3. Bachner also calls our attention, in her chapter "Savage Marks," to the anthropological insights into inscription that haunt deconstructive terrain, especially around questions of gender and race. She traces how marks of gender and race have been thought to be inscribed upon the body.

40 José Esteban Muñoz critiques the "burden of liveness" in performance art for racially marked artists. See his *Disidentifications: Queers of Color and the Performance of Politics* (Minneapolis: University of Minnesota Press, 1999).

41 Antonio Viego, *Dead Subjects: Toward a Politics of Loss in Latino Studies* (Durham, NC: Duke University Press, 2007), 15.

42 Antonio Viego writes, "The challenge for us would be to craft analyses that can read for the historical specificity and texture of loss that is constitutive of subjectivity in relation to those losses that can be attributed to the unequal distribution of social and material resources, losses that continually appear to accrue more on the side of some people than others." Viego, 50.

43 A skeptic of the linguistic turn, Christopher Breu reminds us, "The referential function of language is the crucial way in which the materiality of language intersects with other forms of materiality and attempts to be adequate to them. One of the problems with the linguistic turn was its insistence, following Saussure, that reference should be bracketed. What I am resisting instead is the notion that the referent can be fully adequate to what it refers." But if a referent is what is referred to, then here we have a slight elision between signified and referent. And this elision warrants a reconsideration of how much we have eschewed and eclipsed matters of signified concepts and material referents. The matter of reference entangles the conceptual work of signifieds because of the abyss that remains between "the referent" and how a sign's signified conceptual work refers, thus morphing how we understand the supposed referent. My emphasis on catachresis encourages this reading where reference itself may not originate from the supposed "referents"—since catachresis exposes the discomfit of referentiality. Christopher Breu, *Insistence of the Material: Literature in the Age of Biopolitics* (Minneapolis: University of Minnesota Press, 2014), 184.

44 Jacques Derrida, "Deconstruction in America," interview by James Creech, Peggy Kamuf, and Jane Todd, *Critical Exchange* 17 (Winter 1985): 20.

45 Chuh writes,
> I have for some time been attuned to my irritation with "aboutness," partly because of the regularity and normativity of the practices and questions organized by and around it. This plays out in such ordinary academic activities as the creation of doctoral exam lists, course titling, and departmental hiring practices, all of which still largely follow the dogmatism of mastery-of-field ideology. It seems to me that the determination of what something (a novel, a field of study, a lecture) is "about" often is conducted as a way of avoiding engagement with "difference," especially with racialized difference. I'm pointing attention to how aboutness functions as an assessment of relevance and within the racialized economy of academic knowledge (canonical knowledge reproducing whiteness continues to center the US academy and thus ensures that higher education maintain its long tradition of contributing to the reproduction of social inequality) preserves the (racist) epistemologies of (neo)liberalism through a reproductive logic that is utterly unqueer. (Kandice Chuh, "It's Not about Anything," *Social Text* 32, no. 4 [2014]: 127.)

46 Rey Chow makes this point emphatically in the introduction to *Ethics after Idealism: Theory, Culture, Ethnicity, Reading* (Bloomington: Indiana University Press, 1998).

47 The following work on catachresis was previously published in Christina A. León, "Risking Catachresis: Reading Race, Reference, and Grammar in 'Women,'" *Diacritics* 49, no. 1 (2021): 61–71. For the purposes of this introduction, the excerpts have been edited to concern issues beyond the category of "woman."

48 See Rodriguez, *Latinx Literature Unbound*; Ortiz, *Latinx Literature Now*; and Vázquez, *Triangulations*.

49 For more on this dilemma in the work of Xandra Ibarra, see Christina A. León, "Forms of Opacity: Roaches, Blood, and Being Stuck in Xandra Ibarra's Corpus," *ASAP/Journal* 2, no. 2 (2017): 369–94.

50 My thinking of *imposition* as a concept to truly tarry with at the level of ontology is indebted to Judith Rodríguez's forthcoming manuscript, *Impositions: The Aesthetic Blackening of Puerto Rico and Its Diaspora*.

51 See Viego, *Dead Subjects*.

52 See Viego.

53 See Rey Chow, "The Fascist Longings in Our Midst," in *Ethics after Idealism: Theory, Culture, Ethnicity, Reading* (Bloomington: Indiana University Press, 1998), 14–32.

54 Chow, *Ethics after Idealism*, 32.

55 Denise Ferreira da Silva, *Toward a Global Idea of Race* (Minneapolis: University of Minnesota Press, 2007), xviii.

56 Da Silva, xxxi.

57 Patricia Parker, "Metaphor and Catachresis," in *The Ends of Rhetoric: History, Theory, Practice*, ed. John B. Bender and David E. Wellbery (Stanford, CA: Stanford University Press, 1990), 60.

58 Gerard Posselt, "The Tropological Economy of Catachresis," in *Metaphors of Economy*, ed. Nicole Bracker and Stefan Herbrechter (Boston, MA: BRILL, 2005), 86.
59 Often aligned with a Derridean notion of language, *catachresis* is a term that has had a strange relationship to the troping of language. For Derrida, it signals the originary incompleteness and indeterminacy of language. For Paul de Man, it is a term that reconfigures metaphor into amalgams. And Andrej Warminski draws our attention to the thinking of de Manian inscriptions that carry the materiality of language itself. If Derrida's insights on catachresis and metaphor are helpful here, and I think they are, it's because of a particular kind of commitment both to understanding figuration and its valuation, its economy. One turn of the screw that takes Saussure out of his axiomatic claim that signs are arbitrary is that this makes sense only in a frozen, synchronic view of language—a kind of scientific freeze that would stop all dissemination. Only then could you turn arbitrariness into a static value.
60 Parker, "Metaphor and Catachresis," 61.
61 Parker, 73.
62 Raquel Salas Rivera, *the tertiary / lo terciario*, 2nd ed. (Blacksburg, VA: Noemi, 2019), 20. Note that in this book, I use Salas Rivera's current publishing name, Roque, which shifted after the publication of many of his texts that I explore.
63 For an excellent exploration of the use of catachresis in the work of Karl Marx, particularly in his theorizations of abstract value, see Sianne Ngai, "Visceral Abstractions," *GLQ* 21, no. 1 (2015): 33–63.
64 In this manner, we see catachresis arise in the work of feminist theorists who range over time and concern: Luce Irigaray, Judith Butler, Gayatri Spivak, Lynne Huffer, and Ranjana Khanna.
65 See Gayatri Spivak, *The Post-colonial Critic: Interviews, Strategies, Dialogue* (New York: Routledge University Press, 1990), 104.
66 See Gayatri Spivak, *"Can the Subaltern Speak?" Marxism and Interpretation of Culture*, ed. Cary Nelson and Lawrence Grossberg (Urbana-Champaign: University of Illinois Press, 1988), 271–313.
67 The relation between need and lack incites questions around the material consequence of catachresis. In Lucretian anthropology, W. H. Shearin traces catachrestic figurations in order to consider the philosopher's notion of divinity: "Thus, in suggesting that Natura is a catachrestic divinity, we emphasize above all two aspects of the trope catachresis: (1) movement (from a proper to an improper sphere) and (2) a unity that yields to (or reveals) diversity. These two features, it should be noted, are not particularly distinct, for—as we have just observed—it may often be a catachrestic linguistic movement that suggests a greater diversity behind an apparent unity." W. H. Shearin, *The Language of Atoms: Performativity and Politics in Lucretius' De Rerum Natura* (Oxford: Oxford University Press, 2015), 169. I find this formulation helpful for thinking of how catachresis operates as one sign that often demands that we materially attend to the particularity and

heterogeneity that underlies its potential referents when that referential relation is nontransparent and tense.
68 Posselt, "Tropological Economy," 56.
69 For a recent debate on the status of metaphor in relation to decoloniality and anti-Blackness, see Eve Tuck and K. Wayne Yang, "Decolonization Is Not a Metaphor," *Decolonization: Indigeneity, Education & Society* 1, no. 1 (2012): 1–40; and Tapji Garba and Sara-Maria Sorentino, "Slavery Is a Metaphor: A Critical Commentary on Eve Tuck and K. Wayne Yang's 'Decolonization Is Not a Metaphor,'" *Antipode* 52, no. 3 (May 2020): 764–82.
70 See Rey Chow, "The Interruption of Referentiality: Poststructuralism and the Conundrum of Critical Multiculturalism," *South Atlantic Quarterly* 101, no. 1 (January 1, 2002): 171–86.
71 Chow, 184.
72 For more on fungibility, in addition to the work of Hortense J. Spillers, see Saidiya V. Hartman, *Scenes of Subjection: Terror, Slavery, and Self-Making in Nineteenth-Century America*, rev. and updated paperback ed. (New York: Norton, 2022); and C. Riley Snorton, *Black on Both Sides: A Racial History of Trans Identity* (Minneapolis: University of Minnesota Press, 2017). For excellent critiques of the racialization of plasticity, see Jackson, *Becoming Human*; and Jules Gill-Peterson, *Histories of the Transgender Child* (Minneapolis: University of Minnesota Press, 2018).
73 Yomaira C. Figueroa-Vázquez writes, "The concept of mestizaje, however, relegates both Blackness and Indigeneity to backwards moves within national imaginaries and nation building projects that seek to move towards whiteness." *Decolonizing Diasporas: Radical Mappings of Afro-Atlantic Literature* (Evanston, IL: Northwestern University Press, 2020), 10.
74 It is in this manner that I seek to think with Ren Ellis Neyra, who asks, "If we imagine Latinx Studies in relation to ecological and sensorial losses that are not gone, but submerged, chimerical, and metamorphosed, and in ethical relation to black and Caribbean studies, then what field concerns and possibilities arise?" *Cry of the Senses*, xv.
75 Judith Butler, *Bodies That Matter: On the Discursive Limits of "Sex"* (New York: Routledge, 2011), 162.
76 Gayatri Spivak, *Outside in the Teaching Machine* (New York: Routledge, 1993), 182.
77 Hortense J. Spillers, "Mama's Baby, Papa's Maybe: An American Grammar Book," *Diacritics* 17, no. 2 (Summer 1987): 65.
78 See Alessandra Raengo, *On the Sleeve of the Visual* (Hanover, NH: Dartmouth College Press, 2013).
79 See Calvin Warren, *Ontological Terror: Blackness, Nihilism, and Emancipation* (Durham, NC: Duke University Press, 2018).
80 Paul de Man, "The Epistemology of Metaphor," *Critical Inquiry* 5, no. 1 (1978): 21.
81 By placing these two fields of discourse in conversation, I am not trying to make them speak the same language, but I am struck by how deconstruction becomes

all the more compelling as a critical project when its theories and chains of citations disseminate beyond sedimented chains of citation. In this way, I am interested in the thinkers aforementioned who enable deconstructive thought in fields and areas not traditionally deconstructed. Mila Zuo articulates the import of this project: "A new kind of (nonwesternized) deconstructive theory around identity grapples with the textures of linguistic indeterminacy as well as attending to ontoethical concerns within different cosmological orders." Mila Zuo, *Vulgar Beauty: Acting Chinese in the Global Sensorium* (Durham, NC: Duke University Press, 2022), 22.

82 In this manner, my work resonates with Lee Edelman's provocations in *Bad Education: Why Queer Theory Teaches Us Nothing* (Durham, NC: Duke University Press, 2022). There, Edelman extends his previous work to consider how terms like *queer*, *Black*, *a*, and *trans* all operate as catachresis and evince a strange nonidentitarian negativity afoot in terms understood as "a catachrestic name of a social being" (19). I find Edelman's argument helpful in how it tarries with Afro-pessimism and queer theory and how it shows that catachresis can create the veneer of positivism. Yet I remain concerned about exceptionalizing certain terms over others as catachrestic. I also worry about the assignation of ontological negation that may seem to be explained by way of rhetorical terms. My work hopes to emphasize two important incommensurabilities: the incommensurability between linguistic and ontological privation and the incommensurability in how one's identitarian inscription has differential material effect. While queerness and Blackness may both refer catachrestically, and this may afford some insights into the strange negativity of symbolic orders, my concern is that the material differences that befall those living under these inscriptions may become flattened.

83 Barbara Christian, *Black Feminist Criticism* (Oxford, UK: Pergamon, 1985), xi. I cite this ending to show how theory and reading take place as material processes rush onward. Full quotation: "I think how the articulation of theory is a gathering place, sometimes a point of rest as the process rushes on, insisting that you follow."

84 Chow, "Interruption of Referentiality," 185.

85 On de-idealized reading and disturbing attachments, see Kadji Amin, *Disturbing Attachments: Genet, Modern Pederasty, and Queer History* (Durham, NC: Duke University Press, 2017).

86 Chow, *Ethics after Idealism*, xxii.

87 Walter Benjamin, "The Work of Art in the Age of Its Technological Reproducibility," trans. Harry Zohn and Edmund Jephcott, in *Selected Writings*, ed. Howard Eiland and Michael Jennings, vol. 4. (Cambridge, MA: Harvard University Press, 2003), 269.

88 Benjamin, 270.

89 See Chow, "Fascist Longings."

90 See Kandice Chuh, *The Difference Aesthetics Makes: On the Humanities "After Man"* (Durham, NC: Duke University Press, 2019).

91 Edwidge Danticat, *Create Dangerously: The Immigrant Artist at Work* (Princeton, NJ: Princeton University Press, 2010), 10.

92 Rodriguez, *Latinx Literature Unbound*.

93 *Dos alas* refers to the poetry of Lola Rodríguez de Tío, who writes, "Cuba y Puerto Rico son // de un pájaro las dos alas" or "Cuba and Puerto Rico are // two wings of the same bird," from *Mi libro de Cuba*. While meant to be a broader ethos of Caribbean liberation, the mythos here can exceptionalize Cuba and Puerto Rico both within the Hispanophone Caribbean and throughout the reception of Hispanophone diaspora in the US. See Lola Rodríguez de Tío, *Mi libro de Cuba: Poesías* (Havana: Imprenta La Moderna, 1893), 5. My emphasis on these two islands and their diasporas is not meant to be exhaustive or representative of latinidad.

94 For excellent work on the Dominican Republic, see Dixa Ramírez, *Colonial Phantoms: Belonging and Refusal in the Domincan Americas, from the 19th Century to Present* (New York: New York University Press, 2018); Silvio Torres-Saillant, *Caribbean Poetics: Toward an Aesthetic of West Indian Literature* (Cambridge: Cambridge University Press, 1997); and Lorgia García-Peña, *The Borders of Dominicanidad: Race, Nation, and Archives of Contradiction* (Durham, NC: Duke University Press, 2016).

95 See Miriam Jiménez Román and Juan Flores, eds., *The Afro-Latin@ Reader: History and Culture in the United States* (Durham, NC: Duke University Press, 2010). In addition to this foundational anthology, recent work remaps questions of latinidad in relation to diaspora, Blackness, brownness, and Africa. See Claudia Milian, *Latining America: Black-Brown Passages and the Coloring of Latino/a Studies* (Athens: University of Georgia Press, 2013); Figueroa-Vásquez, *Decolonizing Diasporas*; Lorgia García-Peña, *Translating Blackness: Latinx Colonialities in Global Perspective* (Durham, NC: Duke University Press, 2022); and Sarah Quesada, *The African Heritage of Latinx and Caribbean Literature* (Cambridge: Cambridge University Press, 2022).

96 See Maritza Cárdenas, "Querying Central America(n) from the US Diaspora," in *Critical Dialogues in Latinx Studies: A Reader*, ed. Ana Y. Ramos-Zayas and Mérida M. Rúa (New York: New York University Press, 2021), 81–93.

1. SOURCE MATERIALS

1 During the early eighties, Mendieta traveled to Cuba several times as part of a group of Cuban Americans born in Cuba who were interested in creating a relationship with the island: Mendieta was first able to return to her homeland in January 1980 as a member of the Círculo de Cultura Cubana (Cuban Cultural Circle).

2 In this manner, Mendieta, though not a self-described filmmaker, documented over one hundred films of her earth-body-art and *siluetas* over the span of her short career. According to Chrissie Iles, "This body of films is the largest to be produced by any artists working during the 1970s." "Subtle Bodies: The Invisible

Films of Ana Mendieta," in *Mendieta: Earth Body*, ed. Olga Viso (Washington, DC: Hirshhorn Museum and Sculpture Garden, 2004), 205.
3 Bonnie Clearwater, ed., *Ana Mendieta: A Book of Works* (Miami: Grassfield, 1993), 41.
4 José Quiroga, *Cuban Palimpsests* (Minneapolis: University of Minnesota Press, 2005), 176.
5 Mary Pat Brady names density as a resistance to the pretense of mastery and mono-worlding that lies behind the colonial apparatus of scale. Mary Pat Brady, *Scales of Captivity: Racial Capitalism and the Latinx Child* (Durham, NC: Duke University Press, 2022), 246.
6 Jodi A. Byrd, *The Transit of Empire: Indigenous Critiques of Colonialism* (Minneapolis: University of Minnesota Press, 2011), 51. While we currently see decolonization as a metaphor that's problematically employed, so too do we know that natives have operated as powerful colonial metaphors: "The 'native' remains an object, a metaphor through which these institutions can confront their complicity in colonialist practices, and is never granted agency or presence beyond its usefulness as sign in the cosmopole of the global North" (51).
7 Leticia Alvarado analyzes Mendieta's use of aesthetic abjection, noting her relative privilege to do work in Mexico via the affordances of being a creative tied to the University of Iowa and a newly minted citizen. Alvarado's work on Mendieta's dubious figuration of primitivism echoes my own concerns about thinking about her cave works as her own "source" or referential to her life. Likewise, Alvarado's readings distance Mendieta from critiques of essentialism and chorus with my own disinterest in such facile dismissal. Whereas Alvarado centers abjection, my chapter here is more concerned with how we read figurations of fundament, source, and origin. See Leticia Alvarado, *Abject Performances: Aesthetic Strategies in Latino Cultural Production* (Durham, NC: Duke University Press, 2018).
8 In particular, Baracoa is a stronghold of Taíno communities. A local historian and director of the municipal museum calls the area *Cuba profunda* or "deep Cuba." José Barreiro explains, "Baracoa is still considered the gateway to indigenous Cuba. When Hartmann refers to *Cuba profunda*, he is signaling this reality: despite all the claims of Native people's extinction in the Caribbean, in this region, encompassing the thick mountain chains inland from Baracoa to Guantánamo, and through the wider sierras, a Cuban indigenous presence is still recognizable." See José Barreiro, "Indigenous Cuba: Hidden in Plain Sight," *American Indian* 18, no. 4 (Winter 2017), www.AmericanIndianMagazine.org.
9 Barreiro traces the Rojas-Ramírez families in particular, revealing a telling missionary and state engulfment: "San Luis de los Caneyes (El Caney), near Santiago de Cuba, became the origin and survival place for the Rojas-Ramírez families for three centuries. These newly liberated or recently isolated Indian families were granted the names Rojas and Ramirez, *en masse*, in baptisms under a Spanish governor and a Bishop with those last names." Barreiro, "Indigenous Cuba."

10 See José Barreiro, *Dreaming with Mother Earth: The Life and Wisdom of Native Cuban Cacique Panchito Ramirez Rojas* (New York: Editorial Campana, 2018). For a Puerto Rican exploration of a very similar figure of the *jíbaro/indio/Boricua*, see Sherina Feliciano-Santos, *A Contested Caribbean Indigeneity: Language, Social Practice, and Identity within Puerto Rican Taíno Activism* (New Brunswick, NJ: Rutgers University Press, 2021).

11 Barreiro writes, "As elsewhere, the discussion of indigeneity is impacted by new genetic studies, which for Cuba reveal that 34.5 percent of the general population is inheritor of Native-American mitochondrial DNA. The highest levels are found in the eastern region of Cuba: Holguín (59 percent) and Las Tunas (58 percent). This news has dealt a frontal blow to the historical dictum of early Native extinction." "Indigenous Cuba." As we can see from these figures, such statistics vary in location, so that scale becomes a problem for decoding how we read DNA as an inscription.

12 Kimberly TallBear, *Native American DNA: Tribal Belonging and the False Promise of Genetic Science* (Minneapolis: University of Minnesota Press, 2013), 6–7. TallBear continues,

> This faith in originality would seem to be at odds with the doctrine of evolution, of change over time, of becoming. The populations and population-specified markers that are identified and studied mirror the cultural, racial, ethnic, national, and tribal understandings of the humans who study them. Native American, sub-Saharan African, European, and East Asian DNAs are constituted as scientific objects by laboratory methods and devices, and also by discourses or particular ideas and vocabularies of race, ethnicity, nation, family, and tribe. For and by whom are such categories defined? How have continental-level race categories come to matter? And why do they matter more than the "peoples" that condition indigenous narratives, knowledges, and claims? (6)

13 Fray Ramón Pané, *An Account of the Antiquities of the Indians*, ed. José Juan Arrom (Durham, NC: Duke University Press, 1999).

14 For more on the work of José Barreiro and the Taíno resurgence, see the Caribbean Indigenous Legacies Project, updated March 24, 2016, https://global.si.edu.

15 Éduoard Glissant, *Poetics of Relation* (Ann Arbor: University of Michigan Press, 1997), 73: "This second Plantation matrix, after that of the slave ship, is where we must return to track our difficult and opaque sources."

16 See Vanessa Agard-Jones, "What the Sands Remember," *GLQ: A Journal of Lesbian and Gay Studies* 18, nos. 2–3 (June 1, 2012); and Tiffany Lethabo King, *The Black Shoals: Offshore Formations of Black and Native Studies* (Durham, NC: Duke University Press, 2019).

17 See Katherine McKittrick, *Demonic Grounds: Black Women and the Cartographies of Struggle* (Durham, NC: Duke University Press, 2006); and Kathryn Yusoff, *A Billion Black Anthropocenes or None* (Minneapolis: University of Minnesota Press, 2019).

18. Zakkiyah Iman Jackson, "Outer Worlds: The Persistence of Race in Movement beyond the Human," *GLQ: A Journal of Lesbian and Gay Studies* 21, nos. 2–3 (2015): 217.
19. See Roberto Zurbano, "For Blacks in Cuba, the Revolution Hasn't Begun," *New York Times*, March 23, 2013, www.nytimes.com.
20. Mira Schor, *Wet: On Painting, Feminism, and Art Culture* (Durham, NC: Duke University Press, 1997), 66.
21. Jane Blocker, *Where Is Ana Mendieta? Identity, Performativity, and Exile* (Durham, NC: Duke University Press, 1999).
22. Diana Fuss, *Essentially Speaking: Feminism, Nature, and Speaking* (New York: Routledge, 1989).
23. Eve Kosofsky Sedgwick, *Touching Feeling: Affect, Pedagogy, Performativity* (Durham, NC: Duke University Press, 2003).
24. Carolee Schneemann, "Regarding Ana Mendieta," *Women & Performance: A Journal of Feminist Theory* 21, no. 2 (2011): 185.
25. Schneemann, 186.
26. Ellen Tepfer, "The Presence of Absence: Beyond the 'Great Goddess' in Ana Mendieta's *Silueta Series*," *Women & Performance: A Journal of Feminist Theory* 12, no. 2 (January 2002): 246.
27. "Perhaps the way in which Mendieta's work refuses to fit comfortably into what some feminists see as an either/or determination of essentialism, as opposed to a post-structuralist account of female subjectivity, or an art characterized by emotional expression as opposed to an art practice marked by theoretical and formal rigor, can suggest another way—a third way—a neither/nor for thinking through feminist art." Tepfer, "Presence of Absence," 246–47.
28. Olga M. Viso, ed., *Unseen Mendieta: The Unpublished Works of Ana Mendieta* (Munich: Prestel, 2008), 82.
29. Ana Mendieta's typewritten artist statement, the Estate of Ana Mendieta Collection Archives, 1984, Galerie LeLong, New York, NY.
30. Octavio Paz, *The Labyrinth of Solitude and Other Writings* (New York: Grove, 1985), 20.
31. María de Los Angeles Torres, "Finding Ana," *Latino Studies* 3 (2005): 430.
32. See Antonio Viego, *Dead Subjects: Toward a Politics of Loss in Latino Studies* (Durham, NC: Duke University Press, 2007).
33. Viso, *Unseen*, 89.
34. Viso, 81.
35. Quiroga, *Cuban Palimpsests*, 193.
36. Elise Rasmussen quoted in Haley Mlotek, "Tracing Ana," *New Inquiry*, March 24, 2014, www.thenewinquiry.com.
37. Laura Roulet, "Ana Mendieta as Cultural Connector with Cuba," *American Art* 26, no. 2 (2012): 23.
38. Camnitzer, quoted in Roulet, 23.
39. Bedia, quoted in Roulet, 10.
40. Roulet, 24.

41 Carlos A. Cruz, "Ana Mendieta's Art: A Journey through Her Life," in *Latina Legacies: Identity, Biography, and Community*, ed. Vicki Ruiz and Virginia Sánchez Korrol (Oxford: Oxford University Press, 2005), 223.

42 Toward the very end of Obama's tenure as president, he signed an executive order reversing what had been known as the "wet foot, dry foot" policy. This policy, formally known as the Cuban Adjustment Act, written into US law in 1962, granted Cubans seeking residency and citizenship in the US a streamlined path to citizenship and the automatic policy of asylum. Of course, this policy did not extend to other migrants from the Caribbean, Latin America, and/or Central America. Such a policy drove mass amounts of Cubans to take to rafts, traversing the ninety miles between Cuba and Florida, hoping to land a foot on dry land, thus securing entry to and asylum in the US. Obama's executive order put an end to one aspect of Cuban exceptionalism. But following the significant number of anti-immigrant, bilious remarks from the Trump administration, along with blank threats to Cuba that once again blamed a small island for global politics, migration has not only become more untenable, but we also now see, within a matter of years, Cubans locked up in detention centers.

43 See Quiroga, *Cuban Palimpsests*.

44 "Pienso en los caballos de los conquistadores cubriendo a las yeguas, pienso en el desconocido son del areíto desaparecido por toda la eternidad, ciertamente debo esforzarme a fin de poner en claro el primer contacto carnal en este país, y el primer muerto." (I think of the conquistadors' stallions mounting their mares, I think of the forever lost sound of the *areíto*, I need to try to make sense of the first carnal contact in this country, and the first death.) Virgilio Piñera, *La isla en peso / The Whole Island*, trans. Mark Weiss (Exeter: Shearsman, 2010), 14, 15. Here we see the mythos of Indigenous extinction stitched into an account of the "whole island."

45 See Edward Kamau Brathwaite, "The African Presence in Caribbean Literature," *Daedalus* 103, no. 2 (1974): 73–109.

46 José Juan Arrom and Manuel Antonio García Arévalo, *Cimarrón / José Juan Arrom, Manuel A. García Arévalo* (Santo Domingo, República Dominicana: Ediciones Fundación García-Arévalo, 1986), 56–57. I am grateful to Charmaine Branch and Angela Brown for alerting me to this quote through their excellent curatorial project "Símaran: Reading with Taíno Objects."

47 Sylvia Wynter, "Unsettling the Coloniality of Being/Power/Truth/Freedom: Towards the Human, after Man, Its Overrepresentation—an Argument," *CR: The New Centennial Review* 3, no. 3 (2003): 267.

48 My usage of exorbitance here is meant to indicate how there are forms of racialization and coloniality indexed here that exceed Mendieta's own positionality. For more on how Blackness is exorbitant to thought, see Nahum D. Chandler's "Of Exorbitance: The Problem of the Negro as a Problem for Thought," *Criticism* 50, no. 3 (2009): 345–410; and Zakiyyah Iman Jackson, who argues that anti-Blackness "constructs black(ened) humanity as the privation and exorbitance of form." Zakiyyah Iman Jackson, *Becoming Human: Matter and Meaning in an Antiblack World* (New York: New York University Press, 2020), 35.

49 Alberto Alvarez de Zayas, "Agave Jarucoensis A. Alvarez: Una Nueva Especie de Cuba Occidental," *Revista del Jardín Botánico Nacional* 1, no. 1 (1980): 5–11.
50 For more on Mendieta's works in Miami, see Christina A. León, "Trace Alignment: Object Relations after Ana Mendieta," *Post45 Contemporaries*, December 9, 2019, https://post45.org.
51 During Mendieta's lifetime, the park did not appear as it does today. Families would come to picnic, and youth groups would enjoy field trips to the park. There was even a bench in front of one of the sites, and it was landscaped—unlike today. Artist Gustavo Pérez Monzón worked at this park, which is how Mendieta was introduced to the locale.
52 Dana Luciano, "Speaking Substances," *Los Angeles Review of Books*, April 12, 2016, www.lareviewofbooks.org.
53 Elizabeth Povinelli has written about how rocks frustrate the binary of life and death, showing us that rocks metabolize and that some of their origins may be found in bacteria. See Elizabeth Povinelli's "Can Rocks Die? Life and Death inside the Carbon Imaginary," in *Geontologies: A Requiem to Late Liberalism* (Durham, NC: Duke University Press, 2016).
54 Lynne Huffer, "Foucault's Fossils: Life Itself and the Return to Nature in Feminist Philosophy," in *Anthropocene Feminism*, ed. Richard A. Grusin (Minneapolis: University of Minnesota Press, 2017), 85.
55 Susan Sontag, *On Photography* (New York: Picador, 2001), 3.
56 See Luce Irigaray, *Speculum of the Other Woman* (Ithaca, NY: Cornell University Press, 1985).
57 As Yusoff writes, "The origins of the Anthropocene continue to erase and dissimulate violent histories of encounter, dispossession, and death in the geographical imagination. This geologic prehistory has everything to do with the Anthropocene as a condition of the present; it is the material history that constitutes the present in all its geotraumas and thus should be embraced, reworked, and reconstituted in terms of agency *for* the present, *for the end of this world* and the possibility of others, because the world is already turning to face the storm, writing its weather for the geology next time." *Billion Black Anthropocenes*, 92.
58 Yusoff, 96.
59 See Axelle Karera, "Blackness and the Pitfalls of Anthropocene Ethics," *Critical Philosophy of Race* 7, no. 1 (2019): 50. Karera emphatically puts a pause on the critical tendency to assume a relational, perhaps species wide and beyond, ethical connection resultant from the threat of an uninhabitable planet. She writes, "One is thus pressed to inquire how can a global ethics of care be possible when fundamental questions of racial culpability are eluded in the name of a shortsighted conception of 'becoming' and an aggrandized notion of ontological relationality—both of which remain unwilling to sustain engagements with their violent racial foundations" (44).
60 For how ecological and vitalist concerns tend to utilize Blackness as compost for sustainable futures, see Dixa Ramírez-D'Oleo, *This Will Not Be Generative* (Cambridge: Cambridge University Press, 2023).

61 Jacques Derrida, *Margins of Philosophy*, trans. Alan Bass (Brighton, UK: Harvester 1982), 256; Gayatri Spivak, "Poststructuralism, Marginality, Postcoloniality, and Value," in *Literary Theory Today*, ed. Peter Collier and Helga Geyer-Ryan (Ithaca, NY: Cornell University Press, 1990), 225.

62 Barbara Johnson, "A Hound, a Bay Horse, and a Turtle Dove," in *A World of Difference* (Baltimore: Johns Hopkins University Press, 1987), 53.

63 Lynne Huffer, *Maternal Pasts, Feminist Futures: Nostalgia, Ethics, and the Question of Difference* (Stanford, CA: Stanford University Press, 1998), 157n18.

64 Irigaray, *Speculum*, 253.

65 Naomi Schor, "The Essentialism Which Is Not One," in *Bad Objects: Essays Popular and Unpopular* (Durham, NC: Duke University Press, 1995), 55.

66 María Josefina Saldaña-Portillo, *Indian Given: Racial Geographies across Mexico and the United States* (Durham, NC: Duke University Press, 2016), 30.

67 Vicki Kirby, *Quantum Anthropologies: Life at Large* (Durham, NC: Duke University Press, 2011), 88.

68 Kirby, 88.

69 See Derek Walcott, "The Sea Is History," *Paris Review*, no. 74 (1978), www.theparisreview.org. See also Edward Kamau Braithwaite, *Sun Poem* (Oxford: Oxford University Press, 1982).

70 See Wai Chee Dimock, *Through Other Continents: American Literature across Deep Time* (Princeton, NJ: Princeton University Press, 2008).

71 Ana Mendieta's typewritten artist statement, undated, the Estate of Ana Mendieta Collection Archives, Galerie LeLong, New York, NY.

72 Mendieta, quoted in Clearwater, *Ana Mendieta*, 41.

2. EXORBITANT DUST

1 Ruiz writes, "I am most concerned with how these tight locations unveil something about Ricanness that is profoundly temporal and on loop in an act of eternal recurrence." Sandra Ruiz, *Ricanness: Enduring Time in Anticolonial Performance* (New York: New York University Press, 2019), 33. This modernization campaign would kick up quite a lot of dust in the midcentury, laying down roads and opening up commerce for a few decades. This would only temporarily shuttle Puerto Rico up to a US notion of modernity and infrastructure. After tax loopholes closed up, the island would be left in enormous debt, a debt that a recognized state or municipality of the US would never have to repay. Rather, Puerto Rico's status as an unincorporated commonwealth makes it ineligible to file for bankruptcy, allowing tax loopholes to create not just tax havens for US companies but also manufactured economic precarity for the island when those loopholes close. These material strictures are compounded by a most pervasive extractive force and isolation thanks to the Jones Act.

2 Ramos Otero, "Ficción e historia: Texto y pretexto de la autobiografía," *El Mundo*, October 14, 1990.

3   Manuel Ramos Otero, *Papiros de babel: Antología de la poesía Puertorriqueña en Nueva York*, ed. Pedro López Adorno (Rio Piedras: Editorial de la Universidad de Puerto Rico, 1991).
4   The first major critical reprise of Ramos Otero finds itself in Juan Gelpí, *Literatura y paternalismo en Puerto Rico* (Rio Piedras: Editorial de la Universidad de Puerto Rico, 1993), where he shows how Ramos Otero breaks from paternalistic approaches to the literary canon of Puerto Rico through an emphasis on the transitory.
5   Lawrence La Fountain-Stokes, *Queer Ricans: Cultures and Sexualities in the Diaspora* (Minneapolis: University of Minnesota Press, 2009), 62.
6   See Arnaldo Cruz-Malavé, "Para virar al macho: La autobiografía como subversión en la cuentística de Manuel Ramos Otero," *Revista Iberoamericana* 59, no. 162 (June 11, 1993): 239–63; and Jossianna Arroyo, "Exilio y tránsitos entre la Norzagaray y Christopher Street: Acercamientos a una poética del deseo homosexual en Manuel Ramos Otero," *Revista Iberoamericana* 67, no. 194 (June 8, 2001): 31–54.
7   Michael Marder, *Dust* (New York: Bloomsbury, 2017), 62.
8   Manuel Ramos Otero, interview with Marithelma Costa, *Hispamérica* 20, no. 59 (August 1991): 59–67 (italics mine).
9   For more on atmospheric reading, see Jesse Oak Taylor, *The Sky of Our Manufacture: The London Fog in British Fiction from Dickens to Woolf* (Charlottesville: University of Virginia Press, 2016).
10 For a more recent archipelagic reprisal of the Hispanophone Caribbean, see Yolanda Martínez-San Miguel, "Colonial and Mexican Archipelagoes: Reimagining Colonial Caribbean Studies," in *Archipelagic American Studies*, ed. Brian Russell Roberts and Michelle Ann Stephens (Durham, NC: Duke University Press, 2017), 155–73.
11 Though the majority of Ramos Otero's writing life was spent in the United States, he is seldom integrated into the canon of US Latinx letters. He is a curious omission in *The Norton Anthology of Latino Literature*, ed. Ilan Stavans, Edna Acosta Belén, and Edna Acosta-Belén (New York: Norton, 2011). While many of his Puerto Rican and Nuyorican contemporaries, like Rosario Ferré and Pedro Pietri, grace the pages of the canon-making anthology, Ramos Otero lingers on the fringes of both US and Puerto Rican letters.
12 His only published novel, *La novelabingo*, was reprinted in 2010. Furthermore, his work is prominently featured in a 2010 anthology of queer Puerto Rican literature from the island and its diaspora: *Los otros cuerpos: Antología de temática gay, lésbica y queer* (San Juan: Editorial Tiempo Nuevo, 2010). The literary collective Colectivo Literario Homoerótica has become a galvanizing presence in Puerto Rico, ensuring that queer Puerto Rican literary production has an ongoing place in the island's literary circles. More recently, Ramos Otero's works have been compiled into two very helpful collections centering on his essays and short stories. For essays and writings, see Manuel Ramos Otero, *No tener miedo a las palabras* (San Juan: Folium, 2020). For Ramos Otero's short stories, see Manuel Ramos Otero, *Cuentos "completos": Manuel Ramos Otero*, ed. Arnaldo M. Cruz Malavé (San Juan: Editorial del Instituto de Cultura Puertorriqueña, 2023).

13 For an excellent discussion of the use of *polvo* in Manuel Ramos Otero's work as it relates to Lorca and Whitman, see Mark Staebler, "Inter-(Homo)-Textuality: Manuel Ramos Otero and the Nuyorican Intersection of Tradition," *Caribbean Studies* 27, nos. 3/4 (December 1994): 331–45. Staebler writes that "Ramos Otero appropriates Whitman's image of the individual within the cosmos, the single blade of life in the timelessness of eternity. But his dominant metaphor is dust, '*polvo*'" (333).
14 Mónica Lladó-Ortega, "A Community in Transit: The Performative Gestures of Manuel Ramos Otero's Narrative Triptych," in *Hispanic Caribbean Literature of Migration*, ed. Vanessa Pérez Rosario (New York: Palgrave Macmillan, 2010), 123.
15 Further along in this chapter, I will return to the question of visuality as it pertains to translation via the critical work of Rey Chow.
16 It is important to note that "Hollywood" is used in the title of the story in relation to memory and nostalgia. Susan Sontag, "Notes on 'Camp,'" in *Camp: Queer Aesthetics and the Performing Subject; A Reader*, ed. Fabio Cleto (Edinburgh: Edinburgh University Press, 2022), 57.
17 Manuel Ramos Otero, "Hollywood Memorabilia," in *Concierto de metal para un recuerdo y otras orgías de soledad* (San Juan: Cultural, 1971), 93. English translations of this story are taken from Manuel Ramos Otero, "Hollywood Memorabilia," trans. Gregory Kolovakos, *Callaloo* 15, no. 4 (1992): 973–78. Subsequent citations will cite the Spanish page first, then the English page, separating them with a slash.
18 Ramos Otero, 96/975.
19 Ramos Otero, 93/973.
20 Ramos Otero, 93/973.
21 Ramos Otero's essay, *Culonacizión*, deals explicitly with capitalism and its effects on Puerto Rican culture. See Manuel Ramos Otero, "De la colonización a la culonacizión," *Cupey* 8, nos. 1–2 (1991): 63–79.
22 Ramos Otero, "Hollywood Memorabilia," 93/973.
23 Sontag, "Notes on 'Camp,'" 60.
24 Ramos Otero, "Hollywood Memorabilia," 95/974.
25 Ramos Otero, 98/976.
26 Philip Core, "From Camp: The Lie That Tells the Truth," in Cleto, *Camp*, 80–81.
27 Ramos Otero, "Hollywood Memorabilia," 98/976–77.
28 Argentine and queer writer Manuel Puig also featured a very similar camp aesthetic in his fiction.
29 For a history of early Latina Hollywood starlets, see Steve Starr, *Starrlight: Glamorous Latin Movie Stars of Early Hollywood* (Chicago: First Flight, 2010). This book contains biographical accounts of Maria Montez, Rita Hayworth, Lupe Velez, Carmen Miranda, and Dolores del Rio.
30 José Esteban Muñoz, *Disidentifications: Queers of Color and the Performance of Politics* (Minneapolis: University of Minnesota Press, 1999), 127.
31 Ramos Otero, "Hollywood Memorabilia," 94/974.

32   This allusion to Stein's infamous rose lines comes from the poem "Sacred Emily." The poem appears in Gertrude Stein, *Geography and Plays* (Boston, MA: Four Seas Press, 1922).
33   Kadji Amin writes that "deidealization may not immediately enable a muscular and decisive politics, but it does have consequences for politicized thought. On the most basic level, it calls for an acknowledgment of the 'complex personhood' of queer, racialized, and subaltern persons too often assigned the psychically flat role of righting the ills of an unjust social order and denied the right to be damaged, psychically complex, or merely otherwise occupied. Deidealization does, however, require scholars to acknowledge a break between scholarly and political practice." Amin, *Disturbing Attachments: Genet, Modern Pederasty, and Queer History* (Durham, NC: Duke University Press, 2017), 31.
34   Ramos Otero, "Hollywood Memorabilia," 94/974.
35   In note thirty-six of Sontag's "Notes on 'Camp,'" she writes, "And third among the great creative sensibilities is Camp: the sensibility of failed seriousness, of the theatricalization of experience. Camp refuses both the harmonies of traditional seriousness and the risks of fully identifying with extreme states of feeling." "Notes on 'Camp,'" 62. The "theatricalization of experience" is precisely how Manuel Ramos Otero keeps autobiography from being read as either "traditional seriousness" or full identification.
36   *Queen Christina* was produced and directed by Rouben Mamoulian in 1933. The film was billed as Greta Garbo's return to the screen after an eighteen-month hiatus from Hollywood. Her career had declined as a result of the rising popularity of "talkies." The film is loosely based on the life of seventeenth-century queen Christina of Sweden. The film grossed over $2,500,000, making it one of Garbo's most commercially successful films.
37   Ramos Otero, "Hollywood Memorabilia," 99/977.
38   As a figure of survival, Garbo's character in *Queen Christina* takes an ambivalent form. She holds open the space of question and does not foreclose ambivalence. In the final scene of the film, her face becomes an unwavering ellipsis—she does not blink, and she does not show much emotion.
39   Ramos Otero, "Hollywood Memorabilia," 99/977–78.
40   The dispersal rendered in the English translation fails to capture the Spanish original of *desvanecerse*. A reflexive verb, *desvanecerse* is not the opposite of *vanecerse*, even though it is preceded with the undoing prefix of *des-*. It is a word that can mean "dispersal" and would often be used to show how things fade or how fog dissipates. It has a temporal character that shows how matter erodes, separates, or thins over time, ever spreading rather than disappearing altogether.
41   Marder, *Dust*, 19.
42   Ramos Otero, "Ficción e historia," 23.
43   Walter Benjamin, "The Task of the Translator," trans. Harry Zohn, in *Selected Writings*, vol. 1: 1913–1926 (Cambridge, MA: Belknap Press, 2004), 254.

44 "Information, however, lays claim to prompt verifiability. The prime requirement is that it appear 'understandable in itself.'" He concludes this paragraph by stating: "If the art of storytelling has become rare, the dissemination of information has had a decisive share in the state of affairs." Walter Benjamin, "The Storyteller," trans. Harry Zohn, in *Selected Writings*, vol. 3: 1935–1938 (Cambridge, MA: Belknap Press, 2006), 147.
45 Benjamin, "Task of the Translator," 256.
46 "The idea of life and afterlife in works of art should be treated should be regarded with an entirely unmetaphorical objectivity. Even in times of narrowly prejudiced thought there was an inkling that life was not limited to organic corporeality." Benjamin, 254.
47 Benjamin, 258.
48 Benjamin, 258–59.
49 Benjamin, 254.
50 Rey Chow, "Film as Ethnography: Or, Translation between Cultures in the Postcolonial World," in *The Rey Chow Reader*, ed. Paul Bowman (New York: Columbia University Press, 2010), 153.
51 Chow, 156.
52 Chow, 166.
53 Paul de Man, "Autobiography as De-facement," in *Rhetoric of Romanticism* (New York: Columbia University Press, 1986), 69.
54 Ramos Otero, "Ficción e historia," 22.
55 de Man, "Autobiography," 69.
56 "Autobiography, then, is not a genre or a mode, but a figure of reading or of understanding that occurs, to some degree, in all texts. The autobiographical moment happens as an alignment between the two subjects involved in the process of reading in which they determine each other by mutual reflexive substitution." De Man, "Autobiography," 70.
57 de man, "Autobiography," 76.
58 Manuel Ramos Otero, *El libro de la muerte* (Rio Piedras, Puerto Rico: Cultura, 1985).
59 Sylvia Molloy, *At Face Value: Autobiographical Writing in Spanish America* (Cambridge: Cambridge University Press, 1991), 2.
60 Molloy, 5.
61 Marithelma Costa and Manuel Ramos Otero, "Manuel Ramos Otero," *Hispamérica* 20, no. 59 (1991): 66–67.
62 Machado Sáez writes, "The postcolonial imperative of ethically depicting Caribbean history and subjectivities comes into conflict with the horizon of expectation created by reader reception, and this creative tension inspires the market aesthetics of Caribbean diasporic writing." Elena Machado Sáez, *Market Aesthetics: The Purchase of the Past in Caribbean Diasporic Fiction* (Charlottesville: University of Virginia Press, 2015), 197.
63 Ramos Otero, "Ficción e historia," 23.

64 Ramos Otero notes the temporal rims of a dusty tongue with the adjective *polvorosa*—which I have chosen to translate as "dusty" instead of the clumsy, but also more specific, translation of "dust-ful." In this quote, the page is embodied through skin signaled as dusty by the descriptor *polvorienta*—which, again, I have translated as "dusty." But this form of dustiness is one that is actively dusting, decaying, and crumbling at the edges.

65 Manuel Ramos Otero, *Invitación al polvo* (Río Piedras, Puerto Rico: Editorial Plaza Mayor, 1991) 64.

66 Ramos Otero, 64.

67 Ramos Otero, 64.

68 Ramos Otero, 64–65.

69 Nancy Tomes, *The Gospel of Germs: Men, Women, and the Microbe in American Life* (Cambridge, MA: Harvard University Press, 2002), 96. I am grateful to Kyla Wazana Tompkins for pointing me toward this helpful source and history.

70 Tomes, 97.

71 Tomes, 259.

72 "There is a grave melody that marks the territory of the book and the island, and a tale melody that seems to put forth a precarious afterlife that escapes the grave melody. Ramos Otero's melodies escape fossilized communitarian and individualistic melodies to offer an impersonal literature in the face of the disaster of history." Luis Othoniel Rosa, "Grave Melodies: Literature and Afterlife in Manuel Ramos Otero," *Revista Hispánica Moderna* 64, no. 2 (2011): 179.

73 Ramos Otero, *Invitación al polvo*, 62. English translation is from Manuel Ramos Otero, "Nobility of Blood," in *Puerto Rican Poetry: A Selection from Aboriginal to Contemporary Times*, ed. and trans. Robert Márquez (Amherst: University of Massachusetts Press, 2007), 295.

74 Ramos Otero, *Invitación al polvo*, 47.

75 The full quotation follows: "God is dead. God remains dead. And we have killed him. How shall we comfort ourselves, the murderers of all murderers? What was holiest and mightiest of all that the world has yet owned has bled to death under our knives: who will wipe this blood off us? What water is there for us to clean ourselves? What festivals of atonement, what sacred games shall we have to invent? Is not the greatness of this deed too great for us? Must we ourselves not become gods simply to appear worthy of it?" Friedrich Wilhelm Nietzsche, *The Gay Science*, trans. Walter Arnold Kaufmann (New York: Vintage, 1974), 181.

76 For more on a queer thinking of *suciedad*, see Deborah Vargas, "Ruminations on Lo Sucio as a Latino Queer Analytic," *American Quarterly* 66, no. 3 (2014): 715–26.

77 See Éduoard Glissant, *Caribbean Discourse: Selected Essays*, trans. J. Michael Dash (Charlottesville: University Press of Virginia, 1989), x.

78 In his memorial essay on Glissant, J. Michael Dash writes, "In response to this dream of theoretical coherence or aesthetic order, Glissant insisted on the ungraspable specificity of a world in which all elementary particles were interrelated." "Remembering Édouard Glissant," *Callaloo* 34, no. 3 (2011): 673.

79 Édouard Glissant, *Poetics of Relation* (Ann Arbor: University of Michigan Press, 1997), 185.
80 I imagine dust as a material metaphor that works in tandem and tension with Vanessa Agard-Jones's work on sand and queer desire in the Caribbean. Her theorization of sand works centers on individuals who do not, whether by choice or circumstance, flee the Caribbean to emphasize their queerness in exile. For her, sand works as a kind of archive: "Rather than invoke ideas about absence and invisibility as the condition of same-sex desiring and gender-transgressing people, turning to sand as a metaphor for the repository of memory may help our analyses engage more fine-grained and ephemeral presences than our usual archives would allow." Vanessa Agard-Jones, "What the Sands Remember," *GLQ: A Journal of Lesbian and Gay Studies* 18, nos. 2–3 (June 1, 2012): 340.
81 In this manner, too, dust becomes exorbitant beyond Ramos Otero's writing, showing us the Africanist presence in the matter of dust. For more on how Blackness is exorbitant to thought, see Nahum D. Chandler, "Of Exorbitance: The Problem of the Negro as a Problem for Thought," *Criticism* 50, no. 3 (2009): 345–410.
82 Edward Kamau Brathwaite, "The African Presence in Caribbean Literature," *Daedalus* 103, no. 2 (1974), 73–109.
83 Yarimar Bonilla, "La Calima: Diasporic Dust," May 8, 2019, https://yarimarbonilla.com.
84 Bonilla.
85 Instead of thinking in terms of identity and agency, Puar considers force and assemblage in her latest book, *The Right to Maim*: "I therefore do not offer debility as an identity; it is instead a form of massification." Puar's conceptualization of debility leads us away from neoliberal identity and more into the massification of dust. Jasbir K. Puar, *The Right to Maim: Debility, Capacity, Disability* (Durham, NC: Duke University Press, 2017), xvii.
86 Gayatri Gopinath, *Unruly Visions: The Aesthetic Practices of Queer Diaspora* (Durham, NC: Duke University Press, 2018), 17.
87 Karen Barad, "Troubling Time/s and Ecologies of Nothingness: Re-turning, Remembering, and Facing the Incalculable," *New Formations* 92 (2017): 56.
88 Vanessa Agard-Jones asks, "What it can mean to pay equal attention to the rooted, to those Caribbean people who build lives for themselves right where they are, under conditions of both intense contradiction and sometimes, too, intense joy." "What the Sands Remember," 327.
89 Agard-Jones, 340.
90 See Nishant Kishore et al., "Mortality in Puerto Rico after Hurricane Maria," *New England Journal of Medicine* 379, no. 2 (July 12, 2018): 162–70.
91 For more on activism within the colonially policed space of Puerto Rico, see Marisol LeBrón, *Policing Life and Death: Race, Violence, and Resistance in Puerto Rico* (Oakland: University of California Press, 2019). For more on the devastating fallout of Hurricane Maria as the ongoing and accelerated disaster of colonial disenfranchisement in Puerto Rico, see Yarimar Bonilla and Marisol LeBrón, eds., *Aftershocks of Disaster: Puerto Rico before and after the Storm* (Chicago, IL: Haymarket, 2019).

92 See Jih-Fei Cheng, Alexandra Juhasz, and Nishant Shahani, eds., *AIDS and the Distribution of Crises* (Durham, NC: Duke University Press, 2020); and Bonilla and LeBrón, *Aftershocks*.
93 William Wendell Haver, *The Body of This Death: Historicity and Sociality in the Time of AIDS* (Stanford: Stanford University Press, 1987).

3. GUT CHECKS

1 *The Rest I Make Up*, directed by Michelle Memran (New York: Piece by Piece Productions, 2018), www.kanopy.com.
2 Eric Mayes Garcia turns from identity to affect to think about a 1975 play by Fornés, *Cap-a-Pie*, in his wonderful article "Feeling Brown like You: Creación Colectiva and Latinx Affect in Fornés's *Cap-a-Pie*," *Chiricú Journal: Latina/o Literatures, Arts, and Cultures* 3, no. 1 (Fall 2018): 23.
3 I am certainly not the first to remark on this conundrum of matriarchy. Gwendolyn Akler puts it this way:

> Irene's legacy as a Latinx matriarch remains complex. Her understanding of the institutional leverage of her pedagogical home at INTAR (International Arts Relations, Inc.) has nurtured an entire generation of playwrights who credit her as their intellectual mentor. Yet she sidestepped any static and simple limitations of training "Latino" playwrights. She rarely posited herself as a woman of color in her work or her framing of it, even as she was a mentor to some of the late twentieth century's most influential Latina writers. She also never hid her own status as a lesbian (most notably as partner to Susan Sontag), but this was not readily raised in her artistic community and there are only two instances of lesbian relationships in her work. (Gwendolyn Alker, "Fornesian Animality: María Irene Fornés's Challenge to a Politics of Identity," *Journal of Dramatic Theory and Criticism* 35, no. 1 [2020]: 12.)

4 By using the maternal function, I am explicitly referencing the work of Elissa Marder in *The Mother in the Age of Mechanical Reproduction: Psychoanalysis, Photography, Deconstruction* (New York: Fordham University Press, 2012).
5 Brian Herrera reads James Baldwin alongside María Irene Fornés in order to see how both offer us prescient lessons about the ruses of representation and the difficulties of being in collaboration. For more, see Brian Herrera, "The Dramatist's Call to Action: The Provocative Prescience of James Baldwin and María Irene Fornés," *Theater* 49, no. 1 (February 2019): 78–95.
6 See Elizabeth Wilson's *Psychosomatic: Feminism and the Neurological Body* (Durham, NC: Duke University Press, 2004), and *Gut Feminism* (Durham, NC: Duke University Press, 2015).
7 María Irene Fornés, interview by Maria M. Delgado, *Conducting a Life: Reflections on the Theatre of Maria Irene Fornes*, ed. Maria M. Delgado and Caridad Svich (Lyme, NH: Smith and Kraus, 1999), 268.
8 For more on centering accent in our thinking, reading, and listening, see Pooja Rangan, Akshya Saxena, Ragini Tharoor Srinivasan, and Pavitra Sundar, *Thinking*

with an Accent: Toward a New Object, Method, and Practice (Oakland: University of California Press, 2023).
9. María Irene Fornés, interview by David Savran, *In Their Own Words: Contemporary American Playwrights* (New York: Theatre Communications Group, 1988), 68.
10. For more on Fornés's time studying with Hans Hofmann, see Christina A. León, "Space Cadets: Fornés and Hans Hoffman," *Fornés in Context*, ed. Anne García Romero and Brian Herrera (Cambridge: Cambridge University Press, forthcoming 2024).
11. Fornés, interview by Savran, 58.
12. Kandice Chuh, "It's Not about Anything," *Social Text* 32, no. 4 (2014): 127.
13. Chuh, 127.
14. Chuh, 133.
15. María Irene Fornés, "Creative Danger," in *The Theater of Maria Irene Fornes*, ed. Marc Robinson (Baltimore: Johns Hopkins University Press, 1999), 233.
16. Fornés, 232.
17. Susan Sontag, preface to *Plays*, by María Irene Fornés (New York: PAJ, 1986), 8.
18. Sontag, 8.
19. In *The Sense of Brown*, José Esteban Muñoz remarks upon Fornés's language: "It may be her resistance to the capture of Anglo-American theater's prevailing discourses of realism and naturalism. But I think of her language, which is both strangely minimalist and excessive, as a kind of illegitimate speech, to invoke Jacques Ranciere." *The Sense of Brown*, ed. Tavia Amolo Ochieng' Nyongó and Joshua Takano Chambers-Letson (Durham, NC: Duke University Press, 2020), 126.
20. Tiffany Ana López, "The Conduct of Life," in Delgado and Svich, *Conducting a Life*, 152.
21. María Irene Fornés, *Fefu and Her Friends* (New York: PAJ, 1978), 4.
22. Alexandra T. Vazquez, *Listening in Detail: Performances of Cuban Music* (Durham, NC: Duke University Press, 2013), 22.
23. Vazquez, 24.
24. Vazquez, 23.
25. Vazquez, 25.
26. Fornés, *Fefu*, 7.
27. Fornés, 10.
28. Fornés, 15.
29. Fornés, 15.
30. Fornés, 15.
31. Fornés, 16.
32. Fornés, 16.
33. Savran, *In Their Own Words*, 58–59.
34. Fornés, *Fefu*, 17.
35. Fornés, 17.
36. Fornés, 17.
37. Fornés, 17.

38 Fornés, 22.
39 María Irene Fornés, interview by Bonnie Marranca, *Performing Arts Journal* 2, no. 3 (1978): 109.
40 Fornés, interview by Marranca, 109.
41 My use of the term *bodymind* owes to the work of Margaret Price, who reintroduces pain into disability and crip studies. See "The Bodymind Problem and the Possibilities of Pain," *Hypatia* 30, no. 1 (2015): 268–84. She writes, "Bodymind is a term I picked up several years ago while reading in trauma studies. . . . According to this approach, because mental and physical processes not only affect each other but also give rise to each other—that is, because they tend to act as one, even though they are conventionally understood as two—it makes more sense to refer to them together, in a single term" (269). As we will see, hysterical figures warrant the usage of *bodymind* because the two (body and mind) often "act as one."
42 Wilson, *Gut Feminism*, 59.
43 Anna Mollow, "Criphystemologies: What Disability Theory Needs to Know about Hysteria," *Journal of Literary & Cultural Disability Studies* 8, no. 2 (January 2014): 199–200.
44 Scott T. Cummings, *Maria Irene Fornes* (New York: Routledge, 2013), 69.
45 Fornés, interview by Marranca, 107.
46 María Irene Fornés, "Notes on Fefu," in *The Theater of Maria Irene Fornes*, ed. Marc Robinson (Baltimore: Johns Hopkins University Press, 1999), 200.
47 See Richard Schechner, *Environmental Theater* (New York: Hawton, 1973).
48 Jadie Stillwell, "In a New Production of an Old Play, *Fefu and Her Friends* Go beneath the Surface," *Interview Magazine*, November 26, 2019, www.interviewmagazine.com.
49 For more on a Latinx thinking of choreography, see Ramón H. Rivera-Servera, *Performing Queer Latinidad: Dance, Sexuality, Politics* (Ann Arbor: University of Michigan Press, 2012). Rivera-Servera shows how performance and choreography mark queer Latinx political interventions in the 1990s and 2000s.
50 Murray Piper, "'They Are Well Together. Women Are Not': Productive Ambivalence and Female Hom(m)osociality in *Fefu and Her Friends*," *Modern Drama* 44, no. 4 (2001): 401.
51 Fornés, *Fefu*, 31.
52 Fornés, 38.
53 For an example of this, see W. B. Worthan, "*Still Playing Games*: Ideology and Performance in the Theater of Maria Irene Fornes," in *Feminine Focus: The New Women Playwrights*, ed. Enoch Brater (New York: Oxford University Press, 1989), 167–85.
54 For instance, Penny Farfan looks at the question of hysteria in *Fefu and Her Friends* but still relies on a feminist understanding of hysteria that registers hysterics as silent: "Elaine Showalter has written that 'hysteria and feminism exist on a kind of continuum' and that '[i]f we see the hysterical woman as one end of the spectrum of a female avant-garde struggling to redefine women's place in the social order, then we can also see feminism as the other end of the spectrum, the alternative to hysterical silence, and the determination to speak and act for women in the public

world.'" Penny Farfan, "Feminism, Metatheatricality, and *Mise-en-Scène* in Maria Irene Fornes's *Fefu and Her Friends*," *Modern Drama* 40, no. 4 (1997): 444. But hysterics feature noisy and busy bodies—somatically communicating in a manner that defies how we understand relationship in a minded body, creating a more nuanced relation between external force and the internal metabolization, ingestion, and transmogrification of those forces.

55 It's worth noting that the year of the play, 1977, influences this play, which is meant to be set in the 1930s. While Fornés yearns for a return to a moment before human behavior was on display for a kind of psychological interpretation, the milieu of 1970s feminist movements surfaces through the play's second act, which allows one to see the effects of what we may call consciousness-raising. Indeed, many of the characters revisit their education to see how they've been punished for being too smart or antinormative or, in the case of Sue, having a working-class difference that sets them apart. Fornés explains, "I had attended several consciousness-raising meetings where I had discovered many things I had experiences as a woman were things that many other women shared." Fornés, interview by Delgado, 258. These conversations do not always bring the women nearer to one another—this is, after all, dangerous terrain.

56 Sami Schalk refines this point by taking the metaphoricity and materiality of disability as entwined. Despite the problematic usage of ableist metaphors (i.e., someone is blind to a cause), Schalk challenges us to see how the literal and the figurative commingle in (dis)ability metaphors and figurations: "This is why reading representations of disability as simultaneously metaphor and materiality is so essential—disability oscillates between abstraction and material meanings due to its social history. In other words, because (dis)ability has been used by dominant social discourses to reference, define, and regulate other social systems, it requires reading for the metaphorical, allegorical, or otherwise abstract ways in which its fictional representation is implicated in gender, race, class, and sexuality concerns as both discursive signifier and material effect." Samantha Dawn Schalk, *Bodyminds Reimagined: (Dis)Ability, Race, and Gender in Black Women's Speculative Fiction* (Durham, NC: Duke University Press, 2018), 44.

57 Fornés, *Fefu*, 33.
58 Fornés, 33–34.
59 Sarah Ruhl, "Six Small Thoughts on Fornes, the Problem of Intention, and Willfulness," *Theatre Topics* 11, no. 2 (2001): 202.
60 Ruhl, 194.
61 Sara Ahmed, *Willful Subjects* (Durham, NC: Duke University Press, 2014), 140.
62 Fornés, "Notes on Fefu," 201.
63 Jorge Ignacio Cortiñas, "'Fefu' and Her Pleasures," *American Theater*, January 8, 2021, www.americantheatre.org.
64 Fornés, *Fefu*, 43.
65 Fornés, 43.
66 Fornés, 43–44.
67 Wiegman carefully traces the critical tendencies of these fields built on identity knowledges by exploring the politics assumed, the concepts afforded, and the

place of social justice in these fields of study. See Robyn Wiegman, *Object Lessons* (Durham, NC: Duke University Press, 2012).
68 Farfan, "Feminism," 446.
69 See Roy Pérez, "Fornés and the Avant-Garde," in *Fornés in Context* (Cambridge: Cambridge University Press, forthcoming 2024).
70 Randi Koppen, "Formalism and the Return to the Body: Stein's and Fornes's Aesthetic of Significant Form," *New Literary History* 28, no. 4 (1997): 791–809.
71 Jonathan Goldberg and Michael Moon, eds., "Melanie Klein and the Difference Affect Makes," in *The Weather in Proust*, by Eve Kosofsky Sedgwick (Durham, NC: Duke University Press, 2012), 126.
72 Goldberg and Moon, 126.
73 Cummings, *Maria Irene Fornes*, xx.
74 María Irene Fornés, "Creative Danger: Exploring the Woman's Voice in Drama," *American Theater*, September 1, 1985, www.americantheatre.org.
75 Edwidge Danticat, *Create Dangerously: The Immigrant Artist at Work* (Princeton, NJ: Princeton University Press, 2010), 10.
76 Fornés, "Creative Danger: Exploring the Woman's Voice in Drama."
77 Fornés.
78 María Irene Fornés, "Writing and Aging: *from* 'Ages of the Avant-Garde,'" *PAJ: A Journal of Performance and Art* 41, no. 1 (2019): 5.
79 Anne García-Romero beautifully captures Fornés's daughterly dedication: "While she did have lesbian partners throughout her life, Fornes never had children of her own. She was, however, a loyal daughter to her mother, Carmen Fornes (1891–1994), for whom she was a caregiver in her later years until Carmen died at 103. Though frail and eventually deaf, Carmen Fornes remained an active presence in Fornés's professional career." *The Fornes Frame: Contemporary Latina Playwrights and the Legacy of Maria Irene Fornes* (Tucson: University of Arizona Press, 2016), 53.
80 Fornes, "Writing and Aging," 5.
81 Viego importantly figures the hysteric's discourse as one that brings "some noise regarding how the production of knowledge is conceptualized in the university—the role of knowledge, its purpose, whom does it serve—I liken Latino studies critique to Lacan's 'hysteric's discourse.'" Viego, *Dead Subjects: Toward a Politics of Loss in Latino Studies* (Durham, NC: Duke University Press, 2007), 113. While this chapter is more concerned with aspects of Kleinian inflections on feminist and queer theory, I concur with much of Viego's psychoanalytic thinking that contends with symptoms and that, rather than seeking a cure or purity, looks to create new symptoms that challenge masterful discourse. This intervention of the hysteric's discourse crucially follows from Viego's hope that, citing Richard T. Ford, our task in the classroom should not reproduce our identities and that we should not desire to reproduce ourselves through coercive mimetics or phallic extension. This point resonates powerfully with Stephen Best's insights in *None like Us: Blackness, Belonging, Aesthetic Life* (Durham, NC: Duke University Press, 2018).

4. LOSING THE PACK

1 Justin Torres, *We the Animals* (New York: Mariner, 2011), 1.
2 Torres, 1.
3 Torres, 3.
4 Torres, 2–3.
5 While my reading lands less on Torres's rearticulation of Latinx masculinity, it is worth noting how the opening, stabbing lines operate as a kind of introduction that is undercut by the feminine. My reading will attend to figurations of birthing and maternity that exceed the feminine. For a reading that tarries with masculinity elegantly, see Nicolás Ramos Flores, "Queer Intimacy and the Disruption of Latinx Masculinity in Justin Torres's *We the Animals* (2011)," *Chiricú Journal: Latina/o Literatures, Arts, and Cultures* 6, no. 2 (July 2022): 5–23.
6 Iván A. Ramos, *Unbelonging: Inauthentic Sounds in Mexican and Latinx Aesthetics* (New York: New York University Press, 2023). 17.
7 See Mary Pat Brady, *Scales of Captivity: Racial Capitalism and the Latinx Child* (Durham, NC: Duke University Press, 2022), 240.
8 Torres, *We the Animals*, 4.
9 Torres, 6.
10 Torres, 6.
11 Torres, 7.
12 Elissa Marder, *The Mother in the Age of Mechanical Reproduction: Psychoanalysis, Photography, Deconstruction* (New York: Fordham University Press, 2012), 5.
13 Marder, 2.
14 For more on Black maternity and mothering specifically, see Sara Clarke Kaplan, *The Black Reproductive: Unfree Labor and Insurgent Motherhood* (Minneapolis: University of Minnesota Press, 2021); Jennifer C. Nash, *Birthing Black Mothers* (Durham, NC: Duke University Press, 2021); and Zakiyyah Iman Jackson, *Becoming Human: Matter and Meaning in an Antiblack World* (New York: New York University Press, 2020).
15 Amber Jamilla Musser, *Sensual Excess: Queer Femininity and Brown Jouissance* (New York: New York University Press, 2018), 172.
16 Richard T. Rodríguez, "Oedipal Wrecks: Queer Ecologies in Justin Torres's *We the Animals*," in *Latinx Environmentalisms: Place, Justice, and the Decolonial*, ed. Sarah D. Wald et al. (Philadelphia: Temple University Press, 2019), 267–80.
17 Cathy J. Cohen, "Punks, Bulldaggers, and Welfare Queens: The Radical Potential of Queer Politics?," *GLQ: A Journal of Lesbian and Gay Studies* 3, no. 4 (May 1, 1997): 437–65.
18 See Melanie Klein's *Love, Guilt and Reparation: And Other Works 1921–1945* (London: Hogarth). My thinking on Klein is indebted to Sedgwick's work in "The Difference Affect Makes" as well as in *Touching Feeling*.
19 Torres, *We the Animals*, 8–9.
20 Torres, 3.

21 Juana María Rodríguez, *Sexual Futures, Queer Gestures, and Other Latina Longings* (New York: New York University Press, 2014), 99.
22 Rodríguez, 105.
23 Alexandra T. Vazquez, *Listening in Detail: Performances of Cuban Music* (Durham, NC: Duke University Press, 2013), 143–45.
24 My thinking of this unsovereign lament of masculinity is indebted to insights from bell hooks's *Feminism Is for Everybody: Passionate Politics* (London: Pluto, 2000), as well as Zakiyyah Iman Jackson's stunning reading of Paul D's encounter with Mister the rooster in *Beloved* in "Losing Manhood: Plasticity, Animality, and Opacity in the (Neo) Slave Narrative" in *Becoming Human*.
25 Torres, *We the Animals*, 10.
26 Torres, 10.
27 Rodríguez, *Sexual Futures*, 105.
28 Torres, *We the Animals*, 11.
29 Mel Chen, *Animacies: Biopolitics, Racial Mattering, and Queer Affect* (Durham, NC: Duke University Press, 2012), 30.
30 Chen, 70.
31 Chen, 40.
32 The invocation of three kings here certainly corresponds to the New Testament of the Bible but is more markedly celebrated in Latin American Catholicism and, hence, bears a particular kind of inflection in this text.
33 Torres, *We the Animals*, 12.
34 Torres, 13–14.
35 Torres, 15.
36 Torres, 16.
37 Torres, 17.
38 Torres, 23.
39 For more on Frankenstein's relation to gender, see Barbara Johnson, "My Monster/My Self," *Diacritics* 12, no. 2 (1982): 2–10. See also Susan Stryker, "My Words to Victor Frankenstein above the Village of Chamounix: Performing Transgender Rage," *GLQ: A Journal of Lesbian and Gay Studies* 1, no. 3 (1994): 237–54.
40 Torres, *We the Animals*, 24.
41 Here, I take issue with the figures that Bersani uses to support his polemic in "Is the Rectum a Grave?" in *Is the Rectum a Grave? And Other Essays* (Chicago: University of Chicago Press, 2010), 3–30. Specifically, I take issue with the figures used to set up Bersani's argument, the female, supine sex worker and the visibility of Black folks recasts white, gay male subjectivity, if unwittingly, at the center of radical queer politics. To be sure, much of queer theory's movements have been helpfully complicated by Bersani's thoughts on psychoanalysis, negativity, and the death drive. But I want to be attentive to how many theorists use figures of women and Black people in order to launch a thought that may unwittingly leave those figures outside of their theorization.

42 This monstrous progeny is birthed through misogyny. The boys seem to feel both rage and shame and utter disappointment at their parents for not being to be able to save them from either interpersonal or structural violence. The narrative of *Frankenstein* figures a relationship to the monstrosity of parenthood, aligning with Melanie Klein's object relations, which account for quotidian interpersonal violence that enmeshes the unconscious (that which is other on a psychic level to the self) with behavior or what we may call symptoms, empirical action, or behavior. I'm less interested in reifying a psychoanalytic insight but am instead culling a piece of wisdom about how violence works from theorists who have found the most banal forms of interpersonal violence that would indeed resonate forcefully with forms of disenfranchisement that are both material and symbolic. Or rather, incommensurate structures of disenfranchisement should deepen an attention to psychoanalytic notions of loss in such terrains.

43 My use of withholding here is indebted to Vivian L. Huang's writing on withholding as an aesthetic form of inscrutability. See Vivian L. Huang, *Surface Relations: Queer Forms of Asian American Inscrutability* (Durham, NC: Duke University Press, 2022).

44 Torres, *We the Animals*, 25.

45 Torres, 26.

46 Torres, 26.

47 My thinking on biocentrism is informed by Sylvia Wynter. See Wynter's "Unsettling the Coloniality of Being/Power/Truth/Freedom: Towards the Human, after Man, Its Overrepresentation—an Argument," *CR: The New Centennial Review* 3, no. 3 (2003): 266–70.

48 Torres, *We the Animals*, 26–27.

49 For more on the anecdote, see Jane Gallop, *Anecdotal Theory* (Durham, NC: Duke University Press, 2002).

50 Torres, *We the Animals*, 27.

51 Torres, 28–29.

52 In *Touching Feeling*, Sedgwick invokes the promise of Melanie Klein and Silvan Tomkins because their notion of the psyche, as well as development, is not so predicated on an Oedipal schema. For Klein, people do not develop on a trajectory of maturation but, rather, waver between paranoid and reparative. Kleinian psychoanalysis often features the inevitability of violence within one's mind and always in relation to others and thus maps onto Torres's novel in helpful ways.

53 Torres, *We the Animals*, 30.

54 Torres, 30.

55 This mention of a Cadillac is not incidental but is instead haunted by the anti-Asian sentiment aroused by the decline of the auto industry in the early eighties in the United States. Torres, 31.

56 Torres, 32.

57 See Kevin Everod Quashie, *The Sovereignty of Quiet: Beyond Resistance in Black Culture* (New Brunswick, NJ: Rutgers University Press, 2012).

58 Torres, *We the Animals*, 34.
59 Torres, 34.
60 Torres, 34.
61 See Oscar Zeta Acosta, *The Revolt of the Cockroach People* (New York: Vintage, 1989).
62 Torres, *We the Animals*, 35.
63 Torres, 37–38.
64 Chen, *Animacies*, 106.
65 Chen, 89. Chen's work here choruses in an opposite manner to Zakiyyah Iman Jackson's important insights in *Becoming Human*. If Chen shows how animality has a cline of slippages, then Jackson shows how blackened persons are not always rendered non-human or animal, but "sub, supra, and human *simultaneously*" (35).
66 Torres, *We the Animals*, 54.
67 Torres, 60.
68 Torres, 66–67.
69 It bears noting that in Puerto Rico, the word for duck, *pato*, is slang for a gay man.
70 Torres, *We the Animals*, 67.
71 Torres, 68.
72 Torres, 68.
73 Torres, 69.
74 Torres, 70.
75 Torres, 71.
76 Torres, 71.
77 In volume 2 of *The Beast and the Sovereign*, Jacques Derrida writes, "There is no world, there are only islands." *The Beast and the Sovereign*, Vol. 2, trans. Geoffrey Bennington, ed. Michel Lisse, Marie-Louise Mallet, and Ginette Michaud (Chicago: University of Chicago Press, 2011), 9. We may read the islands of the Caribbean as an imaginary thought most fully through the diaspora. Michelle Cliff reminds us that "first of all, the Caribbean doesn't exist as an entity; it exists all over the world. It started in diaspora and it continues in diaspora." Michelle Cliff, interview by Meryl F. Schwartz, *Contemporary Literature* 34, no. 4 (1993): 597. What I mean to emphasize here is that the Caribbean is very far from *We the Animals*, and it's notable that this scene is, perhaps, some of the only island imagery we get in this novel.
78 Torres, *We the Animals*, 71.
79 Torres, 72.
80 Torres, 90.
81 Torres, 96.
82 Torres, 97.
83 Torres, 96.
84 Torres, 96–97.
85 Torres, 97.
86 Torres, 100.

87 Torres, 101.
88 Torres, 102.
89 Torres, 104.
90 Torres, 105.
91 Torres, 108.
92 Torres, 111.
93 Torres, 105.
94 Carlos Ulises Decena, *Tacit Subjects: Belonging and Same-Sex Desire among Dominican Immigrant Men* (Durham, NC: Duke University Press, 2011).
95 Torres, *We the Animals*, 110.
96 Torres, 113.
97 Jacques Derrida, *The Animal That Therefore I Am*, ed. Marie-Louise Mallet, trans. David Wills (New York: Fordham University Press, 2008), 3.
98 Torres, *We the Animals*, 116.
99 Torres, 118.
100 Torres, 118.
101 When I read this closing vignette, I cannot help but read an allusion to queer animality in Baldwin's *Giovanni's Room*: "There were, of course, *les folles*, always dressed in the most improbable combinations, screaming like parrots the details of their latest love affairs, their love affairs always seemed to be hilarious. Occasionally, one would swoop in, quite late in the evening, to convey that he—but they always called each other 'she'—had just spent time with a celebrated movie star, or boxer. Then all of the others closed in on this newcomer and they looked like a peacock garden and sounded like a barnyard." *Giovanni's Room* (New York: Vintage, 2013), 26–27.
102 My thinking of ipseity is indebted to Ronald Mendoza-de Jesús's work that tarries with a Derridian emphasis on ipseity that reveals how much of mastery and sovereignty cohere in the figure of the self that knows itself. See Ronald Mendoza-de Jesús, *Catastrophic Historicism: Reading Julia de Burgos Dangerously* (New York: Fordham University Press, 2023), 137–40.
103 Antonio Viego, *Dead Subjects: Toward a Politics of Loss in Latino Studies* (Durham, NC: Duke University Press, 2007), 29.
104 In "Refusing the Referendum," Marion Christina Rohrleitner reads Torres's novel alongside Jack Halberstam's work on the wild, saying that the narrator's "refusal to be confined" in normative modes leads him to "not a zoo, but an island where the 'wild things' roam freely." "Refusing the Referendum: Queer Latino Masculinities and Utopian Citizenship in Justin Torres' *We the Animals*," *European Journal of American Studies* 11, no. 3 (January 24, 2017), 10.
105 What I mean to make plain here is that the novel refuses the confessional mode in a book that traffics in queer desire. I read this move alongside Foucault's insights in *The History of Sexuality, Volume 1*, in order to consider that what we think of as liberation may too easily require that we show how much we've been repressed. It is my argument that Torres's novel does not show repression and

move toward liberation, but dwells in a less ideal place that most of us inhabit. Michel Foucault, *The History of Sexuality: An Introduction*, vol. 1, trans. Robert Hurley (New York: Vintage, 1990).

106 Rey Chow, *The Protestant Ethnic and the Spirit of Capitalism* (New York: Columbia University Press, 2002), 115.

107 I should note that my reading of the novel and, indeed, my reading of Glissantian opacity veers sharply away from a similarly framed argument in the work of Zorimar Rivera Montes. Rivera Montes writes, "The novel's open-ended, opaque ending marks Torres's project of queer liberation: a liberation that eludes recognition and difference in the terms granted by the normative order, showing the potential of opacity as a political strategy." "'For Opacity': Queerness and Latinidad in Justin Torres' *We the Animals*," *Latino Studies* 18, no. 2 (June 2020): 218–34. Instead of transforming the ending's ambivalence and opacity into a politics of liberation, my reading stays with the ambivalence in order to register the losses detailed in the book. I do not think opacity follows after representation, as Rivera Montes formulates earlier in this article, but is a fundamental problem for representation. Similarly, while many of Rivera Montes's readings follow the text of Torres very carefully, I remain unconvinced that one can glean an actionable politics from the novel.

108 Alphonso Lingis, "Animal Body, Inhuman Face," *Social Semiotics* 7, no. 2 (1997): 113–26.

109 For more on the entwined categories of madness and queerness, see Lynne Huffer, *Mad for Foucault: Rethinking the Foundations of Queer Theory* (New York: Columbia University Press, 2010).

CODA. KNOTS IN THE THROAT

1 Raquel Salas Rivera, *Preguntas frecuentes / Frequently Asked Questions* (San Juan: La Impresora, 2019).

2 Raquel Salas Rivera, "A Note on Translation," *Waxwing*, Fall 2016, www.waxwingmag.org.

3 I say "a figure of untranslatability" because it is rendered so in Salas Rivera's translation notes. I should note that the word, *adoquines*, can be translated to "cobblestones." In this manner, it is not untranslatable in the manner that would garner it an entry into the *Dictionary of Untranslatables: A Philosophical Lexicon*, ed. Barbara Cassin, trans. Steven Randall et al. (Princeton, NJ: Princeton University Press, 2014).

4 This excerpt is translated from a thorough report on the history of Old San Juan's pavements and the provenance of the *adoquines*. See Rafael Calderín, *Los adoquines de escoria en San Juan* (self-pub., Issuu, 2015), 26.

5 Calderín, 26.

6 Lolita Buckner Inniss, "Ships' Ballast," in *International Law's Objects*, ed. Jessie Hohmann and Daniel Joyce (Oxford: Oxford University Press, 2018).

7 Buckner Inniss, 432.

8 Contemporary ballasting mechanisms in boats no longer use solid materials and instead use water. However, the problem of ballasted movement remains, since the water used to ballast modern ships often creates pollution and toxicity in oceanic waters, threatening coral reefs.
9 For my reading of Salas Rivera's catachrestic and incommensurate invocations of loss, see Christina A León, "Risking Catachresis: Reading Race, Reference, and Grammar in 'Women,'" *Diacritics* 49, no. 1 (November 2, 2021): 61–71.
10 Raquel Salas Rivera, *the tertiary / lo terciario*, 2nd ed. (Blacksburg, VA: Noemi, 2019), 20.
11 For an excellent analysis of Salas Rivera's self-translation in concert with other Latinx self-translators, see Rachel Galvin, "Transcreation and Self-Translation in Contemporary Latinx Poetry," *Critical Inquiry* 49, no. 1 (2022): 28–54.
12 Salas Rivera, "Note on Translation."
13 Rocío Zambrana, *Colonial Debts: The Case of Puerto Rico* (Durham, NC: Duke University Press, 2021).
14 See Neetu Khanna, *The Visceral Logics of Decolonization* (Durham, NC: Duke University Press, 2020). Here, Khanna provides a rich and compelling reading of decolonial affect as having knotted and entangled meanings issuing from structural dispossession, coloniality, and the mind-body's refusals and metabolizations of such impositions.
15 See Meredith Lee, "Generating Blackness: Unsettling the American Grammar of Trans Politics," *Journal of Black Sexuality and Relationships* 3, no. 3 (2017): 81–90; and Riley, *Black on Both Sides: A Racial History of Trans Identity* (Minneapolis: University of Minnesota Press, 2017).
16 Eva Hayward and Che Gossett, "IMPOSSIBILITY OF THAT," *Angelaki* 22, no. 2 (April 3, 2017): 17.
17 In 2021, La Impresora relocated to Isabela, Puerto Rico.
18 See Judith Butler, "Gender in Translation: Beyond Monolingualism," *philoSOPHIA* 9, no. 1 (2019): 1–25. Here, Butler makes the argument that all gender is a translation and that gender, as a concept understood contemporaneously, issues first from English, because of John Money's sexological and gender research.
19 For more on traps in trans studies, see Reina Gossett, Eric A. Stanley, and Johanna Burton, eds., *Trap Door: Trans Cultural Production and the Politics of Visibility* (Cambridge, MA: MIT Press, 2017). See also Francisco Galarte, *Brown Trans Figurations: Rethinking Race, Gender, and Sexuality in Chicanx/Latinx Studies* (Austin: University of Texas Press, 2021).
20 Galarte, *Brown Trans Figurations*.
21 Salas Rivera, "Note on Translation."
22 Here, I am referencing two key writings that think the ravages of coloniality and tourism in relation to the Caribbean's undeniable beauty: Suzanne Césaire, "Le grand camouflage," in *Le grand camouflage*, ed. Daniel Maximin (Paris: Seuil, 2009); and Jamaica Kincaid, *A Small Place* (New York: Farrar, Straus and Giroux, 2000).

23 Jeannine Murray-Román, "Errors in the Exchange: Debt, Self-Translation, and the Speculative Poesis of Raquel Salas Rivera," *CR: The New Centennial Review* 20, no. 1 (2020): 88.
24 Raquel Salas Rivera, *Preguntas frecuentes*.
25 See Eve Tuck and K. Wayne Yang, "Decolonization Is Not a Metaphor," *Decolonization: Indigeneity, Education & Society* 1, no. 1 (2012): 1–40.
26 By making this claim, I want to emphasize the lingua franca. I recognize that the Caribbean, and Puerto Rico, have indigenous languages that are being taught, revived, and disseminated through organizations and education.
27 For instance, see Jonathan Rosa, *Looking like a Language, Sounding like a Race: Raciolinguistic Ideologies and the Learning of Latinidad* (New York: Oxford University Press, 2019).
28 Galarte, *Brown Trans Figurations*, 130.

INDEX

Note: Page numbers followed by *f* refer to figures.

abstraction, 6–7, 12, 67, 121; disability and, 278n56; visual, 3
accent, 21, 44, 142–43, 146, 148, 275n8; Spanish, 232
adoquines, 46, 225–30, 236–37, 239–43, 245–46, 285nn3–4. *See also* ballast
aesthetics, 5–7, 39–41, 93; anticipatable, 120; history and, 117; market, 272n62; monstrous, 29; persistence and, 113; politics and, 147; vignette, 186, 222
affect, 5, 8, 41, 63, 146, 166, 184, 256n35, 275n2; analogical, 167; archive of, 107; decolonial, 230, 286n14; Kleinian psychoanalysis and, 170; negative, 142; pedagogy of, 213; reflexive, 141
Agard-Jones, Vanessa, 59, 136, 264n16, 274n80, 274n88
agriculture, 82, 97
AIDS, 92–93, 103, 125–26, 137; Ramos Otero and, 43, 98–99, 101, 113, 122, 124–25, 127–31, 133, 136
alterity, 14, 35, 41, 66; abstract, 5; fetishes of, 29; radical, 27, 256n38
ambivalence, 122, 125, 146, 152, 178, 179, 185, 218, 222, 271n38, 285n107; of animality, 41, 204–5; of dust/*polvo*, 131, 135, 137
Americanity, 59, 87
Americas, the, 49, 57, 59, 82, 86, 89, 243; latinidad in, 47
Andre, Carl, 51–52, 54, 68
animacy, 178–79, 190–91, 200–201, 204, 216; of language, 187, 190, 206
animality, 44–45, 178–79, 190–91, 199–200, 202, 204, 206, 283n65; ambivalence of, 41, 45, 205; in *Giovanni's Room*, 284n101; queerness of, 185; of *We the Animals*, 181, 217–18, 220
animals, 159, 178–79, 200, 204–6, 209, 211, 217, 219–20, 222; domesticated, 72; humanimals, 190; movements of, 45. *See also We the Animals*
Anthropocene, 82, 267n56
anticolonial movements, 5, 46, 224, 241
Arawak language, 55, 72

Arrom, José Juan, 58, 65, 72
art, 10, 17, 41, 115, 120, 148, 166, 171, 272n46; caves and, 76, 81–82, 84; in Cuba, 61, 67–68; difference and, 175; feminist, 61, 63, 265n27; Fornés and, 172–73; inscriptions and, 4; institutions, 69; Latinx, 3, 24, 47; masses and, 40; matter and, 6; Mendieta's, 50, 53–54, 62, 64–65, 84, 88, 262n2, 265n27; performance, 49, 257n40; queer; Sánchez's, 13; of storytelling, 272n44; Taíno, 76, 82; underrepresented, 35, 145. *See also* Benjamin, Walter; New York City: art scene / art world
Atlantic Ocean, 81, 94, 127, 132
Austin, J. L., 118, 255n27
autobiography, 20–23, 98, 107, 111, 113–14, 117–19, 272n56; Latinx, 255n30; Ramos Otero and, 21, 43, 93–96, 101–2, 108, 113–20, 271n35. *See also* De Man, Paul

Bachner, Andrea, 26, 254n12, 257n39
ballast, 46, 224–31, 239–41, 286n8
Barad, Karen, 136, 255n21
Barreiro, José, 58, 263–64nn8–11, 264n14
Barthes, Roland, 11, 112
Bedia, José, 67–68
belonging, 64, 178–80, 187, 197, 200, 206, 208; animality and, 41, 221; loss of, 215, 218; metaphors of, 44; Spanish language as guarantor of, 21
Beltrán, Cristina, 4, 6, 15, 254n8
Benjamin, Walter, 21, 39–40; "The Task of the Translator," 114–16
Bersani, Leo, 197, 281n41. *See also* psychoanalysis
bildungsroman, 45, 179–80, 198, 218, 221
biographical hermeneutic, 20, 23, 54, 120; critique of, 19, 171
biography, 19–20, 52, 54, 107, 117, 119, 171
biological matter, 44, 50, 81
Blackness, 60, 179, 260n73, 261n82, 262n95, 266n48, 267n59, 274n81; anti-Blackness, 59, 61, 89, 110, 260n69, 266n48
Blain-Cruz, Lileana, 148, 159–60

289

Blocker, Jane, 52, 62
Bonilla, Yarimar, 134–35, 274n91
Brady, Mary Pat, 18, 180, 255n26, 255n29, 263n5, 280n7
Braithwaite, Edward, 87, 268n69
brownness, 51, 179, 262n95
burden of liveness, 26, 257n40
Butler, Judith, 4, 35, 254n12; *Bodies That Matter*, 37; catachresis and, 259n64; "Gender in Translation: Beyond Monolingualism," 286n18; *Giving an Account of Oneself*, 22
Byrd, Jodi, 52, 255n26

caciques, 55, 58
camp, 101, 103–4, 106–11, 116, 270n28, 271n35
capitalism, 105, 182, 270n21; racial, 40, 45, 180–81, 199, 212
Caribbean, the, 55, 81, 96, 136, 151, 274n80, 283n77; African presence in, 59, 72; AIDS in, 128; atmospherics of, 132; beauty of, 286n22; dust storms and, 133–34; ecologies of dust in, 94; indigeneity in, 56–57, 72; Indigenous languages in, 287n26; Indigenous peoples in, 57–58; Indigenous presence in, 56; limestone and, 87; migrants from, 266n42; Native peoples' extinction in, 263n8; Puerto Rico and, 210, 243; race in, 57; suffering of, 240
carnality, 60, 142
Castro, Fidel, 84, 143; regime of, 69
catachresis, 30–40, 48, 84–86, 257n43, 258n47, 259n59, 261n82; feminist theorists and, 259n63; language and, 201; Latinx as, 28; in Marx, 259n63; material consequence of, 259n67. *See also* De Man, Paul; Derrida, Jacques
caves, 42, 51, 65–67, 69, 74, 76, 78–89; catachrestic, 85, 88; in Taíno mythology, 76
Césaire, Suzanne, 240, 286n22
Chen, Mel, 190–91, 201, 206, 283n65
childhood, 181, 194–95, 198, 204
Chow, Rey, 17, 28–29, 35, 39–40, 116, 220, 258n46, 270n15
Chuh, Kandice, 28, 40, 145–46, 258n45, 261n90
cimarrón, 71–72, 73f
climate change, 43, 134
colonial contact, 42, 57–59, 65
colonialism, 17; British, 226; historical inheritance of, 64; settler, 59, 83
coloniality, 17, 19, 27, 43, 50, 56, 81–82, 85, 92, 236–37, 240–46, 266n48; ballast and, 227–28; Cuba and, 70, 88; decolonial affect and, 286n14; descriptive logic of, 74; effects of, 131; Latinx and, 36; materials of, 224, 231; nuclear, 239, 245–46; Puerto Rico and, 15, 33, 224, 229; queerness and, 93, 132; queer relations and, 136; racial capitalism and, 180;

Sodom as allegorical translation of, 130; of Spanish, 16; time of, 87; tourism and, 286n22; violent, 64
Columbus, Christopher, 57–58, 72
consumption, 17; of the Global North, 46, 235; of monolingual English speakers, 228; voyeuristic, 5
Cortiñas, Jorge Ignacio, 140, 166
cosmologies, 42, 58, 60, 88, 244; Indigenous, 59
critical Black studies, 36, 38, 47
critical race studies, 5, 28, 179
Cuba, 15, 47, 61, 71–72, 84, 88, 266n42; *Agave Jarucoensis*, 74; Baracoa, 58, 263n8; Blackness in, 60; Fornés and, 143; Guantánamo, 55, 58, 263n8; Havana, 49, 61, 66–67, 69–70, 142; indigeneity in, 42, 55, 264n11; Indigenous peoples in, 49, 55–56, 58–59, 263n9; Mendieta and, 42, 50–54, 65–69, 75, 76–78, 87, 262n1; Puerto Rico and, 262n93; Sánchez and, 3, 10–11; Special Period, 59, 70. *See also* Castro, Fidel; *guajiro*; Jaruco
Cuban Cultural Circle (Círculo de Cultura Cubana), 68, 262n1
Cuban exiles, 50, 66, 87, 143
Cuban Revolution, 50, 53, 59, 61, 66, 96, 114

Danticat, Edwidge, 18, 41, 173
Da Silva, Denise Ferreira, 7, 29–30, 39
death, 43, 83, 86, 95, 98–99, 104, 118, 130, 135, 137–38, 266n44; Anthropocene and, 267n56; desire and, 122–23, 125; dust/*polvo* and, 92, 101, 113, 115, 121–22, 136; in *Fefu and Her Friends*, 168–69; glamorized, 110; HIV/AIDS and, 98, 103, 113, 126, 131; Hollywood and, 106, 111; Indigenous, 59; Mendieta's, 49, 51–52, 54; Ramos Otero's, 43, 94, 98, 103, 111, 114, 122, 125–26; rocks and, 81, 267n52; social, 134; of the subject, 30; in *We the Animals*, 214
death drive, 125, 281n41
debt, 182, 207; Puerto Rico's, 33, 96, 236, 268n1; Salas Rivera and, 230, 243
decoloniality, 243, 260n69
deconstruction, 18, 38, 260n81; catachresis and, 34; *différance* and, 36; reference and, 27
De Man, Paul, 4, 38, 117–18; on catachresis, 259n59. *See also* deconstruction
Derrida, Jacques, 4, 11, 18, 27, 86, 206; *The Animal That Therefore I Am*, 217–18; *The Beast and the Sovereign*, 283n77; on catachresis, 84, 259n59; *Of Grammatology*, 8; "Signature, Event, Context," 255n27, 256n38. *See also* deconstruction
desire, 17; dust and, 113; kinship and, 180; lack of, 34; loss and, 179; pronouns and, 121; queer, 97, 136, 274n80, 284n105; Ramos

Otero's work and, 43, 94, 101, 105–6, 108, 112, 121–23, 125, 131–32; Sánchez and, 3; traces of, 23
diaspora, 10–11, 17, 41–42, 94, 122, 133, 135–36, 187; Afro-Caribbean, 189; Caribbean, 283n77; Cuban, 69, 144, 262n93; latinidad and, 262n95; Puerto Rican, 188, 224, 236, 262n93, 269n12
disability, 17, 155–56, 164, 278n56; in *Fefu and Her Friends* (Fornés), 153; studies, 155, 277n41
différance, 35–36, 256n38
Dimock, Wai Chee, 87, 268n70
discipline, 17, 212
disenfranchisement, 5, 32, 34, 36, 54, 216, 241, 282n42; in Puerto Rico, 274n91
displacement, 59, 134
dispossession, 7, 33, 46, 60, 81, 83, 92, 207, 222, 267n56; grammars of, 20; of land, 59; neoliberal, 96; ontological, 110; structural, 221, 286n14; transatlantic slave trade and, 134
DNA, 56, 82, 264nn11–12
Dominican Republic, 47, 82, 262n94
dust/*polvo*, 41–43, 92–98, 101, 103–4, 112–15, 120–23, 127, 131–38, 268n1, 270n13, 273n64, 274nn80–81; colonial, 245; massification of, 274n85; Ramos Otero's writing and, 274n81. *See also* poetics: of dust; theory: dust; writing: dust/dusty

ecology, 142, 204; animal, 45; Cuba's, 42, 59
encomienda, 55, 58–59
erasure, 50; Indigenous, 83; linguistic, 236
Enlightenment, 45, 130, 169, 179
equivalence, 84, 232; nonequivalence, 241
eroticism, 10, 12
essentialism, 52, 62–64, 85, 263n7, 265n27; strategic, 34
ethnicity, 3, 17–18, 255n21, 264n12
exile, 51, 53, 65–66, 86; forced, 53–54; queerness in, 136, 274n80. *See also* Cuban exiles
exposure, 46, 84, 88, 93–94, 121, 131; of dust, 137; of madness, 165; to pornography, 212; shame and, 189; translation and, 224–25, 228
extinction, 19, 59, 81; Indigenous/Native, 50, 52, 263n8, 264n11, 266n44; narrative, 58
extraction, 17, 59–60, 81, 134, 255n22; English language and, 236; exposure as, 46, 228; forced, 88; translation as, 46

fascism, 29, 40, 239–41, 245–46
fecundity, 11, 42
Fefu and Her Friends (Fornés), 44–45, 141–42, 145–54, 156–69, 277n54, 278n55. *See also* hysteria
feminine, the, 10, 82, 86, 195–96, 203, 280n5

femininity, 13, 52, 62, 64, 178, 197; fetishism and, 61
feminism, 68, 146; Anglo-American, 85; bad, 62; Black, 37–38; hysteria and, 163, 277n54
figuration, 6, 35, 38, 48, 83–87, 118, 130, 201, 229, 246; animal, 190, 200; catachresis as, 31; of dust/*polvo*, 92–93, 102, 115, 138; of Fornés, 174–75; Indigenous, 36; of life, 210; limestone as, 60; mutt as, 190; of primitivism, 263n7; of trans and anticolonial movements, 241; valuation of, 259n59; of "x," 235
figurative, the, 4, 43, 84, 99, 278n56
figurativity, 3, 5, 7, 10, 41; tropes as, 32
film, 116; Fornés and, 139–40, 174; Mendieta and, 49, 66; Ramos Otero and, 97, 111. *See also* Queen Christina
finitude, 81, 83, 86, 93, 121, 209; freedom and, 123; lithic, 88; Mendieta and, 50–51, 53; poetics of, 120; Ramos Otero and, 43, 129–32, 136
form, 5–6, 10, 99, 266n48; aesthetic, 96, 235, 282n43; generic, 234; human, 34; the inscriptive and, 253n4, 256n36; organic, 3; poetic, 129, 232; pointillist, 2; translation as, 116
formalism, 5–6
Fornés, María Irene, 44–45, 139–49, 151, 153–54, 156–59, 164–66, 169–76, 275n2, 275n5, 279n79; Hofmann and, 144, 276n10; language of, 276n19. *See also Fefu and Her Friends*; Sontag, Susan
fossils, 57, 81, 138

Galarte, Francisco, 235, 244, 253n5, 286n19
Garbo, Greta, 105, 111–12, 271n36, 271n38
gender, 6, 17, 19, 27, 40, 142, 179, 185, 206, 234, 278n56; animality and, 191; binaries, 95, 244; difference, 5, 255n21; *Fefu and Her Friends* and, 150, 160, 163, 167, 169; Frankenstein and, 281n39; grammar(s) and, 21, 24, 46, 223, 235, 238; inscription and, 9; Klein and, 170; Latinx and, 36; Mendieta's work and, 62; pronouns and, 18, 221, 232; race and, 257n39; racialized, 29, 35, 222; Ramos Otero's work and, 114, 137; rhetoric of, 24; Salas Rivera's work and, 230, 241–43; Sánchez's work and, 3, 10; studies, 5, 18, 28, 167; trans and, 231; translation and, 160, 224, 233, 235, 240, 244–45, 286n18; in *We the Animals*, 184–87, 196–97, 216–17
genocide, 83, 127, 130
geography, 60, 65, 83, 199
geology, 60, 82–83, 267n56
Glissant, Édouard, 29, 59, 132–33, 190, 273n78, 285n107
graffiti, 75, 137

grammar(s), 5–9, 20, 37–38, 191, 198; catachresis and, 34; colonial, 224, 231, 241, 244–46; difference and, 41; gender and, 21, 24, 46, 223, 235, 238; laws of, 116; of loss, 215; Puerto Rican, 236, 244; race and, 24, 238; of raciality, 36; reference and, 13; sedimented, 4, 26; transparency and, 30
guajiro, 55, 58, 70
guilt, 18, 130, 194

Haiti, 41, 127
heritage, 188–90, 197, 206, 210, 215
heterosexism, 45, 199, 208
heterosexuality, 111, 180
HIV, 92–93, 98, 103, 113, 126–27, 130–31, 137; Ramos Otero and, 43, 118, 122, 124–25, 133, 136
Hofmann, Hans, 144, 276n10
Hollywood, 101, 106, 108, 270n16, 271n36; golden-age starlets of, 103–4, 111; Latina starlets of, 270n29; old, 107
Huffer, Lynne, 81, 85, 259n64, 285n109
humanism, 44, 179; critique of, 180; illiberal, 40; liberal, 178, 181, 206; myths of, 45, 186
humanities, 5–6, 15, 17, 40
humanity, 36, 40; animality and, 178; black(ened), 266n48; first woman of, 77; origins of, 84
Hurricane Maria, 43, 92–93, 103, 131, 133, 136–37, 274n91
hysteria, 141–42, 155, 163–64, 168–69, 277–78n54

idealism, 5, 36, 246; ethics after, 39; materiality and, 68
identity, 3, 12, 18, 35, 106, 129–30, 143, 146, 219, 274n85, 275n2; categories, 16, 140, 147, 221; content, 165; deconstructive theory around, 261n81; difference and, 41; Fornés's, 140–41; God's, 131; knowledges, 167, 278n67; latinidad and, 15; markers, 4, 19, 39, 141; as metaphor, 32; narrative, 217; politics, 98, 167; politics and, 45, 175; sexual, 112; shared, 45, 169; signifiers of, 17
ideology, 19; aesthetic, 5; mastery-of-field, 258n45
imperialism, 83; of English, 16–17, 243; nuclear coloniality under, 245–46; US, 130, 228, 236, 243
index, 9, 13; material, 228
indigeneity, 36, 52, 71, 85–86, 88; anti-indigenuity, 89; in the Caribbean, 56, 58, 72; in Cuba, 42, 50–51, 55, 264n11; *mestizaje* and, 260n73
Indigenous languages, 55, 57, 287n26
Indigenous people, 49, 55, 57, 59. See also Taíno
infrastructure, 96, 209–10; colonial, 228, 243, 245; human, 212; Old San Juan's, 225–26; public health, 126; of translation, 46; twenty-first-century, 70; US notion of, 268n1

inheritance, 185, 206; of colonialism, 64; Taíno, 51; willfulness as, 165
INTAR (International Arts Relations, Inc.), 44, 140, 144, 275n3
intimacy, 49, 51, 93, 159, 169, 185
Iowa, 49, 51, 53, 60, 65; University of, 263n7
Irigaray, Luce, 82, 85, 259n64, 267n55
Italy, 54, 65
iterability, 18, 36, 256n38

Jackson, Zakkiyah Iman, 60, 255n21, 260n72, 266n48, 280n14, 281n24, 283n65
Jaruco, 51–52, 56, 64–67, 69–71, 74–76, 79, 84, 243; histories of, 80; limestone in, 42, 49, 52, 55, 60, 65, 75f–76f, 82
jíbaro, 55, 96, 264n10
Johnson, Barbara, 85, 281n39
Jones Act, 92, 268n1
justice, 202; equal, 117; social, 36, 279n67

Karera, Axelle, 83, 267n58
Khanna, Neetu, 230, 286n14
Kincaid, Jamaica, 240, 286n22
Klein, Melanie, 170–71, 185, 280n18, 282n42, 282n52. See also psychoanalysis
knowledge, 18, 88, 167, 169–70, 175, 220; academic, 258n45; authoritative, 22; extraction of, 148, 163; hierarchies of, 17; hysteria and, 155; language and, 199; objective, 200; personal, 145; production of, 52, 279n81; rational, 165; Taíno, 58

labor, 34; carceral, 83; forced, 81, 134; linguistic, 230; maternal, 182; performative, 166; stolen, 59; of thought, 146; translation, 46, 235
Lacan, Jacques, 11, 26, 279n81
Las Casas, Bartolomé de, 57–58
Latinx, 3–4, 14–16, 18–19, 23–25, 27–28, 36, 39, 44, 46–48, 221, 243, 246, 255n26; debates on, 254n20; Hispanic and, 255n28; "x" of, 224, 229, 235, 242, 244. See also art: Latinx; literature: Latinx; playwriting: Latinx
Latinx studies, 65, 88, 167, 229, 253n5; Afro-Latinx studies, 47; institutionalization of, 3; Latinx literary studies, 5, 18, 98; Viego and, 26, 29, 175, 219
liberation, 3, 5, 17, 48, 58, 120–22; poetics of finitude without, 120; telos of, 120
limestone, 41, 49–50, 52–53, 55, 59–60, 66, 72, 81, 84, 86–88; in caves, 42, 49, 65, 76–77, 80, 81–82, 87, 243; oolitic, 65, 79. See also Jaruco; Mendieta, Ana
linguistics, 25, 206; general, 24; variation, 190
linguistic turn, 5, 7, 11–13, 24, 27–28, 254n10, 257n39; Breu on, 257n43; deconstruction and, 34
Lippard, Lucy, 61, 68

INDEX | 293

literary studies, 5; Latinx, 18, 98
literary theory, 18, 28
literature, 4, 40, 115, 119; impersonal, 273n72; Latinx, 3, 18, 41, 47; queer Puerto Rican, 269n12; underrepresented, 20, 35, 145
liveness. *See* burden of liveness
loss, 26–27, 29, 45–46, 50, 88, 179, 202, 220, 222, 242–43, 246, 257n42; catachresis and, 32–33; caves and, 81, 86; covering up of, 156; Cuba and, 60; of ego, 168, 173; language and, 189, 215–16; of memory, 174; need and, 36; personal, 221; politics of, 201, 219; psychoanalytic notions of, 282n42; Salas Rivera and, 286n9; translation and, 229–30

Maceo, Antonio, 55, 68
Machado Sáez, Elena, 120, 272n62
manhood, 151, 192, 195, 218
Marder, Elissa, 184, 275n4
Marder, Michael, 97, 113
Marx, Karl, 33–34, 243, 259n63
masculinity, 178, 190, 214–15, 281n24; Latinx, 280n5; liberal humanist standards of, 185; telos of, 209; white, 189–90
material, the, 4, 20, 52, 88, 145
materiality, 3, 35, 42, 48, 82, 88, 246; ballast and, 227; desire and, 131; diaspora and, 135; of disability, 278n56; force of, 85; of hysterics, 155; idealism and, 68; of inscription, 19, 27; within Jaruco, 56; of language, 4, 13, 26–27, 257n43, 259n59; the poetic and, 243; posthuman, 125; referential, 25; semiotics and, 239, 245; signification and, 257n39
maternal, the, 82, 185
maternal function, 141, 174, 184, 275n4
maternity, 76, 182, 184–86, 280n5; Black, 280n14
Mayes-Garcia, Eric, 140, 275n2
McKittrick, Katherine, 60, 82–83, 264n17
meaning, 9, 31–32, 242, 245; of *adoquines*, 228; catachresis and, 36; *différance* and, 35; disability and, 156; dust and, 121; entangled, 241; extracting, 145, 154; for humanimals, 190; language and, 39; making, 29, 37, 86, 116, 187; matter and, 6, 16, 41, 84, 255n21; neoliberal individual and, 138; proper, 38, 85; reference and, 13; sedimentations of, 26; signified as, 8; suspension of, 172
mediation, 93, 121–22; aesthetic, 43, 99, 102, 246; autobiography as, 20, 114, 119
Memran, Michelle, 174–75; *The Rest I Make Up*, 139
Mendieta, Ana, 49–54, 56–57, 59–69, 74–79, 82–89, 265n27, 266n48, 267n50; aesthetic abjection and, 263n7; *Bacayu (Light of Day)*, 76, 77f; *Ceiba Fetish*, 75; Cuba and, 42, 50–54, 65–69, 75, 77–78, 87, 262n1;

Esculturas Rupestres, 42, 49–50, 52, 64–65, 68, 75, 243; *Guanaroca (First Woman)*, 77–78, 78f; *Maroya* (I), 76; *Silueta* series, 51, 63–64, 79, 262n2. *See also* Andre, Carl; caves; exile; Iowa; Jaruco; privilege
mestizaje, 55, 57, 86, 260n73; myths of, 36
metaphor, 7, 25, 31–32, 85, 246, 259n59, 260n69; abuse of, 32, 35, 84; *adoquines* as, 242; decolonization and, 245, 263n6; disability as, 278n56; dust as, 92–93, 133, 136, 270n13, 274n80; of heritage, 189; horsepower as, 70; as idealism, 36; latinidad as, 4; motherly role as, 145; sand as, 136, 274n80; scale as, 255n26. *See also* catachresis
metaphysics, 219; of presence, 23, 28, 63; of purity, 55; Western, 60
Mexico, 54, 65, 133, 263n7; US border with, 15
Miami, 15, 69, 75, 267n50; Cuban exile community in, 67; diocese of, 53
migration, 2, 53–54, 205; Central American, 47; Cuban, 15, 53, 266n42; dust, 134; forced, 19, 24, 59; Fornés's story of, 144
modernity, 36, 70, 83, 87, 128; of Havana, 67; in Puerto Rico, 96; US notion of, 268n1
Molloy, Sylvia, 118, 155
Moraga, Cherríe, 44, 140
motherhood, 184–86, 195
multiplicity, 102, 180, 185–86, 221
Muñoz, José Esteban, 51, 108, 145–46, 257n40, 276n19. *See also* burden of liveness
mutt, 188, 190, 215; life, 214–15
mythology, 36, 56, 190; of the Black Other, 74; genealogical, 42; Taíno, 76, 84

nationalism, 69, 87, 167; ethnonationalism, 188; homonationalism, 103, 135, 240
negativity, 24–25, 33, 110, 281n41; nonidentitarian, 261n82
never-never time, 182–83, 186, 193, 209
New York City: art scene / art world, 54, 67; El Museo del Barrio, 68; Fornés and, 44, 144–45, 157; Guggenheim Museum, 66; Latinx, 140; Puerto Rican communities in, 179; Ramos Otero and, 95, 97–98, 103–4, 108, 125, 127; Sánchez and, 10, 12

Obama, Barack, 69, 266n42
Old San Juan, 137; roads, 46, 224–26, 228–31, 237, 239, 241, 246, 285n4. See also *adoquines*
orphanhood, 54, 64
Ortiz, Ricardo, 18, 255n24

Pané, Ramón, 57–58, 65
pedagogy, 41, 140, 167; of affect and licentiousness, 213; corporeal, 44; ethics and, 147; Fornés and, 147, 165, 172, 174–75; Klein and, 170; of Muñoz, 145–46; visceral, 142

294 | INDEX

performance, 4, 60, 277n49; art, 49, 257n40; fascism and, 246; gender as, 35; migration as, 134; studies, 145
performativity, 36, 102, 191; gender, 35
pinkwashing, 103, 240
plantation matrix, 15, 59
playwriting, 44, 144; Fornés's, 146, 157; Latinx, 140–41, 175
poetics, 94–95, 213, 237, 239, 241, 244; of autobiography, 21, 96; of dust, 93, 102, 137; of life, 138; Ramos Otero's, 92–93, 119–20, 137; Salas Rivera's, 228–30, 236, 243–44, 246; Stein's, 170
poetry, 246; Ramos Otero's, 21, 43, 93–95, 99, 101, 118–19, 122, 129; Rodríguez de Tío's, 262n93; Salas Rivera's, 223–24, 228–30, 235, 242, 244
politics, 86, 104, 109–10, 112, 220; aestheticization of, 39–40, 246; biopolitics, 127; camp and, 106–8; Cold War, 42; Cuba's, 61, 69; deidealization and, 271n33; disinterest in, 106; essentialism and, 62; Fornés and, 147; gay liberal, 179; gender, 241; geopolitics, 83; global, 266n42; identity, 98, 167; identity and, 45, 278n67; of liberation, 285n107; logics of, 84; loss and, 179; of loss, 201, 219; Muñoz's queer optic and, 145; necropolitics, 127; normative, 109; queer, 217, 281n41; rational, 160; representational, 174; viscera and, 142
polvo. See dust/*polvo*
porosity, 43, 93–94, 99, 122, 125, 132, 135; of dust, 137; between fiction and history, 114; of the self, 113; of skin and the gut, 163
positivism, 27–28, 35; catachresis and, 261n82; essentialism as form of, 62
postcolonial studies, 5, 28, 167
poverty, 96, 146, 202, 214
precarity, 92–93, 103, 127, 132, 135, 268n1; after Hurricane María, 131; of the Puerto Rican and queer condition, 113; of Spanish, 243
presence, 60, 80; absence of, 256n38; African, 72; Africanist, 274n81; Afro-Caribbean, 58; Indigenous, 36, 50, 52, 56, 59, 263n6, 263n8; of Mendieta, 78; metaphysics of, 23, 28, 63
privilege, 53, 62, 151; heteronormative, 185; relative, 11, 54, 110, 263n7
progress, 43, 180, 182, 232; narratives, 58, 61, 69; neoliberal, 45
pronouns, 9, 21, 33, 45, 193, 198, 207–8, 217–19, 231–32; gendered, 196; queerness of, 221
prosopopoeia, 38, 118
psychoanalysis, 130, 154; Bersani on, 281n41; Kleinian, 170, 282n52; Spillers and, 219
Puar, Jasbir, 135, 274n85
Puerto Rico, 55, 82, 189, 210, 228–30, 234–36, 283n69; Colectivo Literario Homoerótica, 269n12; colonialism and, 226; Cuba and, 262n93; debt and, 33; diaspora and, 47, 94, 98; dust and, 133–34; Hurricane María and, 103, 133, 136, 274n91; language and, 34, 242–44, 287n26; mid-century, 3, 15; modernization and, 268n1; Ramos Otero and, 43, 92, 96–98, 125, 127, 132, 269n4; Salas Rivera's return to, 46, 224; *soberano* protests in, 241; US and, 239; Vieques, 239, 245. See also *adoquines*; *jíbaro*; Old San Juan; Spanish language
purity, 55, 69, 279n81; critique of, 127; genealogical, 56; god of, 125

Queen Christina (Mamoulian), 111, 271n36, 271n38
queerness, 11–13, 45, 93, 132, 179, 181, 185, 194, 197, 222, 239, 261n82; in exile, 136, 274n80; madness and, 285n109; Otero's, 92, 125, 127; of pronouns, 221; Salas Riveras and, 240, 244–45; of Torres's writing, 218
queer studies, 28, 217
Quiroga, José, 50, 66, 79, 266n43

race, 9, 17–19, 21, 26, 36, 40, 52, 137, 179, 206; animality and, 41, 45, 200, 204; in the Caribbean, 57; coloniality and, 81; debt and, 230; disability and, 278n56; DNA as marker of, 56; *Fefu and Her Friends* and, 163; femininity and, 62; grammars of, 24; HIV/AIDS and, 126; in "Hollywood Memorabilia" (Ramos Otero), 108; inscription and, 257n39; Klein and, 170; maternal function and, 185; mixing, 214–15; mythologies of, 5; new materialisms and, 255n21; the performative and, 191; pronouns and, 221; referentiality and, 13, 28; Spanish language and, 243; teaching, 167; vocabularies of, 264n12
raciality, 7, 29, 35–36, 184, 210
racialization, 6, 27, 92, 185, 214, 266n48; ethnic, 210; gendered, 60; of plasticity, 260n72; relationality and, 4; structural violence as, 202; of Torres's writing, 218
racism, 17, 61, 108–9, 208
Ramos Otero, Manuel, 21, 42–43, 92–99, 101–5, 107–9, 111–22, 125–38, 269n4, 269nn11–12, 270n13, 273n64, 274n81; "De la colonización a la culonización," 270n21; "Ficción e historia: Texto y pretexto de la autobiografía," 93–94, 114; "Hollywood Memorabilia," 93, 103–8, 111–13, 131 (*see also* Hollywood); *Invitación al polvo*, 92–93, 99–101, 122, 127, 131; melodies of, 273n72. *See also* AIDS; autobiography; desire; dust/*polvo*; finitude; HIV; poetics; poetry; Spanish language; writing
real, the, 26–27, 246
realism, 44, 120, 140, 157, 276n19

reference, 7–8, 13, 19, 29, 31, 35, 243, 257n43; *adoquines* and, 225, 228–29, 246; association and, 254n9; autobiography and, 117, 119; biography and, 171; of bombs, 240, 245; catachresis and, 37; cline, 191; Derrida on, 27; frames of, 4, 20; future anterior and, 65; beyond gender, 21; inevitability of, 39; language and, 30; Latinx and, 14, 28; material, 245–46; race and, 36

referentiality, 12–13, 19, 22–23, 27, 41, 95, 102, 104, 117, 191, 228, 241, 246; animal metaphors and, 220; catachresis and, 32, 35, 37, 39; as colonial problem, 46; discomfit of, 257n43; figuration and, 84; grammatical, 9; pure, 121; race and, 13, 28; theory of, 213

representation, 3, 7, 9, 28–30, 34, 36, 47, 116, 201, 203, 244; burden of, 26; fictional, 278n56; Fornés and, 170; life and, 23; opacity and, 285n107; political, 51, 58; ruses of, 275n5; as signification, 8; truth and, 81; videotaped, 212; visual, 101–2, 118; of woman, 62

resistance, 44, 56, 168, 197; figurative, 225; hysteria and, 169; to meaning, 156; movements, 241, 244; political, 165; of Spanish, 243; student, 17, 110; Taíno and Afro-Cuban, 42; to translation, 226; to transportation, 228, 242; tropological, 45, 178

return, 64–66, 88; exile and, 51, 65–66; to formalisms and aesthetics, 5; impossibility and, 134; maternity and, 76; Mendieta's, 50, 52–53, 65–66, 74, 84–85, 87; origin and, 52–53; of the repressed, 32; Salas Rivera's, 224, 241

revolution, 109–10, 112. *See also* Cuban Revolution

rhetoric, 5–6, 8, 13, 20; anticommunist, 53; catachresis as form of, 31; political, 37; psychoanalysis as, 219; purebred, 186; of race and gender, 24

Salas Rivera, Roque, 223–24, 228–32, 234–37, 240–46, 259n62, 285n3; *Preguntas frecuentes / Frequently Asked Questions*, 46, 224, 231–33, 239, 245; *the tertiary / lo terciario*, 33; *X/Ex/Exis*, 46, 224, 237, 239, 242–43, 245. See also *adoquines*; loss; poetics: Salas Rivera's; queerness; translation

Sánchez, Zilia, 1–4, 7–13, 24–25, 67, 254n9; *El significado del significante*, 1f, 3, 7, 9, 254n9

San Francisco, 103, 127

Santería, 58, 60

Sarduy, Severo, 10–12

Saussure, Ferdinand de, 5, 24–26, 257n43, 259n59

Schneeman, Carolee, 61, 63

Schor, Mira, 61, 85

Sedgwick, Eve Kosofsky, 62, 170–71, 221, 280n18, 282n52

semiotics, 5, 8, 11, 239, 245; of the body, 187; cultural, 14, 108; dance and, 188; of gesture, 190; post-Saussurian, 25; Spanish, 230

sex, 10, 26, 122, 198–200, 206, 212, 217; referentiality and, 13

sexism, 17, 155. *See also* heterosexism

sexuality, 12, 17–18, 98, 137, 167, 278n56; open, 97; philosophies of, 10; proper, 96

shame, 181, 187–89, 200, 204, 206–9, 213, 215, 217, 282n42

sidoso, 43, 92, 124, 128–29, 132

sign, 24–25, 27, 39

signification, 7, 18, 25, 39, 52, 203, 227, 257n39; erotic, 3; limits of, 38; representation as, 8; resignification, 35

signified, 8–9, 25, 27, 35, 145, 254n10; referent and, 24, 257n43; of the signifier, 3, 7–9, 13, 24; status of, 7, 25; transcendental, 17–18, 27. *See also* Sánchez, Zilia: *El significado del significante*

signifier, 13–14, 25–27, 145, 278n56; catachresis and, 32, 35; the racial as transparent, 29; signified of, 7–9, 24

slavery, 42, 83; aftermath of, 240; transatlantic, 227

slave trade: African, 57; transatlantic, 58, 87, 134, 227

solitude, 64, 67, 103–4, 112, 130, 214, 222

Sontag, Susan, 81, 106–7, 111; Fornés and, 144–46, 275n3; "Notes on 'Camp,'" 271n35. *See also* camp

sovereignty, 130, 256n35, 284n102; critique of, 127; narrative, 104; of quiet, 203; self-sovereignty, 95; tribal, 56

Spain, 10, 55, 58, 210

Spanish language, 24, 34, 43, 46, 92, 101, 225, 228, 271n40; Castilian, 57; coloniality of, 16, 243; double nos and, 33; as guarantor of belonging, 21; as heritage language, 189; Ramos Otero's writing and, 98, 104, 107–8, 270n17; Salas Rivera's writing and, 229–30, 232–36, 239, 241–45; speakers of, 148, 215, 229. See also *adoquines*; dust/*polvo*

Spillers, Hortense J., 4, 219, 254n12, 260n72; "'All the Things You Could Be by Now, If Sigmund Freud's Wife Was Your Mother': Psychoanalysis and Race," 253n3; "Mama's Baby, Papa's Maybe," 37

Spivak, Gayatri, 34, 37, 84–85, 259nn64–66

Sretenovic, Vesela, 11–12

Stein, Gertrude, 109–10, 271n32; poetics of, 170

sterilization, 15, 96

Strasberg, Lee, 98, 103

subjectivity, 26, 45, 93–94, 181, 265n27; female, 265n27; interior, 219; loss and, 257n42; male, 281n41; neoliberal, 92; sovereign, 130, 197; violence of, 185, 202

supplementarity, 9, 27, 39
Svich, Caridad, 44, 140

Taíno: community, 55, 263n8; culture, 56, 82; goddess effigies, 42, 65; iconography, 51; inheritance, 51; languages, 57, 72; mythology, 49, 65, 76, 77, 84; peoples, 55, 57–58, 76, 82, 87; resistance, 42; resurgence, 264n14
TallBear, Kim, 56, 264n12
Tel Quel, 7–8, 11–12
theater, 98, 140, 144–45, 169–70, 172, 174–75; environmental, 158–59. See also Fornés, María Irene
theory, 7, 10, 68, 74, 261n83; of cathexis, 162; deconstructive, 261n81; De Man's, 118; dust, 125–26; essentialist, 63; feminist, 63, 142, 155, 279n81; of gender, 62; germ, 126; inscription and, 4–6; Klein and, 170; of Latinx narratology, 221; literary, 18, 28; new materialist media, 81; quantum field, 135; queer, 261n82, 279n81, 281n41; referentiality and, 39, 213
Tomes, Nancy, 125–26
Torres, Justin, 44, 65, 178, 220, 280n5, 285n107. See also We the Animals
trace structure, 7, 27, 83, 86, 142, 256n38
translation, 21, 32, 34, 46, 52, 57, 104, 114–17, 120–22, 225, 234, 238–40, 242, 271n40; adoquines and, 236–37, 285n3; aesthetic, 95; (auto)biography as, 20–21, 93–94, 96, 107, 114–16, 119; camp as, 106–8, 110; challenges of, 57; of coloniality, 130; diaspora and, 189; difference and, 230; dust and, 43; as exposure, 46; gender and, 160, 224, 233, 235, 240, 244–45, 286n18; gendered, 223; genealogical, 85; literary, 102; resistance to, 226, 228; self-translation, 46, 224, 232, 286n11; theatrical, 142; as transformation, 238; transgender and, 231; visuality and, 270n15
trans movements, 46, 224, 236, 241
transparency, 20, 22, 29–30, 37
trans people, 231–32, 237–38
trans studies, 28, 235, 286n19
trauma, 142, 216; exilic, 62; intergenerational, 190; studies, 277n41
tropes, 5, 7, 32, 46, 201; baby, 200; in the Caribbean, 136; childhood as, 198; of Darwinian evolution, 221; dust/polvo as, 41, 92, 103, 131, 136; of finitude, 43; in Fornés, 142, 174; of humanism, 179; of insects, 204; Latinx as, 28; material, 6, 48; psychoanalysis as series of, 219; in Salas Rivera, 223, 240; solitude as, 112; triumph as, 219; in We the Animals (Torres), 181. See also catachresis; prosopopoeia
Trump, Donald, 69; administration of, 266n42
Tuck, Eve, 242, 245, 260n69, 287n25

Ulloa, Alfonso de, 57–58
untranslatability, 225, 236, 241–42, 285n3. See also translation

Vazquez, Alexandra, 148, 187
Viego, Antonio, 26–27, 29, 175, 179, 201, 219, 257n42, 279n81
violence, 44–45, 52, 60, 93, 169–71, 194–95, 282n52; adoquines and, 228–29, 246; of bombs, 246; of Cuba, 61; of English, 231; Fefu and Her Friends and, 149, 152, 157, 168; femininity and, 64; foundational, 59; grounding, 89; heritage as, 190; histories of, 87; of language, 13, 27, 235–36, 241, 244; originary, 37, 155; structural, 45, 201–2, 282n42; subjectivity as, 202; surplus, 83; transphobic, 235, 240; in We the Animals, 181, 185, 195, 201, 204, 207, 213–14, 219, 221–22; against women, 54; between women, 141
visibility, 15, 29, 121, 133, 217; of Black folks, 281n41; trap of, 235
Viso, Olga, 64–66

Walcott, Derek, 87, 268n69
We the Animals (Torres), 45, 177–89, 191–222, 282n52, 283n77, 284nn104–5
whiteness, 56, 86, 178, 212, 215–16, 260n73; Asian American subjects and, 256n31; canonical knowledge and, 258n45; femininity and, 197; nonwhiteness, 26
Wiegman, Robyn, 167, 253n6, 278–79n67
Wilson, Elizabeth, 141–42, 155, 169, 275n6
women, 111–12, 172–73, 212–13, 277–78nn54–55, 281n41; bodies of, 54; catachresis and, 84; Fefu and Her Friends and, 44, 141, 146–47, 149–54, 156, 159–67, 169; Fornés's relationships with, 144; Hollywood, 108; as master word, 34; Puerto Rican, 96; subordination of, 169
writing, 4, 6, 27, 113, 125, 127, 129, 139–40, 147, 148, 151, 156, 157, 175; affects, 8; autobiographical, 116–19; Caribbean diasporic, 272n62; différance and, 256n38; dust/dusty, 96, 101–2, 120–21, 132, 136; exercises, 145; figurative dimensions of, 117, 119; Fornés's, 140, 142, 172–73; beyond the grave, 110; Irigaray's, 85; about Latinx peoples, 41; life, 20; limestone and, 81; modes of, 21–22, 118; posthumous, 122, 138; Ramos Otero's, 92, 94–95, 98–99, 102–4, 114, 116, 119, 122, 126, 131–32, 135–36, 269n11, 274n81; rock, 51; supplementarity of, 9; Torres's, 218
Wynter, Sylvia, 7, 40, 74, 83, 282n47

Yang, K. Wayne, 242, 260n69, 287n25
Yusoff, Kathryn, 60, 82–83, 267n56

ABOUT THE AUTHOR

Christina A. León is Assistant Professor of Literature at Duke University. She specializes in Latinx and Caribbean literatures, in addition to critical engagements with literary, feminist, queer, anticolonial, and critical race theories. Her writing can be found in *Women & Performance*, *ASAP/Journal*, *Diacritics*, *GLQ*, *Representations*, *Small Axe*, and *Post45*.

Milton Keynes UK
Ingram Content Group UK Ltd.
UKHW011608160724
445471UK00001B/1